Chancellorsville

Military Campaigns of the Civil War

Chancellorsville

The Battle and Its Aftermath

Edited by Gary W. Gallagher

The University of North Carolina Press

Chapel Hill and London

© 1996
The University of North Carolina Press
All rights reserved
Manufactured in the United States of America
Library of Congress Cataloging-in-Publication Data
Chancellorsville : the battle and its aftermath / edited by
Gary W. Gallagher.
p. cm. — (Military campaigns of the Civil War)
Includes bibliographical references and index.
ISBN 0-8078-2275-2 (cloth: alk. paper)
1. Chancellorsville (Va.), Battle of, 1863.   I. Gallagher,
Gary W.   II. Series.
E475.35.C47   1996
973.7′34—dc20   95-43508
                          CIP
The paper in this book meets the guidelines
for permanence and durability of the Committee on
Production Guidelines for Book Longevity of the
Council on Library Resources.

00 99 98 97 96   5 4 3 2 1

For

Norma Lois Peterson

and

John E. McDaniel,

who set an admirable

standard of scholarship

and teaching for their

students to emulate

Contents

Introduction

R. E. Lee's stunning tactical victory at Chancellorsville capped a remarkable eleven-month period during which he built the Army of Northern Virginia into a self-confident and formidable weapon. Conditioned to expect success after defeating the Army of the Potomac at the Seven Days battles, Second Manassas, and Fredericksburg, the officers and men of Lee's army entered the spring of 1863 with abundant faith in their commander and his principal lieutenants. Their triumph at Chancellorsville cemented a bond with Lee unrivaled on either side during the Civil War. Even the costly defeat at Gettysburg two months later failed to weaken that bond, which sustained the Army of Northern Virginia for nearly two more years. Beyond its effect on the internal dynamics of the Confederate army, Chancellorsville contributed to a growing impression among white southerners that the future of their incipient nation lay with Lee and his men in Virginia. The comments of a British observer in March 1865 suggest that faith in Lee's ability to carry Confederate hopes for independence—a legacy of Chancellorsville and other victories in 1862–63—continued during the final grinding year of the conflict: "*Genl R. E. Lee* . . . [is] the idol of his soldiers & the Hope of His Country. . . . The prestige which surrounds his person & the almost fanatical belief in his judgement & capacity . . . is the one idea of an entire people."[1]

The sheer odds against Confederate success at Chancellorsville elevated the battle to a special position among Lee's victories. Union general Joseph Hooker had rebuilt and reinspirited the Army of the Potomac in the wake of Ambrose E. Burnside's removal from command in January 1863. Hooker entered the Chancellorsville campaign at the head of a force with ample equipment, strong discipline, and high morale. He pronounced it "the finest army on the planet," and as astute an observer as Confederate artillerist Edward Porter Alexander spoke of it after the war as "Hooker's great army—the greatest this country had ever seen."[2] During the difficult winter, Lee had dispersed his cavalry to secure sufficient fodder and detached two divisions under James Longstreet to Southside Virginia to forage on a wide scale and block threatened enemy movements from Norfolk or the Carolina coast. Lee could count on the redoubtable spirit of his men, but he knew their ranks were dangerously thin to hold off a determined enemy offensive. With more than 133,000 men to Lee's 61,000, Hooker enjoyed the widest margin of manpower of any Union general who had fought against the Army of Northern Virginia to that point in the conflict.[3]

Hooker added an impressive strategic blueprint to his material advantages. He envisioned marching the bulk of his army up the Rappahannock River in a wide turning movement around Lee's left. A sizable force under John Sedgwick would cross the Rappahannock opposite Lee at Fredericksburg to hold the Confederates in place. As a third element in the plan, Federal cavalry under George Stoneman also would swing around Lee's left before striking south toward Richmond to disrupt communications, destroy bridges, and spread confusion. If all went well, Lee would be caught between Hooker's powerful turning column to the west and Sedgwick's troops in his front. Confederate options, thought Hooker, would be limited to a retreat toward Richmond complicated by Stoneman's activities or desperate assaults against one or both of the major components of the Army of the Potomac.

The outline of the campaign that unfolded after Hooker's first infantry marched upriver on April 27, 1863, is well known. The Federals succeeded in crossing the Rappahannock and Rapidan rivers without significant delays, and by the evening of April 30, the flanking force had reached the crossroads of Chancellorsville, ten miles in Lee's rear. There Hooker's soldiers found themselves in the midst of the Wilderness of Spotsylvania, a scrub forest heavily cut over to feed small iron furnaces in the area. With few roads, infrequent clearings, and dense underbrush that severely limited military movement, the Wilderness posed an obstacle to Hooker's plan. But the northern units at Chancellorsville had to move only a few miles eastward to break free of the limiting woods. Once in open country, they could bring the full weight of their numbers and equipment to bear against Lee's army. Hooker brimmed with confidence on the night of April 30. "It is with heartfelt satisfaction the commanding general announces to the army," he stated in a message that would soon ring hollow, "that the operations of the last three days have determined that our enemy must either ingloriously fly, or come out from behind his defenses and give us battle on our own ground, where certain destruction awaits him."[4]

Lee refused to follow Hooker's script, responding instead with a series of typically audacious moves. Assigning roughly 10,000 men under Jubal A. Early the task of watching Sedgwick at Fredericksburg, Lee and "Stonewall" Jackson hurried the rest of the Army of Northern Virginia westward to stop Hooker. The decisive moment of the campaign occurred on the morning of May 1, when the vanguards of Hooker's and Lee's forces collided near Zoan Church on the road between Chancellorsville and Fredericksburg. This clash seemed to drain all offensive spirit from Hooker, who immediately ordered a withdrawal to Chancellorsville. Like a frightened child bravely announcing in the dark that ghosts do not exist, Hooker told Darius N. Couch, who led the Union Second Corps, that he had "Lee just where I want him; he must fight me on my own ground." "The retrograde movement had prepared me for something of the kind," recalled Couch after the war, "but to hear from his own lips that the advantages gained by the successful marches of his lieutenants were to culminate in fighting a defensive battle in that nest of thickets was too much, and I retired from his presence with the belief that my commanding general was a whipped man."[5]

Lee and Jackson decided on a bold flanking maneuver of their own on the night of May 1, which Jackson executed successfully the next day. Although Jackson's attack on May 2 routed the Federal Eleventh Corps, the bulk of Hooker's army remained between the two pieces of Lee's force at Chancellorsville (a third piece of the Army of Northern Virginia remained at Fredericksburg under Early). Hooker failed to exploit this opening, pulling his men into a tighter defensive position in the face of heavy Confederate assaults on May 3. When Lee learned on that day of Sedgwick's success in breaching Early's line at Fredericksburg, he divided his army a third time. Leaving 25,000 men under "Jeb" Stuart to keep an eye on Hooker, Lee concentrated the balance of his men several miles west of Fredericksburg at Salem Church, where the Confederates won a fumbling victory against Sedgwick on May 4. By the morning of May 6, the Army of the Potomac had retreated to the north bank of the Rappahannock, conceding to Lee control of the field and returning the strategic situation to precisely the same circumstances that had existed at the outset of the campaign.

Chancellorsville presents a number of striking contrasts. Lee had crafted a victory that is often termed his "masterpiece" but at a cost of nearly 22 percent of his army, including Stonewall Jackson, who was shot by his own men in the confusing aftermath of the famous flank attack on May 2 and died eight days later. "At Chancellorsville we gained another victory," Lee commented later that summer. "Our people were wild with delight—I, on the contrary, was more depressed than after Fredericksburg; our loss was severe, and again we had gained not an inch of ground and the enemy could not be pursued."[6] The staggering human toll and Lee's failure to achieve any decisive strategic result must be weighed against Chancellorsville's powerful influence on morale within the Army of Northern Virginia and throughout the Confederacy. The battle also deepened Lee's staunch respect for his men and their ability to accomplish the apparently impossible—a circumstance that would influence his actions two months later at Gettysburg.

On the Union side, immense promise gave way to bitter disappointment in just eight days. Once again, the largest and most famous army of the republic had suffered ignominious defeat in Virginia. Many soldiers in the Army of the Potomac, disgusted with Hooker's decision to withdraw on May 1, believed they had not been given a chance to win the battle. A number of Hooker's subordinates shared this view. On the home front, Abraham Lincoln realized on May 6 that Hooker had failed. A newspaperman recorded the president's reaction: "My God! my God!" said an anguished Lincoln, "What will the country say?" Republican senator Charles Sumner of Massachusetts, who had expected much from Hooker, similarly described the president as "extremely dejected" and admitted to Secretary of the Navy Gideon Welles that he himself believed "all is lost."[7]

Chancellorsville offers the best example during the Civil War of one army commander's utter domination of another. "The most striking feature to me of the military history of the battle," wrote Porter Alexander, "is the perfect collapse of the moral courage of Hooker . . . as soon as he found himself in the actual presence of Lee & Jackson." A recent historian of the campaign agrees: "At no other time between Sumter and Appomattox," suggests Ernest B. Furgurson, "did moral character so decisively affect a battle."[8] Two scenes on the morning of May 3 captured perfectly the relative situations of the two generals. At the Bullock house, an unsteady Hooker lay on a blanket sipping brandy after being injured a few minutes earlier by a Confederate artillery shell that had crashed into a pillar at the Chancellor house near which he had been standing. At almost exactly the same moment, Lee rode into the clearing near Chancellorsville to watch the two wings of his army reunite after several hours of severe fighting. As his soldiers cheered wildly at the appearance of their chief, Lee "sat in the full realization of all that soldiers dream of—triumph," remembered Charles Marshall of his staff in an often-quoted postwar account of the moment. "As I looked upon him in the complete fruition of the success which his genius, courage, and confidence in his army had won," continued Marshall, "I thought that it must have been from such a scene that men in ancient days rose to the dignity of gods."[9]

Most accounts of Chancellorsville emphasize the generalships of Hooker, Lee, and Jackson; the Confederate flank attack on May 2 and the calamity it visited on O. O. Howard's Eleventh Corps; and the heavy fighting around the crossroads at the Chancellor house on May 3. Like other volumes in the Military Campaigns of the Civil War series, this collection of essays addresses less well known dimensions of the campaign, brings new evidence or a different interpretive twist to bear on other topics, and extends the discussion beyond strategic and tactical questions in an effort to demonstrate the various possibilities for fruitful examination of Civil War military events.

John J. Hennessy leads off with an examination of the Army of the Potomac on the eve of the campaign. He analyzes the factors that led soldiers to recover their enthusiasm for the war after the bitter reverse at Fredericksburg in mid-

December 1862 and the "Mud March" the following month. Covering issues as diffuse as the quality of rations and the men's response to emancipation and to the possible enrollment of black men as northern soldiers, Hennessy portrays an army that possessed remarkable recuperative powers. The role of politics in shaping the army's high command stands in sharp relief. Hennessy makes a strong case that caution in discussing volatile political issues counted for more than effective leadership on the battlefield in determining who received assignments to lead the eight Federal corps. He also leaves little doubt that at this level the Army of the Potomac lagged far behind its opponent in quality of leadership.

The second essay examines Jubal A. Early's performance as Confederate commander at the eastern end of the battlefield. Although it was slighted in newspaper accounts at the time and is often relegated to the status of a sideshow by modern writers, the fighting at Second Fredericksburg and Salem Church constituted a major element of the campaign. Early served capably but following the battle became embroiled in a controversy with William Barksdale, one of his subordinates, that forced Lee to intervene. Expressing concern at the time and during the postwar years about the written record of his actions at Chancellorsville, Early manifested his understanding that the printed word, rather than what actually happened, would determine how later generations viewed the operations along the Rappahannock in April and May 1863.

George Stoneman's cavalry raid often is adjudged one of the more egregious Union failures during the campaign.[10] Poorly conceived by Hooker and indifferently executed by Stoneman, according to the common argument, it denied the Army of the Potomac vital cavalry screening while garnering no compensatory advantage. A. Wilson Greene takes issue with much of the conventional interpretation, dismissing, for example, the notion that the presence of more Federal cavalry would have changed the tactical situation on Hooker's right flank on May 2. Although making no extravagant claims about the positive impact of Stoneman's activities, Greene points to a number of solid accomplishments. More significantly, he argues persuasively that Stoneman's raid rather than Brandy Station marked the beginning of a transformation within the ranks of the Union cavalry. Long ridiculed by their opponents and even by comrades in the Army of the Potomac, northern troopers emerged from Chancellorsville with an enhanced self-confidence that would serve them well when Lee marched into Pennsylvania in June.

The loss of Stonewall Jackson muted Confederate joy over the victory at Chancellorsville. "*Stonewall Jackson is dead,*" wrote a South Carolina woman who exhibited a typical reaction. "The mournful tidings are swept over the length and breadth of our land by the electric wires with crushing effect."[11]

Prior to Robert K. Krick's essay detailing Jackson's final movements on the battlefield, no one has fully explained what happened to Lee's great lieutenant in the chaotic woods west of Chancellorsville on the night of May 2. Krick's mastery of the sources, many of them quite obscure, yields a fascinating reconstruction of the general's reconnaissance along the Orange Plank Road and smaller side roads, the fateful volley from a North Carolina regiment that wreaked havoc on two parties of Confederate horsemen, and the painful injuries Jackson suffered while being carried to safety. Seldom can historians say that a topic has been treated definitively, but in the case of Krick's essay, that superlative is well deserved.

Winfield Scott Hancock's Union division fought much of the battle of Chancellorsville not far from where Jackson was wounded. In contrast to the men of O. O. Howard's Eleventh Corps, whose stampede on May 2 invited the glare of attention, Hancock's soldiers labored in relative obscurity. Carol Reardon brings their accomplishments to center stage, revealing that steady troops under accomplished officers could confront a variety of problems in splendid fashion. Imbued with a sense of work well done, many men in Hancock's division recrossed the Rappahannock nursing bitter feelings toward their commanding general. They had matched the rebels blow for blow in the smoke-filled woods, and they believed Hooker's errors alone had permitted Lee to exert his dominance. Reardon's essay suggests a range of Union responses to the defeat at Chancellorsville and should alert readers to the danger of generalizing about the impact of any one battle on an army's rank and file.

Facing the enemy amid the forbidding terrain of the Wilderness chastened many men less than the specter of having to undergo treatment for a wound. James I. Robertson, Jr., analyzes the delivery of medical care to the wounded of both armies, thus picking up the story of Chancellorsville where most other historians have left off. Thousands of men endured great suffering in springless ambulances or languished without attention for prolonged periods; once in the apparent safety of field hospitals, they encountered surgeons overwhelmed by the scale of the slaughter, often lacking adequate supplies of drugs and bandages, and helpless to mend much of the human wreckage that jammed their operating tables. The horror of the battle's aftermath defies evocation, but Robertson's essay conveys more than a glimmer of what Walt Whitman (who nursed Union wounded from Chancellorsville) called "these butcher's shambles."

Reputations as well as bodies could suffer irreparable damage in battle, and no charge struck nearer the vitals than cowardice in the face of the enemy. On May 2, 1863, Col. Emory F. Best and his 23rd Georgia Infantry received orders to guard the rear of Jackson's flanking column. Well before the Confederate Second Corps mounted its assault late that afternoon, Best and his regiment experienced a humiliating debacle, in the course of which the colonel abandoned his men and approximately 250 Confederates surrendered. In an essay based on testimony from Best's court-martial and other manuscript sources, Keith A. Bohannon assesses the ways in which political influence, widely divergent versions of what transpired, and, perhaps most important, notions about personal courage helped determine the fate of the accused. Denied the glory savored by most of Lee's soldiers after Chancellorsville, Best and other members of the 23rd who fled on May 2 also stood outside the circle of Lost Cause heroes after the war. Years after the conflict, Bohannon reveals, some of them continued to seek absolution from their fellow white southerners.

Sue Chancellor saw her childhood world literally blown apart when the armies collided around her family's home in early May 1863. James Marten uses the experiences at Chancellorsville of this fourteen-year-old girl and a Union drummer boy named Robert as points of departure to investigate the meaning of the battle and the war for children on both sides. A number of themes emerge from Marten's essay, among them the greater impact of the war on southern white children than on their northern counterparts, the ways in which adults sought to mold young people's understanding of the conflict, and the indelible nature of children's wartime memories. Adults made the decisions that precipitated the conflict and orchestrated its destruction and slaughter, but Marten's essay reminds readers that the national tragedy also left a profound mark on the generation of children who lived through it.

The essays in this volume do not present a chronicle of movements or a systematic review of all command decisions at Chancellorsville. Instead, readers will find insights relating to the political and military background of the campaign, tactical developments on selected parts of the battlefield, the experiences of officers and soldiers, and some of the ways in which the battle reverberated beyond May 1863 and Spotsylvania County, Virginia. In touching on a handful of the myriad facets of this complex event, the authors implicitly underscore the fact that many opportunities beckon historians interested in Civil War military campaigns.

It was a pleasure to work with the contributors to this volume, each of whom cheerfully complied with all editorial requests. George Skoch prepared the maps from sometimes crude sketches supplied by the editor, demonstrating that a talented person can bring order out of chaos. Individuals who assisted some of the contributors are acknowledged at the end of several essays. Finally, I wish to thank the Research and Graduate Studies Office of the College of the Liberal Arts at Pennsylvania State University, which provided support for the preparation of maps and illustrations.

1. Thomas Conolly, *An Irishman in Dixie: Thomas Conolly's Diary of the Fall of the Confederacy*, ed. Nelson D. Lankford (Columbia: University of South Carolina Press, 1988), 52.

2. Walter H. Hebert, *Fighting Joe Hooker* (Indianapolis: Bobbs-Merrill, 1944), 183 (Hooker's quotation was from an interview with Pennsylvania politician Alexander K. McClure); Edward Porter Alexander, *Fighting for the Confederacy: The Personal Recollections of General Edward Porter Alexander*, ed. Gary W. Gallagher (Chapel Hill: University of North Carolina Press, 1989), 195.

3. The troop strengths are from John Bigelow, Jr., *The Campaign of Chancellorsville: A Strategic and Tactical Study* (New Haven, Conn.: Yale University Press, 1910), 473–75.

4. U.S. War Department, *The War of the Rebellion: A Compilation of the Official Records of the Union and Confederate Armies*, 127 vols., index, and atlas (Washington, D.C.: GPO, 1880–1901), ser. 1, 25(1):171.

5. Darius N. Couch, "The Chancellorsville Campaign," in *Battles and Leaders of the Civil War*, ed. Robert Underwood Johnson and Clarence Clough Buel, 4 vols. (New York: Century, 1887–88), 3:161.

6. Henry Heth, "Letter from Major-General Henry Heth, of A. P. Hill's Corps, A.N.V.," in *Southern Historical Society Papers*, ed. J. William Jones and others, 52 vols. (1876–1959; reprint, with 3-vol. index, Wilmington, N.C.: Broadfoot, 1990–92), 4:154. Lee made these comments to Maj. John Seddon, who related them to Heth.

7. James M. McPherson, *Battle Cry of Freedom: The Civil War Era* (New York: Oxford University Press, 1988), 645 (quoting Noah Brooks); Gideon Welles, *Diary of Gideon Welles: Secretary of the Navy under Lincoln and Johnson*, ed. Howard K. Beale, 3 vols. (New York: W. W. Norton, 1960), 1:293.

8. Alexander, *Fighting for the Confederacy*, 216; Ernest B. Furgurson, *Chancellorsville 1863: The Souls of the Brave* (New York: Alfred A. Knopf, 1992), 132.

9. Charles Marshall, *An Aide-de-Camp of Lee; Being the Papers of Colonel Charles Marshall, Sometime Aide-de-Camp, Military Secretary, and Assistant Adjutant General on the Staff of Robert E. Lee, 1862–1865*, ed. Sir Frederick Maurice (Boston: Little, Brown, 1927), 173.

10. For a typically negative view, see Patricia L. Faust, ed., *Historical Times Illustrated Encyclopedia of the Civil War* (New York: Harper & Row, 1986), 721: "The raid was an unrelieved failure . . . one of Hooker's worst mistakes in the campaign."

11. Emma Holmes, *The Diary of Miss Emma Holmes, 1861–1866*, ed. John F. Marszalek (Baton Rouge: Louisiana State University Press, 1979), 255.

Chancellorsville

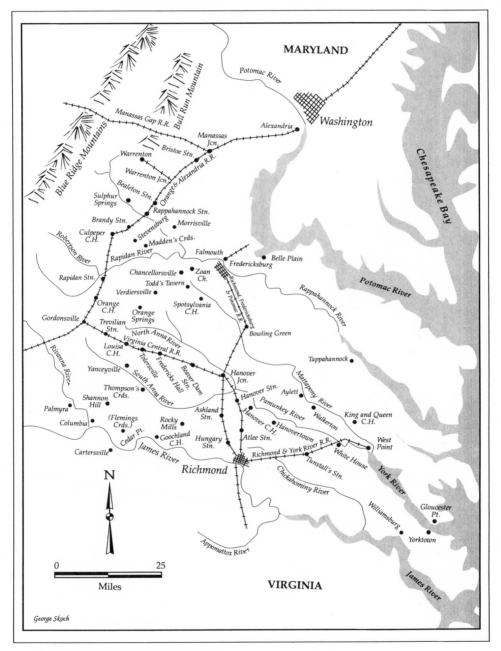

Theater of operations, April–May 1863

We Shall Make Richmond Howl

THE ARMY OF THE POTOMAC ON THE EVE OF CHANCELLORSVILLE

John J. Hennessy

ON JANUARY 27, 1863, Maj. Gen. Joseph Hooker took command of perhaps the saddest, angriest, most grumbly army that ever marched under America's postrevolutionary flag. Pontoons and wagons by the hundreds lay hopelessly mired along the roads of Stafford County, a depressing legacy of Ambrose E. Burnside's recently failed Mud March. Soldiers huddled gloomily in tents and huts. Men of all ranks groused loudly in letters read in countless drawing rooms across the North. "An entire army struck with melancholy," wrote an officer of the 140th New York. "Enthusiasm all evaporated—the army of the Potomac never sings, never shouts, and I wish I could say, never swears. . . . There is no concealing the fact," he explained, that "the mind of the army, just now, is a sort of intellectual marsh in which False Report grows fat, and sweeps up and down with a perfect audacity and fierceness." "At present the army is fast approaching a mob," another soldier told the readers of his local newspaper—a revelation hardly calculated to uplift the spirits of an already distressed homefolk. So restless had the army become, wrote a Connecticut correspondent, that "some of us have forgotten the distinction between a good government and its sometimes corrupt agents; and in our personal indignation, we have lost sight, for the moment, of our correct principles."[1]

More than a few commentators-in-ranks suggested the breakup of the army altogether. "I like the idea for my part," wrote a man of the 155th Pennsylvania, "& I think they may as well abandon this part of Virginia's bloody soil." Charles Francis Adams, Jr., the wealthy, educated, and blooded colonel of the 1st Massachusetts Cavalry, saw the army's dispersal as a necessity, lest, he warned, "some day they [the government] will have it marching on Washington."[2] Others foresaw the diminution of the army by the more insidious problem of desertion. Commenting in January on the high rate in his unit (the 121st New York), a soldier wrote that the deserters "had the good wishes of the whole regiment, almost without exception. Men here attach no disgrace to desertion."[3]

The sources of the discontent that so afflicted the Army of the Potomac in January 1863 went far beyond simple defeat on the battlefield (although surely victories would have been a swift antidote to the army's unhappiness). Letters of the period reflect an astonishing breadth of complaints—some rooted within the army, some without.[4] Many grievances were fundamental, such as the lack of paychecks. Regiments and batteries had not seen the paymaster for months. An artillery officer noted bitterly, "The voting of millions into the public Treasury failed to open a channel to [the] Battery . . . and into the pockets of one hundred and thirty brave defenders of that Treasury." Other complaints stemmed from the soldier's typical wintertime lament about physical discomfort. And even for these grievances the men found fault with the government. "The severity of the winter is nothing compared with the frigidity of our hearts toward the administration . . . for keeping men all winter in shelter tents and feeding them hard tacks and salt beef," wrote a man of the 44th New York. "It is an outrage on humanity and one that will live in the hearts of those composing the Army of the Potomac until disease and the bullet have consummated its extinction."[5]

Such a litany of woes naturally reflected on the army's leaders, and soldiers hardly could be faulted for a lack of confidence in their generals that winter. Quizzical whispers about the army's generalship had started in the wake of Antietam, when even privates recognized the opportunity lost when Lee's army slipped away due to Union idleness on September 18.[6] Burnside's defeat at Fredericksburg transformed the whispers into a roar of dissatisfaction. "From want of confidence in its leaders and *from no other reason*, the army is fearfully demoralized," reported a New York Zouave to his homefolk. Gouverneur Warren, who would be Hooker's chief topographical engineer, fairly fumed when he addressed the subject in a letter to his brother in January: "There seems to be an infatuation or a destiny that rushes our men at a breastwork as a moth does at a candle. . . . The bravery of our men is *quailing* before these things. We might as well rush our steamboats at full speed against the sea coast fortifications." Then he uttered the lament expressed thousands of times that winter: "Why can we not have generalship that will put [us] on equal footing with our enemies?"[7]

Generalship—performance on the battlefield—was one thing; leadership—the ability to motivate and inspire—was another, and the army at the moment lacked both. The problem was not merely that another George B. McClellan had not yet emerged but that the entire high command of the army was in a state of wholesale transformation. With the relief of Edwin Vose Sumner, William B. Franklin, and W. F. "Baldy" Smith in late January, only five of the nineteen corps and division commanders who had been with the army at the outset of the Seven Days battles in June 1862 remained.[8] Hooker's appointment gave the army its third commander in three months. "I dislike these constant changes," wrote Col. Walter Phelps of the 22nd New York. "I know they have a bad influence on the troops in the field."[9]

Of those who had departed, enough had left in a blaze of controversy (including Fitz John Porter, Franklin, and Smith) to give the impression that the high command of the Army of the Potomac was a volatile, boiling pot of intrigue. "The army, now, does not know under whom it is fighting," Charles Francis Adams, Jr., told his diplomat-father. "[The] Government has taken from it every single one of its old familiar battle names." Those who remained in the high command inspired only marginal confidence among their men. "The army seems to be overburdened with second rate men in high positions," offered Rufus Dawes of the 6th Wisconsin. "Common place [men] and whiskey are too much in power for the most hopeful future. This winter is, indeed, the Valley Forge of the war."[10]

A good part of the discontent with the current leadership had to do with the men's affinity for George B. McClellan, the army's past commander and "first love" in terms of both time and stature. Judging from the volume of ink expended on the subject in the soldiers' letters throughout December 1862 and January 1863, the army suffered from a serious bout of nostalgia, pining for the "good old days" when "Little Mac" commanded and all the soldiers fought entirely for love of country. "Our men do not fight with the same vim and élan that they used to," ran a typical complaint. "I believe about one half of our army fight for the money . . . not for patriotism."[11]

The depression stemmed not just from McClellan's absence but also from what the soldiers viewed as a broad-based assault on everyone closely associated with their beloved first commander. Porter, Franklin, and "Baldy" Smith all had been close confidants of McClellan. To some observers, the administration seemed bent on purging the army of McClellan's influence. For its part, the army seemed equally fervent in its desire for McClellan's return. Gouverneur Warren expressed a common conviction to his brother: "We *must* have McClellan back with unlimited and unfettered powers. His name is a tower of strength here."[12]

The perceived obstruction of McClellan's program by the administration drove Alexander Webb to label the men in Washington "fools" and "idiots." Soon to be a brigade commander in the Second Corps, Webb declared, "I despise them more intensely than I do the Rebels." But Régis de Trobriand saw the administration's meddling in a less insidious light, attributing it simply to the proximity of the army to the nation's capital: "[The] Army of the Potomac was the army of the President, the army of the Senate, the army of the House of Representatives, the army of the press and of the tribune, somewhat the army of every one. Everybody meddled in its affairs."[13]

Besides going badly that winter for the Army of the Potomac, the war in Virginia also was changing dramatically. It had metamorphosed from a straightforward effort to restore the Union into a struggle that would alter American society. These changes, combined with growing war-weariness at home, made the Union of 1863 a cauldron of division and discontent.

The fissures that rent society divided the army as well. Lincoln's issuance of the Emancipation Proclamation stimulated an avalanche of commentary. Although opinions spanned the spectrum, letters written during the first weeks of January make clear that much of the army saw the proclamation as a disquieting prospect rather than the trumpet of a grand crusade. Francis Pierce of the 108th New York declared flatly, "I will not jeopardize my life or become an invalid for life . . . simply to restore 3,000,000 *brutes* to freedom." "Formerly when a rebel on picket or any other place asked me, 'What are you fighting for?,'" he explained, "I could answer, proudly too, *for the restoration of the Union*—now when one asks me I have to hang my head or else answer, *for the nigger*." A soldier-correspondent for an Indiana newspaper wrote that the new proclamation "caused me an hour's hearty laugh, two hour's steady cry, [and] four hours big with mad." He laughed, he said, "because I am now certain of seeing [Lincoln] in an insane asylum." He cried because Lincoln "did not kill himself when a youth splitting rails." And, he wrote, "I choked with wrath to think that he has command of the old ship of state for twenty six long months to come."[14]

A corollary of emancipation was the government's effort to create African American regiments. The specter of black troops joining the Army of the Potomac threw many a soldier into swivets of often-racist protest. "I tell you it will ruin the army," wrote a Jerseyman. "If a negro regiment were to come and camp near an old regiment out here, the men would kill half of them. The men do nothing but curse the President now." The surgeon of the 105th Pennsylvania likewise declared that his regiment, "though composed almost entirely of Republicans, would charge and drive [a black regiment] with more delight than they would the rebels. . . . You have no idea how greatly the common soldiers are prejudiced against the Negro."[15]

Others took a more enlightened view (although truly noble opinions, by modern standards, were rare): "I am a firm friend to the cause of organizing an army of fifty thousand negroes," commented one soldier. "Our enemies use them, why not we?" Wrote another man with a practical eye, "*Anything* which tends to shorten and put down this conflict I am in favor of employing." Similarly, the chaplain of the 26th New Jersey stated, "Let him fight, or make him fight; he ought to fight. He has as much or more at stake in this war than any one else."[16]

Debates about abolition, the Emancipation Proclamation, and the use of African American soldiers flourished in the army, but on one issue the soldiers reached agreement: they reviled those at home, including newspapers, who in their view undercut the Union war effort. (This was ironical because much of the discontent at home grew out of dissatisfaction over the same issues that divided the army.) To those toiling at the front, domestic unhappiness with the war effort seemed pervasive; the army felt acutely a lack of support for its immense sacrifices. The defeat at Fredericksburg, the disastrous Mud March, and the issuance of Lincoln's proclamation coincided with the emergence of an ever-growing peace movement in the North. Although the soldiers often sympathized with the views of the Peace Democrats on an issue-by-issue basis, they could not abide talk of peace without a restored Union. Indeed, few words generated more outrage among Union troops that winter than "Copperhead."

No matter how low the army's morale or how harsh the debate over the proper path to victory, the soldiers never lost collective sight of the war's ultimate objective. Robert Gould Shaw of the 2nd Massachusetts (who saw things in a far more liberal light than most in the army) declared, "I had rather stay here all my life (though, in this case, I should pray for a short one) than give up to the South." The army almost unanimously viewed the antiwar agitators with contempt—"mean low bred cowardly traitors and scoundrels," as Pennsylvanian James Miller put it. Wrote a normally genteel and pious surgeon of the 121st New York, "I hate them worse than the enemies in front, and would sooner see a field strewn with their blackened, putrid carcasses, than those who we are fighting down here." Indeed, many soldiers promised just such a result: "After this war is over . . . we will take vengeance on those cowardly skunks that are a disgrace to our country," wrote Miller.[17]

*Maj. Gen. Joseph Hooker (*fourth from the left in the front row*) and staff. Maj. Gen. Daniel Butterfield, the army's chief of staff, is seated to the right of Hooker; chief of artillery Brig. Gen. Henry Jackson Hunt is seated second from the left. Francis Trevelyan Miller, ed.,* The Photographic History of the Civil War, *10 vols. (New York: Review of Reviews, 1911), 2:109*

These agents of domestic discontent expressed their views in the many anti-administration newspapers that circulated throughout the army, and it seemed to many that the perfidious press (as the officers, especially, saw it) was determined to stir the pot of unrest. Before he took command of the army, Hooker had written to Secretary of War Edwin M. Stanton, "I wish that you could choke the newspapers. They are a nuisance in their effect on certain minds." One of Burnside's staff officers agreed that the quashing of the press "would be one of the greatest victories we have gained. The ill effect of their constant criticism . . . is seen in camp every day."[18]

Never in its forty-seven months of existence would the Army of the Potomac have so much to disapprove of as it had that January. Its generals, its government, its food, the cold, emancipation, the specter of black troops, Copperheads, the press—almost every aspect of the war effort and the condition of the army brought discontent in some form at every level of command. Each issue left a scrape on the army's body, and those wounds oozed freely as Hooker assumed command. Lamented one forlorn Yankee cavalryman that dark winter, "Oh my country, how my heart bleeds for your welfare."[19]

Into this "intellectual marsh" of discontent strode "Fighting Joe" Hooker. Tall, muscular, erect, and almost always described as "florid," Hooker bore himself as a man much younger than his forty-eight years. "Anybody would feel like cheering when he rode by at the head of his staff," recorded Carl Schurz.[20] During the antebellum years, he had served in the Regular Army after graduating in the class of 1837 at West Point, dabbled in politics as a Democrat, failed at farming, and finally found success as superintendent of military roads in Oregon. When the war broke out, he hurried east, lacking nothing in the way of confidence or boldness. After First Manassas he had declared to Lincoln, "I was at Bull Run the other day, Mr. President, and it is no vanity in me to say that I am a d— sight better general than any you had on that field." Eighteen months later Lincoln had come to believe Hooker's boast, appointing him on January 27, 1863, to command the republic's largest army.[21]

Hooker's military brethren knew him best for three prominent qualities. The most positive of the three was his aggressiveness. In an army full of passive, mediocre officers, Hooker's was one of the few resumés that reflected a consistent record of aggression. History has looked kindly on this record, but in some respects it has not been subjected to sufficient examination. At Williamsburg, Hooker initiated a battle that should not have been waged under the circumstances and nearly lost his division. Fellow division commander Philip Kearny said of him, "Hooker has been beaten, because he did not know his mind." At Antietam, his overaggressiveness on the evening of September 16 put his corps almost among the Confederate pickets. This faulty position hamstrung him on the morning of September 17, preventing flexibility regarding either the nature or the timing of the attacks against Lee's left. Admittedly, he had done well at Glendale and South Mountain, but the quiet perception persisted in the high command that Fighting Joe sometimes did a little too much fighting too soon. "His bravery is unquestioned," wrote his former chief of artillery Charles Wainwright, "but he has not so far shown himself anything of a tactician." "I am not prepared to say as to his abilities for carrying on a campaign and commanding a large army," added George G. Meade. "I should fear his judgment and prudence, as he is apt to think the only thing to be done is to pitch in and fight." After Chancellorsville, the irony of this prebattle reputation could not have been lost on anyone.[22]

Another characteristic that brought Hooker notice among his colleagues was a penchant for—some said obsession with—self-promotion. Hooker paid assiduous attention to his connections in the press and Congress. The papers of members of the cabinet, House, and Senate are liberally strewn with missives from Fighting Joe espousing his own accomplishments.[23]

Distinguishing Hooker from other self-advocates in the Army of the Potomac was his relentless denigration of others to his own benefit. Régis de Trobriand remembered that he "was accustomed to criticise freely, with more sharpness than discretion . . . the conduct and acts of his superiors." Few viewed this habit as Hooker himself did: "I was *pronounced* in my opinions . . . for the sake of the *cause* and the *country*," he wrote after the war, "cherishing no ill-feeling towards the persons, or parties, implicated, or in any way reflecting on their merits, or demerits, but simply [to] have the attention of the authorities called . . . so that the mistakes might be remedied." He did all this, he claimed, "utterly regardless of any influence it might have on myself."[24]

Most of Hooker's contemporaries did not see his backbiting in so noble a light. John Gibbon considered him "an intriguer" who "sacrificed his soldierly principles whenever such sacrifice could gain him political influence to further his own ends." McClellan called him a "good soldier and an unreliable man," an opinion elaborated upon by Ulysses S. Grant, who regarded him as "dangerous." "He was not subordinate to his superiors," Grant wrote after the war. "He was ambitious to the extent of caring nothing for the rights of others."[25]

A third trait, Hooker's political changeability, simultaneously alienated many of his military brethren and worked to his benefit. Hooker usually told those in power exactly what they wanted to hear. This was especially onerous (and anomalous) in a high command largely and faithfully conservative in its political views. Meade noticed Hooker's chameleon tendencies even before Fighting Joe achieved command. "Hooker is a democrat and an anti-abolitionist—that is to say, he was," Meade wrote in October 1862. "What he will be, when the command of the army is held out to him, is more than anyone can tell, because I fear he is open to temptation and liable to be seduced by flattery." Lincoln sensed all of this too. In his letter of appointment, he acknowledged elevating Hooker despite the record of intrigue. "I much fear that the spirit which you have aided to infuse into the Army, of criticizing their commander, and withholding confidence from him, will now turn on you," Lincoln warned.[26]

Hooker's appointment stimulated mixed reviews from the army and did little to uplift the spirits of downtrodden men. W. T. H. Brooks, division commander in the Sixth Corps, probably penned the majority opinion when he wrote unenthusiastically, "I think the country may safely expect a better account of [Hooker] and the Army of the Potomac than was rendered by its late commander." A man of the Ninth Corps wrote home on the day of the appointment, "Everybody appears entirely indifferent to the matter. Heroes of many defeats, we are not inclined to give gratuitous confidence to anyone." Others showed less ambivalence. Henry Abbott of the 20th Massachusetts could not conceal his disdain for his fellow Bay Stater: "Hooker is nothing more than a smart, driving, plucky Yankee, inordinately vain & I imagine from the way he has converted himself to the administration, entirely unscrupulous. . . . We all expect [he] will soon make a grand failure & patiently wait for it."[27]

The simple fact that they were forced to endure yet another change outraged some. "Are the chuckle heads at Washington beside themselves: will they never be done with their awkward bungling?" queried a member of the soon-to-be-detached Ninth Corps. "The President must be crazy," concluded this man in anguish. A wag in the Eleventh Corps used vivid colloquialism to record his displeasure: "When a man is hauling a heavy load up hill, he has no time to stop and swap jackasses."[28]

The army's discontent indicated the magnitude of the task facing Hooker in early 1863. He could do nothing about such causes of discord as frustration with government policy, emancipation, the raising of black regiments, and the railings of Copperheads. He could only hope to hold the army together long enough to allow these wounds—which were hemorrhaging badly in January—to scab over. He would succeed by focusing his energy on those sources of pain that were within his power to address.

Hooker inherited an army whose administration had atrophied. Under Burnside, the quality and quantity of rations had diminished. "In less than a week after Burnside took command," one soldier had written, "we saw a difference in rations, etc. We were never short before."[29] The principles of sanitation had been discarded. Illness had increased. Paymasters had vanished. Immediately on taking command, Hooker, with his new chief of staff Daniel Butterfield, undertook to resuscitate the army—to perform a military triple bypass on their heartsick patient.

Sensing that the morale of the army mirrored its collective health, Hooker first attended to the physical condition of his troops. His primary agent of change in this area—and the unseen hero of the army's rebirth—was medical director Jonathan Letterman. Writing of Letterman after the war, Hooker offered uncommonly unrestrained praise: "I doubt if any army had his superior in technical and profound knowledge of his profession, and in administrative ability and devotion. Many a man in that army was indebted to him for their lives, without even knowing it."[30]

To a modern eye, the measures Letterman enacted in February and March 1863 seem elementary. Subscribing to the belief in the storied correlation between hunger and happiness, he urged improvement of the army's diet. Through Hooker, he ordered bakeries constructed, and soon the smell of fresh bread wafted across the camps at Falmouth. By mid-February the men already had noticed improvements. "Fighting Joe Hooker is . . . becoming favorite with us," exclaimed a correspondent in the 108th New York, "because he has ordered that we shall have fresh bread four days a week—instead of Baltimore pavements. . . . Bravo for Joe Hooker."[31] Letterman also prompted the regular provision of vegetables, which were supplied to the camps at least twice per week in February. James Crole, an Irish staff officer in the new Cavalry Corps, declared, "I like old Joe Hooker better now than I did two months ago and I think every Irishman in the army is of the same opinion. . . . We get more potatoes in a week now than we used to get in a month."[32]

Sanitation also improved under Letterman's direction. He mandated the rotation of campsites, improvement of drainage ditches, removal of latrines from living areas and the vicinity of water supplies, and the regular airing of tents, huts, and bedding. In early April he even persuaded Hooker to order every soldier in the army to wash both their clothes and themselves. Those who failed to do so would be arrested. This prompted a grudging compliment from a formerly dubious New York artilleryman: "General Hooker is bound to have this army start forth in good style with clean clothes, at least."[33]

These measures stimulated dramatic results. In February alone, cases of diarrhea in the army dropped 32 percent, typhoid, 28 percent. Scurvy, common in January, virtually disappeared by April. Between February 1 and March 28, only 800 men left the army due to illness. For these remarkable accomplishments by Letterman, Hooker received much of the public praise. "I am fully disposed to give General Hooker credit for every good thing he does," wrote Charles Morse of the 2nd Massachusetts in mid-March. "I believe that the army was never in better condition . . . than it is now, very different from what it was a month ago."[34]

While Letterman massaged the army's physical body back to health, Hooker devoted himself to rehabilitating its psyche and organization. He first attacked desertion, the most serious and obvious symptom of the army's sickness. When Hooker took command, 29 percent (76,878) of the army was absent, half of them without leave. Two hundred more were leaving each day.[35] To stem the flow, Hooker took many steps. In the belief that the treasured "boxes to the soldiers from home" often included civilian clothes and other inducements to desert, Hooker started inspecting the packages. He also improved patrols along routes to the North and increased the pace of courts-martial for those caught deserting. In March, at Hooker's urging, Lincoln issued an amnesty proclamation for deserters that lured many back to the rolls. By April, the number of men absent from the army had dropped to 48,638—23.5 percent of the army's total strength. Hooker's efforts had yielded an 18 percent drop in the absentee rate.[36]

Hooker's other measures worked directly on the army's disgruntled frame of mind. He instituted a system of furloughs—a measure initially opposed by President Lincoln, who predicted the furloughed men, once gone, would never return. Hooker persisted and was eventually granted a three-week trial. For every 100 men in a regiment, two soldiers with "the most excellent record for attention to all duties" could be furloughed at a time for up to ten days. Regiments with outstanding records might receive additional privileges. An Ohioan described comrades "filled with joyous anticipation" at the prospect of leaves, and Henry Abbott of the 20th Massachusetts, an incessant critic of Burnside, gave the new army commander great credit for "employing the spirit of emulation, the most powerful governing spirit of . . . American troops." Although only a small percentage of the army benefited directly from the system, virtually all accounts confirm that it achieved the desired effect. In alluding to the furloughs, Hooker himself proudly told a postwar correspondent, "You know the results."[37]

Anyone familiar with Hooker's image in the press was not surprised that in addition to improving the army's food, he also improved its drink. He arranged that regiments returning from picket would receive a ration of whiskey. Although the men hailed the measure, it nonetheless stimulated rueful comment. John Haley of the 17th Maine (one of the army's most entertaining diarists), recorded in February: "General Hooker is a firm believer in spirits of this kind, and, if rumor is true, he and his staff devote a great deal of time to 'inspecting quarts.' "[38]

The most famous of Hooker's measures concerned corps badges. Although these simple metal disks eventually would become prized possessions (of both their original owners and later collectors), they owed their genesis to a negative motivation. Hooker wanted to be able to identify a laggard's unit and hence easily bring the responsible officer to heel for the army's straggling problem. Before Chancellorsville, the corps badges stimulated little comment from their wearers. After the battle, references to the emblems were common. Hooker later wrote that they had a "*magical* effect on the discipline and conduct of our troops. . . . The badge became very precious in the estimation of the soldier, and to this day [1876] they value them more than anything beside."[39]

Despite disdain for his predecessors in the army's command, Hooker did not hesitate to steal arrows from their quivers. For example, his practice of staging regular reviews and inspections had been a favorite device used by George B. McClellan to encourage the army to see itself in a positive light. "Inspecting and reviews are the order of the day," wrote a Twelfth Corps soldier with mixed pleasure and fatigue, noting that "we have had no less than six within the last three weeks." The greatest of the spectacles occurred in early April, when President Lincoln visited the army and spent several days reviewing its eight corps. The reviews provoked a small flood of commentary on the appearance of the president, his wife, and his son Tad; more important for the

*Grand review of the Army of the Potomac, April 1862 (sketch by Edwin Forbes).
Library of Congress*

army, they stimulated positive reflection on the immense spectacle presented by its component parts. This week of reviews was not a defining moment in the army's history (as had been the first grand review at Bailey's Crossroads in the fall of 1861), but soldiers undoubtedly were heartened by the spectacle. Charles Morse of the 2nd Massachusetts concluded that "the Army of the Potomac is a collection of as fine troops, I firmly believe, as there are in the world. I believe the day will come when it will be a proud thing for any one to say he belonged to it."[40]

The Army of the Potomac also took a different organizational form under Hooker. Some of his structural changes would continue to benefit the army; others would quietly fade away; and a few would fail abjectly. Without question, Hooker made his greatest contribution in this regard by combining the cavalry into a single corps. This step culminated a steady course of consolidating the army's mounted units begun by John Pope the previous summer. Pope had formed the Army of Virginia's cavalry into brigades; McClellan later created a division. Hooker melded the army's cavalry into a corps of 17,000 riders. Used wisely, it could be a formidable, perhaps decisive, weapon in the campaign ahead.[41]

In his most dramatic measure, Hooker abolished Burnside's grand divisions. Under the old system, the army commander had to communicate with only grand division commanders (each grand division consisted of two corps). Hooker saw that arrangement as cumbersome—"impeding rather than facilitating the dispatch of [the army's] current business," he wrote—and predicted that the character of the impending campaign would be "adverse to the movement and operations of heavy columns" (whatever that meant). Instead, Hooker chose to deal directly with all eight corps commanders. Oliver Otis Howard postulated that Hooker adopted this arrangement for the same reason McClellan had: "I think General Hooker . . . enjoyed maneuvering several independent bodies."[42]

Whatever Hooker's reasoning, the reorganization must be judged a step backward for the Army of the Potomac. The yardstick for this judgment is the organization of the armies in Virginia that achieved decisive success during the war: Lee's in 1862 and 1863 and Meade's in 1864 and 1865. Both of these commanders organized their armies in large chunks—two, three, sometimes four corps at most. Each found that the arrangement offered sufficient flexibility while at the same time facilitating the delivery of large numbers of men to the point of contact on the battlefield. To be sure, organization alone could not accomplish this, but organization alone could *discourage* it. The effective management of eight corps in an offensive role on a battlefield would prove to be beyond the ability of any commander in this war; of this, Hooker became a vivid example.

Another of Hooker's organizational blunders concerned the reconfiguration of his artillery. For months, the tendency in both Union and Confederate armies had been to consolidate batteries at the corps level while maintaining an army reserve. Hooker reversed this trend. He stripped his chief of artillery, Henry Jackson Hunt (a strong McClellan man whom Hooker called "opinionated but able"), of all line authority and dispersed the army's batteries to divisions. Hooker took this step not for sound tactical reasons but rather to sustain the warm feelings between the infantry and batteries. He later explained, "In my old Brigade and Division I found that my men had learned to regard their batteries with a feeling of devotion, which I considered contributed greatly to our success."[43]

This change naturally pained Hunt no end, for it showed that Hooker had little grasp of evolving artillery tactics. The measure severely reduced the ability of the army's artillery to achieve a decisive concentration of fire on the battlefield. With no more than four batteries assigned to any one division—and hence assigned to work together—serendipity would play a key role in determining whether the Federals managed any significant massing of firepower. Hooker would learn this lesson quickly at Chancellorsville. On May 3, in the midst of battle, he would attempt to correct the situation by giving Col. Charles Wainwright of the First Corps control of the army's batteries. By May 13, Hooker had abolished his own reform. Hunt returned to command, and the trend toward the consolidation of the army's artillery into brigades resumed.[44]

A final error of Hooker's—less serious but much commented upon—was the addition of 2,000 pack mules to the army's rolls. The theory (based, perhaps, on the positive British experience during the Crimean War) was that the small army of mules would shuttle matériel between the wagon trains and the front, easing the flow of supplies and disencumbering the army of part of its huge complement of wagons. The mule-shuttle would also eliminate the rumbling of wagons near the front, giving the enemy one less hint at the army's activities. Theoretical benefits aside, few outside army headquarters embraced the idea. Charles Wainwright commented that Hooker "has got quite a new kink in his head." Another man suggested that the scheme was more "a whim . . . based upon old Californian notions than a real practical ideal."[45]

The plan proved to be impractical largely because of the difficulties of managing mules. None of the army's mules had been broken as pack animals, and even when properly trained, they could be single-minded beasts. Wainwright noted in the midst of the retraining regimen that there was "great amusement in the trains, trying to get the mules accustomed to their new burdens, and the men used to their animals." The mules also had to be loaded and unloaded at each stop—a time-consuming chore—and six mules with packs could carry far less than six mules hauling a wagon. The same amount of freight thus would consume more space in the road under the new scheme. The mule reform failed and in the spring of 1863 quietly faded away.[46]

The transformation of the Army of the Potomac during the first months of Hooker's command was by any measure impressive. The force that stood poised to march on April 27, 1863, was healthy, motivated, and hopeful. The grumbling that had resounded through the ranks in January had diminished greatly.[47] Although Hooker's structural changes earned mixed reviews, he deserves considerable credit for the turnaround. Contrary to his image—and in sharp contrast to the methods of McClellan—he had not tried to pull the army upward by the force of his personality, concentrating instead on correcting organizational defects concerning food, sanitation, and leaves. Apart from Hooker's actions, several happy circumstances abetted the army's recovery. Most important, the soldiers enjoyed their first truly relaxed and extended period of inaction in almost a year. Rest in itself was surely responsible for some of the rehabilitation.[48]

The break from campaigning seemed all the sweeter because it followed the most tumultuous period in the army's life—an ordeal that extended from the end of the Seven Days battles to Hooker's ascension. During that time the high command believed itself constantly threatened by increasingly radical politicians in the cabinet and the halls of Congress. The army's original leadership (men such as McClellan, Porter, Baldy Smith, Franklin, and even Sumner) had been removed, as most of the rank and file saw it, by political machinations. At all levels, and especially among the army's largely Democratic high command, resentment ran deep against the meddling men of Washington.[49]

Because the Radical Republicans embraced Hooker, the new commander suffered little of the external agitation that had beset McClellan. Sinister letters to and between members of the Joint Committee on the Conduct of the War largely stopped—at least those that included criticism of the commander of the Army of the Potomac. An almost tranquil atmosphere surrounded the army during the spring of 1863.

Another advantage Hooker enjoyed over his predecessors concerned intrigue within the army. Most notably, he did not have to combat the greatest intriguer the Army of the Potomac ever knew—Joe Hooker. Whereas Burnside had suffered the agitations of many who wished to have him removed, Hooker functioned without threat of internal subversion. As Hooker led his soldiers toward Spotsylvania County's Wilderness that spring, he did so without the aura of backbiting that had demoralized the army in December and January.[50]

Finally, Hooker presided over the diminishing ripples of controversy caused by the more radical turn the war had taken in late 1862 and early 1863. This is not to say that most soldiers had come to embrace emancipation, the prospect of black troops, or the 1862 mandate to confiscate Confederate property (although many reveled in the confiscation measure, for, if practiced cleverly, it could benefit them considerably in the form of increased victuals and other niceties). But during Hooker's first months in command, they had accepted these measures as faits accomplis, and many saw them as useful. Any great social change invariably engenders controversy followed by sometimes-grudging and always-gradual acceptance. So it was with the Army of the Potomac. In January, vicious commentary on the Emancipation Proclamation and the prospect of black regiments prevailed. By May and June, letters home contained relatively few such references.

The result of this happy marriage between Hooker's effective administration and fortuitous circumstances was the creation of an army both able and willing to do battle. Wrote Wilbur Fisk of the 2nd Vermont, "Confidence in the government, and respect for it, is reestablished." And Frank Haskell of the Second Corps concluded, "The army is in magnificent condition—If it cannot do well, what hope can the country have?"[51]

The focus thus far has been on the heart and mind of the army. What of its subordinate commanders and the organizations they led? The high command that took the field with Joe Hooker in May 1863 reflected changes that had taken place in the army during the previous nine months. It differed considerably from the body that had toiled under McClellan in 1862.[52] Of the ninety-four officers who marched into battle that spring, only twenty had held brigade or division commands with the army in June 1862. Forty—43 percent—would be leading brigades or divisions for the first time. More than 64 percent had attended college; 42 percent had gone to West Point; 17 percent were lawyers. About 30 percent had combat experience in the Mexican War (down from more than 50 percent in June 1862), and at an average age of about forty, the officers of 1863 were younger by two years than their counterparts of 1862.[53]

The officers of May 1863 had learned some vivid lessons during the past year. Hooker vowed to rid the army of any attachment to George B. McClellan's conservative mode of war but by his own admission failed.[54] Officers devoted to McClellan had come to realize that their views were out of step with the political atmosphere in Washington. They had seen Charles Stone wrongly arrested and imprisoned in early 1862, making him the first victim of the Joint Committee on the Conduct of the War. They had seen Fitz John Porter wrongly court-martialed and dismissed. They had seen McClellan relentlessly persecuted and (to their eyes) harassed. They had seen William B. Franklin and Baldy Smith banished. All these men possessed similar political views—views that represented the outlook of many others in the high command. Those of the old guard who remained—John F. Reynolds, George G. Meade, John Sedgwick, Darius N. Couch, Henry W. Slocum, and others—realized that the prevailing political winds blew against them. They had learned that success and longevity in the Army of the Potomac depended as much on the ability to maneuver in the political field as on the ability to maneuver on the battlefield and that mixing duty and loud expressions of objectionable political views must be avoided.[55]

Which men would play prominent roles in Hooker's six-day adventure at Chancellorsville? First and perhaps most important was Maj. Gen. Daniel Butterfield, Hooker's chief of staff and one of two men—the other being Daniel E. Sickles—widely believed to have constituted the army commander's innermost circle. Known best as the supposed composer of "Taps," Butterfield is today something of an enigma (no body of his papers or any revealing writings exist). The fastest-rising nonprofessional soldier in the army in 1862, Butterfield had progressed from brigade command to head the Fifth Corps in just three months, outdistancing the likes of Sedgwick, George Sykes, Couch, Winfield S. Hancock, Warren, and Charles Griffin.

A New Yorker, Butterfield owed his rise to a combination of organizational skills and smart politics rather than to outstanding performance on the battlefield. First, he established a sterling record as a regimental and brigade commander during the war's first winter. Porter wrote of him that he "had his brigade in such good order as to make it a model for the best organization." The glow from those heady days remained with Butterfield for months.[56] Like the miscreant Hiram Berdan, he also paid assiduous attention to his connections with the big-city press, especially the *New York Times*, which regularly featured accounts of his exploits. Friendships with Secretary of the Treasury Salmon P. Chase and Senator Henry Wilson of Massachusetts further boosted his career. Finally, Butterfield owed much to Fighting Joe Hooker himself, who proved to be a loyal champion in his dealings with Congress and the cabinet.[57]

Butterfield undeniably did good work as Hooker's chief of staff. Indeed, none of the army's chiefs of staff would ever wield greater influence. Washington Roebling called him "Hooker's brains" and maintained that "Hooker was simply the beau sabreur, posing before the rank and file." This was surely too strong a statement, but even corps commander Darius Couch—one of Hooker's most bitter enemies—conceded that Butterfield "proved himself very efficient."[58]

It is equally true, however, that many of Butterfield's colleagues considered him pretentious and obnoxious. In May Charles Wainwright, who had expected good things of the army's chief staff man, concluded that Butterfield "does not seem to have practical common sense in all points" and "is most thoroughly hated by all . . . as a meddling, over-conceited fellow." Others saw him as a "humbug." McClellan called him "a sycophant, an intriguer, & of low tastes & associations." Charles Francis Adams wrote pointedly, "Sickles, Butterfield, and Hooker are the disgrace and bane of this army. They are our three humbugs, intriguers and demagogues."[59]

Daniel E. Sickles was another member of the high command who owed his station in part to Hooker's influence and friendship (it is likely true, too, that Hooker owed his position in part to Sickles's influence, for Sickles had close connections with Lincoln, especially Mrs. Lincoln, with whom one man said he was "very spooney.")[60] Early in the war, he had commanded a brigade under Hooker. When Hooker took charge of the army, he put his friend at the head of the Third Corps—a move that rankled several of Sickles's seniors, especially O. O. Howard, whom Hooker passed over. Grumbling, however, swayed Hooker not at all, and Dan Sickles would quickly gain station as one of Hooker's inner circle.[61] Brigade commander Régis de Trobriand commented that Sickles "brings to the service of his ambition a clear view, a practical judgment, and a deep knowledge of political tactics."[62]

It is difficult to overstate the singularity of Sickles's background. Before the war he had reputedly carried on an affair with his future mother-in-law. Later, as a New York congressman, he murdered his wife's paramour, Philip Barton Key, then to the shock of Victorian America took his wife back. Edwin M. Stanton represented him in the subsequent legal spectacular and managed to gain his acquittal on the grounds of temporary insanity. A modern biographer's characterization of him is most apt: "He was always in some sort of crisis, be it financial, legislative, sexual, or homicidal."[63]

Dan Sickles inspired a moderate reaction from no one. Few outside his own corps found much to praise. Brig. Gen. Alpheus S. Williams of the Twelfth Corps expressed a typical opinion: "A 'Sickles' would beat Napoleon in winning glory not earned. He is a hero without an heroic deed! Literally made by scribblers." G. K. Warren declared him "morally debased, and of no military experience"; he maintained that Sickles received his command solely because "he is smart as a political maneuverer." Staff officer Frank Haskell of the Second Corps called him "a man after show, and notoriety, and newspaper fame, and the adulation of the mob!"[64]

But within the Third Corps, Sickles engendered mostly warm devotion. His brigade commander, the Frenchman Régis de Trobriand, called him "one of the striking figures of this war. . . . In many ways a typical American. He was gifted in a high degree with that multiplicity of faculties which has given rise to the saying that a Yankee is ready for everything." From the ranks came like praise. John Haley of the 17th Maine wrote in his diary, "He is a gamey looking bird" and "a fine specimen of majestic indifference." Haley saw the murder of Key in a positive light: "A person who has the nerve to do that might be expected to show good qualities as a general where daredeviltry is a factor." So it would prove to be, for although Sickles brought little skill or finesse to the battlefield, he did display courage, thus endearing himself to the Third Corps.[65]

Beyond Hooker's confidential elite were the rest of the army's corps commanders. History must adjudge them collectively as a mediocre but interesting group of men. Pennsylvanian John Fulton Reynolds commanded the First Corps, a unit that had formerly belonged to the hated Irvin McDowell and hence had been something of a pariah. At Antietam, however, the First Corps had earned its way into the Army of the Potomac with a bloody performance. At that time it had been under Hooker's command, but Reynolds had taken over before Fredericksburg, and now the corps stood solidly in the army's mainstream (a status not accorded the Ninth, Eleventh, and Twelfth corps).

Reynolds had been a candidate for command of the army but, when canvassed, had demanded too much autonomy to suit the Washington set. This was no disappointment to some in Congress. Like so many of his cohorts, Reynolds was widely viewed as a conservative of the McClellan ilk and consequently had received the hostile attention of some members of the Joint Committee on the Conduct of the War. Indeed, Senator Benjamin F. Wade, who chaired the committee, recently had proclaimed his intention to see that Reynolds was removed from the army. But unlike many of his colleagues, Reynolds

Maj. Gen. Daniel Edgar Sickles. Robert Underwood Johnson and Clarence Clough Buel,
eds., Battles and Leaders of the Civil War, 4 vols. (New York: Century, 1887–88), 3:296

was *quietly* Democratic—just as he was quiet about most things. This simple
fact distinguished him in many eyes. "General Reynolds is very different from
Hooker, in that he never expresses an opinion about other officers," recorded
artilleryman Wainwright. "I can get nothing out of him."[66]

Reynolds was probably the most respected man in the Army of the Potomac
(no negative comments about him from his contemporaries have been found).

He attained this status despite a combat record that included only one bright spot—Second Manassas, where he was the best of a mediocre cast of division commanders. Admiration for him derived in part from his direct, unpretentious, even Spartan manner. "General Reynolds obeys orders literally himself, and expects all under him to do the same," recorded Wainwright. Frank Haskell called Reynolds "one of the *soldier* generals of the army, a man whose soul was in his country's work." McClellan termed him "remarkably brave and intelligent, an honest, true gentleman." Hooker would eventually view Reynolds as the best corps commander in the army (supplanting Meade). Of his performance in the Gettysburg campaign, Hooker wrote, "I have never had an officer under me acquit himself so handsomely."[67]

The commander of the Second Corps was Maj. Gen. Darius Nash Couch, an enigmatic, thirty-five-year-old Pennsylvanian who must rank as one of the most obscure of the army's long-term corps commanders. Couch had been with the army from the outset, serving almost invisibly as a division commander. He owed his lofty position as the army's second in command to seniority, his competent if unspectacular performance, the boosterism of Pennsylvania governor Andrew Gregg Curtin, and his pleasing, unpretentious personality. A Second Corps staff officer wrote that he was "a very quiet, sensible, competent officer, but looks more like a Methodist minister than a soldier." Second Corps historian Francis A. Walker recalled that Couch's "unaffected modesty found expression in every tone, look, and gesture" and that he "shrank from every form of display." Walker noted especially Couch's "strongly conservative temper, which led him carefully to scrutinize every project that involved a possible collision with the enemy, and to take unwearying pains to gain an advantage or avert a peril."[68]

If Walker's description of Couch's battlefield methods sounds like a prescription for war written by George B. McClellan, that should be no surprise, for McClellan had few more devoted admirers in the army than Darius Couch.[69] Conversely, Joe Hooker had no harsher critic than Couch—especially in Chancellorsville's aftermath. To his credit, Couch bucked the army's norm by making no effort to infect others with his own disgruntlement; the cancerous tumor of discontent that had doomed Burnside did not develop under Hooker. Instead, once Couch had had enough of Hooker by the end of May, he simply requested reassignment. Thus he passed from the annals of the Army of the Potomac.[70]

George G. Meade would command a corps in battle for the first time at Chancellorsville. If the original Army of the Potomac had a foundation, it was Meade's new command, the Fifth Corps. In 1862 it had been the domain of Fitz John Porter, McClellan's favorite; on the Peninsula it had done some of the army's heaviest fighting. The corps also included the army's only—and highly touted—division of Regular Army troops. With Porter's dismissal and subsequent court-martial, the luster of the Fifth Corps had faded somewhat, but it remained one of the army's mainstays.

Of all the corps commanders at Chancellorsville, the army likely knew the least about Meade. He had performed tolerably well on several battlefields but had gained little notice outside of his native Pennsylvania. Certainly his appearance did nothing to elevate him in the public's or the army's view. An Ohio correspondent described him as "a man who impresses you rather as a thoughtful student than as a dashing soldier." Tall, with "fibres . . . all of the long and sinewy kind," wrote Frank Haskell, "it would be difficult to make him look well dressed." Josiah Favill of Hancock's staff added: "[He] is a very careful officer. . . . He has none of the dash and brilliancy which is necessary to popularity." Meade was an officer of conservative political and military views who in 1862 had hailed McClellan with enthusiasm. The past year, however, had taught Meade and many others the importance of restraint in their political expressions. He therefore appears in the historical record as nonpolitical, and indeed, his contemporaries saw him as such. For his part, Hooker viewed Meade as the best corps commander in the long columns that marched to Chancellorsville.[71]

Strongly identified with its former commanders Baldy Smith and William B. Franklin, the Sixth Corps had to this point in the war done relatively little fighting. It had been on the periphery during the Peninsula battles, had missed Second Manassas, had been in reserve at Antietam, and had served in support at Fredericksburg. Hooker once declared that the Sixth Corps had "*all* the *good* generals." If so, they were—and are—largely anonymous men such as William T. H. Brooks, John Newton, David Russell, and Albion Howe.[72]

John Sedgwick had returned to the army after his serious Antietam wound and now commanded the Sixth Corps under Hooker. To most observers, two things distinguished this forty-nine-year-old, portly old regular from Connecticut: his devotion to McClellan and his manner. In an army full of McClellan's admirers, none would carry his fealty so far. This despite the fact that Sedgwick and McClellan were not intimates. Scarcely acquainted at the war's outset, the two had never even visited socially. Sedgwick's devotion derived from his commitment to McClellan's conservative philosophy and McClellan's official commitment to Sedgwick's standing in the army. Sedgwick was daring enough to harbor Little Mac's brother on his staff. More dramatically, in September 1863 he stimulated a movement within the army to raise $20,000 for a "testimonial" to McClellan. It is not difficult to imagine Lincoln's reaction to such a large donation from the army in honor of the man likely to be his opponent in

Maj. Gen. John Sedgwick. Francis Trevelyan Miller, ed., The Photographic History of the Civil War, *10 vols. (New York: Review of Reviews, 1911), 10:129*

the next election. Somehow Sedgwick managed to survive this gross faux pas. At his death in May 1864, he would be the army's longest-tenured corps commander.[73]

Sedgwick's personality offended few and pleased most. No other general in the army prompted such consistently warm comment from subordinates and colleagues. One staff officer called him "a pure and great-hearted man, a brave and skilful soldier. From the commander to the lowest private he had no enemy in this army." Descriptions akin to Morris Schaff's were common: "His whole manner breathed of gentleness and sweetness, and in his broad breast was a boy's heart."[74]

But John Sedgwick was no beau sabreur. "He was an old bachelor with oddities," wrote Abner Small of the 16th Maine, "addicted to practical jokes and endless games of solitaire." Physically, Small recorded, he was "rather careless of his personal appearance, and habitually crowning his rough head, when not on parade, with a hat that looked like a beehive of straw." His demeanor could be brusque, sometimes frightening. "I have heard that a smile occasionally invaded his scrubby beard, but I never saw one there," remembered Small. "His official manner sent chills down the backs of the rank and file." Still, wrote Haskell of Wisconsin, "he looks, and is, honest and modest.— [You] might see at once, why his men . . . call him 'Uncle John,' not to his face, of course, but among themselves."[75]

Like so many in the army, Sedgwick did not owe his position to accomplishments on the battlefield. Indeed, his most notable moment had been an assault at Antietam during which his command suffered the greatest disaster to befall any division in the army's history, losing 2,200 men in just forty minutes. His reputation survived that blot largely because his corps commander, Edwin V. Sumner, rightly shouldered the blame, but doubts about Sedgwick's ability lingered in some quarters. On the eve of Chancellorsville, the army's provost marshal general, Marsena R. Patrick, wrote, "*Sedgwick*, I fear, is not good enough a general for that position [corps command]. He is a good honest fellow & that is all." A West Point classmate, Hooker claimed that Sedgwick suffered from an "utter deficiency in the topographical faculty, and consequently his great distrust in exercising on the field important commands." Hooker would wrongly name Sedgwick as one of the three culprits for the failure at Chancellorsville.[76]

The most interesting addition to the army's corps command in the spring of 1863 was Maj. Gen. Oliver Otis Howard, the new leader of the Eleventh Corps. Young, righteous, pious, and unquestionably brave (he had lost an arm at Fair Oaks), Howard was badly suited to his new command. The Eleventh Corps was the army's stepchild. It included many German regiments, and its roll of colonels and brigadiers included names such as von Gilsa, Schurz, Schimmelfennig, and Krzyzanowski. Although it had seen action in the Shenandoah Valley under John C. Frémont and at Second Manassas under Franz Sigel (whom the German troops adored), it had yet to fight a battle in the Army of the Potomac. This, combined with strong prejudice against "Dutch" regiments among the rest of the army, made the Eleventh Corps the target of countless derisive comments.

Howard's arrival displeased most of the corps, especially the German units. Some of these men would have been dissatisfied with anyone who was not Franz Sigel or Carl Schurz, but Howard's personality and habits exacerbated the situation. Most objectionable were his patronizing attempts to spread the "Good Word" among the troops. One of his former officers remembered, "Howard talked down to us ('My men—') with the tone and manner of an itinerant preacher." He reveled in giving sermons and holding religious services, sometimes keeping the men shivering in the cold for an hour or more. All this led an army quartermaster to conclude that he "appeared more concerned with saving the souls of his men and of the enemy, than with the care of their bodies." He lacked, the soldier said, "an intuitive knowledge of men."[77]

The men of the Eleventh Corps found expression for their displeasure by greeting each other with "Boys, let us pray" or "Tracts now" and by using "Oh Lord!" and "Oh Jesus!" instead of their normal expletives. Carl Schurz, an Eleventh Corps division commander and an aspirant to corps command, recalled that Howard "did not impress me as an intellectually strong man. A certain looseness of mental operations, a marked uncertainty in forming definite conclusions became evident in conversations." The men "did not take to him," wrote Schurz. "They looked at him with dubious curiosity; not a cheer could be started when he rode along the front. And I do not know whether he liked the men he commanded better than they liked him."[78]

Not only did Howard attempt to convert much of his new command, but he also brought with him a small wave of new, non-German commanders—an obvious attempt to "Americanize" the army's melting-pot corps. Charles Devens, a cultured Bay Stater who had formerly commanded a brigade in the Sixth Corps, took over Brig. Gen. Nathaniel McLean's division. McLean had not discredited himself in either of his major engagements (McDowell and Second Manassas), and his demotion to brigade command left his men sour. Devens's manner did nothing to assuage their dyspepsia. He was, Schurz wrote, "somewhat too austere and distant to make the officers and men of the division easily forget the injustice."[79]

Francis Channing Barlow also joined the Eleventh Corps as a brigade commander—his first such posting. Barlow's arrival caused less upset than Devens's, but he and his men shared a mutual distrust. Some thought Barlow, a

Harvard graduate from a wealthy New York family, had bought his way into brigade command. Others bridled at his disciplinary methods. For Barlow's part, he would come to despise the Eleventh Corps, especially the Germans. "I am convinced that we can do nothing with these German Regts," Barlow declared flatly after Gettysburg. "I never will set foot in the 11th Corps again." The arrival of Howard, Devens, and Barlow was clearly anything but therapeutic for the corps that would find itself in the most critical position at Chancellorsville.[80]

Beyond their vital position on the battlefield, Howard and his corps would play a major role in the historiographical saga of the Chancellorsville campaign. They would emerge as the scapegoat every unsuccessful operation needs—the failed part that caused the entire machine to break down. For the rest of his life, Hooker would vilify Howard for his performance at Chancellorsville. He likened him to McClellan and called him "a hypocrite . . . totally incompetent . . . a perfect old woman . . . a bad man." Hooker would maintain that the battle's result stemmed "from the imbecility and want of soldiership on the part of [the Eleventh Corps'] commander." Although Hooker failed to tarnish Howard's reputation appreciably, by implication he did taint that of the Eleventh Corps. Most of the army blamed the defeat squarely on "the Germans." Unjust though this may have been, it had the important result of allowing Hooker to maintain credibility and the army to retain some measure of its prebattle élan. The Army of the Potomac would recover quickly after Chancellorsville, in part because the Eleventh Corps served as its emotional punching bag.[81]

Like the Eleventh Corps, the Twelfth Corps stood outside the army's mainstream. These were the men of Nathaniel P. Banks, the Shenandoah Valley, and Cedar Mountain. They had fought with the Army of the Potomac only at Antietam and for several months afterward had been detached in Maryland and northern Virginia.

Maj. Gen. Henry Warner Slocum commanded the Twelfth Corps. A West Point graduate and prewar lawyer, Slocum had been with the army from its first days and had been wounded at First Manassas, where he had led the 27th New York. His battle record as division commander counted two significant episodes: heavy fighting at Gaines's Mill that ended in defeat and light fighting at Crampton's Gap that ended in victory. McClellan's assessment of his abilities seems accurate and is seconded by others: "Slocum was a good soldier and possessed very fair ability." Division commander Alpheus S. Williams called him "a hard nut to corrupt." Frank Haskell, whose post-Gettysburg writings include some of the best characterizations of the army's officers, described him thus: "Slocum is small, rather spare, with black straight hair. . . . His movements are quick and angular,—and he dresses with sufficient degree of elegance." His sharp features matched a similar demeanor. Engineer Washington

The Army of the Potomac on the march toward Chancellorsville, April 28, 1863 (engraving based on a sketch by Edwin Forbes). Pack mules move alongside the soldiers. Paul F. Mottelay and T. Campbell-Copeland, eds., The Soldier in Our Civil War, 2 *vols. (New York: Stanley Bradley, 1893), 2:101*

Roebling, who had occasion to know Slocum well after the war, referred to him as "a little acid & tart, apt to snap you up."[82]

Slocum joined Couch and Sedgwick as an ardent supporter of McClellan, and like Couch, he would become one of Hooker's toughest critics. He undoubtedly claimed some satisfaction when Hooker left the army in late June, but it was a pyrrhic victory. In a few months, Slocum and his corps would be transferred to Tennessee, where his new commander would be Fighting Joe Hooker.[83]

This was the Army of the Potomac on the eve of Chancellorsville. Whereas in January it had been snarly, hungry, and shrinking, in April it was large, well-fed, well-organized (though with some flaws), and for the most part happy. The army's commander generally stood in high esteem, although he elicited none of the affection inspired by McClellan. Beneath Hooker, men of moderate standing led the army's component parts—solid men with neither gold stars nor black marks on their records.

At the end of April, the army was ready. The warm sun shone brightly; the mud of the last few months had vanished. On April 27 staff officers and couriers spread throughout the camps with marching orders. The next morning men by the thousands ripped canvases from their winter huts and prepared to march. Numa Barned of the 73rd Pennsylvania spoke for many when he wrote, "I am well and expect to be in Richmond soon if Joe Hooker leads the way and don't stick in the mud. . . . I am in hopes we shall make Richmond howl this time."[84]

Three months before, in the midst of the darkest winter the Army of the Potomac ever knew, soldiers had spurned such optimistic declamations. But time and Joe Hooker had worked a dramatic transformation. Now the army seemed willing to give Hooker whatever he might ask for. Only one question remained: Would Fighting Joe Hooker give the army the only thing it asked of him? Would he deliver the army to victory?

NOTES

1. Letter of "Adjutant," Rochester *Democrat and American*, February 2, 1862; letter of "Marker" (27th New York), Rochester *Union and Advertiser*, February 7, 1863; letter of [Samuel Wheelock Fiske], February 25, 1863, in Samuel Wheelock Fiske, *Mr. Dunne Browne's Experiences in the Army* (Boston, 1866), 119. Testimony on the army's melancholia after Fredericksburg and the Mud March is voluminous. Three excellent recently published sources are Daniel M. Holt, *A Surgeon's Civil War: The Letters and Diary of Daniel M. Holt, M.D.*, ed. James M. Greiner, Janet L. Coryell, and James R. Smither (Kent, Ohio: Kent State University Press, 1994), 63; Robert Gould Shaw, *Blue-Eyed Child of Fortune: The Civil War Letters of Colonel Robert Gould Shaw*, ed. Russell F. Duncan (Athens: University of Georgia Press, 1992); and Henry L. Abbott, *Fallen Leaves: The Civil War Letters of Henry L. Abbott*, ed. Robert Garth Scott (Kent, Ohio: Kent State University Press, 1992), 155, 167–68.

2. Henry W. Grubbs to "Dear Cornelia," February 1, 1863, Henry W. Grubbs Letters, bound vol. 210, Fredericksburg and Spotsylvania National Military Park Library, Fredericksburg, Va. (repository hereafter cited as FSNMP); Charles Francis Adams, Jr., to his father, January 30, 1863, in *A Cycle of Adams Letters*, ed. Worthington Chauncey Ford, 2 vols. (Boston: Houghton Mifflin, 1920), 1:250. For additional commentary on the army's possible breakup, see letter of "W. C." (13th New York), Rochester *Democrat and American*, February 26, 1863, and Cornelius Moore, *Cornie: The Civil War Letters of Lt. Cornelius Moore* (57th New York), ed. Gilbert C. Moore, Jr. (n.p., 1989), 82.

3. Letter of "F. E. F.," *Herkimer County Journal* (Little Falls, N.Y.), February 5, 1863. For other commentary on desertion, see letter of George Breck (Reynolds's Battery), Rochester *Union and Advertiser*, January 12, 1863; Charles Harvey Brewster, *When This Cruel War Is Over: The Civil War Letters of Charles Harvey Brewster*, ed. David W. Blight (Amherst: University of Massachusetts Press, 1992), 211–12; Blake McKelvey, ed., "Civil War Letters of Francis Edwin Pierce of the 108th New York Volunteer Infantry," *The Rochester Historical Society Publications: Rochester in the Civil War* (Rochester: Rochester Historical Society, 1944), 168; and letter of "W. C.," Rochester *Democrat and American*, February 7, 1863.

4. Although contemporary testimony on morale confirms that the army's collective psyche was severely depressed, it should be noted that more optimistic accounts, though rare, show that not everyone shared a gloomy assessment. Col. Walter Phelps of the 22nd New York (First Corps), for example, wrote to "E" (his wife) on January 29, 1863: "I hear

much said about the demoralization of the army. I have never seen anything of the kind in this division, it may exist elsewhere, but I don't believe it" (Walter Phelps Letters, bound vol. 215, FSNMP).

5. Letter of Lt. George Breck, Rochester *Union and Advertiser*, December 30, 1862; James R. Woodworth to Phebe (his wife), February 5, 1863, James R. Woodworth Papers, Schoff Collection, William L. Clements Library, University of Michigan, Ann Arbor, Mich. (repository hereafter cited as CLUM). For a good discussion of the pay issue, see A. Wilson Greene, "Morale, Maneuver, and Mud: The Army of the Potomac, December 16, 1862– January 26, 1863," in *The Fredericksburg Campaign: Decision on the Rappahannock*, ed. Gary W. Gallagher (Chapel Hill: University of North Carolina Press, 1995), 175, 191.

6. For a sampling of this commentary, see Shaw, *Blue-Eyed Child of Fortune*, 277, and David Hunter Strother, *A Virginia Yankee in the Civil War: The Diaries of David Hunter Strother*, ed. Cecil D. Eby (Chapel Hill: University of North Carolina Press, 1961), 113. For a spirited defense of McClellan's inaction, see Fitz John Porter to Manton Marble, September 30, 1862, Manton Marble Papers, vol. 3, Library of Congress, Washington, D.C. (repository hereafter cited as LC).

7. Edward King Wightman, *From Antietam to Fort Fisher: The Civil War Letters of Edward King Wightman, 1862–1865*, ed. Edward G. Longacre (Rutherford, N.J.: Fairleigh Dickinson University Press, 1985), 106; Gouverneur K. Warren to his brother, January 10, 1863, Gouverneur K. Warren Papers, New York State Library, Albany, N.Y. (repository hereafter cited as NYSL).

8. The figures include McDowell's corps, which in January 1863 constituted the First Corps of the Army of the Potomac. The five holdovers—all now exercising different commands—were John Sedgwick, Hooker, Darius N. Couch, George Sykes, and Henry W. Slocum.

9. Walter Phelps to "E," February 2, 1862, Phelps Letters, FSNMP.

10. Charles Francis Adams, Jr., to his father, January 30, 1863, in Ford, *Adams Letters*, 1:250; Rufus Dawes, *Service with the Sixth Wisconsin Volunteers* (1890; reprint, Dayton, Ohio: Morningside, 1984), 115.

11. Jacob W. Haas to his brother, December 18, 1862, Jacob Haas Papers, Civil War Miscellaneous Collection, U.S. Army Military History Institute, Carlisle Barracks, Pa. (repository hereafter cited as USAMHI).

12. Gouverneur K. Warren to his brother, December 17, 1862, Warren Papers, NYSL. See also David M. Cory, ed., "A Brooklyn Soldier a Century Ago: The Letters of John Vliet" (14th Brooklyn), *Long Island Journal of History* 3 (Fall 1963): 4; Daniel E. Woodward, ed., "The Civil War of a Pennsylvania Trooper," *Pennsylvania Magazine of History and Biography* 87 (January 1963): 51; and letter of Henry Ropes, December 24, 1862, in "Letters from the Harvard Regiments," ed. Anthony Milano, *Civil War: The Magazine of the Civil War Society* 13 (June 1988): 57.

13. Alexander Webb to his father, August 14, 1862, Alexander S. Webb Papers, Yale University, New Haven, Conn.; Régis de Trobriand, *Four Years with the Army of the Potomac* (1889; reprint, Gaithersburg, Md.: Ron R. Van Sickle Military Books, 1988), 417.

14. McKelvey, "Letters of Francis Edwin Pierce," 167–68; "The Fourteenth Indiana Regiment, Peninsular Campaign to Chancellorsville, Letters to the *Vincennes Western Sun*: Prock's Letters from the Eastern Front," *Indiana Magazine of History* 33 (1937): 341. For like commentary, see Horace Emerson (2nd Wisconsin) to his brother, January 31, 1863, Horace Emerson Papers, CLUM, and Jacob Haas (96th Pennsylvania) to his brother, January 13,

1863, Jacob Haas Diary and Letters, Harrisburg Civil War Round Table Collection, USAMHI.

15. Hugh P. Roden to his family, February 16, 1863, Hugh P. Roden Letters, Schoff Collection, CLUM; Paul Fatout, ed., *Letters of a Civil War Surgeon* (West Lafayette, Ind.: Purdue University Studies, 1961), 53. An Irishman of the 28th Massachusetts predicted that black troops "will meet as hot a reception in their retreat as in their advance. . . . They are looked upon as the principal cause of this war" (Peter Welsh, *Irish Green and Union Blue: The Civil War Letters of Peter Welsh*, ed. Lawrence F. Kohl [New York: Fordham University Press, 1986], 62).

16. Letter of "M. S. D." (34th New York), *Herkimer County Journal* (Little Falls, N.Y.), February 11, 1863; Holt, *A Surgeon's Civil War*, 47; Alan A. Siegel, *For the Glory of the Union: Myth, Reality, and the Media in Civil War New Jersey* (Rutherford, N.J.: Fairleigh Dickinson University Press, 1984), 140.

17. Shaw, *Blue-Eyed Child of Fortune*, 271; James T. Miller (11th Pennsylvania) to his family, March 30, 1863, Miller Family Papers, Schoff Collection, CLUM; Holt, *A Surgeon's Civil War*, 81. David Acheson of the 14th Pennsylvania addressed this topic in March 1863: "The Army of the Potomac is, I believe, the most democratic army we have, and yet if called upon to give an opinion concerning the copperheads of the north, it would give forth such a cry of hatred and disgust as would make the traitors tremble" (Sara Gould Walters, *Inscription at Gettysburg* [Gettysburg, Pa.: Thomas Publications, 1991], 72).

18. Joseph Hooker to Edwin M. Stanton, December 4, 1862, Edwin M. Stanton Papers, microfilm roll 4, LC; Daniel Larned to his uncle, January 1, 1863, Daniel Larned Papers, LC.

19. Woodward, "Civil War of a Pennsylvania Trooper," 51.

20. *Harper's Weekly*, February 7, 1863; Charles S. Wainwright, *A Diary of Battle: The Personal Journals of Colonel Charles S. Wainwright, 1861–1865*, ed. Allan Nevins (New York: Harcourt, Brace & World, 1962), 12; Carl Schurz, *The Reminiscences of Carl Schurz*, 3 vols. (New York: McClure, 1893), 2:403.

21. Walter H. Hebert, *Fighting Joe Hooker* (1944; reprint, Gaithersburg, Md.: Butternut, 1987), 40–45; John Bigelow, Jr., *The Campaign of Chancellorsville: A Strategic and Tactical Study* (New Haven, Conn.: Yale University Press, 1910), 5.

22. Philip Kearny, *Letters from the Peninsula: The Civil War Letters of General Philip Kearny*, ed. William B. Styple (Kearny, N.J.: Belle Grove Publishing, 1988), 86; Wainwright, *Diary of Battle*, 112; George G. Meade, ed., *The Life and Letters of George Gordon Meade*, 2 vols. (1913; reprint, Baltimore, Md.: Butternut and Blue, 1994), 1:319.

23. For examples of Hooker's self-promotion, see Joseph Hooker to Senator John Conover Ten Eyck, May 16, 1862, Schoff Collection, CLUM, and Joseph Hooker to Edwin M. Stanton, December 4, 1862, Stanton Papers, microfilm roll 4, LC. Evidence of Hooker's influence with the press is found in the dozens of articles about him that appeared in papers large and small across the North after Antietam.

24. De Trobriand, *Four Years*, 413–14; Joseph Hooker to Samuel P. Bates, April 2, 1877, Samuel P. Bates Papers, Pennsylvania State Archives, Harrisburg, Pa. (repository hereafter cited as PSA). For similar commentary on Hooker's tendency to denigrate others, see Wainwright, *Diary of Battle*, 66.

25. George B. McClellan Papers, vol. D-9, microfilm roll 71, LC; Ulysses S. Grant, *Personal Memoirs of U. S. Grant*, 2 vols. (New York: Charles L. Webster, 1885–86), 2:539.

26. Meade, *Life and Letters*, 1:319. For the text of Lincoln's letter of appointment, see U.S. War Department, *The War of the Rebellion: A Compilation of the Official Records of the*

Union and Confederate Armies, 127 vols., index, and atlas (Washington, D.C.: GPO, 1880–1901), 25(1):4 (hereafter cited as *OR*; all references are to series 1).

27. W. T. H. Brooks to his wife, February 17, 1862, William T. H. Brooks Papers, USAMHI; William Thompson Lusk, *War Letters of William Thompson Lusk* (New York: Privately printed, 1909), 274; Abbott, *Fallen Leaves*, 165.

28. Wightman, *From Antietam to Fort Fisher*, 106; letter of Theodore A. Dodge (119th New York), January 28, 1863, Theodore A. Dodge Papers, LC. For other vivid or useful commentary, see Carl M. Becker and Ritchie Thomas, eds., *Hearth and Knapsack: The Ladley Letters, 1857–1880* (Athens: Ohio University Press, 1988), 84, 88, and Robert G. Carter, *Four Brothers in Blue; or, Sunshine and Shadows of the War of the Rebellion, A Story of the Great Civil War from Bull Run to Appomattox* (1913; reprint, Austin: University of Texas Press, 1978), 230–31.

29. Letter of "Scorer" (13th New York), Rochester *Union and Advertiser*, January 20, 1863.

30. Joseph Hooker to Samuel P. Bates, February 18, 1879, Bates Papers, PSA.

31. Letter from unknown member of 108th New York, Rochester *Democrat and American*, February 20, 1863. For descriptions of some of the bakeries, see letter of "Scorer," Rochester *Union and Advertiser*, February 26, 1863; Walters, *Inscription at Gettysburg*, 76; and Siegel, *For the Glory of the Union*, 127 (which quotes a soldier who proclaimed that the bread produced by the bakeries was "fully equal to any that we have ever tasted").

32. James Crole to Hiram Averell, April 12, 1863, William Woods Averell Papers, NYSL. Wrote David Acheson of the 140th New York, "All the boys are satisfied that Hooker intends to keep them fat if he don't do anything else" (Walters, *Inscription at Gettysburg*, 62).

33. Letter of George Breck, Rochester *Union and Advertiser*, April 17, 1863. For a summary of Letterman's improvements, see *OR* 25(1):239–40, and Bigelow, *Campaign of Chancellorsville*, 39–51.

34. Charles F. Morse, *Letters Written During the Civil War* (Boston, 1898), 121–22. See also letter of "W. C.," Rochester *Democrat and American*, March 16, 1863.

35. See *OR* 25(2):15, 77–78. On January 31, 1863, 87,330 out of 326,750 soldiers were absent from the army, but this figure includes Heintzelman's forces in the Washington defenses (ibid., 29). The subtraction of the number of Heintzelman's troops yields the figure given in the text for January 31.

36. Daniel Butterfield's testimony, March 28, 1863, in U.S. Congress, *Report of the Joint Committee on the Conduct of the War, at the Second Session Thirty-Eighth Congress* (Washington, D.C.: GPO, 1865), 73; Siegel, *For the Glory of the Union*, 138; letter of "W. C.," Rochester *Democrat and American*, February 7, 1863; Brewster, *When This Cruel War Is Over*, 212. The reader should note that the army suffered the detachment of significant numbers of troops between January 31 and April 30, 1863 (the entire Ninth Corps and the Pennsylvania Reserve division), which renders invalid any simple comparison of numbers absent on those two dates. The 18 percent drop is derived not from a comparison of absolute numbers but from a comparison of the relative absentee rates of the two dates—29 percent in January, 23.5 percent in April.

37. *OR* 25(2):11–12; Abbott, *Fallen Leaves*, 170; William Aughinbaugh journal, February 6, 1863, CLUM; letter of George Breck, Rochester *Union and Advertiser*, February 14, 1863; Joseph Hooker to Samuel P. Bates, December 8, 1876, Bates Papers, PSA. According to this system, officers were permitted to take furloughs at a regulated rate but were threatened with dismissal if they visited Washington "without the consent of the War Department." This

measure sought to reduce the political play of officers in the nation's capital—an unsurprising response to the crescendo of politicking that had occurred in December and January. See *OR* 25(2):57.

38. John Haley, *The Rebel Yell and Yankee Hurrah: The Civil War Journal of a Maine Volunteer*, ed. Ruth L. Silliker (Camden, Maine: Down East Books, 1985), 73; Bigelow, *Campaign of Chancellorsville*, 39–51.

39. Joseph Hooker to Samuel P. Bates, December 8, 1876, Bates Papers, PSA. See also letter of George Breck, Rochester *Union and Advertiser*, March 30, 1863.

40. James T. Miller (111th Pennsylvania) to his parents, March 28, 1863, Schoff Collection, CLUM; Alpheus S. Williams, *From the Cannon's Mouth: The Civil War Letters of General Alpheus S. Williams*, ed. Milo M. Quaife (Detroit: Wayne State University Press, 1959), 169; Morse, *Letters*, 126. Among the hundreds of accounts of the Lincoln reviews, two of the best are found in letter of Lt. George Breck, Rochester *Union and Advertiser*, April 17, 1863, and P. J. Staudenraus, ed., *Mr. Lincoln's Washington: Selections from the Writings of Noah Brooks, Civil War Correspondent* (New York: Thomas Yoseloff, 1967), 147–64. The only men in the army seemingly dissatisfied with Hooker's measures were the clerks, who had to deal with "multifarious and voluminous reports" (Theodore A. Dodge journal, February 10, 1863, LC).

41. For strengths and the consolidation order, see *OR* 25(2):320, 51–52.

42. *OR* 25(2):51; O. O. Howard, *Autobiography of Oliver Otis Howard, Major General*, 2 vols. (New York: Baker & Taylor, 1907), 1:381.

43. Joseph Hooker to Samuel P. Bates, February 18, 1879, August 28, 1876, Bates Papers, PSA.

44. Wainwright, *Diary of Battle*, 175–76, 194, 206. For the May 12 order rescinding Hooker's earlier reorganization and restoring Hunt and his corps artillery chiefs to line command, see *OR* 25(2):471–72. See also L. Van Loan Naisawald, *Grape and Canister: The Story of the Field Artillery of the Army of the Potomac* (1960; reprint, Washington, D.C.: Zenger, 1983), 272–74. In his report after Chancellorsville, Hunt boldly excoriated Hooker's attempt at reorganization: "I doubt if the history of modern armies can exhibit a parallel instance of such palpable crippling of a great arm of the service" (*OR* 25[1]:252–53).

45. Wainwright, *Diary of Battle*, 174; letter of D. D. Jones (88th Pennsylvania), April 7, 1863, D. D. Jones Papers, MOLLUS War Library and Museum, Philadelphia, Pa.

46. Wainwright, *Diary of Battle*, 174. For a good summary of the disadvantages of the mule scheme, see Bigelow, *Campaign of Chancellorsville*, 44–45.

47. By mid-April, only two issues stimulated regular moaning. First, many men still pined for the departed McClellan, though this likely concerned Hooker not at all. See Henry Ropes (20th Massachusetts) to John C. Ropes, April 17, 25, 1863, Henry Ropes Papers, Boston Public Library, Boston, Mass., and letter of George Breck, Rochester *Union and Advertiser*, March 13, 1863. The second and more important issue concerned the impending expiration of enlistments for regiments that had signed up for two years or for nine months—nearly one-fifth of the army. Not only would the expiration materially affect Hooker's strength, but also many of the individual regiments found fault with the government's method of determining when their enlistments would expire (the men invariably wanted their terms to be calculated from the date they entered state service; the national government preferred to use the date the men entered federal service—a difference of anywhere from four to ten weeks). Throughout April, Hooker was forced to deal with unrest in these units, including several instances of outright mutiny. See Meade, *Life and Letters*, 1:367; Cory,

"Brooklyn Soldier," 16, 19; John Gibbon, *Personal Recollections of the Civil War* (1928; reprint, Dayton, Ohio: Morningside, 1988), 112–13; Dawes, *Service with the Sixth Wisconsin*, 135; and Wainwright, *Diary of Battle*, 184.

48. The army had rested for a month and a half after Antietam, but in many ways those six weeks were stressful. The public and politicians clamored constantly for faster action, and letters of the period include regular commentary on the supposed imminence of the coming campaign. Physical restoration may have come to the army after Antietam; mental restoration surely did not.

49. By far the most vivid and valuable reflection of the gulf that existed between the army's high command and the government can be found in Fitz John Porter to Manton Marble, editor of the *New York World*, April 26, May 21, June 20, September 30, 1862, Marble Papers, LC.

50. The most comprehensive treatment of the December–January infighting appears in Greene, "Morale, Maneuver, and Mud."

51. Wilbur Fisk, *Hard Marching Every Day: The Civil War Letters of Private Wilbur Fisk, 1861–1865*, ed. Ruth Rosenblatt and Emil Rosenblatt (Lawrence: University Press of Kansas, 1992), 69; Frank L. Byrne and Thomas Weaver, eds., *Haskell of Gettysburg: His Life and Civil War Papers* (Madison: State Historical Society of Wisconsin, 1970), 58.

52. For the purposes of this study, the Union high command is defined as all men leading brigades, divisions, or corps. This assessment does not include the cavalry. I have left that to the able pen of A. Wilson Greene elsewhere in this volume.

53. These statistics are based on an analysis of the high command as it appears in *OR* 25(1):156–70. It includes only those officers who commanded units at the outset of the campaign, not those who ascended to command during the campaign itself. Because relevant biographical information on a handful of brigade commanders could not be found, the numbers given in the text must be considered somewhat tentative.

54. Perhaps the three best examples of officers with a conservative mentality are John Sedgwick, Second Corps division commander John Gibbon, and William Thomas Harbaugh Brooks of the Sixth Corps. Each left a set of letters that reflects his views during this period. See John Sedgwick, *Correspondence of John Sedgwick, Major General*, 2 vols. ([New York]: Printed for C. and E. B. Stoeckel [by the De Vinne Press], 1903); John Gibbon Papers, Historical Society of Pennsylvania, Philadelphia, Pa. (repository hereafter cited as HSP), which reflect both Gibbon's and Brooks's attitudes; and Brooks Papers, USAMHI. For Hooker's desire to rid the army's subordinates of "all the weaknesses that had been inspired in their character through the weakness and infirmities of" McClellan, see Joseph Hooker to Samuel P. Bates, December 24, 1878, Bates Papers, PSA.

55. For the Stone case, in addition to the voluminous testimony before the Joint Committee on the Conduct of the War, see Charles Stone to Benson J. Lossing, November 5, 1866, Schoff Collection, CLUM, and Stephen W. Sears, "The Ordeal of General Stone," *Military History Quarterly* 7 (Winter 1994): 47–56 (I am indebted to Stephen Sears for supplying me with a copy of this excellent article in advance of its publication). By far the best assessment of the Fitz John Porter court-martial is Henry Gabler, "The Fitz John Porter Case: Politics and Military Justice" (Ph.D. dissertation, City University of New York, 1979). For commentary on Franklin and Smith, see Greene, "Morale, Maneuver, and Mud," 183, 189, 206–13. The best expression of the growing awareness of the need to steer clear of politics appears in a letter from Winfield Scott Hancock to his wife in May 1863. Hancock wrote that he had "been approached again in connection with the command of the Army of the Potomac." He

would not accept the command, he said, because "I do not belong to that class of generals whom the Republicans care to bolster up. I should be sacrificed" ([Almira Russell Hancock], *Reminiscences of Winfield Scott Hancock by His Wife* [New York: Charles L. Webster, 1887], 94–95).

56. Undated memorandum by Fitz John Porter, microfilm roll 3 (container 7), frame 4, and unsigned, undated account by Fitz John Porter, roll 25 (container 53), frame 284, Fitz John Porter Papers, LC. See also Wainwright, *Diary of Battle*, 162.

57. For example, see Joseph Hooker to Edwin M. Stanton, December 28, 1862, Stanton Papers, LC, and Joseph Hooker to Senator Henry Wilson, March 4, 1863, George Hay Stuart Papers, LC. Other evidence of Hooker's support of Daniel Butterfield is in Meade, *Life and Letters*, 1:339, 341. Butterfield did not neglect to engage in a little of his own self-boosterism. See Daniel Butterfield to Edwin M. Stanton, January 24, 1863, Stanton Papers, LC.

58. Washington Roebling to John Bigelow, December 9, 1910, John Bigelow Papers, LC; Darius N. Couch, "The Chancellorsville Campaign," in *Battles and Leaders of the Civil War*, ed. Robert Underwood Johnson and Clarence Clough Buel, 4 vols. (New York: Century, 1887–88), 3:154. For other positive comments, see Wainwright, *Diary of Battle*, 162, and letter of George Breck, Rochester *Union and Advertiser*, April 7, 1863. It should be noted that Wainwright's opinion as expressed in *Diary of Battle* would change over time.

59. Wainwright, *Diary of Battle*, 215. McClellan's unvarnished comments on his officers appear in the McClellan Papers, vol. D-9, microfilm roll 71, LC. For the Adams quotation, see Ford, *Adams Letters*, 2:14. See also Henry W. Slocum to Joseph Howland, May 29, 1863, Joseph Howland Papers, New-York Historical Society, New York, N.Y. (repository hereafter cited as NYHS). Slocum wrote that "Sickles & Butterfield are [Hooker's] born companions, and everything is conducted as might be expected under such leaders."

60. Wainwright, *Diary of Battle*, 93.

61. W. A. Swanberg, *Sickles the Incredible* (1956; reprint, Gettysburg, Pa.: Stan Clarke Military Books, 1991), 167–76. For the suggestion that Hooker and Sickles benefited equally from each other's influence, see Meade, *Life and Letters*, 1:350. For the perception that Sickles stood in Hooker's inner circle, see Joseph J. Bartlett to Joseph Howland, April 5, 1863, and Henry W. Slocum to Joseph Howland, May 29, 1863, Howland Papers, NYHS, and Ford, *Adams Letters*, 2:14.

62. De Trobriand, *Four Years*, 426.

63. W. A. Swanberg, quoted in Wainwright, *Diary of Battle*, 17n. For other commentary, see Byrne and Weaver, *Haskell of Gettysburg*, 84–85; Robert McAllister, *The Civil War Letters of General Robert McAllister*, ed. James I. Robertson, Jr. (New Brunswick, N.J.: Rutgers University Press, 1965), 212; and Thomas Ward Osborn, *No Middle Ground: Thomas Ward Osborn's Letters from the Field*, ed. Herb S. Crumb and Katherine Dhalle (Hamilton, N.Y.: Edmonston Publishing, 1993), 50.

64. Williams, *From the Cannon's Mouth*, 203; G. K. Warren to his fiancée Emily, April 17, 1863, Warren Papers, NYSL; Byrne and Weaver, *Haskell of Gettysburg*, 117.

65. De Trobriand, *Four Years*, 426; Haley, *Rebel Yell and Yankee Hurrah*, 74, 82, 102.

66. "To Chancellorsville with the Iron Brigade: The Diary of Colonel Henry A. Morrow, Part I," *Civil War Times Illustrated* 14 (January 1976): 15; Wainwright, *Diary of Battle*, 229, 149, 155. See also Meade, *Life and Letters*, 1:342–43.

67. Wainwright, *Diary of Battle*, 181; Byrne and Weaver, *Haskell of Gettysburg*, 100; George B. McClellan, *McClellan's Own Story* (New York: Charles L. Webster, 1887), 140; Joseph Hooker to Samuel P. Bates, May 30, 1878, Bates Papers, PSA.

68. Josiah M. Favill, *The Diary of a Young Officer Serving with the Armies of the United States during the War of the Rebellion* (Chicago: R. R. Donnelley & Sons, 1909), 236; Francis A. Walker, *History of the Second Army Corps in the Army of the Potomac* (1886; reprint, Gaithersburg, Md.: Butternut, 1985), 129. For other commentary on Couch, see letter of Oliver Edwards, June 4, 1862, Lewis Leigh Collection, USAMHI, and *A Memorial of Paul Joseph Revere and Edward H. R. Revere* (1874; reprint, Clinton, Mass.: W. J. Coulter, 1913), 171.

69. McClellan called Couch "an honest, faithful, and laborious man, a brave, modest, and valuable officer" (McClellan, *McClellan's Own Story*, 139). See also Abbott, *Fallen Leaves*, 172–73.

70. See Meade, *Life and Letters*, 1:373–74.

71. Whitelaw Reid, *A Radical View: The Agate Dispatches of Whitelaw Reid*, ed. James G. Smart, 2 vols. (Memphis, Tenn.: Memphis State University Press, 1976), 2:17, 23; Byrne and Weaver, *Haskell of Gettysburg*, 261; Favill, *Diary of a Young Officer*, 236; Joseph Hooker to Samuel P. Bates, May 30, 1878, Bates Papers, PSA. See also Milton E. Fowler, ed., *Dear Folks at Home: The Civil War Letters of Leo and John W. Faller* (Carlisle, Pa.: Cumberland County Historical Society, 1963), 38–39, 71, 81, and Albert D. Richardson, *The Secret Service: The Field, the Dungeon, and the Escape* (Hartford, Conn.: American Publishing Company, 1865), 281. A careful reading of Meade's letters in *Life and Letters* reveals a man acutely aware of the political environment in which he operated.

72. John Gibbon to his wife, March 31, 1863, Gibbon Papers, HSP.

73. Sedgwick, *Correspondence*, 2:43–44, 155; McClellan, *McClellan's Own Story*, 140.

74. Theodore Lyman, *Meade's Headquarters, 1863–1865: Letters of Colonel Theodore Lyman from the Wilderness to Appomattox*, ed. George R. Agassiz (Boston: Atlantic Monthly Press, 1922), 108; Morris Schaff, *The Battle of the Wilderness* (1910; reprint, Gaithersburg, Md.: Butternut, 1986), 43. For a similar comment, see Mason W. Tyler, *Recollections of the Civil War* (New York: G. P. Putnam's Sons, 1912), 74.

75. Abner Small, *The Road to Richmond: The Civil War Memoirs of Major Abner Small of the Sixteenth Maine Volunteers, Together with a Diary Which He Kept When He Was a Prisoner of War*, ed. Harold Adams Small (Berkeley: University of California Press, 1939), 30; Byrne and Weaver, *Haskell of Gettysburg*, 132–33. George T. Stevens of the 77th New York recorded that Sedgwick "needed not the insignia of rank to command the deference of those about him" (George T. Stevens, *Three Years in the Sixth Corps* [New York: D. Van Nostrand, 1867], 186).

76. Marsena R. Patrick, *Inside Lincoln's Army: The Diary of Marsena Rudolph Patrick, Provost Marshal General, Army of the Potomac*, ed. David S. Sparks (New York: Thomas Yoseloff, 1964), 236; Joseph Hooker to Samuel P. Bates, November 29, December 24, 1878, Bates Papers, PSA. In the latter letter, Hooker wrote, "Genl. Sedgwick having been a classmate of mine had infirmities of which I was fully conscious at the time of calling on him for this service [the crossing at Fredericksburg and movement toward Lee's rear at Chancellorsville], but which as circumstances were I could not avoid, though it was done reluctantly and almost with trembling."

77. Small, *Road to Richmond*, 9; William G. Le Duc, *Recollections of a Civil War Quartermaster* (St. Paul, Minn.: North Central Publishing Company, 1963), 98; Abbott, *Fallen Leaves*, 148–49, 152. See also Abner Doubleday, *Chancellorsville and Gettysburg* (New York: Charles Scribner's Sons, 1876), 3. Three of the above sources refer to Howard as the "Havelock of the army." Le Duc added, "By officers and men he was regarded as a tin

soldier; by the church people, generally . . . he was thought to be a great hero" (Le Duc, *Recollections of a Civil War Quartermaster*, 98).

78. Baron Otto von Fritsch, "A Modern Soldier of Fortune: The Diary of Baron von Fritsch," p. 145, LC; Schurz, *Reminiscences*, 3:404–5. See also Justus M. Silliman, *A New Canaan Private in the Civil War: Letters of Justus M. Silliman, 17th Connecticut Volunteers*, ed. Edward Marcus (New Canaan, Conn.: New Canaan Historical Society, 1984), 21; Thomas L. Livermore, *Days and Events, 1860–1866* (Boston: Houghton Mifflin, 1920), 29; and Byrne and Weaver, *Haskell of Gettysburg*, 133. Howard recorded of his appointment to the corps: "I soon found that my past record was not known there . . . and that I was not at first getting the earnest and loyal support of the entire command" (Howard, *Autobiography*, 1:348–49).

79. Schurz, *Reminiscences*, 2:405; Joseph Hooker to Samuel P. Bates, July 20, 1878, Bates Papers, PSA.

80. Letter of John Cate (33rd Massachusetts), April 20, 1863, John Cate Letters, bound vol. 183, FSNMP; Schurz, *Reminiscences*, 2:406; letters of Francis C. Barlow, April 24, May 8, July (undated), August 5, 12, 1863, Francis C. Barlow Papers, Massachusetts Historical Society, Boston, Mass. The former colonel of the 20th Maine, Adelbert Ames—"a very strict, stern man, but a noble officer, brave and decided," observed Maj. Holman S. Melcher of that regiment—also joined the Eleventh Corps as a brigade commander at this time. On Ames, see Wainwright, *Diary of Battle*, 242, and Holman S. Melcher, *With a Flash of His Sword: The Writings of Major Holman S. Melcher, 20th Maine Infantry*, ed. William B. Melcher (Kearny, N.J.: Belle Grove Publishing, 1994), 20, 32–33.

81. Joseph Hooker to Samuel P. Bates, December 24, 1878, Bates Papers, PSA. Hooker's quotation on Howard appears in *Historical Magazine*, 3rd ser., 2 (October 1873): 253. Hooker never directly blamed anyone in the Eleventh Corps other than Howard and Devens; however, the complaints against the Eleventh Corps from the rest of the army are voluminous. For some of the more colorful comments, see Adolfo Fernandez de la Cavada diary, May 7, 1863, HSP; Moore, *Cornie*, 103; Fatout, *Letters of a Civil War Surgeon*, 61; and Robert S. Robertson, *Diary of the War by Robert S. Robertson, 93rd N.Y. Vols. . . . 1861–2–3–4*, ed. Charles N. Walker and Rosemary Walker (Fort Wayne, Ind., 1965), 98. According to Schurz, the abuse left the corps shaken. "The spirit of this corps is broken, and something must be done to revive it," he wrote on May 17. "Too much humiliation destroys the morale of men" (Carl Schurz to Joseph Hooker, May 17, 1863, Carl Schurz Papers, LC).

82. McClellan Papers, vol. D-9, microfilm roll 71, LC; Williams, *From the Cannon's Mouth*, 141, 319; Byrne and Weaver, *Haskell of Gettysburg*, 133; Washington Roebling to John Bigelow, December 16, 1910, Bigelow Papers, LC. See also Holt, *A Surgeon's Civil War*, 20.

83. For Slocum's harsh comments on Hooker, see Henry W. Slocum to Joseph Howland, May 29, 1863, Howland Papers, NYHS. In Tennessee, Slocum tendered his resignation rather than serve directly under Hooker. He was assigned responsibility for protecting the railroad between Nashville and Chattanooga, a duty that removed him from Hooker's control.

84. Numa Barned (73rd Pennsylvania) to Emma (his sister), March 27, 1863, Numa Barned Papers, CLUM.

East of Chancellorsville

JUBAL A. EARLY AT SECOND FREDERICKSBURG AND SALEM CHURCH

Gary W. Gallagher

JUBAL A. EARLY had been living in Canada for more than two years when he composed a letter to R. E. Lee in late November 1868. Begging Lee's indulgence for the intrusion, Early devoted most of this long missive to his role during the Chancellorsville campaign. "I think your official report, which I never saw until I came to this country, does not do full justice to my command," stated Early in carefully chosen words, "but that was my fault in not furnishing you the means of doing so." The report he had forwarded to Lee at the time had been far too brief, he conceded, a sketch "merely intended to aid you in giving the [War] department a brief account of the operations in advance of the official reports." Early had expected in his final report "to show . . . what my command had actually done," but the army's subsequent movement into Pennsylvania and other events had prevented his preparing a fuller account. While in Canada, Early had written a detailed narrative of his part in the campaign, a copy of which he now sent to Lee in the hope that it would set the record straight and assist the general in writing a history of the Army of Northern Virginia. "The most that is left to us is the history of our struggle, and I think that ought to be accurately written," observed Early in language that foreshadowed his later activities as the preeminent Lost Cause controversialist. "We lost nearly everything but honor, and that should be religiously guarded."[1]

Early's postwar sensitivity about Chancellorsville mirrored his attitude immediately after the battle. The campaign marked his first assignment by Lee to semi-independent command, and from the beginning, he sought to place his actions in the best possible light. An examination of Early's conduct during the operation, his subsequent debates with William Barksdale, and his reaction to later writings concerning Second Fredericksburg and Salem Church is useful on several levels. In strictly military terms, it sheds light on Early's characteristics as a soldier and provides a useful context for comparing him with more senior officers such as Lafayette McLaws. The independence, decisiveness, and complex relationship with his troops that he manifested during the 1864 Shenandoah Valley campaign can be detected in the fighting along the Rappahannock River in 1863. Early's dispute with Barksdale not only reveals that controversies among comrades often tainted even stunning victories but also demonstrates how Lee disciplined subordinates to control destructive backbiting. Finally, Early's close attention to the treatment of Chancellorsville in official reports and later writings reveals how well he understood that the printed record—rather than the deeds themselves—shapes the long-term understanding of historical events.

Early seemed an unlikely candidate for a leading role at Chancellorsville. He entered the campaign as the army's junior major general, although he could claim considerable accomplishment as a brigade commander as well as success, while still a brigadier, leading the wounded Richard S. Ewell's division during the last part of the Maryland campaign and at the battle of Fredericksburg. Highly ambitious and quick to criticize officers who had advanced more quickly, Early openly sought promotion during late 1862. Both Lee and Stonewall Jackson recommended him for a major generalcy that fall, the latter remarking that Early "manages his men well in camp and also in action." Promotion came in January 1863, eliciting a typically acidic reaction from the new major general: "I know you will think that I am so much tickled with my promotion that I have given up grumbling," Early commented to Ewell, "but the truth is that it comes after so many have been made over me, that it looks very much like they were picking up the scraps now, & the greatest gratification I have in the matter is that others acknowledge the justice of my promotion."[2]

Despite Early's enviable record as a brigadier, senior division commanders

Maj. Gen. Jubal Anderson Early. Robert Underwood Johnson and Clarence Clough Buel, eds., Battles and Leaders of the Civil War, *4 vols. (New York: Century, 1887–88), 4:529*

such as A. P. Hill, Lafayette McLaws, and Richard H. Anderson seemed better choices to carry out critical elements of Lee's plan to thwart Joseph Hooker. But Lee discerned in Early, whom he affectionately called "My Bad Old Man,"[3] a capacity for command without close supervision and entrusted him with responsibilities during the campaign second only to those he placed in Jackson's hands. Chancellorsville anticipated the deployment of Early and the Second Corps to the Shenandoah Valley in June 1864, affording unmistakable evidence of Lee's belief that Early could function effectively when separated from the main army. Among all of the corps commanders in the Army of Northern Virginia, only Jackson and Early received assignments that bespoke Lee's confidence in their ability to succeed under such circumstances.[4] Robert Stiles addressed this phenomenon in his often-cited memoirs: "[Early's] native intellect, his mental training, his sagacity, his resource, his self-reliant, self-directing strength, were all very great, and the commanding general reposed the utmost confidence in him. This he indicated by selecting him so frequently for independent command, and to fill the most critical, difficult, and I had almost said hopeless, positions, in the execution of his own great plans; as for example, when he left him at Fredericksburg with nine thousand men to neutralize Sedgwick with thirty thousand."[5]

Early's generalship in opposing Sedgwick raised questions in 1863 that have persisted in modern literature. Charged with watching Lee's eastern flank, he failed to hold the lines behind which the Army of Northern Virginia had vanquished Ambrose E. Burnside's Federals the previous December in the battle of Fredericksburg. He thus presided over a disappointing element in the larger Confederate success at Chancellorsville. Were his deployments faulty? Did he respond effectively to a succession of Federal threats on May 2–3? What role did he play in the lethargic Confederate effort at Salem Church on May 3–4? In short, did his performance justify Lee's confidence that he was the man to hold the Rappahannock River opposite Fredericksburg while the bulk of the army marched west to confront Joseph Hooker?

The campaign opened for Early just past daylight on a mist and fog enshrouded April 29, 1863, with word that Federal infantry had crossed the Rappahannock River on pontoons below Fredericksburg near the mouth of Deep Run. He immediately moved his division, a portion of which had been picketing that stretch of the river, into position along the Richmond, Fredericksburg & Potomac Railroad between Hamilton's Crossing on the right and Deep Run on the left. Three regiments moved east to the Richmond Stage Road as skirmishers. Soon came news of another Federal pontoon bridge farther downstream at Smithfield, the home of the Pratt family. Alerted by Maj. Samuel Hale of Early's staff, Brig. Gen. Harry Hays hurried his brigade of five

Louisiana regiments toward the river. The 6th Louisiana relieved the 13th Georgia of Brig. Gen. John B. Gordon's brigade in rifle pits near the Rappahannock, holding the Federals at bay for more than an hour. By then, thousands of northern soldiers were on the Confederate side of the river at Deep Run, and a division crossed at the lower site by late morning. Jedediah Hotchkiss noted that he heard reports of musketry and cannon fire from Early's portion of the field at 6:30 or 7:00 A.M., adding that "we fired some artillery at them, soon after they came over, and did some damage to them."[6]

In an account of this artillery action, a gunner from the Rockbridge Artillery described a meeting between Early and Lee on Prospect Hill. "The enemy's infantry having formed on our side near the river, under Gen. Early's order, we opened on them, and they soon retired under the bank," recalled David E. Moore many years after the war. "Soon after the firing commenced Gen Lee came up and said 'Gen. Early what are you making all this racket about?' Gen. Early replied 'the Yankees have crossed the river again' and Gen Lee said 'oh the troublesome fellows.' This was the beginning of the artillery firing preceding the Battle of Chancellorsville."[7] Moore's reconstructed dialogue may be apocryphal, but it seems likely that Lee must have approved of Early's prompt response to the Federal crossings.

For the remainder of April 29 and into the next day, the Confederate commander watched Union movements on both sides of the Rappahannock, pondered intelligence from his cavalry about Federals marching upriver, and eventually decided that Hooker's main blow would come from the west. "It was, therefore, determined to leave sufficient troops to hold our lines," explained Lee, employing his usual passive voice, "and with the main body of the army to give battle to the approaching column." Most of the Confederate soldiers would take the roads westward toward Chancellorsville before the sun rose on May 1. To Jubal Early fell the task of holding the enemy in check along the long riverfront at Fredericksburg.[8]

How did Lee define "sufficient force" to oppose an enemy estimated at 30,000 men or more? Early would have approximately 7,500 men in the four brigades of his own division, comprising Hays's Louisianians, Gordon's five Georgia regiments, Brig. Gen. Robert F. Hoke's four regiments and one battalion of North Carolinians, and William "Extra Billy" Smith's four Virginia regiments, as well as the four batteries of Col. R. Snowden Andrews's artillery battalion. Also placed under his command were 1,500 Mississippians in the four regiments of Brig. Gen. William Barksdale's brigade from McLaws's division, three companies of the Washington Artillery, and part of the army's general artillery reserve under Brig. Gen. William Nelson Pendleton. After careful study of his division's field returns and other documents after the war,

Early estimated his strength to have been 9,000 infantry and 45 guns. His figure for the infantry probably was accurate, but he perhaps underestimated the number of guns.[9] Whatever the exact total, many Confederates who recognized the obviously superior strength of their foe thought it too small. Looking back on the battle after the war, an officer in Smith's brigade assessed somewhat bitterly Lee's expectations of Early: "Our division occupied a line of battle of sufficient length to require forty thousand troops and as was always the case Gen. Early was selected to lead a forlorn hope."[10]

Early received specific instructions from his chief on the morning of May 1. Before departing to join the troops who would confront Hooker, "General Lee instructed me to watch the enemy and try to hold him; to conceal the weakness of my force, and if compelled to yield before overpowering numbers, to fall back towards Guiney's depot where our supplies were, protecting them and the railroad." Should Sedgwick withdraw all or a significant part of his strength, Early was to "join the main body of the army . . . , leaving at Fredericksburg only such force as might be necessary to protect the town against any force the enemy might leave behind." These instructions allowed Early considerable discretion, although Lee suggested that a bombardment by long-range artillery on May 2 might provoke the Federals into revealing their strength.[11]

Early was familiar with the terrain he would defend. Essentially duplicating the line 75,000 men in the Army of Northern Virginia had held the preceding December, Early's position stretched more than six miles from Hamilton's Crossing on the Richmond, Fredericksburg & Potomac Railroad line to Taylor's Hill on the Rappahannock River. Deep Run divided the field into northern and southern zones; Hazel Run wound eastward to join the Rappahannock just south of Fredericksburg. Howison's Hill rose a mile and a half west of the mouth of Deep Run, the first of a string of excellent defensive positions that included, in order from south to north, Lee's Hill, Willis's Hill, Marye's Heights, Cemetery Hill, Stansbury's Hill, and Taylor's Hill. On December 13, 1862, the Federals had achieved their only breakthrough between Deep Run and Hamilton's Crossing, after which Early had played a key role in restoring the broken Confederate line. The bloody repulses for which First Fredericksburg became infamous in the Federal army occurred at the foot of Willis's Hill and Marye's Heights.

The immediate situation and memories of First Fredericksburg influenced Early's positioning of men and guns. His division held the ground between Deep Run and Hamilton's Crossing, where thousands of Federals had entrenched west of the Rappahannock at the pontoon sites. Barksdale's regiments with supporting artillery stretched between Lee's Hill and the Orange Plank Road just north of Marye's Heights; this had been the strongest part of the

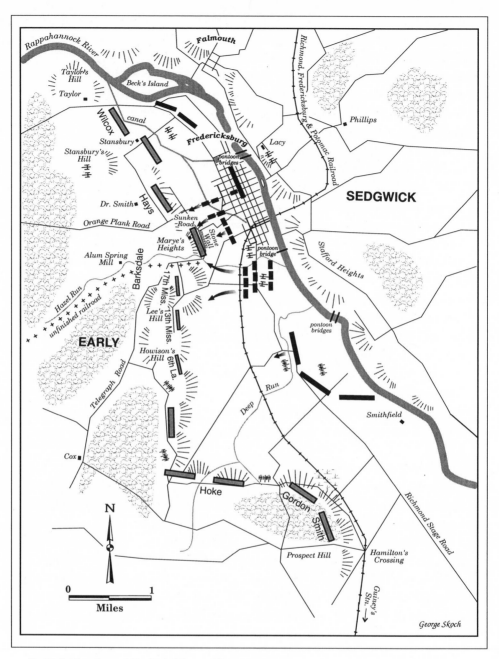

Battlefield at Second Fredericksburg, May 3, 1863

Confederate line in December, and as yet no Federals had crossed the river at Fredericksburg. Artillery and skirmishers alone protected the area between Lee's Hill and Deep Run, while the line north of the Plank Road lay vacant. Pendleton concurred with Early's allocation of guns to the various parts of the line. Although far from ideal in terms of the number of men available along the extensive line, Early's dispositions made sense in the context of the existing Federal threat and the experience of the preceding December.[12]

May 1 passed quietly at Fredericksburg. Federal units mounted weak demonstrations in the course of the day, but no firing broke the silence along the river. The enemy remained entrenched at their bridgeheads and in obvious strength on the east side of the Rappahannock.[13] To the west, Lee and Jackson met Hooker's advancing columns at the edge of the Wilderness, seized the initiative, and ended the day near the crossroads at Chancellorsville.

Dawn on Saturday, May 2, revealed another uneventful scene. Pendleton arrived at Early's headquarters shortly after sunrise. Early informed the artillerist that "by General Lee's order, you would, within half an hour, feel the enemy by opening on him your long-range guns" and that he intended to start two brigades toward Lee if the Federals failed to respond aggressively to the fire.[14] Soon Confederate guns pounded the crossing points. Later in the morning, Pendleton and Barksdale reported Federals concentrating near Falmouth and suggested it might be premature to send reinforcements to Lee. Early joined them on Lee's Hill, whence he hoped to discern what the Union activity across the river portended. "At about 11 o'clock A.M.," Early later wrote, "Colonel R. H. Chilton, of General Lee's staff, came to me with a verbal order to move immediately up towards Chancellorsville with my whole force, except a brigade of infantry and a part of Pendleton's reserve artillery." Those left behind would hold the enemy as long as possible, then retire in the direction of Spotsylvania Court House.[15]

Early protested that such a movement would be detected immediately, inviting a Federal assault against the remaining defenders. Pendleton added his own objections. Chilton "repeated his orders with great distinctness in the presence of General Pendleton," observed Early after the war, "and in reply to questions from us, said that there could be no mistake in his orders." In the midst of this tense conversation, Early learned that the enemy had abandoned their bridgehead at Smithfield but had retained the one at the mouth of Deep Run. The Federals at Falmouth might be preparing to march toward Hooker, he conceded to Chilton, but thousands of them still menaced Fredericksburg. Moreover, he believed, "we were then keeping away from the army, opposed to General Lee, a much larger body of troops than my force could engage or neutralize if united to the army near Chancellorsville." Chilton ended the discussion by observing that Lee had considered all the points raised by Early and Pendleton, "but he was satisfied the great battle had to be fought upon the left, and had determined to get all the available force there." That settled the matter. Full of misgivings but a loyal subordinate, Early immediately issued orders that Hays's brigade and one of Barksdale's regiments remain at Fredericksburg and that the rest of the soldiers march to reinforce Lee. Pendleton would stay behind to oversee the removal of most of the guns.[16]

Because of the need to mask the movement, it took several hours to set the division in motion. The head of the column was approaching the Plank Road just before dark when Early received a note from Lee indicating that Chilton had misrepresented his wishes: Early was to withdraw from Fredericksburg only if he could do so safely.[17] In language vindicating Early's own military judgment, Lee also granted his lieutenant the latitude to remain in place if he believed he could tie down a large number of Federals, which would "do as much or perhaps more service than by joining him." Certain that the enemy at Fredericksburg had discovered his withdrawal, Early decided to press on. His lead units had progressed about a mile west on the Plank Road when a courier from Barksdale brought word that Federals had advanced in force against Hays and Pendleton. An artillerist who overheard this message delivered to Early recalled that "General Pendleton said if he did not come to his relief he would lose all the artillery." Barksdale already had turned back with his regiments, as had John B. Gordon, who offered to assist Barksdale without orders from Early. A divided command would accomplish little, reasoned Early, and he "determined to return at once to my former position," sending Major Hale to apprise Lee of his decision and another messenger to Barksdale. "We regained our former lines without trouble about ten or eleven o'clock at night," wrote Early about the conclusion of a stressful countermarch. "Barksdale occupied his old position and Hays returned during the night to the right of my line." While the Confederates were hurrying back to Fredericksburg, thought Early, Sedgwick "might have smashed every thing to pieces, but for his excessive caution."[18]

May 3 unfolded as a series of crises. William Barksdale appeared at Early's headquarters before sunrise to report Federals crossing the river at Fredericksburg. The previous evening Barksdale had complained about Early's inattention to his part of the line, remarking that it was hard to "sleep with a million of armed Yankees all around him."[19] Early dispatched Hays's brigade to bolster Barksdale, giving the latter authority for its placement. Daylight revealed that Sedgwick had shifted his entire force to the west side of the river. The Federals manifestly contemplated a major blow—but where? Although musketry and cannon fire had broken out to the north, Early still believed his right, where Federals were visible in the largest number, to be the most vulnerable. The valley of Deep Run also lay open to attack. He considered Barksdale's position the "strongest in natural and artificial defences & . . . better guarded by artillery" than any other part of the line. Col. Benjamin G. Humphreys of the 21st Mississippi, whose soldiers manned the trenches on Marye's Heights and had helped repulse two feeble Union assaults before 7:00 A.M. on May 3, agreed that initial Federal dispositions "seemed to justify the suspicians of Gen. Early, that the real attack would be made at Hamilton Station, and that the attack at Marye's Hill was only a feint and a feeler."[20]

The Confederates blunted a Federal demonstration against Deep Run shortly after sunrise, after which "heavy bodies of infantry were seen passing up towards Fredericksburg." Confederates opposite the town believed a major attack soon would be directed against them. Four of Hays's regiments went into line on Barksdale's left, north of the Plank Road, while the 6th Louisiana extended his right to Howison's Hill. Cadmus M. Wilcox, whose brigade had been covering Banks Ford, arrived at Taylor's Hill and promised further assistance should Barksdale require it. Early heard about the failed assaults against Marye's Heights from Barksdale and Pendleton but worried that the movement of Federals toward Fredericksburg might presage a more serious effort in that quarter. The brigades of Hoke, Gordon, and Smith, in that order left to right, maintained positions between Deep Run and Hamilton's Crossing. Watching the battlefield from a point on Hoke's line, Early sent Lt. William G. Calloway of his staff to Lee's Hill to warn Barksdale and Pendleton of the Federal shift upriver and to "ascertain how they were getting on." When the aide failed to return expeditiously, Early rode toward Lee's Hill himself.[21]

Three riders met him en route to Lee's Hill. The first announced that Federals had been reported on Marye's Heights; the second, a courier from Pendleton, reported that northern attacks had been repulsed. Within minutes of hearing the cheering news from Pendleton, Early saw Calloway spurring toward him. His aide had just left Lee's Hill, where Barksdale and Pendleton had expressed confidence in their ability to hold off the enemy. But shortly after leaving the generals, Calloway had seen "that the enemy certainly had carried the heights."[22] Early eventually would learn that Sedgwick had sent columns against Stansbury's Hill, Lee's Hill, and Marye's Heights and that the Federals, at first repulsed at all points, had carried Barksdale's center by massing overwhelming strength opposite the 18th Mississippi and three companies of the 21st Mississippi holding the Sunken Road. Eight pieces of artillery and a significant number of prisoners fell into Federal hands.[23]

There would be time later to digest the particulars; for now, Sedgwick's success had compromised the entire Confederate line and Early acted quickly to limit the damage. He ordered Gordon to hasten forward from his position on

Dead Mississippians and the debris of battle behind the stone wall at the foot of Marye's Heights, May 3, 1863. Francis Trevelyan Miller, ed., The Photographic History of the Civil War, *10 vols. (New York: Review of Reviews, 1911), 2:123*

the right, then made his way to the Telegraph Road, where he rallied some guns that, together with elements of Barksdale's command and the 6th Louisiana, slowed the enemy's progress. Early directed a fighting withdrawal along the Telegraph Road, instructing Barksdale to make a stand at the Cox house, some two miles in the rear of Lee's Hill. There the men of Gordon's and Hays's brigades, supported by artillery, would join the Mississippians. Satisfied that the line at Cox's house could hold, Early rode to his right, where he directed Smith and Hoke to move their brigades and Andrews his battalion of artillery into positions closer to Barksdale. "We quickly and with good order formed a line of battle at right angles with our former one," stated a soldier in the 38th Georgia of Gordon's brigade, "and by the time that it was formed it was late at night." Early returned to the Cox house briefly before riding across Hazel Run to observe the Federals, who at first were moving slowly westward and eventually halted along the Plank Road.[24]

As he returned from his reconnaissance of Sedgwick's column, Early met Maj. Ellison L. Costin of Lafayette McLaws's staff at Hazel Run. Lt. Andrew L. Pitzer of Early's staff, who had been present on Lee's Hill when Marye's Heights fell, had ridden immediately to apprise Lee of the situation, and the commanding general had dispatched McLaws to help stop Sedgwick. Early had fulfilled his primary mission of holding Sedgwick in check while Lee dealt with the main Union force, but now the eastern component of Hooker's army required greater attention. That afternoon, elements of McLaws's division joined Cadmus Wilcox's brigade, which had disputed the Federal advance westward from Fredericksburg for several hours, to turn Sedgwick back near Salem Church. Costin conveyed Lee's wish that Early and McLaws cooperate to attack Sedgwick;[25] however, only an hour of daylight remained, too little time for Smith's and Hoke's troops to take position. Early immediately sent a note to McLaws informing him that he would gather his forces that night and attack the Federals early the next morning with the goal of driving them from Lee's Hill and Marye's Heights, cutting them off from Fredericksburg, and pressing their left flank north of the Plank Road. In the course of the advance, he would extend his left to touch McLaws's right. "I asked General McLaws' cooperation in this plan," Early wrote in his memoirs. "During the night, I received a note from him assenting to my plan and containing General Lee's approval of it also."[26]

McLaws confirmed in his official report and a postwar narrative that Early proposed to retake the high ground on May 4 and that Lee approved the plan, but neither account mentions Early's request that McLaws cooperate in a more general assault. Yet in a message to McLaws dated midnight on May 3, Lee supported Early's plan "if it is practicable" and expressed a desire that if possible McLaws press the Federals "so as to prevent their concentrating on General Early."[27]

Expecting opposition from Federals on Lee's Hill and Marye's Heights, Early planned to employ his full force. Gordon's brigade would advance along the Telegraph Road with Barksdale's and Smith's behind it as a second line; the brigades of Hays and Hoke would cross to the north bank of Hazel Run and then move east along that stream. The initial assaults would cut the Federal connection to Fredericksburg, after which Early expected Gordon and Smith to move north toward the Rappahannock and then west along the Plank Road while Hays and Hoke, shifting their focus to the north, would attack toward the Plank Road while extending their left to unite with McLaws's right flank. Barksdale's brigade would hold Marye's Heights and Lee's Hill against any Federal move from the east.[28] The goal was to force Sedgwick out of his strong position, which approximated a huge "U" with its flanks anchored on the

Rappahannock near Banks Ford and Taylor's Hill and its middle bulging across the Plank Road with its center north of the Downman house.

Early positioned Gordon's brigade at first light before accompanying Hoke's and Hays's brigades to their starting point north of Hazel Run. Expecting to accompany Gordon's men, he returned to find that the Georgian already had begun his movement. Surprised by Gordon's departure, Early ordered Barksdale and Smith to follow at once. Gordon's advance went beautifully, encountering no Federals on Lee's Hill and clearing Marye's Heights and Cemetery Hill with a rapid and nearly bloodless dash against Federals posted along the Plank Road west of the Marye house. "For two miles we saw not a Yankee," wrote Adj. William C. Mathews of the 38th Georgia, "but on ascending a hill near the old plank road we got a sight of them in line of battle behind the road that afforded some protection to them. . . . Before we could get near the road the Yankees were going like a parcel of sheep through the woods, having wounded but three in our regiment." Another of Gordon's men remarked that "the yankees made the poorest stand in this fight I ever saw. . . . I never saw yankees Skeedadle so in all my life."[29] Early directed Smith's brigade across Hazel Run to support Gordon and sent Barksdale's brigade, which Early later claimed had halted without orders a mile behind Lee's Hill, to occupy the Sunken Road below Marye's Heights and then push into Fredericksburg to capture a train of Federal wagons. Irritated at the time that Barksdale made no aggressive move toward the wagons, Early later discovered that a division of Federal troops had occupied the town.[30]

Early had isolated Sedgwick from Fredericksburg and anxiously listened for the sounds of firing on McLaws's front. Gordon and Smith were north of the Plank Road opposite Federals who had dug in facing east and southeast. Thinking Sedgwick's left might lack proper artillery support, Early ordered Smith to "feel the enemy on the heights on the Plank Road, above Fredericksburg." Heavy artillery from Taylor's Hill greeted Smith's soldiers, and Early instructed them to withdraw.[31] It was shortly after 8:00 A.M., and Early had made an excellent start on the plan sketched the previous night. More success could come only with McLaws's assistance, so Early sent Lieutenant Pitzer to ask the Georgian to open his attack. The messenger assured McLaws that Hoke's and Hays's brigades could be moved rapidly into position to connect on his right and that once the battle shifted toward the west, Early would commit Gordon and Smith as well. In his report, McLaws stated that "General Early sent me word by his staff officer that, if I would attack in front, he would advance two brigades and strike at the flank and rear of the enemy. I agreed to advance, provided he would first attack, and did advance my right (Kershaw and Wofford) to co-operate with him; but finding my force was insufficient for a

Salem Church looking south from the Orange Plank Road (engraving based on 1884 photograph). A prominent landmark during the fighting on May 3–4, 1863, the church was crowded with wounded receiving medical treatment after the battle. Robert Underwood Johnson and Clarence Clough Buel, eds., Battles and Leaders of the Civil War, *4 vols. (New York: Century, 1887–88), 3:230*

front attack, I withdrew to my line of the evening previous, General Early not attacking, as I could hear." In fact, none of McLaws's men took any aggressive action. McLaws did inform Lee of Early's request "and my objections to it and asked for additional forces." Receiving word that the balance of R. H. Anderson's division was on its way from Chancellorsville, McLaws "directed that no attack should be made until General Anderson arrived."[32]

Pitzer related all of this to Early, whose cue to join a general attack against Sedgwick would be the firing of three cannons in rapid succession. Soon Hoke settled into position southeast of the Downman house with Hays on his right near Alum Spring Mill. Anderson's brigades arrived at Salem Church before noon, as did Lee himself, who probably believed his presence necessary to prod McLaws into action.[33] Early's troops were ready by that time, but several hours dragged by as Anderson's brigades deployed between McLaws and Early. Edward Porter Alexander, whose artillery battalion stood ready to support the Confederate offensive, recalled Lee's ill humor at the delay. Based on Lee's conversations with him and with others within his earshot, Alexander later suggested three possible causes of the general's pique: "1st. That a great deal of valuable time had been already uselessly lost by somebody, some how, no particulars being given. 2nd. Nobody knew exactly how or where the en-

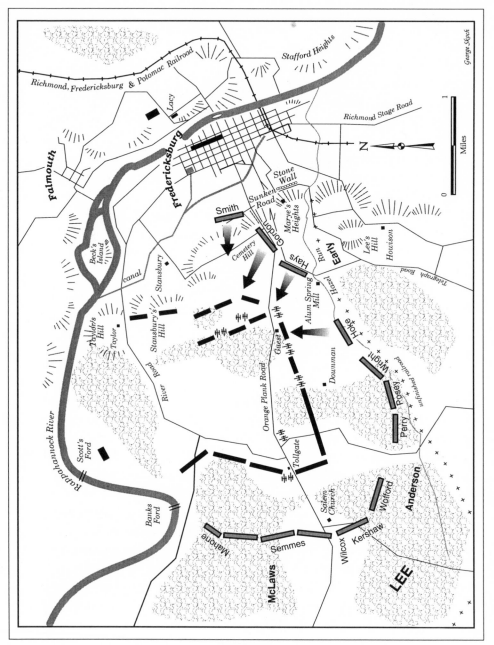

Battlefields at Fredericksburg and Salem Church, May 4, 1863

emy's line of battle ran & it was somebody's duty to know. 3rd. That it now devolved on him personally to use up a lot more time to find out all about the enemy before we could move a peg."[34]

Lee presently joined Early along Hoke's line to discuss the impending attack. The Confederate commander found at least one of his major generals prepared to take action. Early explained that he planned for Hoke and Hays to advance to the Plank Road, where they would pivot to the west, with Hays continuing the assault along the north side and Hoke along the south side of that thoroughfare. Gordon would strike toward the Taylor house, turning Sedgwick's left flank, while "Extra Billy" Smith's brigade remained in reserve as potential reinforcements. If McLaws and Anderson applied simultaneous pressure, Sedgwick's line surely must give way. Lee approved the plan, directed Early to commence as soon as he heard the three-gun signal, then returned to Anderson's sector about 2:00 P.M.[35]

Capt. Richard Watson York of the 6th North Carolina in Hoke's brigade later asserted that Lee's appearance reinvigorated many of Early's soldiers. Because of the "marching and countermarching" of the preceding two days, the "men and officers became thoroughly demoralized. They had lost confidence in every body." The Federal position looked strong, and rumors circulated that "Gen. Early was drunk and was going to order a charge which would be disastrous." Although York knew the rumor "was utterly false," the unit never had seemed so "utterly and generally demoralised—I confess I, myself, to some extent participated." As soon as the men detected Lee's presence, "every man instinctively commenced getting ready. The word soon went down the line 'All is right, Uncle Robert is here. We will whip them.' "[36]

Following Lee's departure, another four hours crawled by before the three signal guns announced the opening of the attack. Whether inspired by Lee or not, Hoke's soldiers and those of Harry Hays exhibited admirable energy. Hoke's men moved across the plateau between the Downman property and Hazel Run, descended into the creek bottom, then climbed the opposite ridge toward the Plank Road. Hays's brigade kept pace to the right, while Gordon's regiments made progress toward Taylor's Hill. The advance of Hoke's North Carolinians and Hays's Louisianians—the same soldiers who two months hence would struggle up East Cemetery Hill at Gettysburg in another memorable assault—exhilarated Early, who watched from a point near the Telegraph Road opposite Alum Spring Mill and later termed it "a splendid sight."[37] Federal artillery near the Guest house had retired in the face of the attack, and the enemy's infantry also gave ground. Just as the brigades seemed poised to achieve significant success, Hoke received a crippling wound. Col. Isaac E. Avery assumed command but knew nothing of Early's instructions, and the brigade floundered across the Plank Road, drifting rightward into the path of Hays's men. Confusion resulted in the woods north of the road as officers struggled in vain to regain momentum amid increasing darkness. An officer in Hays's brigade insisted that some of the North Carolinians fired into the rear of the Louisiana troops, while Federals poured musketry into their front.[38]

Early had spurred across Hazel Run toward the Plank Road when it seemed his brigades would sweep the enemy from the field. He arrived to find the disorganized men of Hays's brigade withdrawing from the woods. Reorganizing them and Hoke's survivors on open ground below the Guest house, Early also summoned two regiments from Smith's command. By the time they appeared and the other brigades re-formed, "it had become too dark to make any further advance." Nightfall also stopped Gordon, who had reached a position near the Taylor house after driving the enemy back a good distance. After dark, Early met with Lee at the Downman house, receiving instructions to leave Gordon and Hoke perpendicular to the Plank Road facing west and to shift Smith and Hays eastward to go into line on either side of Barksdale's brigade.[39]

That night, Sedgwick recrossed the Rappahannock, frustrating Lee's hope of defeating him decisively. Early shared Lee's disappointment with the result. The brigades of Hoke, Hays, and Gordon "fought the main action" on May 4, Early subsequently asserted, adding that only "two of Anderson's brigades, Posey's and Wright's, became engaged at all." Not until he was re-forming Hays's and Hoke's brigades had he seen "some of Anderson's men coming up and it was then near dark." "Had Anderson attacked with vigor, and McLaws come down," Early concluded, "there would have been no escape for Sedgwick."[40]

Although somewhat unfair to Anderson's men, Early's assessment generally was accurate. McLaws had spent May 4 as a bystander. His muddled report stated that late in the day "distant firing in the direction of Fredericksburg was heard, indicating that the attack had commenced on the extreme right. Night now came rapidly on, and nothing could be observed of our operations." Even more revealing about his utter confusion during the last day's fighting, McLaws's postwar narrative devotes only a single sentence to May 4: "In response [to my message] Gen. Lee came in person with Gen. Anderson's Division and under his direction, as he states in his orders I have quoted, Sedgwick's command was driven over the river." This inept performance did not go unnoticed. While preparing a major speech about Chancellorsville in the late 1870s, Fitzhugh Lee was baffled by McLaws's behavior on May 4. "I am not going to find fault with anybody—because I know the difference between *hind*sight & *fore* sight," Lee wrote Early, "—but between you & I, what was the matter with McLaws in connection with the attack on Sedgwick on Tuesday 4th

May!" Between the lines of R. E. Lee's report anyone could read implicit criticism of McLaws: "The speedy approach of darkness prevented General McLaws from perceiving the success of the attack until the enemy began to recross the river a short distance below Banks' Ford."[41]

The fighting on May 4 closed a week during which Jubal Early stepped into the circle of Lee's primary lieutenants. Newspaper coverage told him what later historical treatment would confirm: the action at Fredericksburg and Salem Church always would remain in the imposing shadow of Lee and Jackson's masterpiece in the Wilderness.[42] Crowded out of the headlines by dramatic details of Jackson's flank attack and Hooker's withdrawal from Chancellorsville, events at Fredericksburg and Salem Church also struck many as unfortunate brushstrokes on an otherwise perfect canvass. Artillerist William Ransom Johnson Pegram, who had fought brilliantly with the Confederate guns at Hazel Grove on May 3, speculated eight days later that "the greatest victory of the war" would have been even more resounding had Early "managed better below at Fredericksburg." On May 3, a gunner with Early's division expressed disgust with the Federal capture of Marye's Heights. "It is thought gross mismanagement somewhere has caused this loss," he wrote, adding that the "surprise was shameful." Silent about whether he blamed Early or Barksdale, this man placed his hope in Lee and Jackson, who according to rumor had whipped the enemy at Chancellorsville and "can very easily wipe out those now on this side of Fredericksburg."[43]

Whatever the consensus of the army's grapevine, Early knew he had the good opinion of his commander. Lee had selected him for an important post with wide discretion, approved his plans on May 3 for an offensive against Sedgwick at Salem Church, and, after seeking him out on May 4, once again sustained his judgment about how best to attack the enemy. Habitually economical with official praise for subordinates, Lee included a sentence in his report certain to gratify Old Jube: "Major General Early performed the important and responsible duty intrusted to him in a manner which reflected credit upon himself and his command."[44]

Early's conduct fully merited Lee's approbation. He had presided over the defense of an extensive line with relatively very few men. He met the initial Federal crossings with dispatch, and, although questioned then and later, his placement of the bulk of his soldiers south of Deep Run was prudent in light of both the Federal deployment and the Confederate experience at First Fredericksburg. Had he massed more troops along the ridges north of Lee's Hill, the area from Deep Run to Hamilton's Crossing would have offered Sedgwick a more tempting target than Barksdale's position offered on May 3. His decision to turn back to Fredericksburg after reaching the Plank Road on May 2 bespoke a grasp of the value of concentrated strength. When Barksdale requested assistance on May 3, Early immediately sent Hays's brigade. In the chaotic aftermath of the Confederate retreat from the hills west of Fredericksburg, Early supplied vigorous personal leadership along the Telegraph Road, maneuvered his brigades into strong positions, and then turned his attention to recapturing the initiative the next day. No evidence of panic accompanied any of his actions through May 3, and on the final day's battle, his aggressiveness stood out among the three major generals on the field.

Some critics have argued that without Cadmus Wilcox's stout service on the afternoon of May 3 none of Early's efforts would have mattered. He also displayed a somewhat ungenerous spirit toward Barksdale and his men. But on balance, Early justified his chief's confidence in him and staked a claim to larger responsibility in the future. The soldierly qualities he exhibited while in direct contact with Lee during the campaign helped bring about his assignment to independent command in the Shenandoah Valley the following summer.[45]

A controversy with Barksdale in the wake of the campaign highlighted Early's sensitivity to criticism as well as his complete deference to Lee. In a letter to the editors of the Richmond *Enquirer* dated May 11, 1863, Early complained about "correspondents ignorant of the real facts, or writing in the interests of particular commands," who had offered flawed accounts of the capture of Marye's Heights. He bridled at the suggestion that he had failed to support the Mississippians defending the heights, calling attention to his transfer of Hays's brigade in prompt response to Barksdale's request for help. Three regiments of Wilcox's brigade added even more strength to the northern end of the line. "This left only three brigades on the long and comparatively weak line from the heights in rear of Fredericksburg to the mouth of the Massaponax to confront the heavy columns of the enemy on this side at the mouth of Deep Run," remarked Early, "while there were two brigades and three regiments of another to defend the strong and comparatively short line in rear of and above Fredericksburg." Moreover, Barksdale benefited from the strongest natural position and the best artillery support along the seven-mile Confederate line, for which Early had no reserves.

Professing to cast no censure on Barksdale's unit, Early nevertheless chose language certain to provoke a response: "I will state that my division did not lose Marye's Hill, but one of my brigades (Gordon's, formerly Lawton's,) recaptured it before 9 o'clock on the next morning, and three of my brigades (Hays's, Hoke's, and Gordon's,) bore the brunt of the fight when the enemy was driven back across the River, Barksdale's brigade and Smith's, of my own division, having been left to keep the enemy in check from the direction of Fredericksburg." He had done all in his power to "avert the disaster, and to correct and retrieve it" and was "willing to abide by the judgment of the commanding General upon my own conduct and that of my division."[46]

Barksdale answered with barely controlled anger on May 13.[47] Resenting the "gratuitous and unfounded" insinuation that members of his brigade had complained to the press, Barksdale had been unaware that Early's "conduct in the late engagements around Fredericksburg had been made the subject of newspaper censure until I saw it announced over his own signature." Barksdale correctly pointed out that when he asked for help on the morning of May 3, his brigade covered a front "of not less than three miles" from Taylor's Hill to Howison's Hill rather than the " 'short line in rear of and to the left of Fredericksburg,' as stated by Gen. Early." Describing in detail his deployment and the course of the battle, he concluded that "it will thus be seen that Marye's hill was defended by one small regiment, three companies and four pieces of artillery, and not by the entire brigade. A more heroic struggle was never made by a mere handful of men against overwhelming odds." Early's letter produced the impression that Gordon's brigade had driven the Federals from a position the Mississippians had failed to hold the day before. "I would scorn to detract from the well-earned reputation of this brigade and its gallant commander," Barksdale asserted, "but the truth is, the enemy had abandoned Marye's heights, and Gen. Gordon took possession without opposition."

Early responded to Barksdale's letter the same day he read it in the *Enquirer*.[48] Surprised at Barksdale's reaction to a letter intended only to deny the rumor that the Mississippians had fought without adequate support on May 3, Early reminded Barksdale that "shortly after the capture of Marye's hill by the enemy, he had stated to me that he had previously felt no uneasiness about the safety of his position, as he deemed it impregnable, but had felt a good deal of anxiety about my position on the right, which had been threatened all morning by a column of the enemy moving up Deep Run." Early loftily observed that he would shun a controversy, "which accords neither with my taste nor sense of military propriety," contenting himself with correcting Barksdale's claims "that the enemy had abandoned Marye's hill on the 4th, and that it was taken possession of without opposition." Barksdale could not have known the situation on the hill because he and his brigade were "in the rear, and out of sight" of the action. Federals arrayed behind the Plank Road had resisted Gordon's advance, with assistance from a pair of nearby brigades on high ground near the upper mill on Hazel Run. After making these comments, Early would "abstain from all further notice of this matter."

Barksdale fired his final volley in mid-June. Flatly denying Early's version of their conversation after the fall of the heights, he insisted that from Lee's Hill he saw no threat along Deep Run to Early's right and neither felt nor expressed

William Barksdale. This is a previously unpublished late-antebellum view (there is no known wartime photograph of Barksdale). National Archives

"solicitude as to his position." A mass of Federals evident in Fredericksburg did inspire doubts about the safety of his own line. As for Gordon's actions on May 4, "I have the amplest testimony in my possession to establish it, that Marye's Hill had been abandoned, and that whatever engagement Gen. Gordon may have had with the enemy on Monday morning, was beyond the plank road, and to the left of Marye's hill." Barksdale simultaneously published a letter dated May 14, 1863, in which Early requested a detailed report of Barksdale's operations so that he could "do full justice to your brigade." "I am satisfied that the carrying [of] Marye's hill could not well have been avoided," stated this letter. "The whole line was exposed for want of reserves, and the enemy made his most determined and desperate effort against the part defended by your brigade. . . . All of our troops, including yours, did their duty under the trying circumstances in which they were placed."[49]

Was there a winner in this episode? Early *had* supported Barksdale on May 3 and justly resented implications to the contrary, but the tone of his letters surely left readers with the sense that Barksdale and his men may have behaved less gallantly than the soldiers of Gordon, Hays, and Hoke. He also misrepresented the length of Barksdale's line and the number of men available at the crucial point. As for Gordon's "fight" on Marye's Heights on May 4, Early's own report, written several days before his first letter to the editors, stated that "Gordon succeeded in capturing Marye's Hill with ease." The problem may have been one of semantics—Federals along the Plank Road certainly did oppose Gordon, but they were not on the part of Marye's Heights associated with the fighting on December 13, 1862, and May 3, 1863. In the absence of corroborating evidence on one side or the other, it is impossible to say which of the men dissembled about the conversation after the Federals captured the heights.

Because Early instigated the exchange and was the senior officer, it reflected most negatively on him. A correspondent for the *Dispatch* whose reporting initially had upset Early mocked the general and reprimanded him for tarnishing the victory: "I see that the *late* Gen. Early—Gen. Jubal—has shown his 'strategy' by poking his nose into a hornet's nest. It is no time for Confederates to quarrel." A friendlier piece in the *Enquirer* lauded the accomplishments of Early, Barksdale, and their soldiers before scolding that "this is no time for bickerings and newspaper controversies among our braves in the field."[50]

A born controversialist (despite his second letter's profession of distaste for such jousting), Early probably would have answered Barksdale's second letter had Lee not intervened. Always eager to quiet friction among his often-disputatious subordinates, the commanding general reprimanded Early for airing grievances in public. "You gave me a mild rebuke for that," Early reminded Lee after the war, "and I never repeated the offence, not even when I was so unjustly assailed in regard to my valley campaign." No evidence reveals whether Barksdale received a similar rebuke from Lee.[51]

In the postwar years, Early paid close attention to writings about the Confederate experience. Believing that his own operations were imperfectly understood, he published a memoir of his 1864 Shenandoah Valley campaign.[52] He sent Lee a copy of this book in the fall of 1866, asking if the general minded his expanding the account to embrace the earlier period of the conflict. "I have no objection to the publication of the narrative of your operations before leaving the Army of N. Va.," replied Lee. "I would recommend however that while giving the facts which you think necessary for your own vindication, that you omit all epithets or remarks calculated to excite bitterness or animosity between different sections of the Country." Widely known as a sarcastic man given to making extreme statements, Early nonetheless approached the task of recording his recollections with the instincts of a scholar. He asked a former aide to gather his military papers and send them to Canada. "I desire to write an account of my whole experiences and observations during the war," explained Early, "and I desire to obtain all the documents in regard to my command which I can." Among the items he mentioned as especially important were reports and other materials relating to the Chancellorsville campaign.[53]

Early sent Lee the portion of his narrative covering Second Fredericksburg and Salem Church in late 1868.[54] In his cover letter, he explained at length that Gordon had met resistance on Marye's Heights on May 4. "General Barksdale felt a little sore about the loss of the heights," he added, "which he need not have done, and seemed to think it necessary, in order to defend his brigade, to depreciate the services of my division." Early hoped Lee would agree that the narrative was fair to everyone involved in this phase of the battle. As for Salem Church, he disputed Richard Anderson's official report, which claimed that Early's and Anderson's brigades encountered only slight resistance on May 4. Hays, Hoke, and Gordon had met fierce fire, suffering heavy losses and inflicting severe injury on the enemy: "My pioneer party, buried, next day, more than 200 of the enemy picked up on the ground on which my brigades had fought."[55]

Early's narrative and his comments to Lee defended the honor of his division against explicit and implied criticisms in earlier published accounts. He probably had seen Benjamin G. Humphreys's piece on Second Fredericksburg in *The Land We Love*, wherein the author scoffed at the notion that Gordon had "recaptured" Marye's Heights: "If 'recaptured' at all, it was by the ladies of Fredericksburg (God bless them,) who were found there quietly searching for wounded Mississippians, by . . . [members of Barksdale's brigade] in advance of Gordon's brigade of Early's division." He certainly had read Edward A.

Pollard's four massive volumes on the Confederate war, the second of which spoke of "two remarkable misfortunes" that diminished Lee's victory at Chancellorsville. "The breaking of our lines at Fredericksburg" caused Lee to cease his pursuit of Hooker at Chancellorsville, averred Pollard, and the failure to trap Sedgwick at Salem Church "robbed us of a complete success." Such passages undoubtedly infuriated Early, who lamented the fact that "newspaper accounts, and Pollard's abominable books furnish the main source of information" about "the operations of Confederate armies."[56]

Early thought more highly of William Allan and Jedediah Hotchkiss's book on Chancellorsville, published in New York City in 1867, but considered it deficient on Second Fredericksburg and Salem Church. "The description of the fighting at Fredericksburg is in accordance with the published reports, and it is not inaccurate," Early commented to Hotchkiss, "but it is not as full or minute as it might have been, had there been the material for writing a fuller account." Blame for the dearth of information lay with Early, who had failed to write a long report. "I now regret it very much," he admitted, "as it has prevented Allan's description from being perfect."[57]

Less than eight months after writing Hotchkiss, Early sent his own narrative of the campaign to Lee. He presumably considered it as close to "perfect" as possible but chose not to publish it during his lifetime. Why would he withhold an account that answered, in restrained and meticulous fashion, every question about his performance along the Rappahannock in April and May 1863? His return to the United States shortly after writing Lee disrupted his routine in the short term, and the need to earn a living as a lawyer left him pressed for time over the next few years. After the mid-1870s, however, a handsome annual income from the Louisiana Lottery freed him to pursue whatever he chose. Yet the narrative remained buried amid his voluminous personal papers.

The editors of *Century Magazine* offered Early a prominent national forum in 1884. Asking him to contribute his reminiscences of the Chancellorsville campaign for their war series, they emphasized their preference for colorful anecdotal material over an "official report" style. Early sniffed at the notion of writing for effect rather than seeking accuracy based on the records. He also disdained the practice of accepting money for military reminiscences (he had donated the meager proceeds from his earlier memoir to a variety of groups and individuals). In declining the invitation, he mentioned "that I had discovered that the practice of paying for articles in regard to the war had produced an immense deal of lying, as when such articles were paid for according to their length, their authors, to eke out their pay, had drawn on their imagination for their facts." Clarence Clough Buel tried to recruit Early again in 1887 when the Century Company decided to publish *Battles and Leaders of the Civil War*.

The books would find a large audience, predicted Buel accurately, and would be used by ordinary people and historians in the future. Despite his concern about history's judgment, Early declined to write a new piece. He gave permission for *Century* to print extracts from his official papers, however, and two excerpts from his *Memoir of the Last Year of the War* appeared in *Battles and Leaders*.[58]

Perhaps Early resisted publishing the portion of his reminiscences dealing with Chancellorsville because he wanted to present the entire story. In her "Editor's Note" to his posthumous *Autobiographical Sketch and Narrative of the War Between the States*, his niece, Ruth H. Early, observed that he worked on the manuscript "to the end of his life." Another clue lies in a letter from the mid-1880s. "I begin to despair of ever having a true history of the war written," he confessed to William H. Payne. "If I were to attempt one, and were to express my honest opinions, I would at once be called a crank." Did he contemplate inserting more inflammatory material into his narrative, having been restrained by Lee's injunction to refrain from sectional controversy? He told Payne that 90 percent of everything written about Grant was untrue and closed with a bitter passage capturing years of frustration with what others had written about the conflict: "I begin to believe . . . ," he said, "that the Muse of history is nothing but a 'lying-bitch.' "[59] With his death in Lynchburg less than a decade later, all control over the assessment of Early's performance during the Chancellorsville campaign passed into the hands of that fickle muse.

NOTES

1. Jubal A. Early to R. E. Lee, November 20, 1868, box 25, folder title "Introductory Chapter (Notes & Pages of a Rough Draft) I," John Warwick Daniel Papers, Alderman Library, University of Virginia, Charlottesville, Va. (repository hereafter cited as UVA).

2. U.S. War Department, *The War of the Rebellion: A Compilation of the Official Records of the Union and Confederate Armies*, 127 vols., index, and atlas (Washington, D.C.: GPO, 1880–1901), 19(2):682 (hereafter cited as *OR*; all references are to series 1); T. J. Jackson to Samuel Cooper, November 21, 1862, box 1, T. J. Jackson File, SHSP, Eleanor S. Brockenbrough Library, Museum of the Confederacy, Richmond, Va.; *OR* 21:1099; Jubal A. Early to Richard S. Ewell, January 23, 1863, James A. Walker Compiled Service Record, microfilm roll 257, National Archives, Washington, D.C.

3. For a wartime reference to Lee's bestowing this nickname on Early, see letter of "Phax," Mobile *Advertiser*, September 15, 1864.

4. James Longstreet exercised independent command at Suffolk in the spring of 1863; however, the strategic circumstances were far less challenging than those confronting Jackson and Early during their semi-independent commands.

5. Robert Stiles, *Four Years under Marse Robert* (1903; reprint, Dayton, Ohio: Morningside, 1977), 188–89.

6. Jubal A. Early, *Lieutenant General Jubal Anderson Early, C.S.A.: Autobiographical*

Sketch and Narrative of the War Between the States (1912; reprint, Wilmington, N.C.: Broadfoot, 1989), 193–94; *OR* 25(1):1000; William J. Seymour, *The Civil War Memoirs of Captain William J. Seymour: Reminiscences of a Louisiana Tiger*, ed. Terry L. Jones (Baton Rouge: Louisiana State University Press, 1991), 48; Jedediah Hotchkiss, *Make Me a Map of the Valley: The Civil War Journal of Stonewall Jackson's Topographer*, ed. Archie P. McDonald (Dallas: Southern Methodist University Press, 1973), 135.

7. David E. Moore to John Warwick Daniel, [1907?], box 22, folder title "Chancellorsville 1907," Daniel Papers, UVA. Moore did not include this anecdote in his *The Story of a Cannoneer under Stonewall Jackson, In Which Is Told the Part Taken by the Rockbridge Artillery in the Army of Northern Virginia* (1907; reprint, Alexandria, Va.: Time-Life Books, 1981).

8. *OR* 25(1):796–97.

9. Early, *Autobiographical Sketch and Narrative*, 198. Early took the strength for his division from the April 20, 1863, trimonthly field return, which he had in his possession in Canada but which was not published in the *Official Records*. In his careful *The Campaign of Chancellorsville: A Strategic and Tactical Study* (New Haven, Conn.: Yale University Press, 1910), 268 (n. 2), John Bigelow, Jr., credits Early with 56 guns.

10. Samuel D. Buck, *With the Old Confeds: Actual Experiences of a Captain in the Line* (Baltimore: H. E. Houck, 1925), 77.

11. Early, *Autobiographical Sketch and Narrative*, 197; *OR* 25(1):811, (2):765.

12. Early, *Autobiographical Sketch and Narrative*, 198–99; William Barksdale to the editors of the *Enquirer*, May 13, 1863, Richmond *Semi-Weekly Enquirer*, May 19, 1863, and Richmond *Daily Dispatch*, May 21, 1863; *OR* 25(1):810–11.

13. Early, *Autobiographical Sketch and Narrative*, 199.

14. *OR* 25(1):811. Although chief of artillery for the army, Pendleton submitted his report through Early, who was overall commander along the Fredericksburg line.

15. Early, *Autobiographical Sketch and Narrative*, 200; *OR* 25(1):811–12, 1001. Pendleton's report also placed the time of the meeting with Chilton at about 11:00 A.M.

16. Early, *Autobiographical Sketch and Narrative*, 201–2; *OR* 25(1):812.

17. No explanation for Chilton's mistake ever was offered. Lee's report stated simply that on May 2 he repeated his orders to Early of May 1, "but by a misapprehension on the part of the officer conveying it, General Early was directed to move unconditionally. . . . The mistake in the transmission of the order being corrected, General Early returned to his original position" (*OR* 25[1]:800).

18. Early, *Autobiographical Sketch and Narrative*, 203–4; Jonathan Thomas Scharf, *The Personal Memoirs of Jonathan Thomas Scharf of the First Maryland Artillery*, ed. Tom Kelley (Baltimore: Butternut & Blue, 1992), 67 (Scharf wrote his memoirs during the war); *OR* 25(1):813–14; Jubal A. Early to Jedediah Hotchkiss, March 24, 1868, Jedediah Hotchkiss Papers, Mss2/H7973/b/2, Virginia Historical Society, Richmond, Va. (repository hereafter cited as VHS).

19. Benjamin G. Humphreys, "Recollections of Fredericksburg, From the Morning of the 29th of April to the 6th of May, 1863," *Land We Love* 3 (October 1867): 448 (an abridged version of this article appeared in J. William Jones and others, eds., *Southern Historical Society Papers*, 52 vols. [1876–1959; reprint, with 3-vol. index, Wilmington, N.C.: Broadfoot, 1990–92], 14:415–28 [hereafter cited as *SHSP*]). The Confederates learned later that the Federals Barksdale reported to Early had marched upriver from the vicinity of Deep Run rather than crossing at Fredericksburg; a pontoon was not in place opposite the Lacy house at Fredericksburg until later in the morning.

20. Early, *Autobiographical Sketch and Narrative*, 204–5; Jubal A. Early to editors of the *Enquirer*, May 11, 1863, Richmond *Daily Dispatch*, May 13, 1863; Humphreys, "Recollections of Fredericksburg," 450.

21. Early, *Autobiographical Sketch and Narrative*, 206, 209; *OR* 25(1):840, 856.

22. Early, *Autobiographical Sketch and Narrative*, 209.

23. For excellent accounts of this fighting, see Humphreys, "Recollections of Fredericksburg"; Ernest B. Furgurson, *Chancellorsville 1863: The Souls of the Brave* (New York: Alfred A. Knopf, 1992), 258–66; and Douglas Southall Freeman, *Lee's Lieutenants: A Study in Command*, 3 vols. (New York: Charles Scribner's Sons, 1942–44), 2:613–18.

24. Early, *Autobiographical Sketch and Narrative*, 209–11; William C. Mathews to "Dear Father," May 8, 1863, (Sandersonville) *Central Georgian*, June 3, 1863.

25. Lee sent a note to Early, dated 7:00 P.M. on May 3, that asked him to join McLaws in the type of attack described by Costin. See *OR* 25(2):769–70.

26. *OR* 25(1):1001; Early, *Autobiographical Sketch and Narrative*, 220.

27. *OR* 25(1):827; Lafayette McLaws, "The Battle of Chancellorsville: The Most Remarkable One of the War," p. 25, undated typescript, folder 31, Lafayette McLaws Papers, #472, Southern Historical Collection, Wilson Library, University of North Carolina, Chapel Hill, N.C.; *OR* 25(2):770.

28. Early, *Autobiographical Sketch and Narrative*, 221–22.

29. Ibid., 223–24; William C. Mathews to "Dear Father," May 8, 1863, (Sandersonville) *Central Georgian*, June 3, 1863; George M. Bandy to William Strain and family, May 15, 1863, in James Parker and others, comps., *The Strain Family* (Toccoa, Ga.: Commercial Printing Company, 1985), 223.

30. Jubal A. Early to R. E. Lee, November 20, 1868, Daniel Papers, UVA; Early, *Autobiographical Sketch and Narrative*, 224–25.

31. *OR* 25(1):1002–3; Early, *Autobiographical Sketch and Narrative*, 225–26. Several dozen members of the 58th Virginia and a few members of the 13th who refused to brave Federal fire to rejoin their comrades became prisoners; the 58th also lost its colors, which Early refused to allow the regiment to replace until it captured a Federal flag.

32. Early, *Autobiographical Sketch and Narrative*, 226–27; *OR* 25(1):1001–2, 827; McLaws, "Battle of Chancellorsville," 26.

33. In *R. E. Lee: A Biography*, 4 vols. (New York: Charles Scribner's Sons, 1934–36), 2:550, Douglas Southall Freeman's discussion of Lee's decision to supervise the battle on his right includes speculation that "perhaps he was the more readily prompted to do this by his knowledge of McLaws, who as senior of the three division commanders would assume command. Lafayette McLaws was a professional soldier, careful of details and not lacking in soldierly qualities, but there was nothing daring, brilliant, or aggressive in his character."

34. Edward Porter Alexander, *Fighting for the Confederacy: The Personal Recollections of General Edward Porter Alexander*, ed. Gary W. Gallagher (Chapel Hill: University of North Carolina Press, 1989), 213.

35. Early, *Autobiographical Sketch and Narrative*, 227–28; Freeman, *R. E. Lee*, 2:554.

36. Richard Watson York to George Washington Custis Lee, November 28, 1872, copy provided by R. K. Krick, Fredericksburg and Spotsylvania National Military Park, Fredericksburg, Va.

37. After the war, Maj. David French Boyd, the commissary officer in Hays's brigade, told a colorful story about Early on the afternoon of May 4: "He and Lee were standing on a little eminence, to see the effect of the charge over that wide, open plateau, swept as it was by

cannon in front and by the heavy batteries on the north side of the Rappahannock; and when Harry Hays burst through two lines of the Federal army as if they were but paper walls, old Jubal in his enthusiasm and joy, forgetting the august presence of Lee, threw his old white hat with black ploom on the ground, exclaiming: 'Those damned Louisiana fellows may steal as much as they please now!'" (David French Boyd, *Reminiscences of the War in Virginia*, ed. T. Michael Parrish [Austin, Tex.: Jenkins, 1989], 34 [Boyd's reminiscences first appeared in New Orleans *Times-Democrat*, January 31, February 7, 1897]). Although Terry L. Jones, *Lee's Tigers: The Louisiana Infantry in the Army of Northern Virginia* (Baton Rouge: Louisiana State University Press, 1987), 155; Furgurson, *Chancellorsville 1863*, 297; and other works cite this appealing anecdote, there is no other evidence that Lee and Early were together during the final assaults on May 4.

38. Early, *Autobiographical Sketch and Narrative*, 229–30; Seymour, *Memoirs*, 55.

39. Early, *Autobiographical Sketch and Narrative*, 232–33; *OR* 25(1):1002.

40. Jubal A. Early to Jedediah Hotchkiss, March 24, 1868, Hotchkiss Papers, Mss2/H7973/b/2, VHS; Jubal A. Early to R. E. Lee, November 20, 1868, Daniel Papers, UVA. See also Early, *Autobiographical Sketch and Narrative*, 230–31.

41. *OR* 25(1):828, 802; McLaws, "Battle of Chancellorsville," 26; Fitzhugh Lee to Jubal A. Early, July 31, 1879, Jubal A. Early Papers, Library of Congress, Washington, D.C. (repository hereafter cited as LC). Lee's address is in *SHSP*, 7:545–85. Confederate artillerist David Gregg McIntosh argued that Early should have attacked Sedgwick's left at Salem Church on May 3, suggesting that his failure to do so may have influenced McLaws's actions on May 4: "It would be uncharitable at this day to impute to McLaws any feeling of pique because of Early's failure. . . . But his conduct is inconsistent with the fine reputation he bore in the Army of Northern Virginia as one of its most tried and experienced division commanders" (David Gregg McIntosh, "The Campaign of Chancellorsville," in *SHSP*, 40:96–97).

42. A canvass of the Richmond *Semi-Weekly Enquirer*, Richmond *Daily Dispatch*, and Richmond *Sentinel* between May 5 and June 1 reveals far greater attention to Chancellorsville than to Second Fredericksburg and Salem Church.

43. William Ransom Johnson Pegram to Mary Pegram, May 11, 1863, in James I. Robertson, Jr., "'The Boy Artillerist': Letters of William Ransom Johnson Pegram, C.S.A.," *Virginia Magazine of History and Biography* 98 (April 1990): 238; William B. Pettit to Arabella Speairs Pettit, May 3, 1863, in Arabella Speairs Pettit and William Beverley Pettit, *Civil War Letters of Arabella Speairs and William Beverley Pettit of Fluvanna County, Virginia, March 1862–March 1865*, ed. Charles W. Turner (Roanoke: Virginia Lithography & Graphics Company, 1988), 106–7.

44. *OR* 25(1):803.

45. For a somewhat uneven analysis of Early's performance at Chancellorsville, see Freeman, *Lee's Lieutenants*, 2:653–54.

46. Jubal A. Early to the editors of the *Enquirer*, May 11, 1863, Richmond *Daily Dispatch*, May 13, 1863. The original letter, which differs in minor ways from the printed version quoted in this essay and which Barksdale read, is in the Early Papers, LC.

47. William Barksdale to the editors of the *Enquirer*, May 13, 1863, Richmond *Semi-Weekly Enquirer*, May 19, 1863, Richmond *Daily Dispatch*, May 21, 1863.

48. Jubal A. Early to the editors of the *Enquirer*, May 19, 1863, Richmond *Semi-Weekly Enquirer*, May 27, 1863. The original, which differs in minor ways from the printed version, is in the Early Papers, LC.

49. William Barksdale to the editors of the *Enquirer*, May 31, 1863, Jubal A. Early to William Barksdale, May 14, 1863, Richmond *Daily Enquirer*, June 15, 1863.

50. Richmond *Daily Dispatch*, May 15, 1863; Richmond *Semi-Weekly Enquirer*, May 15, 1863.

51. Jubal A. Early to R. E. Lee, November 20, 1868, Daniel Papers, UVA.

52. The first edition of Early's *A Memoir of the Last Year of the War for Independence, in the Confederate States of America, Containing an Account of the Operations of His Commands in the Years 1864 and 1865* was published in Toronto by Lovell & Gibson in 1866; subsequent editions were published in Lynchburg, Mobile, and New Orleans.

53. R. E. Lee to Jubal A. Early, October 15, 1866, George H. and Katherine M. Davis Collection, Manuscripts Section, Howard-Tilton Library, Tulane University, New Orleans, La.; Jubal A. Early to John Warwick Daniel, February 17, 1867, John Warwick Daniel Papers, Perkins Library, Duke University, Durham, N.C.

54. Jubal A. Early to R. E. Lee, November 20, 1868, Daniel Papers, UVA. The manuscript Lee received was probably almost identical to chapter 20 in Early, *Autobiographical Sketch and Narrative*.

55. Jubal A. Early to R. E. Lee, November 20, 1868, Daniel Papers, UVA.

56. Humphreys, "Recollections of Fredericksburg," 445; Edward A. Pollard, *Southern History of the War: The Second Year of the War* (1863; reprint, New York: Charles B. Richardson, 1865), 262–63; Jubal A. Early to Jedediah Hotchkiss, March 24, 1868, Hotchkiss Papers, Mss2/H7973/b/2, VHS.

57. William Allan and Jedediah Hotchkiss, *The Battle-Fields of Virginia: Chancellorsville; Embracing the Operations of the Army of Northern Virginia, from the First Battle of Fredericksburg to the Death of Lieutenant-General Jackson* (New York: D. Van Nostrand, 1867). For Early's comments about the book, see Jubal A. Early to Jedediah Hotchkiss, March 24, 1868, Hotchkiss Papers, Mss2/H7973/b/2, VHS.

58. Editors to Jubal A. Early, April 23, May 7, 1884, Robert Underwood Johnson to Jubal A. Early, May 12, 1884, Clarence Clough Buel to Jubal A. Early, April 12, 1887, Early Papers, LC; Jubal A. Early to William H. Payne, August 4, 1885, Hunton Family Papers, Mss1/H9267/a/7, VHS. The excerpts appear in Robert Underwood Johnson and Clarence Clough Buel, eds., *Battles and Leaders of the Civil War*, 4 vols. (New York: Century, 1887–88), 4:492–99, 522–30.

59. Jubal A. Early to William H. Payne, August 4, 1885, Hunton Family Papers, Mss1/H9267/a/7, VHS.

Stoneman's Raid

A. Wilson Greene

THE SUN rose on Friday, May 8, 1863, over a Virginia land-scape alive with spring but brutally scarred by the aftermath of the battle of Chancellorsville. Hundreds of acres of Spotsylvania County betrayed the effects of an engagement that claimed nearly 30,000 casualties, most of them concentrated within the green hell of the Wilderness.[1]

The tentacles of this campaign also stretched into other corners of the Old Dominion. On the Virginia Peninsula near Yorktown, Willard Glazier of the 2nd New York Cavalry enjoyed a sumptuous breakfast, then strolled through the town's old streets, reveling in his unit's status as "the 'lions of the day.'" Edward P. Tobie of the 1st Maine Cavalry rode across Fauquier County toward a bivouac in Bealeton. Tobie looked forward to a sound night's sleep on the last leg of a ten-day adventure that had taken him nearly to the Confederate capital. In camp at Potomac Creek in Stafford County, Col. John B. McIntosh wrote to his friend and recently deposed commander, Brig. Gen. William W. Averell. McIntosh complained about the irresponsible practices of Averell's successor, Brig. Gen. Alfred Pleasonton, in guarding the vanquished Army of the Potomac, now licking its wounds on the north bank of the Rappahannock River.[2]

Each of these Federal troopers had experienced a different aspect of a multifaceted but little understood component of the Chancellorsville campaign known as Stoneman's raid. Maj. Gen. Joseph Hooker had divided his army into three segments in preparation for maneuvers that culminated in one of the war's great battles in early May 1863. The great pincers movement executed by Hooker's two infantry wings left a legacy and a literature appreciated by most students of the Civil War. The conduct of Hooker's cavalry, the third leg of "Fighting Joe's" strategic triangle, remains imperfectly understood. From the first, the operation provoked controversy about its impact and significance. Samuel Hill Merrill of the 1st Maine pronounced Stoneman's expedition "one of the most remarkable achievements in the history of modern warfare," while James Rodney Wood of the 6th U.S. Cavalry thought "no good results attended this raid." Historians have been similarly divided in their views on the execution and import of this chapter of the Chancellorsville saga.[3]

When Hooker assumed control of the Army of the Potomac in January 1863, he instituted a number of useful reforms, including the reorganization of his mounted arm. On February 5 he issued orders creating the army's first full-scale cavalry corps consisting of three divisions and a reserve brigade. He selected Brig. Gen. George Stoneman, an experienced horseman who most recently had led an infantry corps in Hooker's grand division, to direct this new unit. Stoneman's division commanders included Brig. Gen. Alfred Pleasonton, William Woods Averell, and David McMurtrie Gregg. Brig. Gen. John Buford led the reserve brigade of five regular army regiments. The corps numbered some 11,000 troopers present and equipped for duty.[4]

"From the day of its reorganization under Hooker, the cavalry of the Army of the Potomac commenced a new life," one officer commented. Another called the new arrangement "an emancipation" from the restricted role assigned the cavalry by previous commanders.[5] The Federals gained a chance to demonstrate their new independence and élan on March 17 when Averell took 3,000 men up the north bank of the Rappahannock River and crossed 2,200 of them at Kelly's Ford. In what became the first purely cavalry battle in the Eastern Theater involving more than one battalion on each side, Averell met an outnumbered Confederate force under Brig. Gen. Fitzhugh Lee and more than held his own, mortally wounding Maj. Gen. J. E. B. Stuart's handsome young artillerist, Maj. John Pelham, in the bargain. The Unionists disengaged without achieving any strategic advantage and recrossed the Rappahannock in the afternoon, but

Brig. Gen. George Stoneman (shown later in the war as a major general).
Library of Congress

their performance earned praise from Secretary of War Edwin M. Stanton and
various lesser lights. "I got in last night from a most brilliant expedition,"
reported Charles A. Legg of the 1st Massachusetts Cavalry on March 18, an
assessment shared by most of the battle's blue-clad participants. "For the first
time our cavalry had a chance to pit itself against that of the enemy," wrote
Rhode Islander Jacob B. Cooke. "It was a . . . challenge of man against man,
horse against horse, and sabre against sabre. The result was such as to elevate

us in the eyes of the army, to increase our confidence in ourselves and to increase our *esprit de corps*."[6]

In early April President Abraham Lincoln journeyed south from Washington to examine Hooker's revitalized army. On April 6 near the Potomac River above Belle Plain, Stoneman formed his divisions along three lines of a square and orchestrated a review that lasted more than three hours. New Englander Alfred G. Sargent remembered this spectacle as "one of the grandest sights my eyes ever beheld" but noticed that the president looked "pale, haggard and careworn . . . as though there was a heap of trouble on the old man's mind."[7]

Lincoln's worries no doubt included the fate of the spring offensive conceived by Hooker and now on the verge of implementation. Fighting Joe confirmed his plan in a detailed letter to the president on April 11. He intended to use Stoneman's cavalry to sever Gen. Robert E. Lee's communications with Richmond and then pin the rebel army in place until assailed by the Union infantry. He articulated this concept to Stoneman with orders the following day to move his force, except for one brigade, up the Rappahannock on April 13 to crossings above the Orange & Alexandria Railroad. Once on the south bank, Stoneman would meet and disperse Fitz Lee's cavalry near Culpeper, eliminate a small detachment at Gordonsville, then gallop southeast to Hanover Junction astride the Richmond, Fredericksburg & Potomac Railroad, Lee's lifeline. Admonishing Stoneman that his "watchword be fight, and let all your orders be fight, fight, fight," Hooker affirmed the lofty status of the cavalry in his strategic thinking. "It devolves upon you . . . to take the initiative in the forward movement of this grand army, and on you and your noble command must depend in a great measure the extent and brilliancy of our success."[8]

Was Hooker's expectation that 10,000 cavalry could resist Lee's 60,000 infantry along the Richmond, Fredericksburg & Potomac Railroad between Fredericksburg and Richmond reasonable? If the Confederates failed to withdraw and protect their supply line, what might happen to Stoneman's isolated force with the Army of Northern Virginia between it and Hooker? We can never know the answers to these questions because the weather, abetted by Stoneman's own lethargy, prevented his testing Hooker's plan.

The expedition, accompanied by 275 supply wagons sufficient to sustain the column for eight to ten days, left camp at Falmouth and Belle Plain on Monday, April 13, in fair weather. The main body camped that night at Morrisville, a hamlet twenty miles upstream from Fredericksburg. Col. Benjamin F. "Grimes" Davis's brigade, the lone representative of Pleasonton's division, received orders to continue riding that night with the goal of crossing the river at Sulphur Springs. Davis would then move down the south bank, uncovering Beverly Ford and Rappahannock Bridge for Averell, Gregg, and Buford.[9]

Davis crossed the river at two places on April 14 while the rest of the column forged ahead to the vicinity of Beverly Ford. There Gregg skirmished with elements of the 9th and 13th Virginia Cavalry under Brig. Gen. William Henry Fitzhugh "Rooney" Lee, briefly advancing a small party across the railroad bridge at Rappahannock Station before withdrawing to the left bank of the stream. Although the Federals enjoyed overwhelming numerical superiority, Stoneman opted not to press the pesky Confederates until morning, a decision distinctly at odds with the spirit of his orders.[10]

That night, "one of the very worst storms of the season" commenced, raising the Rappahannock an incredible seven feet in a few hours and "converting mere rivulets into torrents making the roads quite impassable." Stoneman canceled the advance and summoned Davis to recross the river. Most of his brigade swam their horses through the swirling waters at Beverly Ford, but two companies of the 3rd Indiana Cavalry waited too long. A force of Virginia horsemen with emptied scabbards slapping at their sides charged the cornered Hoosiers. The bluecoats executed a fighting retreat to the north bank, suffering twenty or thirty casualties at the hands of the onrushing Confederates. A few Yankees drowned in the raging current.[11]

That evening, Lincoln wrote Hooker of his concern with Stoneman's lack of progress, noting that in three days of mostly good weather and without material interference from Stuart, the cavalry had advanced only twenty-five miles. "To reach his point he still has 60 [miles] to go, another river [the Rapidan] to cross, and will be hindered by the enemy. By arithmetic, how many days will it take him to do it?" Hooker defended his lieutenant, a posture that in time he would drastically modify. Admitting that he shared the president's disappointment, the army commander asserted that "I can find nothing in [Stoneman's] conduct . . . requiring my animadversion or censure. We cannot control the elements."[12]

It continued to rain steadily for days, preventing Stoneman from relaunching his offensive. During this interval he kept his regiments busy picketing the river and shifting from camp to camp, concentrating the bulk of his force near Warrenton Junction and drawing his supplies from the Orange & Alexandria Railroad. On April 22, however, Hooker dispatched two messages to cavalry headquarters instructing Stoneman to attempt a crossing the following day. These orders provided a radically different agenda than the one outlined in Hooker's April 12 directive. They said nothing about seizing Hanover Junction or causing and then blocking a retreat by Lee's army. Instead, Hooker suggested that Stoneman "subdivide your command, and let them take different routes, and have some point of meeting on your line of general operations. These detachments can dash off to the right and left, and inflict a vast deal of mischief, and at the same time bewilder the enemy as to the course and intentions of the main body." Although the weather and high water continued to frustrate Stoneman's departure, the legacy of these orders would cast a long shadow on the eventual conduct of his operation.[13]

By April 28, the water had receded sufficiently to permit renewal of the offensive. Once again Hooker sent Stoneman a blueprint for action, the third such document in little more than two weeks. These orders more closely resembled those of April 12, with the primary goal being to gain the Richmond, Fredericksburg & Potomac Railroad in Lee's rear. Stoneman would no longer bear responsibility for compelling the Confederates to abandon the line of the Rappahannock, however; that job now belonged to the infantry. The cavalry was to "cut off the retreat of the enemy" after uniting somewhere near the Pamunkey River, by which Hooker meant that stream's primary tributaries, the North and South Anna rivers. Stoneman would divide his units at the outset of the maneuver. One wing, as originally intended, would move against enemy forces still presumed to be near Culpeper, and the rest of the column would make for Raccoon Ford on the Rapidan River and then Louisa Court House on the Virginia Central Railroad. Stoneman would attempt the crossing that night or at the latest by 8:00 A.M. on April 29. His force would consist of about 7,400 men in six brigades. Pleasonton would remain behind with three regiments, about 1,200 sabers, because, said one trooper, they were considered the least efficient outfits in the corps.[14]

Stoneman methodically gathered his scattered regiments and drew in his pickets during the afternoon of April 28. Some Federal horsemen negotiated as many as twenty-six miles of muddy roads to arrive at the riverbank about 8:00 A.M. They spent the morning searching for a suitable crossing point, causing Capt. Charles F. Adams, Jr., of the 1st Massachusetts Cavalry to "doubt whether we ever should get across that miserable little river." At last they determined that Kelly's Ford offered the best option, and blue-clad riders began moving across the Rappahannock about noon. Some of Stoneman's men used the pontoon bridge laid by Hooker's engineers to accommodate the Eleventh, Twelfth, and Fifth corps, which Hooker had assigned to envelop Lee's left at Chancellorsville. Other troopers employed the ford, while a third column swam its horses through the coursing stream, the water reaching halfway to the animals' withers.[15]

"By dint of great exertion" Stoneman completed his passage by 5:00 P.M. He then gathered his high-level commanders, spread out the maps, and reviewed his operational plans. Consistent with Hooker's orders, Averell would move his division, along with Davis's brigade, toward Culpeper to dispatch Confederate cavalry believed to be in that vicinity. Gregg's division accompanied by

Union cavalry at Kelly's Ford (engraving based on a sketch by Edwin Forbes). Paul F. Mottelay and T. Campbell-Copeland, eds., The Soldier in Our Civil War, *2 vols. (New York: Stanley Bradley, 1893), 2:110*

Buford's brigade would drive southwest toward Stevensburg. A battery of artillery would support each column.[16]

Averell's wing moved forward on the road to Culpeper, where it promptly collided with a small body of Confederates near the Kelly's Ford battlefield. These horsemen from the 13th Virginia were a part of only two brigades, some 2,400 men, available to contest the Union advance, the rest of Stuart's force being either on recruiting duty south of the James River or operating independently in western Virginia. The 1st Rhode Island Cavalry drove its opponents from the field after a brief skirmish, but this minor altercation prompted Stoneman to halt both of his columns until after dark. Averell's men made little further progress that night, failing to reach their objective at Brandy Station, while Gregg and Buford marched a short distance to the vicinity of Madden's Crossroads, where they established a cheerless bivouac in a drizzling rain. Officers prohibited the kindling of fires and horses remained saddled all night, each man taking a one-hour turn holding four mounts while three of his comrades rested. "A few hardtack and a moiety of salt Jewish abomination was all the boys received to quiet their stomachs' demands," grumbled a trooper in the 10th New York Cavalry.[17]

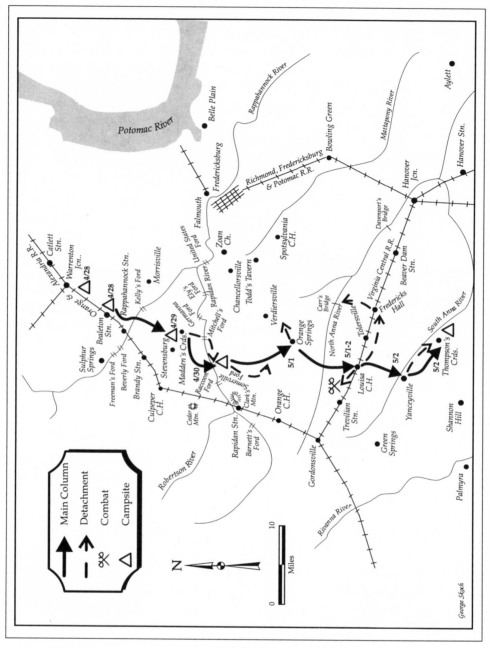

Stoneman's raid, April 28–May 2, 1863: Gregg's and Buford's columns

April 30 dawned under rainy skies. Instructing Averell to take sole responsibility for the Confederates in his front, Stoneman determined to push toward Richmond with Gregg and Buford. To expedite this movement, Stoneman directed that all the pack mules, led horses, and wheeled vehicles other than the artillery be sent toward Hooker's right wing at Germanna Ford. Gregg's and Buford's 3,500 men each carried three days' subsistence on their persons and three days' short forage for their horses, while also packing forty rounds of carbine and twenty rounds of pistol ammunition. At 4:00 A.M. orders arrived to mount and move toward Raccoon Ford. "All felt as though they were going forward to the accomplishment of an object of the greatest importance to the army and the country," stated Stoneman. The chaplain of the 6th Pennsylvania Cavalry described men "jubilant at the prospect before them" but conceded that "visions of Libby prison or Belle Isle, weakened the nerves of some."[18]

Buford's regulars led the way. A squadron of the 5th U.S. Cavalry swam the river at Mitchell's Ford and uncovered the south bank as far as Raccoon Ford, five miles upstream, nabbing more than a dozen prisoners. In the afternoon the sun at last appeared, revealing the quiet beauty of the Culpeper County landscape. The remainder of Buford's brigade with Gregg's division reached Raccoon Ford and negotiated the pounding current with the loss of several men and horses who drowned, the entire command receiving a thorough soaking. The operation continued until well after dark, when the drenched soldiers dismounted on a plateau south of the river.[19]

Nathan Webb of the 1st Maine remembered seeing Generals Stoneman and Gregg on the riverbank urging their troops forward while Col. Judson Kilpatrick implored the men to "keep closed up, keep well up stream." Anticipating an attack, Stoneman advanced pickets in all directions and ordered his troops to spend the night in line of battle. The Union commander learned that Fitz Lee's brigade had crossed the Rapidan at Somerville Ford that morning and ridden toward Fredericksburg. Rooney Lee, however, still lurked somewhere in the vicinity, and the Union position could be seen from the signal station on Clark's Mountain. "It was a season of considerable anxiety to all, and of great fatigue especially to those of us who had been in the saddle several consecutive days and nights," recalled a New Yorker.[20]

Once again Stoneman forbade fires but ungallantly exempted his own headquarters from the proscription. Soon a "noble pile of logs and fence-rails sent up their brilliant and tempting blaze," attracting some bold men of the 1st New Jersey Cavalry who wrangled permission to boil their coffee and dry their uniforms near the cheery flames before contentedly falling asleep in the shadow of the fire's warmth. Other troopers fared less well. "Hungry, wet, and fatigued, we were illy prepared to spend a night in standing to horse," wrote a Pennsylvanian. "A dense fog settled down in the valley . . . it became very cold, and our clothing being wet, we suffered greatly before the morning." Many Union troopers dropped to earth with halter and bridle in hand to snatch a few hours of sleep on the clammy ground.[21]

Stoneman issued orders that the troops be in the saddle at 2:00 A.M. on May 1, but without the assistance of a local guide, the column could not make headway through a thick fog. The Federals rode at dawn under a leaden canopy, Buford's brigade angling in the direction of Orange Court House and Gregg's division, with the 1st New Jersey in the van, aiming toward Orange Springs, ten miles southeast of the courthouse on Riga Run. Troopers mounted on unserviceable horses moved to the rear of the line. Upon reaching the Fredericksburg-Orange Turnpike, Stoneman verified that a large body of enemy cavalry had recently passed in an easterly direction. He then directed Gregg to press toward Louisa Court House while Buford and the headquarters guard followed.[22]

The 1st New Jersey scattered a Confederate picket at Orange Springs shortly after noon, capturing a major and twelve men. Some Federal troopers helped themselves to a supply of boots and shoes in the village, while others foraged successfully for edibles. "Every smokehouse and farmyard near the line of our march, was made to contribute to our comfort. Chickens, ducks, and hams, in great numbers, were secured," said Chaplain Samuel L. Gracey of the 6th Pennsylvania. Gregg learned that a Confederate wagon train had hurried through Orange Springs toward Spotsylvania earlier in the day. The division commander sent Col. Percy Wyndham's brigade in pursuit, but after trotting five miles without catching a glimpse of the fleeing vehicles, Wyndham returned to Orange Springs empty-handed.[23]

The balance of Gregg's column rested in town during the afternoon. Tired horses enjoyed a meal, the sun broke through the clouds, and the sloppy country roads began to dry. At 6:00 P.M. Gregg ordered his men into the saddle once again, then pushed ahead through the night before halting nine hours later slightly less than a mile north of Louisa Court House. "We were all very sleepy and as we rode along would sleep . . . while . . . nodding & swaying, first one side then the other and making all sorts of gyrations," recalled a trooper in the 1st Maine. Buford's men trailed Gregg and after fording the North Anna River at 3:00 A.M. on May 2 encamped on the south bank, unsaddling their horses and building fires for the first time since leaving Warrenton Junction.[24]

General Gregg expected to face a staunch defense at Louisa Court House and planned accordingly. He deployed the four guns of Capt. James M. Robertson's artillery in a commanding position supported by Wyndham's brigade. Gregg told Kilpatrick to form his regiments into three columns aimed respectively at the village and at points one mile above and below the town. Kilpatrick's New Yorkers charged in unison but encountered only token resistance. Taking possession of the depot and storehouses, they tore into the tracks, burning sleepers and twisting rails for a distance of more than five miles. The Unionists occupied Louisa's telegraph office, merrily exchanging messages with Richmond for nearly an hour until the Confederate authorities caught on and terminated their transmissions with "some very decided remarks of disapprobation."[25]

Louisa's citizens, heretofore spared the direct heel of war and characterized by one New Englander as "not remarkable either for intelligence or enterprise," were quite shocked to discover so many Union cavalrymen in their midst. "The inhabitants were . . . considerably at a loss to know from where we came so suddenly," Nathan Webb recorded in his diary. "No doubt some thought we came from the clouds and looked for our wings, horns and forked tails." The terrified residents took some comfort in the fact that the Union troopers confined their destruction to government and military targets. Although private homes were spared, their edible stores became fair game. Various delicacies found their way into Union saddlebags, and the remainder supplied an impromptu feast. "A huge slice of ham in one hand, a fritter . . . in the other, the utter abjuration of knives and spoon, faces all grease or wiped off with their jacket sleeves and all laughing and jolly as kings in their palaces," the Federals exulted in what would be the high point of their grand adventure.[26]

Stoneman arrived in Louisa about 10:00 A.M. Two hours later, while Kilpatrick and Wyndham rampaged through the village, he ordered parts of two companies of the 1st Maine, perhaps fifty men, to ride west along the tracks toward Gordonsville. They advanced only three miles before discovering a line of rebel pickets. The Federals scattered the Confederate vedettes—the advance of Rooney Lee's 9th Virginia—but quickly encountered the main southern line. Lee had reached Gordonsville at 11:00 A.M. and upon learning of Stoneman's presence in Louisa dispatched the 9th Virginia to the rescue. Overwhelmed by their opponents, the small Union force disengaged after losing nearly half their number, most of them captured. Skirmishing continued through the afternoon as both sides received reinforcements, until Lee withdrew his tired troopers to Gordonsville, content to have measured the Union column. The Federals returned to Louisa.[27]

In the meantime, Stoneman ordered the 1st U.S. Cavalry under Capt. Richard S. C. Lord to move east and pillage the Confederate depots at Tolersville and Fredericks Hall, six and twelve miles respectively from Louisa Court House. Lord mustered 251 men and 14 officers, the only troops whose mounts could sustain them on the expedition, and carried out his orders against nominal opposition. Near sunset, a detachment of thirty men galloped to Carr's Bridge, where the main road from Spotsylvania to Goochland Court House crossed the North Anna River, brushed aside a small Confederate outpost, and burned the 200-foot-long span.[28]

Late in the afternoon, Stoneman gathered his regiments at Louisa and put them on the road for the South Anna River at Yanceyville, an establishment consisting of one residence, a gristmill, and a church. Once across this stream, he directed a squadron of fifty men under his staff officer Capt. Wesley Merritt to disable the bridges and fords as far downriver as possible while the main body continued southeast to Thompson's Crossroads. Most of Stoneman's force reached this undistinguished intersection about 10:00 P.M. The 1st Maine lingered at Louisa to deceive any of Lee's observers who may have been concealed on the perimeter: "Just after dark large numbers of fires were built on the hills and in the woods surrounding the village, to convey the idea to the rebels that a large force was going into camp for the night." Shielded by the gloom, the last Federals stole out of Louisa and reached Thompson's Crossroads about midnight. Lord's raiders had not yet returned, nor had the fifty men under Merritt engaged in rendering the South Anna uncrossable.[29]

As Stoneman, Gregg, and Buford gathered at Thompson's Crossroads, a successful romp through Louisa County behind them and the most daring portion of their operation still ahead, the enterprise of Averell's division and Davis's brigade already had ended. On the night of May 2, Averell's command found itself some thirty-six miles northeast of Thompson's Crossroads on the left bank of the Rapidan near Ely's Ford, skirmishing with a mixed Confederate force as a footnote to the events surrounding "Stonewall" Jackson's flank attack and wounding. How they arrived there, completely divorced from the fate of their cavalry comrades, comprises one of the most controversial aspects of Stoneman's raid.

At dawn on April 30, Averell roused his 3,400 men and, after allowing them time to feed and groom their horses, had them in the saddle at 7:00 A.M. Averell had seen copies of Hooker's April 12 orders and the April 28 modifications and had reviewed his column's assignment with Stoneman the previous day at Kelly's Ford. His mission, consistently expressed, included defeating the Confederate cavalry in Culpeper County, operating against the Orange & Alexandria Railroad, and then uniting with the rest of Stoneman's raiders near the Anna rivers to block the Richmond, Fredericksburg & Potomac Railroad.[30]

The road from Kelly's Ford to Culpeper Court House presented "one of the grandest sights" a trooper in the 4th Pennsylvania Cavalry had ever beheld. Skirmishers cantered ahead while supports and the main body followed, using the road and the open fields on either side to expedite their movement. Averell

Brig. Gen. William Woods Averell. Robert Underwood Johnson and Clarence Clough Buel, eds., Battles and Leaders of the Civil War, *4 vols. (New York: Century, 1887–88), 4:484*

encountered only light resistance, scattering a small cluster of rebels at Brandy Station before reaching the county seat about noon. Union soldiers admired the town's impressive spires and stately homes, gaining a favorable impression underscored by the distribution of confiscated Confederate foodstuffs. Averell halted briefly to apportion flour, bacon, and salt to his grateful troopers, then resumed his march past Cedar Mountain battlefield, where bleached bones from the previous summer's casualties lay exposed in grisly greeting. By 8:00 P.M. his lead regiments approached Rapidan Station, a depot on the railroad, where a wooden trestle carried the tracks across the Rapidan River. Confederate artillery and infantry fire from the south bank suddenly brought the Union troopers to the ground, many of them finding soggy shelter in concealed places back from the stream.[31]

Who were these aggressive Confederates? Averell's antagonists belonged to the two Virginia cavalry regiments, supported by one gun, of Rooney Lee's command. Averell outnumbered this demibrigade about three to one, but the young New Yorker believed his opponents presented a much graver threat. On the evening of April 29, Averell had heard from a deserter and intercepted an

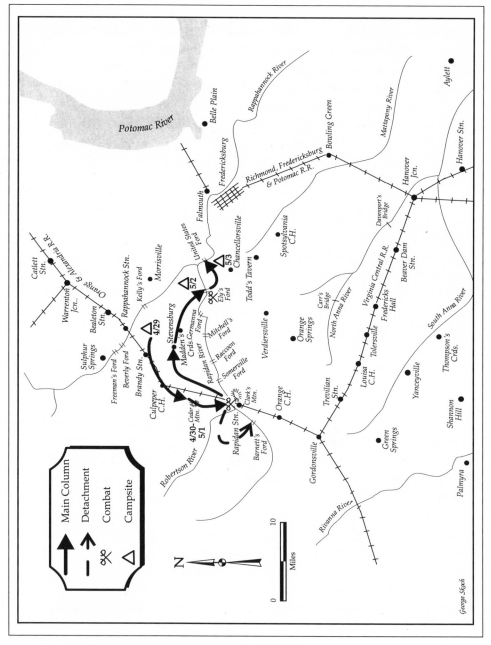

Stoneman's raid, April 29–May 3, 1863: Averell's and Davis's columns

apparently corroborating dispatch that Stuart, with four brigades of cavalry and fifteen pieces of artillery, awaited the Federals near Brandy Station. Estimating the next morning that half of this phantom force had decamped for Stevensburg, Averell still assumed that both Fitz and Rooney Lee's brigades had withdrawn from Culpeper southeast toward the Rapidan. Moreover, while rooting through captured mail in Culpeper, Averell had discovered a document placing Stonewall Jackson in Gordonsville with 25,000 men poised to deflect a Union offensive down the Orange & Alexandria Railroad.[32] Averell had amply demonstrated his timidity when in independent command the previous month at Kelly's Ford. Now a message arrived from Stoneman that virtually guaranteed his caution.

This communiqué provides a key to understanding and evaluating conduct on Averell's part that would result in his removal from command within the week. In it, Stoneman informed his lieutenant that high water had delayed Gregg's and Buford's crossing of the Rapidan and that he wanted Averell to "push the enemy as vigorously as possible, keeping him fully occupied, and, if possible, drive him in the direction of Rapidan Station." Stoneman concluded with the words (written by a staff officer in the third person), "He turns the enemy over to you." Averell already had herded the southern troopers across the river at Rapidan Station and happily concluded that he had anticipated his superior's wishes.[33]

On the morning of May 1, "cannonading and carbine discussions commenced early and lasted all the day." Averell ordered scouts to range up and down the river to ascertain the strength and disposition of the Confederate defense. These men reported and Averell personally confirmed (barely avoiding capture in the process) that the works on the south bank were well sited and controlled all of the river approaches. Sharpshooters made it hot for any Yankee who showed himself on open ground. Rejecting a costly frontal charge against the bridge, Averell planned to ford the river above or below the railroad "where the chances would be in my favor." A diversion aimed at burning the span would mask his real intentions. He deployed marksmen of his own and unlimbered Capt. John C. Tidball's artillery, while pioneers gathered light wood saturated with kerosene oil to fire the bridge. These preparations consumed the entire morning.[34]

About noon a dismounted squadron of the 9th New York Cavalry dashed toward the bridge only to receive a thunderous volley from the opposite shore. The Empire Staters sought cover in a nearby cemetery and exchanged fire with their Confederate opponents. While maintaining this action near the bridge, described as "spirited" by artillerist Tidball, Averell shifted some troops to his right, splashed through the Robertson River, and late in the day approached

Barnett's Ford on the Rapidan some five miles above the railroad crossing. Rooney Lee blocked Averell's gambit by moving men to his left; however, by this time he had received orders to abandon Rapidan Station and ride toward Gordonsville to confront Stoneman's force, now known to be descending on the Virginia Central Railroad. To facilitate his withdrawal, the Virginian advanced Col. Richard L. T. Beale and a detachment of thirty men from the 9th Virginia to create a distraction. This gallant body seized more than two dozen troopers and a captain from the 8th Illinois Cavalry, but a Union counterthrust forced Beale to relinquish his prisoners, leaving behind in the gathering darkness two of his own men and a blazing railroad bridge set aflame by the retiring Confederates.[35]

Averell intended to draw in his right the next morning and cross the Rapidan downstream at Raccoon Ford, either moving to rejoin Stoneman or throwing himself "on the left flank of the enemy's main body, according as circumstances and the news from our army should determine me." A message from Hooker canceled these plans. Reaching Averell at 6:30 A.M. on May 2, the dispatch questioned his presence at Rapidan Station. "If this finds you at that place, you will immediately return to United States Ford, and remain there until further orders," ordered the army chieftain. Understandably wounded by the tone and content of this directive, Averell replied promptly that "I have been engaged with the cavalry of the enemy at that point and in destroying communications," enclosing by way of explanation a copy of Stoneman's April 30 orders. Nevertheless, he quickly dressed out his regiments in marching order and steered them first through Stevensburg then back down the river to Ely's Ford, arriving in camp well after dark. Here Jeb Stuart surprised them with a hit-and-run attack by the 16th North Carolina Infantry supported by the 1st Virginia Cavalry that unnerved the Federal troopers more than it altered the strategic situation.[36]

On Sunday, May 3, Averell moved his force across the Rapidan to United States Ford and conferred with Hooker. The commanding general "did not intimate by his deportment or conversation that he entertained any dissatisfaction" with Averell's performance, other than to quiz him about his activities at Rapidan Station. Later that day, however, Hooker drafted an order relieving Averell and placing his division under Pleasonton. This directive reached a stunned Averell at daylight on May 4. Hooker explained less than a week later that he had removed the unfortunate brigadier because Averell had "entirely disregarded" his orders. "It is no excuse or justification of his course," Hooker continued, "that he received instructions from General Stoneman in conflict with my own. . . . If he disregarded all instructions, it was his duty to do something. If the enemy did not come to him, he should have gone to the enemy. . . . I could excuse General Averell in his disobedience if I could anywhere discover in his operations a desire to find and engage the enemy."[37]

Hooker committed an injustice against Averell. The cavalryman had not disregarded his chief's orders. As expressed on April 12 and repeated on April 28, Averell bore responsibility for operations along the Orange & Alexandria Railroad and against whatever Confederate cavalry defended it. Averell reached the railroad on the morning of April 30 and chased all Confederate opposition out of Culpeper County by day's end. His approach to Rapidan Station, influenced by the erroneous notion that he faced close to an equal number of enemy horsemen, brought him to the very point designated by his superior's orders received that evening. It is to these orders that one must turn for an explanation of Averell's performance.

Stoneman's dispatch was ambiguous and incomplete. It called for Averell to push the Confederates to Rapidan Station and keep them fully occupied. But for what purpose? Did Stoneman seek relief from cavalry threats to the west until his column could bypass the 25,000 Confederate infantry waiting, as Averell suspected, in Gordonsville? How long would Averell be required to keep Lee busy? What circumstances would dictate his next move? How would Averell negotiate the ghostly Gordonsville Confederates and reunite with Gregg and Buford? Indeed, in light of Stoneman's failure to mention a rendezvous on the Pamunkey or elsewhere in his April 30 missive, did the corps commander still envision a concentration along the Richmond, Fredericksburg & Potomac Railroad?

Averell certainly must be faulted for adopting a McClellanesque assessment of enemy strength, and his tactics on May 1, while not as incompetent as usually described, lacked aggression and drive. Yet one can readily understand why the West Pointer believed he had accomplished the initial goals of his expedition in accordance with his changing instructions. Had Hooker not recalled him, Averell might have joined Stoneman in Louisa County and enveloped Rooney Lee along the Virginia Central Railroad east of Gordonsville. As it was, Stoneman would have to cope alone with Lee and the increasingly aroused Confederate detachments deep within enemy lines.[38]

Thompson's Crossroads, or Four Corners, lay on the right bank of the South Anna at the intersection of the Old Mountain Road running west from Richmond to the Blue Ridge and the Cartersville Road connecting Spotsylvania Court House with the James River. As his weary troopers drew rein in the fields and woods around the junction, Stoneman summoned his regimental commanders to a council of war. Displaying a set of maps, some of which may have been captured from the baggage wagon of a Confederate surveying party, Stoneman explained his "previously conceived plan of operations. . . . I gave them to understand that we had dropped in that region of country like a shell, and that I intended to burst it in every direction, expecting each piece or fragment

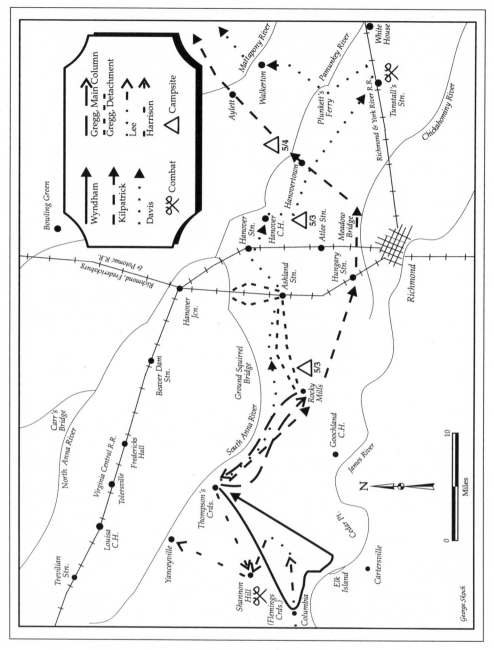

Stoneman's raid, May 3–5, 1863

Inside map legend:

Gregg, Main Column
Gregg, Detachment
Lee
Harrison

Wyndham
Kilpatrick
Davis

Combat
Campsite

Map labels:

Bowling Green

Matiapony River
Aylett
Walkerton
Pamunkey River
Plunkett's Ferry
White House
Tunstall's Stn.
5/4
Hanovertown
Richmond & York River R.R.
Chickahominy River

Richmond, Fredericksburg & Potomac R.R.

Hanover Stn.
Hanover C.H.
5/3
Atlee Stn.
Meadow Bridge

Hanover Jcn.

Beaver Dam Stn.

Ashland Stn.
Hungary Stn.

Richmond

Carr's Bridge
North Anna River

Virginia Central R.R.
Fredericks Hall

Ground Squirrel Bridge

South Anna River

5/3
Rocky Mills

Goochland C.H.

James River

Louisa C.H.
Tolersville

Trevilian Stn.

Yanceyville

Thompson's Crds.

Shannon Hill
(Flemings Crds.)
Columbia

Elk Island
Cedar Pt.

Cartersville

N

10
Miles
0

would do as much harm and create nearly as much terror as would result from sending the whole shell, and thus magnify our small force into overwhelming numbers."[39]

This strategy reflected Hooker's thoughts as expressed on April 22 rather than the April 12 or April 28 conceptions. Despite harboring concerns about Averell's safety and whereabouts and operating with only the vaguest notion of the main army's fate, Stoneman ordered his ten regiments to disperse into seven separate parties.[40] Not only did this render each of his detachments vulnerable to a superior concentration of Confederate cavalry, but it also practically eliminated any chance that Stoneman could delay the Army of Northern Virginia should Hooker induce it to retreat south along its supply line to Richmond. If Hooker's recall of Averell compromised Stoneman's ability to execute his mission, the cavalry commander's own decision to disperse his remaining units crippled it.

Stoneman's plan included sending Col. Percy Wyndham with the 1st New Jersey and most of the 1st Maryland Cavalry to Columbia. There in the southeastern corner of Fluvanna County, Wyndham would dismantle the James River and Kanawha Canal aqueduct over the Rivanna River and then proceed eastward along the canal itself, "doing all the harm possible." The 2nd New York Cavalry under Col. Judson Kilpatrick would aim toward Richmond and the railroad bridges over the Chickahominy River, while Lt. Col. Hasbrouck Davis of the 12th Illinois Cavalry would operate against the Richmond, Fredericksburg & Potomac Railroad at Ashland and the Virginia Central Railroad at Atlee Station. Gregg would take the 1st Maine and 10th New York down the South Anna to "destroy all the road bridges thereon, and, if possible, the two railroad bridges across that river." Capt. Thomas Drummond of the 5th U.S. Cavalry would follow Gregg and mop up any unfinished business. Stoneman had previously released Capt. Wesley Merritt to lead "a flying party" of the fragmented 1st Maryland on a freelance frolic "to do what he thought he could accomplish in the way of destroying bridges, & c." The commander himself would remain at Thompson's Crossroads with a reserve of 500 men from Buford's brigade to act as a rallying point. Stoneman suffered from a painful case of hemorrhoids, and his decision to sit out the day's excitement, figuratively speaking, may have found its motivation in his debility.[41]

Sir Percy Wyndham cultivated a mustache almost two feet wide and a reputation nearly as magnificent. The twenty-nine-year-old Englishman arrived in America in 1861 after serving as a soldier of fortune in the armies of Britain, France, Austria, and Italy. George McClellan liked Wyndham's style and in October arranged for him to receive command of the 1st New Jersey Cavalry. One Confederate described Wyndham as "a stalwart man . . . who strode along with the nonchalant air of one who had wooed Dame Fortune too long to be cast down by her frowns."[42]

At 3:00 A.M. on May 3, Wyndham left Thompson's Crossroads with 400 troopers. Traveling south some fifteen miles on the Cartersville Road, Wyndham's column struck Byrd Creek two miles from Columbia, crossed and then burned the span there, and approached the village between 8:00 and 9:00 A.M. Wyndham deployed the 1st Maryland in reserve on the outskirts of town and sent his Garden Staters pounding through Columbia's streets, vanquishing a tiny Confederate outpost. The Yankees then divided into smaller parties to carry out their mission of destruction. Within ten minutes flames lapped at four bridges across the canal while the Jerseymen and Marylanders demolished canal boats, damaged locks, and confiscated or burned a large accumulation of commissary and quartermaster stores.[43]

Wyndham enjoyed less success with the aqueduct. The solid masonry structure defied destruction by the means at hand, so the Unionists abandoned their work and rode downriver, wrecking "the large and elegant bridge crossing the James River to Elk Island" at Cedar Point. When Maj. Myron H. Beaumont of the 1st New Jersey learned that the aqueduct remained intact, he volunteered to return to Columbia with fifty men and a bag of cartridges to blow it up. Wyndham assented, and the members of the small party retraced their steps to Columbia. Beaumont discovered several barrels of gunpowder and a thousand feet of waterproof fuse hidden in town, suggesting a more efficacious means of accomplishing his task. As he prepared his pyrotechnics, urgent word arrived to evacuate immediately. Confederate cavalrymen were bearing down on Columbia, and the detachment faced imminent capture. The frustrated incendiaries took to their horses and rejoined the main column about 8:00 P.M. after riding some fifty miles in seventeen hours.[44]

The threat to the Federals in Columbia came from Rooney Lee. Leaving Gordonsville in the hands of newly arrived reinforcements, Lee rode south in the morning through Green Springs and on to Palmyra. By evening, his 800 ubiquitous men reached smoldering Columbia. Finding the Yankees gone, Lee pursued on Wyndham's trail. Although the Federals enjoyed an insurmountable lead that night, Lee's persistence would be rewarded on the following day.[45]

In the meantime, the second of Stoneman's bursting shells, the 2nd New York, known in army circles as the "Harris Light," spent most of the day concealed in a pine thicket about ten miles southeast of Thompson's Crossroads. Its commander, Judson Kilpatrick, and fewer than 450 men had as their goal Hungary Station on the Richmond, Fredericksburg & Potomac Railroad but disdained daylight travel for fear of being detected so close to the rebel capital. The troopers found their respite "very refreshing both to men and

Col. Hugh Judson Kilpatrick. Francis Trevelyan Miller, ed., The Photographic History of the Civil War, *10 vols. (New York: Review of Reviews, 1911), 4:284*

beasts," although Kilpatrick's order to discard extra clothing, blankets, and nonessential baggage portended challenging times.[46]

The twenty-seven-year-old Kilpatrick earned a Civil War reputation as "flamboyant, reckless, tempestuous, and even licentious." One Federal officer referred to the young New Jerseyian as "a frothy braggart without brains." In spite of these character flaws, Kilpatrick generated respect and affection from his command. "His clarion voice rings like magic through the ranks, while his busy form, always in the thickest of the fight, elicits the warmest enthusiasm," gushed the regimental historian.[47]

The Harris Light slept little during the night of May 3. Kilpatrick had them mounted and on the move by 2:00 A.M., reaching the depot at Hungary, fifteen miles away, by daybreak. A pair of incredulous Confederate horsemen turned tail at the approach of Kilpatrick's troopers, leaving the Yankees free to torch the station, sever the telegraph line, and dismantle a couple of miles of track. The

Unionists then pushed ahead to the Brook Turnpike, the main highway leading into Richmond from the north. To their delight, they encountered no resistance at the city's outer defenses, where a Confederate battery of artillery fled before them without firing a shot. Kilpatrick cautiously proceeded toward the capital, the first organized Union force to venture so close to the Confederate seat of government. Lt. R. W. Brown, an aide-de-camp to Richmond's provost marshal, confidently drew near the column and asked authoritatively, "What regiment?" Kilpatrick responded, "The Second New York Cavalry . . . and you, sir, are my prisoner." "You're a mighty daring sort of fellows," the stunned lieutenant replied, "but you will certainly be captured before sundown." Kilpatrick acknowledged the possibility of that outcome but affirmed his intention "to do a mighty deal of mischief first." Brown and a dozen of his men received an immediate but humiliating parole.[48]

Kilpatrick's column rode forward until within sight of Richmond's main defenses, the smoke from workshops and the steeples of the capital's churches plainly visible. Artillery frowned at the raiders from strong embrasures, and prudence dictated a change of course. Kilpatrick had reached the road leading east toward the Chickahominy River bridges that carried the Virginia Central Railroad and several wagon roads over that swampy tributary of the James. Reaching these spans, called the Meadow Bridges, and burning them in his wake, Kilpatrick captured a train loaded with supplies, set the cars ablaze, and then pushed the fiery conveyance onto the ruined bridge, whence it plunged spectacularly into the Chickahominy "until the whole thing well-nigh disappeared in the deep mud and water."[49]

Kilpatrick had ventured too far to attempt a return to Thompson's Crossroads. His only refuge lay with Union forces at Yorktown, some sixty miles southeast near the tip of Virginia's Peninsula. The weary New Yorkers accordingly pressed toward Hanovertown on the Pamunkey River, guided by a local black man who knew the shortest route. They commandeered a small flatboat and loaded twenty men and horses per trip until the entire regiment had safely crossed the river. Destroying the ferry after the last man disembarked on the north bank, the invaders disappeared into the wooded countryside of King William County as a Confederate cavalry force from Richmond glared impotently from across the unfordable river. "Cheer after cheer now rent the air," recalled one Federal, "and the skilful manner in which their leader conducted the hazardous enterprise . . . gave him such a hold on the hearts of his men, and such a feeling of confidence in him was inspired, as to raise their enthusiasm to the highest point of admiration." Kilpatrick intercepted and destroyed a train of thirty wagons loaded with bacon and then went into bivouac five miles from the Pamunkey.[50]

Thirty-three-year-old Unitarian minister and lawyer Hasbrouck Davis, Kilpatrick's partner in Stoneman's plan to sever the railroads leading north out of Richmond, led his 12th Illinois out of Thompson's Crossroads before dawn on May 3. His initial target would be Ashland Station about twenty-two miles east on the Richmond, Fredericksburg & Potomac Railroad. The troopers dismantled a bridge across the South Anna River and dispersed an annoying band of guerrillas before reaching Ashland later in the morning. "Words cannot describe the astonishment of the inhabitants at our appearance," remembered Davis. Meeting no interference from the few Confederates who had occupied the settlement, Davis repeated the now-familiar pattern of cutting telegraph wire, warping rails, and wrecking bridges. A train arriving from the north interrupted this routine. Davis effortlessly captured the cars, which proved to be loaded with 250 sick and wounded Confederates from the Chancellorsville battlefield along with a small guard and several officers. Among the latter was Lt. Joseph G. Morrison, Stonewall Jackson's aide and brother-in-law, who was en route to Richmond to collect his sister and escort her to her wounded husband's bedside. Morrison managed to escape the scrutiny of Davis's parole officers and would continue on his mission once the 12th Illinois had finished its work in Ashland.[51]

After some additional minor depredations, Davis moved east to Hanover Station on the Virginia Central Railroad. He arrived about 8:00 P.M. and put his exhausted men to work on the rails, telegraph, bridges, stables, and storehouses. The Illinoisans burned more than 100 wagons laden with supplies and scattered some 1,000 sacks of flour and corn. Typical of Federal behavior throughout Stoneman's operations, private homes remained unharmed. Well after dark, Davis headed south through Hanover Court House to a point within seven miles of Richmond before collapsing at a welcome encampment.[52]

From here, Davis planned to proceed east down the Peninsula toward Williamsburg. Moving along the south bank of the Pamunkey on May 4, he encountered a train on the Richmond & York River Railroad near Tunstall's Station that had ventured out from White House Landing. Its cars contained a regiment of Confederate infantry supported by three pieces of artillery. Davis boldly attempted to overwhelm the fast-deploying riflemen and engaged the rebels in a skirmish along the railroad embankment. Each side suffered casualties, the 12th Illinois losing two men killed and several wounded. Davis wisely terminated the contest and opted to fall back across the Pamunkey, doing so at Plunkett's Ferry a few miles downstream from Hanovertown, where Kilpatrick would cross later in the day. Using a ferry boat much as would the 2nd New York, Davis completed his operation unmolested and proceeded to Walkerton, where he navigated the York River's other major tributary, the Mattapony, without incident.[53]

Kilpatrick and Davis between them had thus broken the Richmond, Fredericksburg & Potomac and Virginia Central railroads in two places each—the Hungary and Ashland stations along the former and the Meadow Bridges and Hanover Station along the latter. Trains had been captured and destroyed, bridges dismantled, telegraphic communications interdicted, and supplies consumed by flames and Yankee appetites. Union horsemen had penetrated Richmond's defenses and taken prisoners, all with minimal losses. Word of the enemy's presence in Hanover County reached the Confederate capital on May 3. The following day, as Kilpatrick cavorted within the city's environs, "the tocsin sounded and the din kept up for several hours" around Capitol Square. Thousands of old men and government clerks rallied to defend Richmond's inner defense line before word arrived that the Union raiders had turned down the Peninsula and away from Richmond. Kilpatrick and Davis thus threw a scare into the Virginia metropolis, but their threatening presence was sufficiently brief to limit the impact of their terror.[54]

General Gregg led the fourth and largest detachment out of Thompson's Crossroads in the predawn darkness of May 3. The thirty-year-old Pennsylvanian, kinsman to his native state's wartime governor, directed the remaining two regiments of Kilpatrick's brigade down the South Anna "for the purpose of destroying the several bridges between Thompson's Four Corners and the Gordonsville and Richmond [Virginia Central] Railroad." The 1st Maine and 10th New York soon encountered the squadron led by Wesley Merritt that had left Louisa the previous evening. Together they continued the ruination of bridges and fords that Merritt had initiated some hours earlier. All told, the Union troopers applied axes and matches to five spans across the South Anna, arriving late in the afternoon at Rocky Mills (present-day Rockville), fifteen miles from the Confederate capital. While pausing to allow his men the opportunity to feed themselves and their mounts, Gregg received a report that only a handful of cavalry guarded the bridge carrying the Richmond, Fredericksburg & Potomac across the South Anna. The division commander ordered Lt. Col. Charles H. Smith of the 1st Maine to select about 100 men from each of the two regiments and, joined by Merritt's eager despoilers, destroy this key piece of Confederate infrastructure.[55]

Waiting until nightfall to conceal his approach, Smith obtained a black guide, whose knowledge of local geography proved less than intimate. "It was a wild ride of several miles, mainly through woods, with no road, and it seemed in no particular direction, and most of the way at a trot," recalled a trooper from the 1st Maine. The marauders struck the tracks near Ashland about 9:00 P.M. and picked up where Hasbrouck Davis's westerners had left off during the day. They targeted "several culverts, 4 large RR buildings, 400 cords of wood, repairing tools of eight men, three locomotives, cut the wire, and damaged things generally," boasted a New Englander. One house along the way yielded a number of prisoners whom Nathan Webb guessed had been "sparking" with the ladies inside: "Such a sheepish woebegone, forsaken lot of mortals I never saw."[56]

Eliminating the South Anna railroad bridge proved far tougher. The Federals discovered that "the enemy had sent a force of infantry and artillery for its protection, this precaution doubtless having resulted from Lieutenant-Colonel Davis' operations at Ashland." Smith's detachment thus returned toward Rocky Mills as "tired nature began to assert its sway." Most of the riders fell asleep, trusting their horses to follow the road. Stumbling into Rocky Mills about 2:00 A.M., the raiders found that their comrades had already departed. All discipline vanished as "arguments, orders, curses, loud and frequent, and even blows, could not keep the men awake." Somehow the exhausted cavalry closed with Gregg's main body an hour later and dismounted in abject fatigue, stealing a few moments of rest. Before dawn on May 4, the enervated troopers resumed their trek toward Thompson's Crossroads, reaching the intersection shortly after noon. "We started back with our plunder which consisted of horses, mules, niggers besides what flour, bacon, grain and tobacco we could well carry," reported William B. Baker of the 1st Maine. "On the whole we had a big time though suffered much from want of sleep."[57]

The last of Stoneman's parties to leave Thompson's Crossroads on May 3 belonged to Buford's brigade. Capt. Thomas Drummond of the 5th U.S. Cavalry "with 200 men and the picked horses from eight companies" trotted down the South Anna to ensure that Gregg and Merritt had done justice to the fords and bridges between the crossroads and the highway leading to Goochland Court House. Another portion of the regiment rode upstream toward Yanceyville to take responsibility for the bridge at that point should its destruction become necessary. These separate missions left Capt. James E. Harrison, the regimental commander, with only 109 men and 10 officers at Thompson's Crossroads in addition to the other undersized units of Buford's reserve brigade.[58]

Although Stoneman no doubt relished his time out of the saddle, he nevertheless spent May 3 "in no little anxiety." Captain Lord with the 1st U.S. Cavalry returned during the day reporting the success of his operations against Tolersville, Fredericks Hall, and Carr's Bridge. Wyndham's men dragged in after dark with tales of triumph at Columbia (except for their failure to ruin the aqueduct). The fate of Kilpatrick, Davis, Gregg, Merritt, and Drummond remained unknown, and Stoneman fretted about threats from Gordonsville to his vulnerable reserve. He accordingly instructed Captain Harrison to move what remained of his regiment six miles west to Fleming's Crossroads, atop Shannon

Hill, where the Three Chopt Road from Richmond intersected the highway between Louisa and Columbia. Harrison reached Shannon Hill about 2:30 A.M. on May 4. He immediately dispersed his tiny force in every direction, retaining a nucleus of twenty-five troopers at Fleming's Crossroads.[59]

In fact, Harrison needed to look in only one direction for danger. Rooney Lee and his 800 men continued to move north through the night on the Cartersville Road from Columbia toward Thompson's Crossroads in dogged pursuit of Wyndham. By dawn Lee's column, with his old regiment, the 9th Virginia, in the vanguard, had reached the Three Chopt Road about four miles east of Shannon Hill and six miles south of Thompson's Crossroads. Lee learned from a local farmer that Wyndham had passed to the north nearly twelve hours earlier, so the Confederate commander decided to rest his men before proceeding. One of the Virginia troopers received permission to forage for his breakfast and discovered Harrison's picket line one mile west of the Confederate bivouac.

This man returned to his unit and reported the presence of an undetermined number of Union cavalry looming on Lee's left flank. The Confederate commander authorized a small contingent to investigate this alarming news, and the patrol clashed with Harrison's alert vedettes. This sparring prompted Harrison to concentrate his men at Fleming's Crossroads while providing Lee a ready target against which to unleash his combative instincts. Neither officer knew that the Confederates would enjoy an eight-to-one advantage in the imminent confrontation.[60]

As the advance of Lee's brigade approached the top of Shannon Hill riding eight abreast on and beside the road, Harrison ordered the forty-five Union troopers then present to barrel down the slope into the charging Confederates. He hoped to check "them for a short time, to enable my pickets to return and to get my led animals off," explained Harrison, but "the shock of the charge was so great that my foremost horses were completely knocked over." After challenging Lee's men hand-to-hand for ten minutes, Harrison realized his force faced overwhelming odds and sounded the retreat. The Yankees dashed back up Shannon Hill, then northward toward Yanceyville with the Virginians in hot pursuit, leaving behind an officer and at least four men killed or wounded. Lee captured more than thirty of Harrison's men, including most of a patrol that did not clear the crossroads in time. These prisoners informed Lee that Stoneman's main force rested at nearby Thompson's Crossroads and easily outnumbered the Confederate brigade. Satisfied with his victory at Shannon Hill, Lee withdrew his jaded men west on the Three Chopt Road toward Gordonsville.[61]

Word of the engagement at Shannon Hill quickly reached Stoneman at Thompson's Crossroads. Joined by the balance of Buford's brigade, he raced west to the rescue, arriving in time to snatch one of Lee's officers and three privates but too late to confront the main Confederate column. Stoneman and Buford remained at Shannon Hill throughout the day, moving north to Yanceyville the next morning. Here along the steep right bank of the South Anna River, Gregg, Wyndham, Merritt, and Drummond rendezvoused with their commander. With most of his force thus reunited for the first time in more than forty-eight hours, Stoneman called another council of war.[62]

Six days had transpired since the cavalry plunged across the Rappahannock at Kelly's Ford. Hooker's orders had stipulated that Stoneman would hear from army headquarters before the cavalry consumed its supplies, but Fighting Joe had not communicated with Stoneman during the entire operation. Moreover, prisoners and civilians repeated "vague rumors" of a Union defeat at Chancellorsville, and the fleeing Confederate infantry that would signal the success of Hooker's plan had been manifestly invisible. With rations exhausted and foraging growing more difficult, neither Davis nor Kilpatrick likely to return to the column, and no inkling of Averell's whereabouts, Stoneman "determined to make . . . our way back to the Army of the Potomac," satisfied that "all that we were sent to perform" had been accomplished.[63]

While Stoneman's self-congratulatory assessment would not go unchallenged, his assumptions about Kilpatrick and Davis proved accurate. The Illinoisans moved down the middle of the Peninsula from Walkerton on May 5, some of the column becoming separated in the process. Their advance reached Gloucester Point opposite Yorktown on May 6.[64]

Kilpatrick experienced a more exciting journey. Reaching the Mattapony at Aylett in the predawn hours of May 5, the New Yorkers surprised 300 enemy troopers, capturing 2 officers and 33 men. After burning more than 50 wagons and a depot loaded with wheat, corn, and commissary goods, Kilpatrick crossed the river on a ferry minutes ahead of pursuing Confederates. That night he reached the tidal Rappahannock upriver from Tappahannock and destroyed yet another train of rebel supplies. The Federals pressed southeast in the dark, fending off bushwhackers and sparring with a force of regular Confederate cavalry.

On the evening of May 6, Kilpatrick spotted a body of horsemen drawn across his front near King and Queen Court House. He deployed skirmishers and advanced in column of squadrons expecting a sharp engagement. A few shots split the night air before Kilpatrick identified his foes as the isolated fraction of the 12th Illinois. "This re[e]ncounter was very pleasing," admitted a New Yorker. "We needed this stimulus exceedingly, for we had been marching all day through a cold drizzling rain, which had dampened our ardor somewhat, and chilled our blood." At 10:00 A.M. the following morning, everyone in

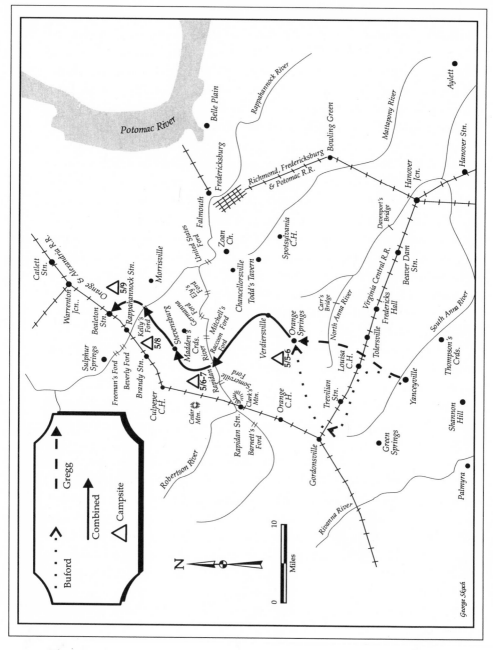

Potomac River

Belle Plain

Rappahannock River

Mattapony River

Aylett

Hanover Stn.

Fredericksburg

Richmond, Fredericksburg & Potomac R.R.

Bowling Green

Hanover Jcn.

Catlett Stn.

Orange & Alexandria R.R.

Warrenton Jcn.

Sulphur Springs

Morrisville

United States Ford

Falmouth

Zoan Ch.

Spotsylvania C.H.

Davenport's Bridge

Beaver Dam Stn.

South Anna River

Rappahannock Stn.

5/9

Bealeton Stn.

Kelly's Ford

Ely's Ford

Chancellorsville

Todd's Tavern

Carr's Bridge

Virginia Central R.R.

Fredericks Hall

Thompson's Crds.

Freeman's Ford

Beverly Ford

Brandy Stn.

5/8

Stevensburg

Madden's Crds.

Mitchell's Ford

Verdiersville

Orange Springs

North Anna River

Louisa C.H.

Tolersville

Yanceyville

Shannon Hill

Culpeper C.H.

5/6-7

Rapidan River

Raccoon Ford

Somerville Ford

5/5-6

Trevilian Stn.

Green Springs

Cedar Mtn.

Clark's Mtn.

Orange C.H.

Gordonsville

Palmyra

Rapidan Stn.

Barnett's Ford

Robertson River

Rivanna River

Gregg
Combined
Buford
Campsite

10
Miles
0
N

George Skoch

Stoneman's raid, May 5–9, 1863

Kilpatrick's tired command received a boost when the New Yorkers and their midwestern comrades rode into Union lines at Gloucester Point. In little more than 100 hours, Kilpatrick had covered nearly 200 miles with a loss of only one officer and thirty-seven men, taking many times that number of Confederates out of the war and causing extensive damage along the way. When Secretary of War Stanton learned of Kilpatrick's and Davis's arrival at Yorktown, he telegraphed his thanks to the raiders for "an achievement unsurpassed for daring and success."[65]

Success for Stoneman would depend upon his ability to navigate the perils of his return trip. "To take the enemy by surprise and penetrate his country was easy enough," Stoneman averred, but "to withdraw from it was a more difficult matter." The Union commander correctly deduced that the bulk of his potential opposition would come from uncounted forces to the west around Gordonsville posted to block an attempt to move against Charlottesville's rich depots and vulnerable bridges. He therefore determined to employ Buford along the Virginia Central Railroad to occupy the Confederates' attention, while under cover of night he and Gregg would retrace their steps north toward the Rapidan.[66]

At Fleming's Crossroads Buford assembled 646 of his strongest horses and mounted picked men from his regular units and the 6th Pennsylvania to execute his perilous mission. Heading north across the bridge at Yanceyville, he hoped to maneuver cross-country south of the railroad to elude Confederate patrols but soon discovered that the terrain would not accommodate the expeditious movement of cavalry. "The only alternative was to march by Louisa," concluded Buford. When the Federals reached that familiar county seat, they discovered that Confederates had restored telegraphic communication with Gordonsville, thirteen miles to the west. The Yankees snipped the lines again and plundered the post office, gaining some "valuable information."[67]

By nightfall they reached Trevilian Station, where water tanks, rails, pumps, handcars, arms, ammunition, and a large supply of subsistence stores fell victim to the well-practiced Union raiders. Buford cautiously advanced scouts toward Gordonsville, approaching to within two miles of the vital junction town. The blue-clad troopers spied a line of infantry and artillery blocking their path, prompting one Federal to believe that "it looked very much as if our time had come." Satisfied that he had done all he could to distract the Confederates, Buford used the moonless sky and a violent downpour to avoid detection and turned northeast toward the North Anna River. "The night was very dark, and much of the way led us through dense woods, intensifying the darkness; and for several hours it was utterly impossible for one to see the person riding immediately in advance, or even the head of the animal upon which he was himself mounted," remembered a Pennsylvanian. The drenched column forded the North Anna about 2:00 A.M. on May 6 and rode all night before stopping near dawn at Orange Springs. "Fires were soon started, coffee prepared," wrote one Federal, "and after a light lunch, we wrapped ourselves in wet blankets and were soon asleep."[68]

Stoneman, Gregg, Wyndham, and the remainder of the Union cavalry, now reduced to fewer than 2,000 sabers in four regiments, lounged at Yanceyville on May 5, although Stoneman did detach 300 men under Capt. Theophilus F. Rodenbaugh and Capt. Thomas Drummond to move across the South Anna downstream and create an additional diversion. Near dusk the troopers mounted and, once across the river, burned the bridge behind them. Suffering from the same inclement weather and impenetrable blackness experienced by Buford's command, the troopers intercepted the Virginia Central Railroad at Tolersville and the North Anna River near the Victoria Iron Works. "It was a dismal ride," confessed a soldier in the 1st Maine, "made more so by the sound of an occasional shot from a guerilla, and the doleful note of a single whippoorwill that followed the column all night long." A comrade noted in his diary that the freezing temperatures caused him to shake "till my flesh was as tender as raw meat." Stoneman reached Orange Springs in mid-morning, resting only three hours during the entire movement, and greeted Buford and his weary men with no little relief.[69]

The miserable march experienced by both Buford and Stoneman on the night of May 5–6 might have been much worse had the Confederates interfered with it in any meaningful way. Rooney Lee had returned to Gordonsville and rested his command after the minor victory at Shannon Hill. The War Department relayed information about Union incursions at Hungary Station, on the Peninsula, at Goochland, and in Louisa. Lee pointed to the lack of clarity of this intelligence by complaining that he "heard by telegram from Richmond that the enemy were everywhere." On May 6 he set out toward the North Anna in pursuit but found that the night's rain, which continued unabated during the day, had swollen the stream beyond fording and that the Federals had destroyed all the bridges. Conceding that Stoneman had escaped him, at least for the time being, Lee returned to Louisa and on May 7 trotted west to Trevilian Station, escorting a few Union stragglers who had tarried south of the river.[70]

In the meantime, Stoneman remounted his command at Orange Springs about noon on May 6 and cautiously probed north toward the Orange and Fredericksburg Plank Road. The slow advance covered just two miles in the afternoon before he called a halt to feed and water the animals. Local blacks now began to report that Hooker had withdrawn across the Rappahannock in defeat—dispiriting news but as yet unconfirmed. The march resumed at 5:00

P.M., inaugurating another night of indescribable wretchedness for the Union troopers. "The rain pouring in torrents, and so dark that at times I could not see my horse's ears, and with the mud so deep that . . . it was with difficulty my saddle horse could extract his feet," reported Captain Robertson of the 2nd U.S. Artillery, who shared the suffering of the fatigued, filthy, and famished privates.[71]

The column reached Verdiersville on the Plank Road at midnight. Rebel scouts operating in the downpour and darkness attempted with some success to misdirect individual Federals away from the column and into captivity. Despite the considerable hardships of a second consecutive night march, many of the troopers managed to sleep in their saddles as their mounts steered a steady course. About 2:00 A.M. on May 7, the head of this mud-splattered parade reached Raccoon Ford, "which to our great joy," said Stoneman, "we found fordable." The last regiment passed into Culpeper County about dawn.[72]

"When we emerged on the bank of the river and found the coast clear we felt greatly relieved," recalled twenty-one-year-old seminarian Nathan Webb. "The Col. had told us we were to remain here six hours. Six long hours! What a time in which to sleep. More than we've had at any one time since we started." Mildred M. Halsey, a resident of the Raccoon Ford area, testified that not all the Federals used this respite for slumber. Watching Union soldiers prowling around her farm, Halsey walked out to the front gate to challenge them. "They look[ed] like the dregs of the earth," observed the countrywoman as the Yankees cheerfully cleaned out her smokehouse.[73]

Stoneman allowed his men to unsaddle their horses and provide the loyal beasts with whatever forage remained. About noon, the column commenced the final leg of its journey toward the Rappahannock. Rain continued to fall as the languid march halted before Kelly's Ford between 9:00 and 10:00 P.M. Three days of precipitation had filled the Rappahannock to swimming depths, and after a halfhearted attempt to negotiate the ford, Stoneman decided to postpone a crossing until daylight. Such a delay, of course, would provide Jeb Stuart an opportunity to trap the Federals between his troopers and the river, a concern shared by many of the Union horsemen. That morning Stoneman had dispatched Lt. Edwin V. Sumner, Jr., an aide on his staff, with a message to Hooker reporting the status of the returning riders. Sumner reached army headquarters at 11:00 P.M. after a harrowing ordeal, but for the first time since April 29, Hooker knew the general disposition of all of his cavalry.[74]

By the end of the day on May 8, the last of that cavalry (excepting Kilpatrick and Davis) reached the north side of the Rappahannock. The only conveyance available at Kelly's Ford was a small punt or scow in which Stoneman attempted to cross his artillery chests. When this experiment failed, the Unionists opted to destroy their ammunition. The teams breasted the current dragging their guns and empty limbers behind them, emerging on the far bank without incident but with gun barrels streaming water like hoses. Gregg and Buford posted strong men on good horses below the ford while the rest of the command coaxed their weakened mounts through the rushing water. "Our horses, being thoroughly exhausted, were scarcely able to stem the swift current of the stream, and in several cases both horse and rider were carried down the river," remembered one participant. The lifeguards rescued all but one man and half a dozen animals. Stoneman waited until the last of his troops had reached the left bank before boarding the little boat and ferrying to safety. By nightfall the command had reached Bealeton on the Orange & Alexandria Railroad, "where we found supplies for man and beast."[75]

In the immediate afterglow of their ten-day adventure, Stoneman and most of his soldiers considered their tribulations a military success. The *New York Herald* reported that the raiders destroyed twenty-two bridges; severed railroads in seven places; burned five canal boats, three depots, and four supply trains; captured more than 300 horses and mules; and cut telegraph lines in five spots. "To the pecuniary loss in the destruction of . . . public stores of all kinds . . . there must be added the money value of some 450 negroes, who came out of the country with the various parties," boasted Stoneman.[76] "Not . . . the least valuable among other results of this expedition is the influence it has had upon the cavalry arm of the service," added the corps commander. This judgment was seconded by a trooper in the 1st New Jersey: "For the first time the cavalry found themselves made useful . . . and treated as something better than military watchmen for the army. They saw that the long desired time had come when they would be permitted to gain honor and reputation, and when they would cease to be tied to the slow moving divisions of infantry without liberty to strike a blow for the cause of the nation. . . . It gave our troopers self-respect, and obliged the enemy to respect them."

A member of the 1st Maine stated simply, "It was ever after a matter of pride with the boys that were on 'Stoneman's Raid.'" Robert E. Lee verified the perception that the operation had shifted the balance of cavalry power in the East. On May 7, even before Stoneman had returned to the Rappahannock, Lee wrote President Jefferson Davis that "unless we can increase the cavalry attached to this army we shall constantly be subject to aggressive expeditions of the enemy similar to those experienced in the last ten days. . . . Every expedition will augment their boldness and increase their means of doing us harm."[77]

Stoneman achieved these physical and moral benefits with minimal casualties. One scholar estimates Union losses in the raid at fewer than 90 killed or wounded and about 300 missing. In his definitive account of the Chancellorsville campaign, John Bigelow, Jr., concludes that Stoneman and Averell lost 189 men from all causes. The major incidents of combat near Louisa Court House, Rapidan Station, Shannon Hill, and Tunstall's Station emptied relatively few saddles. The Confederate capture of exhausted troopers on jaded horses accounted for the bulk of Union losses. In fact, Hooker would experience infinitely more trouble in replacing the horseflesh expended during Stoneman's raid than in alleviating manpower shortages. Stoneman's troops abandoned approximately 1,000 mounts during their journey, shooting most of them so they would not fall into rebel hands. The men compensated when they could by appropriating animals from Virginia farms, but these brood mares, work horses, or mules inadequately replaced Stoneman's well-bred cavalry steeds. For weeks after the campaign, the Army of the Potomac scrambled to remount members of "Company Q."[78]

Stoneman himself considered the operation a triumph. "The desire of the commanding general that I should 'understand that he considers the primary object of your [my] movement the cutting of the enemy's communications with Richmond by the Fredericksburg route, checking his retreat over those lines . . .' was fully complied with . . . as not only the railroad bridges . . . were destroyed, but all the road bridges across the South Anna and several across the North Anna were completely destroyed, placing a ditch, fordable only in a very few places, between the enemy and Richmond." Hooker saw the matter differently. In testimony before the Joint Committee on the Conduct of the War, Fighting Joe reported that "an examination of the instructions General Stoneman received, in connexion [sic] with the official report of his operations, fully sustains me in saying that no officer never [sic] made a greater mistake in construing his orders, and no one ever accomplished less in so doing."[79]

Other initial assessments tended to agree with Stoneman's interpretation. Brig. Gen. Rufus King at Yorktown called the raid "one of the finest feats of the war." Provost Marshal Marsena Patrick considered Stoneman's movements "a complete success." The Newark *Daily Advertiser* reported on "the magnificent exploit performed by Gen. Stoneman's cavalry" and concluded that "the expedition . . . appears to have accomplished all that was required of it." Some saw the matter in a different light, but none more so than Hooker himself. As early as May 10, the army commander complained to Edwin Stanton that "the raid does not appear to have amounted to much," and he bluntly requested a full explanation from Stoneman. After the war, Hooker hardened in his conviction. "I consider Stoneman as justly answerable for my failure at Chancellorsville as Howard," he wrote historian Samuel P. Bates. "Stoneman . . . had married just before a Rebel wife and at the same time was terribly afflicted with the piles, and between the two he had become completely emasculated, and I might as well have had a wet shirt in command of my cavalry. . . . Had Genl. Lee's communications with Richmond been severed, not many of his Army would ever have been returned to that city, provisions or no provisions."[80]

Some troopers adopted this theme in postwar memoirs. W. L. Heermance of the 6th New York Cavalry, which had remained behind with the infantry, concluded that Stoneman's raid "accomplished nothing," while James Rodney Wood agreed that "the raid was a failure strategically. . . . It nearly crippled us as [a] cavalry command. Our horses returned from the raid in a ruinous condition, and the condition of the men was scarcely little better." Historian William Swinton considered the results of the raid "quite insignificant"; a century later, Bruce Catton averred that the operation wasted the Union cavalry.[81]

The evidence supports Stoneman's critics at least in regard to the effort to disrupt communications between Richmond and Lee's army. The Confederates repaired the Richmond, Fredericksburg & Potomac Railroad by May 5 and the Virginia Central Railroad by May 8. By Stoneman's own admission, the Anna rivers could still be forded in several places, and no doubt retreating Confederate infantry would have located those crossings. Moreover, because Lee would switch his supply line to the Shenandoah Valley during the Gettysburg campaign, Confederate authorities had ample opportunity to erase any residual effects of Stoneman's depredations.[82]

In a purely physical sense, then, Stoneman did not deliver the substantial results he proclaimed. Partial explanation may be found in Hooker's ambiguous and conflicting orders, which left Stoneman uncertain about his objectives, Averell's role, and the cavalry's relationship with the army's main operations in the Wilderness. Even today, students of Chancellorsville find it difficult to reconcile strategic reality with Hooker's professed intentions.

We can be sure that the most salutary outcome of Stoneman's raid—increased morale and self-confidence among the Union troopers—appears nowhere in Hooker's explicit objectives or postcampaign analysis. A member of the 10th New York stated that he had little doubt "but the prominence awarded the cavalry by General Hooker was viewed with much concern by the Confederates." A captain in the 13th Virginia of Rooney Lee's brigade agreed: "Stoneman has taken the shine off of Stuart—that raid beat anything [else] the Yankees ever done." A soldier in the 1st Maine echoed these sentiments but added a telling point: "We have made a big raid and done our part for a successful opening of the spring campaign," he wrote. "In the meantime what has Hooker done. Simply failed."[83]

Traditional evaluations of the Federal disaster at Chancellorsville substantially attribute Hooker's undoing to his cavalry's barren contribution. The army commander, the Joint Committee on the Conduct of the War, and Fighting Joe's biographer are among many others who claim that Stoneman's bootless escapade deprived the army of the means to thwart Jackson's flank march and discover Lee's vulnerability on May 2–3. Even if this analysis rings true, the fault must rest not with Stoneman but with Hooker himself. After all, the army commander rather than George Stoneman devised the plan to detach six of seven cavalry brigades.[84]

It may be argued, however, that Hooker retained sufficient cavalry to perform the required tasks at Chancellorsville. Pleasonton provided three regiments, about 1,200 sabers, during the army's operations from April 29 through May 2, after which Averell's brigades arrived as reinforcements. The presence of Stoneman's entire command might not have changed the strategic picture on that critical day. Would Hooker have placed his cavalry beyond the right flank of the Eleventh Corps? How could more cavalry have penetrated the Wilderness tangle any better than did Pleasonton's troopers? Might Gregg and Averell have employed their regiments to greater advantage against Jackson that evening than did Pleasonton? Did not Union infantry spot Jackson's flank march even in the absence of a larger number of mounted troops?[85]

The real responsibility for Union defeat at Chancellorsville rests with Hooker's series of unmitigated battlefield errors, not with the absence of Stoneman's corps. As a New England trooper recognized, "Whether [Hooker] was dissatisfied or not with our raid . . . I think we accomplished as much as he did."[86]

Such an analysis could do Stoneman no good in May 1863. Recognizing Hooker's intention to blame him for the defeat at Chancellorsville, the cavalry chieftain sought a medical leave shortly after the raid's conclusion. Fighting Joe promptly granted the request and two weeks later elevated Pleasonton to command of the corps, ending Stoneman's affiliation with the Army of the Potomac.[87]

Did Hooker treat Stoneman with justice, and has the verdict of history been any fairer? Stoneman clearly opted to obey the strictures of Hooker's April 22 instructions and erred in ignoring the directive circulated on April 28. The "bursting shell" strategy executed at Thompson's Crossroads deprived him of a chance to implement Hooker's conception of blocking Lee's retreat, even though Hooker's own failures would render moot such a contingency (in any case, it is highly doubtful that 10,000 cavalry could have blocked Lee's infantry for very long). Moreover, Stoneman's message to Averell in Culpeper County froze that unfortunate officer and led to Hooker's recall of half of the cavalry before it had the chance to reunite with Gregg and Buford. If any Union cavalry officer can claim unjust treatment during the Chancellorsville campaign, it must be the overdeliberate Averell.

The physical damage inflicted by Stoneman on the Confederate military infrastructure in central Virginia clearly was substantial though ephemeral. Two observations help to place these results in context. First, few if any cavalry raids during the entire war succeeded in doing what Stoneman sought to accomplish—namely, the effective and prolonged disruption of the supply line of a major army through the destruction of a railroad. Second, Ulysses S. Grant sent virtually all of his cavalry under Philip H. Sheridan off on a raid very like Stoneman's almost precisely a year later and with almost precisely the same results. Perhaps Grant joined Hooker in believing cavalry was of little value in direct support of an army operating in the Wilderness.

Overall, Stoneman's raid compares quite well with virtually every other cavalry operation during the first three years of the war—even those remembered as brilliant successes. But its influence on the esprit de corps of the Federal cavalry and the perception of that influence in the minds of official Washington, the army's infantry, and, most importantly, Confederate opponents mark the greatest significance of this neglected episode in Civil War history. Stoneman's raid served as a dress rehearsal for the engagements at Brandy Station and Gettysburg that established first parity and then superiority for the mounted arm of the Army of the Potomac.[88]

ACKNOWLEDGMENTS

Following in the hoofprints of Stoneman and his raiders required the generous help of a number of friends who provided research assistance and advice. The author expresses his thanks to William J. Bernache, David Bosse, John J. Hennessy, Marshall Krolick, Daniel M. Laney, Blake Magner, William Marvel, William Matter, Gen. John P. Murray, Mark Silo, George Skoch, Steve Wright, R. Michael Yost, Allan J. Zellnock, Kathleen J. Ziemer, and Cindy V. Ziperman for tracking down a wide range of unpublished sources consulted in the preparation of this essay. Richard Bowles shared his extensive knowledge of the skirmish at Shannon Hill, and Donald C. Pfanz and Robert K. Krick of the Fredericksburg and Spotsylvania National Military Park assisted me in using the voluminous manuscript copies accumulated by the park's staff. Dr. Richard J. Sommers of the U.S. Army Military History Institute in Carlisle Barracks, Pennsylvania, provided his usual high level of expertise in guiding me through the rich manuscript collections under his care. The staff at the Manuscripts Division of the Library of Congress facilitated my research with professionalism and courtesy. The author also wishes to thank Gary W. Gallagher and William Curley and his staff at Pennsylvania State University at Mont Alto for providing such a pleasing rationale for the preparation of this essay.

1. John Bigelow, Jr., *The Campaign of Chancellorsville: A Strategic and Tactical Study* (New Haven, Conn.: Yale University Press, 1910), 505. Bigelow carefully estimated a total of 30,099 casualties during the campaign. This figure includes losses suffered during operations ancillary to the main battle.

2. Capt. Willard Glazier, *Three Years in the Federal Cavalry* (New York: R. H. Ferguson, 1873), 185; Edward P. Tobie, *History of the First Maine Cavalry* (Boston: First Maine Cavalry Association, 1887), 143; J. B. McIntosh to "My dear friend," May 8, 1863, W. W. Averell Papers, New York State Archives, Albany, N.Y.

3. Samuel H. Merrill, *The Campaigns of the First Maine and First District of Columbia Cavalry* (Portland, Maine: Bailey & Noyes, 1866), 101; James Rodney Wood, Sr., "Civil War Memoirs," p. 41, Maud Wood Park Papers, Manuscript Division, Library of Congress, Washington, D.C. (repository hereafter cited as LC).

4. U.S. War Department, *The War of the Rebellion: A Compilation of the Official Records of the Union and Confederate Armies*, 127 vols., index, and atlas (Washington, D.C.: GPO, 1880–1901), 25(2):51, 320 (hereafter cited as *OR*; all references are to series 1). General Orders No. 4, issued February 12, 1863, designated the organizational structure of the Cavalry Corps (*OR* 25[2]:71–72). The cavalry's order of battle during the campaign may be found in *OR* 25(1):169–70.

5. Theophilus F. Rodenbaugh, *From Everglades to Canon with the Second Dragoons* (New York: D. Van Nostrand, 1875), 285; Benjamin W. Crowninshield, "Cavalry in Virginia during the War of the Rebellion," in *Papers of the Military Historical Society of Massachusetts*, 14 vols. (1895–1918; reprint, Wilmington, N.C.: Broadfoot, 1989–90), 13:11.

6. *OR* 25(2):148; Charles A. Legg to "Dear Parents," March 18, 1863, Charles A. Legg Papers, Perkins Library, Duke University, Durham, N.C.; Jacob B. Cooke, "The Battle of Kelly's Ford, March 17, 1863," in *Personal Narratives of Events in the War of the Rebellion, Being Papers Read Before the Rhode Island Soldiers and Sailors Historical Society*, 3rd ser., no. 11 (Providence, R.I.: Rhode Island Soldiers and Sailors Historical Society, 1887), 11–12. For a good summary of the battle of Kelly's Ford, see Bigelow, *Campaign of Chancellorsville*, 89–105.

7. David McMurtrie Gregg, "Brevet Major General David McMurtrie Gregg," pp. 182–86, David M. Gregg Papers, LC; Alfred G. Sargent to "Dear Folks," April 22, 1863, Alfred G. Sargent Letters, Center for American History, University of Texas, Austin, Tex. Gregg's narrative of the review includes a description of Lincoln's horse bolting, which created some anxious moments until the president could regain control of his mount. "What a furious and exciting ride we have had," Lincoln told Gregg. Sargent served in the 1st Rhode Island Cavalry.

8. *OR* 25(2):199, (1):1066–67. In a postwar letter, Hooker claimed that his "main object in detaching [the cavalry] was to sever Genl. Lee's communications with Richmond, and until that was done, I was unwilling to advance on the enemy as he would only have to fall back, and behind any of the rivers find a stronger position than the one I had driven him from" (Joseph Hooker to Samuel P. Bates, October 5, 1878, Samuel P. Bates Papers, Pennsylvania State Archives, Harrisburg, Pa. [repository hereafter cited as PSA]).

9. *OR* 25(1):1067–68, (2):204–5; Bigelow, *Campaign of Chancellorsville*, 145–47.

10. Bigelow, *Campaign of Chancellorsville*, 147–48; H. B. McClellan, *The Life and Campaigns of Major-General J. E. B. Stuart* (1885; reprint, Little Rock, Ark.: Eagle, 1987), 219–22. Part of Davis's command crossed at Freeman's Ford.

11. Charles S. Wainwright, *A Diary of Battle: The Personal Journals of Colonel Charles S. Wainwright, 1861–1865*, ed. Allan Nevins (New York: Harcourt, Brace & World, 1962), 182; Stephen Z. Starr, *The Union Cavalry in the Civil War*, 3 vols. (Baton Rouge: Louisiana State University Press, 1979–85), 1:353; Marsena R. Patrick diary, April 15, 1863, Marsena Patrick Papers, LC; May 15, 1863, entry, Letterbook, 1863–64, Gregg Papers, LC; Flavius Bellamy to "Dear Brother," April 17, 1863, Flavius Bellamy Papers, Indiana Division, Indiana State Library, Indianapolis, Ind.; Glazier, *Three Years in the Federal Cavalry*, 166–67; McClellan, *J. E. B. Stuart*, 223–24.

12. *OR* 25(2):214, 220.

13. Edward G. Longacre, *Mounted Raids of the Civil War* (South Brunswick, N.J.: A. S. Barnes, 1975), 156; Bigelow, *Campaign of Chancellorsville*, 163; *OR* 25(2):42–44.

14. *OR* 25(1):1065, 1077; Bigelow, *Campaign of Chancellorsville*, 447; Col. Thomas Cruse, "Operations of the Union Cavalry during the Chancellorsville Campaign," p. 35, U.S. Army War College Paper, n.d., U.S. Army Military History Institute, Carlisle Barracks, Pa. (repository hereafter cited as USAMHI); W. N. Pickerill, *History of the Third Indiana Cavalry* (Indianapolis: Aetna, 1906), 69. Pleasonton retained Col. Thomas C. Devin's brigade, which consisted of the 6th New York Cavalry, 8th Pennsylvania Cavalry, and 17th Pennsylvania Cavalry. The 1st Pennsylvania Cavalry guarded the far left of the Union army below Fredericksburg and participated in neither Stoneman's raid nor the battle of Chancellorsville. Hundreds of additional troopers remained behind on detached duty or in the hospital. Thus the force available to Hooker on the eve of the campaign had been significantly diminished.

15. *OR* 25(1):1058; Charles F. Adams, Jr., quoted in Longacre, *Mounted Raids*, 157; Frederick Denison, *Sabres and Spurs: The First Regiment Rhode Island Cavalry in the Civil War, 1861–1865* (Central Falls: First Rhode Island Cavalry Veteran Association, 1876), 221; Bliss Perry, *Life and Letters of Henry Lee Higginson* (Boston: Atlantic Monthly Press, 1921), 187.

16. *OR* 25(1):1058.

17. *OR* 25(1):1075, 1098; Denison, *Sabres and Spurs*, 221–22; McClellan, *J. E. B. Stuart*, 225; Bigelow, *Campaign of Chancellorsville*, 441; Tobie, *First Maine Cavalry*, 134; N. D. Preston, *History of the Tenth Regiment of Cavalry, New York State Volunteers, August 1861 to August 1865* (New York: D. Appleton, 1892), 69–70. Denison described the skirmish a mile above Kelly's Ford as having "almost the dignity of a battle. . . . The dispute was short. They retired to their old position of March 17th, not caring to meet again, as on that sorely remembered day, the charge and steel of the Yankees." McClellan estimates that the two brigades of Fitzhugh and Rooney Lee numbered about 2,000. Fitz Lee himself guessed that the two units counted 2,700 sabers. Bigelow estimates 2,600. I have chosen to credit Rooney Lee with 800 men in his two regiments active during this operation and accept Bigelow's figure of 1,600 in Fitz Lee's brigade. Brig. Gen. William E. Jones's brigade spent the Chancellorsville campaign operating in the Shenandoah Valley and northwestern Virginia. Brig. Gen. Wade Hampton's brigade, according to Stuart's staff officer Heros Von Borcke, "had been left behind for recruiting, most of its dismounted men having been furloughed to their distant homes in Mississippi and the Carolinas to supply themselves with fresh horses" (Heros Von Borcke, *Memoirs of the Confederate War for Independence*, 2 vols. [1866; reprint, Dayton, Ohio: Morningside, 1985], 2:194).

18. *OR* 25(1):1058–59, 1068–69; Bigelow, *Campaign of Chancellorsville*, 441; Rev. S. L. Gracey, *Annals of the Sixth Pennsylvania Cavalry* (Philadelphia: E. H. Butler, 1868), 137.

19. *OR* 25(1):1060, 1088, 1092; Tobie, *First Maine Cavalry*, 135; Glazier, *Three Years in the Federal Cavalry*, 177. The 6th Pennsylvania Cavalry, known as Rush's Lancers, rode with Buford's regulars during the raid as a part of the reserve brigade.

20. Nathan B. Webb diary, April 30, 1863, Schoff Civil War Collection, William L. Clements Library, University of Michigan, Ann Arbor, Mich. (repository hereafter cited as CLUM); *OR* 25(1):1060; Glazier, *Three Years in the Federal Cavalry*, 177.

21. Henry R. Pyne, *The History of the First New Jersey Cavalry* (Trenton, N.J.: J. A. Beecher, 1871), 141–42; Gracey, *Sixth Pennsylvania Cavalry*, 138–39.

22. *OR* 25(1):1060, 1081; Gracey, *Sixth Pennsylvania Cavalry*, 139; Bigelow, *Campaign of Chancellorsville*, 442. Orange Springs, important during Stoneman's raid, no longer appears on maps and is apparently unreachable by road.

23. Gracey, *Sixth Pennsylvania Cavalry*, 139–40; *OR* 25(1):1082.

24. Gracey, *Sixth Pennsylvania Cavalry*, 140; *OR* 25(1):1082; Nathan Webb diary, May 1–2, 1863, CLUM; Bigelow, *Campaign of Chancellorsville*, 442.

25. *OR* 25(1):1082; Gracey, *Sixth Pennsylvania Cavalry*, 140–41.

26. Merrill, *Campaigns*, 96–97; Nathan Webb diary, May 2, 1863, CLUM; Glazier, *Three Years in the Federal Cavalry*, 177.

27. *OR* 25(1):1060, 1082, 1098; Glazier, *Three Years in the Federal Cavalry*, 178; Wells A. Bushnell journal, container 17, bound vol. 1, William Pendleton Palmer Collection, Western Reserve Historical Society, Cleveland, Ohio.

28. *OR* 25(1):1060, 1091; Gracey, *Sixth Pennsylvania Cavalry*, 145–46.

29. *OR* 25(1):1060; Bigelow, *Campaign of Chancellorsville*, 443–44; Nathan Webb diary, May 3, 1863, CLUM; Tobie, *First Maine Cavalry*, 137–38.

30. *OR* 25(1):1074, (2):474; Henry Norton, *Deeds of Daring; or, History of the Eighth N.Y. Volunteer Cavalry* (Norwich, N.Y.: Chenango Telegraph Printing House, 1889), 62.

31. Capt. William Hyndman, *History of a Cavalry Company* (Philadelphia: Jas. B. Rodgers, 1870), 89; Marshall D. Krolick, "The Cavalry in the Chancellorsville Campaign," p. 14, typescript provided by Krolick in the author's possession; Perry, *Henry Lee Higginson*, 187; [Regimental History Committee, comp.], *History of the Third Pennsylvania Cavalry* (Philadelphia: Franklin Printing Company, 1905), 230; *OR* 25(1):1078.

32. *OR* 25(1):1075–78, 1098.

33. *OR* 25(2):352–53, (1):1078.

34. Denison, *Sabres and Spurs*, 222; Perry, *Henry Lee Higginson*, 188; *OR* 25(1):1078–79; Newel Cheney, *History of the Ninth Regiment New York Volunteer Cavalry* (Poland Center, N.Y.: Martin Merz & Son, 1901), 91.

35. Cheney, *Ninth Regiment New York Volunteer Cavalry*, 91–92; "Summary of War Service of John Tidball," pp. 13–14, John Tidball Papers, U.S. Military Academy, West Point, N.Y.; *OR* 25(1):1079, 1098; Abner Hard, *History of the Eighth Cavalry Regiment Illinois Volunteers, During the Great Rebellion* (1868; reprint, Dayton, Ohio: Morningside, 1984), 232. Despite Beale's efforts, and those of the Federals for that matter, fire did not completely destroy the bridge. See Bigelow, *Campaign of Chancellorsville*, 442.

36. *OR* 25(1):1079–80, (2):352; [Regimental History Committee], *Third Pennsylvania Cavalry*, 231; Norton, *Deeds of Daring*, 62–63; John Follmer diary, May 2, 1863, typescript, bound vol. 41, Fredericksburg and Spotsylvania National Military Park Library, Fredericksburg, Va. (repository hereafter cited as FSNMP); Perry, *Henry Lee Higginson*, 188; Bigelow, *Campaign of Chancellorsville*, 322; Von Borcke, *Memoirs*, 2:227–28.

37. *OR* 25(1):1079, 1072–73. Averell was banished to the backwater of the Middle Depart-

ment, where he fought with some success in western Virginia. In 1864 he commanded a cavalry division during a portion of the Shenandoah Valley campaign until relieved again because of lack of aggression, this time by Maj. Gen. Philip H. Sheridan. Although it is true that Averell's performance in pursuit of the defeated Confederates after the battle of Fisher's Hill left much to be desired, Sheridan, like Hooker, unfairly focused his frustration exclusively on Averell.

38. Two of the finest students of the Chancellorsville campaign agree that Stoneman's April 30 order justified Averell's presence at Rapidan Station but find serious fault with Averell's lack of aggressiveness. Averell reported only four officers and a few men wounded (one officer mortally) and two men killed. See *OR* 25(1):1079; Bigelow, *Campaign of Chancellorsville*, 457–58; and Starr, *Union Cavalry*, 1:362–64.

39. Richard Bowles, Jr., "Shannon Hill Encounter," *Goochland County Historical Society Magazine* 17 (1985): 40; Bigelow, *Campaign of Chancellorsville*, 444; *OR* 25(1):1060.

40. *OR* 25(1):1060–61. Kilpatrick and Wyndham each commanded three regiments. Buford led five regiments, but the 1st U.S. Cavalry had been detached at Louisa.

41. *OR* 25(1):1060–61; Ernest B. Furgurson, *Chancellorsville 1863: The Souls of the Brave* (New York: Alfred A. Knopf, 1992), 283.

42. Edward G. Longacre, "Sir Percy Wyndham," *Civil War Times Illustrated* 8 (December 1968): 12, 14.

43. *OR* 25(1):1085; Gracey, *Sixth Pennsylvania Cavalry*, 142–43; Pyne, *First New Jersey Cavalry*, 144–45.

44. *OR* 25(1):1085; Pyne, *First New Jersey Cavalry*, 144–45.

45. *OR* 25(1):1098; Bowles, "Shannon Hill Encounter," 41.

46. James Moore, *Kilpatrick and Our Cavalry* (New York: Hurst, 1865), 47; *OR* 25(1): 1083–84; Glazier, *Three Years in the Federal Cavalry*, 179; Bigelow, *Campaign of Chancellorsville*, 445.

47. Edward G. Longacre, "Judson Kilpatrick," *Civil War Times Illustrated* 10 (April 1971): 25; Glazier, *Three Years in the Federal Cavalry*, 135.

48. *OR* 25(1):1084; Glazier, *Three Years in the Federal Cavalry*, 180–81; Capt. John S. Fair, "The Operations of the Federal and Confederate Cavalry in the Chancellorsville Campaign," p. 95, U.S. Army War College Paper, Session 1911–12, USAMHI; Bigelow, *Campaign of Chancellorsville*, 448.

49. *OR* 25(1):1084; Glazier, *Three Years in the Federal Cavalry*, 181–82.

50. *OR* 25(1):1084; Moore, *Kilpatrick*, 50–51.

51. Roger D. Hunt and Jack R. Brown, *Brevet Brigadier Generals in Blue* (Gaithersburg, Md.: Olde Soldier Books, 1990), 149; *OR* 25(1):1086; Furgurson, *Chancellorsville 1863*, 325.

52. *OR* 25(1):1086–87.

53. *OR* 25(1):1087; Bigelow, *Campaign of Chancellorsville*, 448; Cruse, "Operations of the Union Cavalry," 32.

54. John B. Jones, *A Rebel War Clerk's Diary*, 2 vols. (Philadelphia: J. B. Lippincott, 1866), 1:306–7.

55. Ezra J. Warner, *Generals in Blue: Lives of the Union Commanders* (Baton Rouge: Louisiana State University Press, 1964), 187; *OR* 25(1):1082, 1071; Tobie, *First Maine Cavalry*, 138.

56. *OR* 25(1):1082, 1071; Tobie, *First Maine Cavalry*, 138–39; Nathan Webb diary, May 3, 1863, CLUM.

57. *OR* 25(1):1082; Tobie, *First Maine Cavalry*, 139–40; William B. Baker to "My dear

Mercie," May 10, 1863, typescript, William B. Baker Papers, Southern Historical Collection, Wilson Library, University of North Carolina, Chapel Hill, N.C.

58. *OR* 25(1):1092–93.

59. *OR* 25(1):1061, 1093; Bowles, "Shannon Hill Encounter," 42.

60. Bowles, "Shannon Hill Encounter," 42–43. Today the intersection of the Cartersville Road and Three Chopt Road is called Hadensville.

61. *OR* 25(1):1093, 1098; Bowles, "Shannon Hill Encounter," 43–45, 48 (n. 44). Bowles is by far the most careful student of this engagement. He concludes that although Harrison claimed he made the attack with thirty men, as many as sixty were available on Shannon Hill. Bowles uses forty-five as a compromise figure.

62. *OR* 25(1):1063; Bowles, "Shannon Hill Encounter," 45. Bigelow, *Campaign of Chancellorsville*, 450, states that the council of war took place on the evening of May 4—a conclusion at odds with Stoneman's version of events.

63. *OR* 25(1):1063, 1067.

64. *OR* 25(1):1087, 18:701.

65. *OR* 25(1):1084, (2):452; Glazier, *Three Years in the Federal Cavalry*, 184–85. Kilpatrick remained at Gloucester Point until May 30, returning to Hooker's army at Falmouth the first week of June.

66. *OR* 25(1):1062.

67. *OR* 25(1):1089; E. R. Hagemann, ed., *Fighting Rebels and Redskins: Experiences in Army Life of Colonel George B. Sanford, 1861–1892* (Norman: University of Oklahoma Press, 1969), 202.

68. *OR* 25(1):1089; Hagemann, *Fighting Rebels and Redskins*, 202; Gracey, *Sixth Pennsylvania Cavalry*, 149.

69. Bigelow, *Campaign of Chancellorsville*, 450, 452; Tobie, *First Maine Cavalry*, 141; Nathan Webb diary, May 6, 1863, CLUM.

70. *OR* 25(1):1098–99, (2):776.

71. *OR* 25(1):1062–63, 1096; Tobie, *First Maine Cavalry*, 142.

72. Tobie, *First Maine Cavalry*, 142; Gracey, *Sixth Pennsylvania Cavalry*, 150; *OR* 25(1):1063; Bigelow, *Campaign of Chancellorsville*, 454.

73. Nathan Webb diary, May 7, 1863, CLUM; "Pages from Mildred M. Halsey's Notebook," May 7, 1863, typescript, bound vol. 135, FSNMP.

74. *OR* 25(1):1063, 1096, (2):783–84; Hagemann, *Fighting Rebels and Redskins*, 203; Tobie, *First Maine Cavalry*, 142–43; Bigelow, *Campaign of Chancellorsville*, 454–55.

75. *OR* 25(1):1063, 1096–97; Bigelow, *Campaign of Chancellorsville*, 456; Gracey, *Sixth Pennsylvania Cavalry*, 151.

76. *OR* 25(1):1063–64; *New York Herald*, quoted in Glazier, *Three Years in the Federal Cavalry*, 188.

77. *OR* 25(1):1064, (2):782; Pyne, *First New Jersey Cavalry*, 147; Tobie, *First Maine Cavalry*, 144.

78. Longacre, *Mounted Raids*, 173; Bigelow, *Campaign of Chancellorsville*, 505; Starr, *Union Cavalry*, 1:367. Many of the horses that completed the raid proved unfit for immediate service due to sore backs and "mud fever."

79. *OR* 25(1):1063; Joseph Hooker, quoted in Cruse, "Operations of the Union Cavalry," 34.

80. *OR* 25(2):452; Marsena Patrick diary, May 8, 1863, Patrick Papers, LC; Newark *Daily Advertiser*, May 9, 8, 1863, copy in bound vol. 193, FSNMP; *OR* 25(2):463, 468–69; Joseph

Hooker to Samuel P. Bates, December 24, 1878 (first quotation), n.d. (second quotation), August 24, 1878 (third quotation), Bates Papers, PSA. Hooker made a number of choice comments about Stoneman. On December 24, 1878, he reminded Bates that "when [Stoneman was] placed again on duty in the West . . . he surrendered his command to a band of Georgia Crackers." In an undated letter to Bates, Hooker stated that Stoneman "commenced chasing phantoms and his conduct was criminally insubordinate and trifling."

81. Capt. W. L. Heermance, "The Cavalry at Chancellorsville, May 1865 [*sic*]," in *Personal Recollections of the War of the Rebellion: Addresses Delivered Before the Commandery of the State of New York, Military Order of the Loyal Legion of the United States*, ed. A. Noel Blakeman, 2nd ser. (1897; reprint, Wilmington, N.C.: Broadfoot, 1992), 225; Wood, "Civil War Memoirs," p. 30; William Swinton, *Campaigns of the Army of the Potomac: A Critical History of Operations in Virginia, Maryland and Pennsylvania, from the Commencement to the Close of the War, 1861–1865* (1866; reprint, Secaucus, N.J.: Blue & Grey Press, 1988), 302; Bruce Catton, *Bruce Catton's Civil War* (New York: Fairfax, 1984) (originally published as *Glory Road* [Garden City, N.Y.: Doubleday, 1952]), 347.

82. Longacre, *Mounted Raids*, 172–73; Bigelow, *Campaign of Chancellorsville*, 454, 458–59; *OR* 25(2):780; Maj. Gen. George B. Davis, "The Stoneman Raid," *Journal of the United States Cavalry Association* 24 (January 1914): 550–51.

83. Preston, *Tenth Regiment of Cavalry, New York State Volunteers*, 77; Daniel T. Balfour, *13th Virginia Cavalry* (Lynchburg, Va.: H. E. Howard, 1986), 16; Nathan Webb diary, May 9, 1863, CLUM.

84. Walter H. Hebert, *Fighting Joe Hooker* (1944; reprint, Gaithersburg, Md.: Butternut, 1987), 197–98, 222–23. On April 2, 1877, Hooker wrote Samuel Bates: "I felt I had made a mistake in dispatching the greater part of my cavalry force, to sever Genl. Lee's communications with Richmond" (Bates Papers, PSA).

85. Starr, *Union Cavalry*, 1:360–61. Pleasonton widely claimed that the charge of his 8th Pennsylvania Cavalry was calculated to disrupt Jackson's progress. In fact, the consequences of this maneuver proved as great a shock to the Pennsylvanians as it did to the Confederates.

86. Krolick, "The Cavalry in the Chancellorsville Campaign," 26; Edward Longacre, "The Raid That Failed," *Civil War Times Illustrated* 26 (January 1988): 49.

87. Special Orders No. 137, May 20, 1863, provided Stoneman his leave of absence; General Orders No. 11, May 22, 1863, announced Pleasonton's temporary elevation to corps command; and Special Orders No. 153, June 5, 1863, directed Stoneman to report for further instructions to the adjutant general of the army. On July 28, 1863, Stoneman was appointed chief of the Cavalry Bureau, an administrative post. See *OR* 25(2):513, 27(3):11, for the various orders or references thereto. Hooker admitted to Bates in undated postwar correspondence that he would have preferred Buford to Stoneman had he known of Buford's talents. He might also have preferred Buford to Pleasonton. See Bates Papers, PSA, and Starr, *Union Cavalry*, 1:368 (n. 6).

88. Starr, *Union Cavalry*, 1:361, 365; Krolick, "The Cavalry in the Chancellorsville Campaign," 26–27; Davis, "The Stoneman Raid," 551.

The Smoothbore Volley That Doomed the Confederacy

Robert K. Krick

NINETEEN MEN in two distinct groups rode forward from the coalescing Confederate lines west of Chancellorsville at about 9:00 P.M. on May 2, 1863. Only seven of the nineteen came back untouched, man or horse. Although one of those nearest the offending musket muzzles, Maj. Gen. A. P. Hill escaped among the unscathed handful. Lt. Gen. Thomas J. "Stonewall" Jackson, among those farthest from the flash point, was one of the five men killed or mortally wounded. The capricious paths of a few dozen one-ounce lead balls caroming off the dense shrubbery of Spotsylvania's Wilderness that night had much to do with the course of the Civil War.

From every imaginable perspective, the afternoon of May 2 had been a stunning Confederate success of unprecedented magnitude. Lee and Jackson had crafted between them a dazzling tactical initiative that sent Stonewall covertly all the way across the front of a Federal army that outnumbered the

Last meeting of Generals Lee and Jackson, morning of May 2, 1863. This early engraving correctly shows the two generals mounted during their final brief meeting. Sarah Nicholas Randolph, The Life of Gen. Thomas J. Jackson ("Stonewall" Jackson) *(Philadelphia: J. B. Lippincott, 1876), 304*

southerners by more than 2 to 1. The redoubtable corps commander managed the remarkable march without serious interruption, arrayed his first two divisions in a wide line, and descended upon the Federals like a thunderbolt. Those northerners who rallied bravely against the tide faced an inexorable outflanking by the outriders of Jackson's line, who stretched far beyond the center of the attack in both directions. In this fashion Jackson routed one Union corps, trapped another out of the line, and left the others shaky, uncertain, and vulnerable to be stampeded.

Southern soldiers enjoying the chance to steamroller their enemy observed their legendary leader throughout his victorious advance. Darkness and confusion would lead to disastrous results, causing some southerners to fire mistakenly at Jackson, but during the early evening, everyone knew where he was. The adjutant of a Georgia regiment in the attack's front rank recalled that after the fighting had died down, the ground appeared "to tremble as if shaken by an earthquake, the cheering is so tremendous, caused by Gen. Jackson riding along the line." Members of the 18th North Carolina of James H. Lane's brigade, which within an hour would inadvertently fire on Jackson, saw their hero pass "about twilight." The Tar Heels cheered him and were gratified when Stonewall "took off his hat in recognition of their salutation."[1]

The divisions of Robert E. Rodes and Raleigh E. Colston had carried Jackson's attack forward. Most of A. P. Hill's division, last in the long column during the flanking march, had not maneuvered out of column and into line of battle. As darkness closed in on the victorious but exhausted Confederates, the need to advance fresh and better-organized troops to the front rank became obvious. Lane's five regiments drew the assignment. A. P. Hill ordered Lane to push them forward and then spread them to the right and the left, perpendicular to the Orange Plank Road, in preparation for a novel night attack. The North Carolinians hesitated in the road, uncertain how to form line because "on each side the shrubbery was so dense as to render it impossible to march."[2]

Jackson's plan to attack despite the steadily thickening darkness foundered first on a whimsical exchange of artillery fire. Southern guns in a small roadside clearing near a country schoolhouse and shop to the west of Lane's regiments opened a ranging fire into the woods toward Chancellorsville. The dreadful idea to begin this firing probably originated with an artillery captain eager to make noise. Northern guns responded in far greater numbers, wreaking havoc on the unfortunate North Carolina infantrymen standing in the road in ranks, having arranged themselves as a conveniently enfiladed target. The shot and shell came "as thick as hail." Maj. W. G. Morris of the 37th North Carolina swore that he had "never experi[e]nced such a shelling." General Lane shouted to his men to lie down in the road; most had probably tumbled into the thickets before their general could summon the yell. A lieutenant in the 37th recalled that the troops "buried our faces as close to the ground as possible and I expect some of us rubbed the skin off our noses trying to get under it."[3]

A. P. Hill and Stonewall Jackson ignored the intense fire as they conversed with each other on horseback, so "deeply absorbed" that enemy shells burst "all around[,] . . . plowing up the ground" under their horses' feet, "without either of them taking the slightest notice." Maj. William H. Palmer, Hill's bright and capable chief of staff, managed to locate General Lane in the scrubby underbrush, and the two men quickly agreed that the fire must be halted before the troops could make any further movement. Palmer rode back to the schoolhouse and shut down the Confederate artillery, and the enemy stopped firing as well soon after the provocation ended. The firing had lasted about fifteen minutes.[4]

As soon as the firestorm ceased, Lane moved his five North Carolina regiments into position as ordered. The 28th faced east on his far left, with the 18th just to its right. The right of the 18th anchored on the Orange Plank Road. The 37th continued the front south of the road, with the 7th on its—and the brigade's—right. In accordance with the tactical dogma of the era, Lane provided a healthy screen of skirmishers well to the front in the form of the entire 33rd

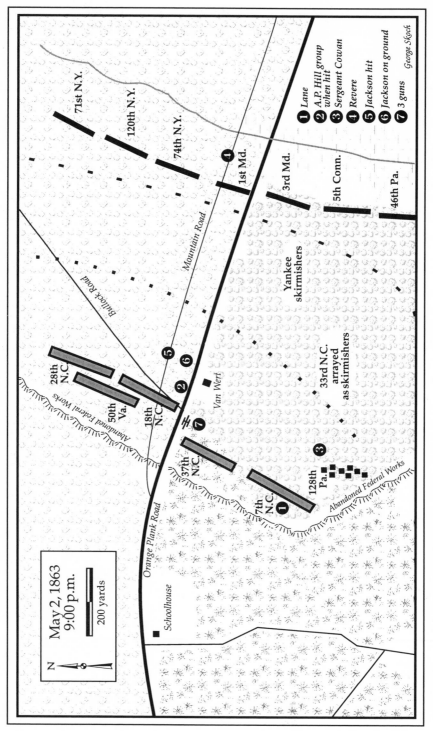

Area of Jackson's reconnaissance, night of May 2, 1863

May 2, 1863
9:00 p.m.

200 yards

N

Schoolhouse

Orange Plank Road

Abandoned Federal Works

7th N.C.

37th N.C.

128th Pa.

Abandoned Federal Works

18th N.C.

50th Va.

28th N.C.

Bullock Road

Van Wert

33rd N.C. arrayed as skirmishers

Mountain Road

1st Md.

71st N.Y.

120th N.Y.

74th N.Y.

3rd Md.

5th Conn.

46th Pa.

Yankee skirmishers

George Skoch

1 Lane
2 A.P. Hill group when hit
3 Sergeant Cowan
4 Revere
5 Jackson hit
6 Jackson on ground
7 3 guns

North Carolina. All of this occurred without the firing of a gun. Crude Federal works of earth and logs paralleled the brigade front, but Lane did not position his men behind that shelter; their mission was to attack, not defend. The 28th and 18th pushed a bit farther to the front on Lane's instructions, poised for the advance that Jackson had ordered. Lane then went to his right to bring the 37th and 7th into the same alignment. Once this was accomplished, the attack could begin.[5]

Three Confederate artillery pieces stood in the road near the middle of Lane's infantry array, each from a horse artillery battery. This mobile arm had served as Jackson's support from the outset of his attack. Four guns of the Lynchburg Beauregard Rifles, under Capt. Marcellus N. Moorman, had stood in the road two miles to the west when Jackson launched his assault. Moorman was at the front at dark with one of those guns, which was commanded by Lt. Robert P. Burwell. The other two belonged to McGregor's Battery and Breathed's Battery (under Lt. Philip P. Johnston). Maj. Robert F. Beckham was the ranking officer present. Jackson's artillery chief, Col. Stapleton Crutchfield, directed the horse artillery pieces to prepare to move to the rear to allow his more conventional batteries to take over.[6]

The most important job in the unfolding Confederate line belonged to the men of the 33rd North Carolina, far out front on the skirmish line. The regiment entered action 480 strong, about 20 percent above the average number of troops in a Confederate regiment at the time. The men of the 33rd recognized that they held "the post of danger, but it was also the post of honor." It became conventional to erroneously accuse Lane of causing Jackson's impending mishap by not sending out skirmishers. Capt. R. E. Wilbourn, whose account of riding alongside Jackson is the most important of the many sources on the event, set the tone: "This lamentable affair was caused by not having any skirmishers or pickets in front of our lines—a piece of negligence unexcusable." In truth, Wilbourn and Jackson never quite reached the well-established, well-situated, and well-instructed line of skirmishers. The 33rd's three field-grade officers spread out to control their unit—the colonel on the road and his two subordinates at the far flanks, all "within short range of the enemy's skirmishers." As the historian of the 7th, on the right of the main line, declared: "Everyone knew they were [there]." The historian of the 37th noted accurately that the 33rd fanned out across "the entire front of the brigade." Lane's line could not have been drawn better.[7]

The setting in which Lane built his line while Stonewall Jackson waited impatiently contrasted starkly with the violence of the afternoon. The front edge of the fluid battle zone was almost eerily calm. "The firing had ceased," Wilbourn wrote, "and all was quiet,—the enemy having in the darkness . . .

disappeared entirely from our sight." In the stillness, Yankee voices shouting commands echoed faintly through the woods from several hundred yards away, making "a great hum of human voices generally." An unsettling exception to the silence was "the mournful cry of the whippoorwill," General Lane recalled, "ringing in my ears from every direction." (The species still fills the Chancellorsville woods with its ominous calls today.) The sun had set at 6:49 P.M., but the moon would be full on May 3, so its brightness was near the peak. Even so, the dense undergrowth produced a darkness in which Lane could not read his watch.[8]

Stonewall Jackson rode restlessly in the rear of the forming brigade, impressing upon every ranking officer he met the importance of exploiting the advantage they had won. Near the schoolhouse he encountered General Rodes, who spiritedly asserted, "My Division behaved splendidly this evening." Jackson agreed and promised to say so in his official report. A bit closer to the front, Stonewall met A. P. Hill, to whom he spoke emphatically: "Press them, Gen. Hill; press them, and cut them off from the United States Ford." Jackson then encountered General Lane, who was calling for Hill in the darkness. Stonewall made clear to the brigadier that he wanted the night attack to go forward: "Push right ahead, Lane, right ahead!" Lane knew better than to solicit further details from his old Virginia Military Institute professor, so he continued to make preparations for the attack. In these encounters, Jackson used a "peculiar wave of the hand" to emphasize his intentions. Wilbourn described this ardent gesticulation as "characteristic of his determination and energy,—throwing forward his body and extending his hand beyond his horse's head, with as much force and earnestness as if he was trying to push forward the column with his hand." The lunge beyond his horse's head, a gesture enthusiastic enough to verge on the acrobatic, clearly conveyed to subordinate observers the general's customary intensity.[9]

Traditional reconstructions of Jackson's ride in front of his forming lines depict his party as accompanied by A. P. Hill, with their staff members intermixed. Both generals did ride to the front, surrounded by aides and couriers. The two men and their accompanying cavalcades were quite widely separated, however, and out of touch with each other. The confusion probably originated in the incontrovertible fact that Capt. James Keith Boswell, Stonewall's topographic engineer, rode next to Hill. This came about at the last minute when Jackson detailed Boswell to help Hill understand the ground. The corps commander had asked Hill how well he knew the road toward the United States Ford (Bullock Road). Even though he was a native of nearby Culpeper, Hill had been away for years on army duty and admitted, "I am entirely unacquainted with the topography of this country." Jackson "instantly replied: 'Capt. Boswell, report to Gen. Hill.'" To his division commander, Stonewall added the admonition: "Allow nothing to stop you; press on to the United States ford." Jackson then moved forward, leaving Boswell behind with Hill.[10]

Hill's gathering entourage, lagging well behind Jackson and his group, eventually numbered ten men. Hill rode on the Plank Road in the center of a three-man cluster, with Captain Boswell on his right and Maj. William H. Palmer on his left. Grouped slightly behind them were seven mounted men:

Capt. Conway Robinson Howard, engineer officer
Lt. Murray Forbes Taylor, aide-de-camp
Capt. Benjamin Watkins Leigh, aide-de-camp
James Fitzgerald Forbes, temporary volunteer aide
Sgt. George W. Tucker, chief courier
Pvt. Richard J. Muse, courier
Pvt. Eugene L. Saunders, courier

Hill's party did not follow Jackson's precise route, nor did it depart at once when Jackson disappeared into the shadowed woods astride his famous mount, Little Sorrel.[11]

Jackson's escort included almost precisely the same number of men as Hill's. The general's brother-in-law, Joseph G. Morrison, described the party as numbering "eight in all." A lieutenant in the 18th North Carolina confirmed the count when he estimated that the Jackson and Hill groups between them totaled "perhaps 20 horsemen"; the two lists given here total nineteen. If Morrison meant eight riders in addition to Jackson, the estimate matches precisely the known participants—all but one of them identified by some other member of the party rather than merely in an autobiographical account:

Capt. Richard Eggleston Wilbourn, signal corps
Capt. William Fitzhugh Randolph, 39th Virginia Cavalry Battalion, which
    supplied couriers
Lt. Joseph G. Morrison, aide-de-camp
William E. Cunliffe, signal corps enlisted man
W. T. Wynn, signal corps enlisted man
Pvt. David Joseph Kyle, 9th Virginia Cavalry
Pvt. Joshua O. Johns, 39th Virginia Cavalry
Pvt. Lloyd T. Smith, 39th Virginia Cavalry

Wilbourn rode at Jackson's left side, with Cunliffe and Wynn immediately behind them. The couriers formed into "columns of two" to extend the cavalcade.[12]

The most important member of Jackson's party for historical purposes was

Stonewall Jackson and staff (clockwise from top right): Robert L. Dabney, William Allan, Alexander S. Pendleton, Joseph G. Morrison, David B. Bridgeford, Henry Kyd Douglas, James Power Smith, Dr. Hunter Holmes McGuire, Jedediah Hotchkiss, and Wells Joseph Hawks. Only Morrison accompanied the general on his reconnaissance after dark on May 2, 1863. Courtesy of Stonewall Jackson Foundation, Lexington, Va.

the man with the least standing at the time—nineteen-year-old Pvt. David Kyle of the 9th Virginia Cavalry. In his admirable *Lee's Lieutenants*, Douglas Southall Freeman attributes special merit to Kyle's account because the veteran had, Freeman learned from a friend, hunted in the area and bought cattle nearby during the 1890s, making Kyle, after the fact, "entirely familiar with the terrain." What Freeman did not know was that David Kyle literally was serving as a scout and guide in his own backyard. He had lived before the war on the Bullock farm that gave the adjacent road its name. But for the dense thickets hugging the ground, Kyle could have seen his own back porch from the route of Jackson's cavalcade. In the smoke-streaked, flaming, chaotic Wilderness that night, David Kyle knew precisely where he was. No one else could have been certain of much.[13]

Private Kyle found himself guiding the legendary Stonewall Jackson around his home-cum-battlefield by a quirky circumstance. At about 3:00 P.M. Brig. Gen. William Henry Fitzhugh "Rooney" Lee, R. E. Lee's son and former commander of the 9th Virginia Cavalry, sent Kyle to deliver a dispatch to Maj. Gen. J. E. B. Stuart. Lee warned the courier that the main roads might be infested with Yankees, so Kyle detoured across country toward Parker's Store, then carefully wound his way northward. He passed Jackson's troops on the Brock Road, then struck out again on byways past Lacy's Mill to Ely's Ford. Kyle found Stuart near the gate to the Ely yard and delivered the dispatch. The general asked about Kyle's leisurely pace, and the young cavalryman explained about the necessarily circuitous route. Stuart asked how well Kyle knew the country. Thomas Frazer Chancellor, another local boy, happened to be standing nearby and piped up, "He knows every hog-path." With that reassurance, Stuart sent Kyle out at 6:30 P.M. with a message for Jackson enclosed in a large sealed envelope.

Kyle circled southwest, then southeast, to reach the intersection of the Orange Plank Road and the Orange Turnpike opposite Wilderness Church. Confused officers there told him he might find Jackson westward on the Plank Road. Within a half-mile, better-informed sources led the courier to retrace his steps. Kyle happened upon Rev. Melzi Chancellor, "a man whome I had known for some time and had confidence in." Chancellor lived at the southeast corner of the intersection and had just returned from guiding Jackson himself, having left the general "on the right hand side near Powells old field . . . the spot which I knew so well," Kyle recalled; he might have said the same about his familiarity with the rest of the scene toward which he now headed.

Just as Kyle neared the field, he saw several horsemen ride into the road and turn toward the front. He hurried to catch up and asked the hindmost where Jackson was. "There he is to the right in front," the aide answered. Kyle spurred forward, saluted the general, and handed over the large envelope. Jackson pulled up Little Sorrel, turned the horse's head to the right road edge, and read what Stuart had sent. As Kyle glanced around the familiar scenes of his youth, he noticed the Hazel Grove road nearby and the schoolhouse farther to the front; he also saw an unfamiliar sight—piles of dead horses in and around the road, the debris from a recent charge by the 8th Pennsylvania Cavalry. When Jackson finished reading, he tersely asked Kyle, "Do you know all of this country?" When the youngster answered positively, Jackson said simply, "Keep along with me," then rode eastward again.[14]

Jackson went forward, impelled by a hunger for information, as his conversations with subordinates make clear. He was, a Stonewall Brigade veteran commented, "always a great hand to wander about. . . . He had to see for himself." Hill followed fifty or more yards behind as a matter of military etiquette. He had been in the middle of the road, surrounded by mounted staff, when Jackson's group headed out. "As soon as . . . Hill saw Jackson ride in front of his lines," one of the former's aides wrote, "he felt it his duty, as a subordinate, to join him, and accordingly he also rode forward."[15]

Both of the regular staff members accompanying Jackson thought, almost certainly erroneously, that their chief was looking for the advanced Confederate skirmish line. They also presumed, undoubtedly in error, that the skirmish line was missing or misaligned. Under a narrow construction, it might be asserted that David Kyle was responsible for the death of Stonewall Jackson because it was Kyle's well-informed and skillful guidance that led the general on what would be a fatal route. Had the local boy not been present, Jackson almost surely would have reconnoitered carefully down the main road. Both Morrison and Wilbourn held this view. In fact, however, Kyle steered Jackson onto the far more appropriate corridor of the Mountain Road and pointed him eastward on that dark tunnel through the brush.[16]

Kyle rode quietly with the Jackson cavalcade beyond the schoolhouse he knew so well and around the curve in the road just east of that point. He noticed reserve infantry in ragged alignment, most of it facing away from the front. After a pause during which Jackson conversed with other officers (evidently the encounters with Lane and Hill), the group moved ahead to another forward infantry line. The men of this thin force responded to a query from Kyle by identifying themselves as members of the 55th Virginia and the 22nd Virginia Battalion, both of Brig. Gen. Henry Heth's brigade. Jackson veered to the left of the main road and halted, the junctions of the Bullock and Mountain roads with the Plank Road visible on either side. Kyle informed the general that one road went to the Bullock house (his home) and the other "ran sorter parallel with the plank road and came out on it about a half a mile below." Probably due to

Stonewall Jackson going forward on the Orange Plank Road in advance of his line of battle. Robert Underwood Johnson and Clarence Clough Buel, eds., Battles and Leaders of the Civil War, *4 vols. (New York: Century, 1887–88), 3:210*

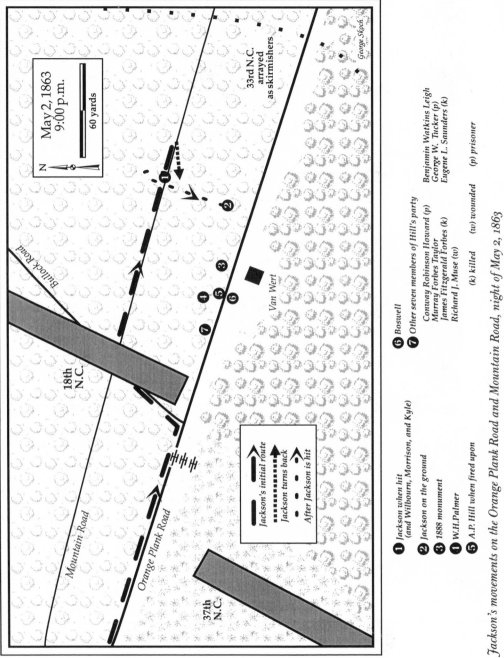

May 2, 1863 9:00 p.m.

60 yards

N

Bullock Road

Mountain Road

Orange Plank Road

18th N.C.

37th N.C.

33rd N.C. arrayed as skirmishers

Van Wert

George Skoch.

❶ *Jackson's initial route*
❷ *Jackson turns back*
❸ *After Jackson is hit*

❶ Jackson when hit (and Wilbourn, Morrison, and Kyle)
❷ Jackson on the ground
❸ 1888 monument
❹ W.H.Palmer
❺ A.P. Hill when fired upon

❻ Boswell
❼ Other seven members of Hill's party

Conway Robinson Howard (p)
Murray Forbes Taylor
James Fitzgerald Forbes (k)
Richard J. Muse (w)

Benjamin Watkins Leigh
George W. Tucker (p)
Eugene L. Saunders (k)

(k) killed   (w) wounded   (p) prisoner

Jackson's movements on the Orange Plank Road and Mountain Road, night of May 2, 1863 suspicion of the strange guide's credentials, Jackson curtly ordered Kyle to lead the way. The boy did so for about 200 yards; at that point the general, satisfied at last, caught up and kept abreast of him.[17]

There can be little doubt that Stonewall Jackson made his eastward ride on the Mountain Road and that he was shot near that corridor and not the main (Orange Plank) road. Whether he took the Mountain Road all the way from the main road, however, or instead went north on the southernmost leg of Bullock Road to reach the Mountain Road, is less certain. Kyle's own account may be interpreted either way, but it is more logical if taken to mean that Jackson took the Mountain Road entirely. Major Palmer's version refers to the Hazel Grove road as being part of the intersection Jackson used, which means that the Mountain Road, being appreciably farther west, must have been his initial route.[18]

The nineteenth-century historian Augustus C. Hamlin, though ardently polemical in northern outlook and primarily concerned with the Federal Eleventh Corps, devoted more careful attention to Jackson's foray than any other early student. Hamlin noted cogently that the cannon fire from Fairview that had recently swept the main road made it an undesirable avenue for reconnaissance. The slightly more northerly road missed that beaten zone and also took Jackson a bit closer to the sensitive enemy sector that interested him. Hamlin sensibly accepted Kyle's account as the best extant and also adduced testimony from two (unidentified) 18th North Carolina officers who "declared that Jackson did not pass by them but turned off to the left of their rear and passed out of view in the forest." Most of the road complex remained distinctly visible ("although long out of use") when Hamlin examined the scene in the 1890s. The Mountain Road maintained a parallel course, "sixty to eighty yards distant" from the Plank Road in the vicinity of Jackson's wounding. Its westernmost leg had disappeared, however, and for that incorrect reason Hamlin concluded (perhaps correctly) that Jackson rode up the beginning of the Bullock Road to reach the Mountain Road.[19]

Jackson and his eight companions continued east on the Mountain Road until nearly to the 33rd North Carolina skirmish line. There is no indication that the skirmishers saw Jackson or that his party saw them, but it seems likely that each knew something of the other's presence. From their advanced vantage point, the southerners listened intently to the sounds of enemy preparations. Ringing axes told of Federal pioneers frantically throwing obstacles in the way of a Confederate advance. Commands echoed distinctly through the woods. After questioning eyewitnesses and cross-checking accounts, Jackson's aide James Power Smith later concluded that Jackson actually "passed the swampy depression and began the ascent of the hill toward Chancellorsville"; an advance that far, however, is hardly credible. Kyle, who was present at the time and far more accurate than Smith, thought the enemy were 200–300 yards distant; he could hear them best from the vicinity of the Fairview clearing south of the main road. "It seemed that the officers were trying to form their men in line," Kyle recalled. In retrospect, the courier estimated that the quiet pause at the apogee of the advance lasted "from two to four minutes." Then Jackson reined Little Sorrel around and started to retrace his steps.[20]

Meanwhile the tactical situation west of the general, and especially southwest beyond the Plank Road, had shifted dangerously. Immediately after Jackson left him, Gen. James H. Lane hurried toward the right of his brigade to prepare it for the mandated advance. The chaos and uncertainty he encountered deflected him from that purpose. A swarm of Federals had by accident curled up between the outer skirmish line, manned by the 33rd North Carolina, and the 7th North Carolina, the regiment farthest to the right in Lane's main line. Most of the disoriented northerners belonged to the 128th Pennsylvania. That unit's Lt. Col. Levi H. Smith tried to unsnarl the confusion by waving a white handkerchief and asking troops in each direction whose cause they favored. The 7th North Carolina promptly corralled Smith, who naively claimed the immunity of a white flag—as though front-line reconnaissances could be executed without risk. "The simpleton imagined Gen. Lane would allow him to return," one Tar Heel chortled. Lt. James W. Emack of the 7th, with help from four subordinates, raked in fully 200 of Smith's regiment as prisoners. Carolinians gleefully harvesting trophy swords and muskets by the armful filled the woods on Lane's right.[21]

The confusion incumbent on the capture of so many enemy soldiers in unexpected proximity contributed to the events that followed. At this critical juncture, a Federal officer rode toward the far right of the 33rd's skirmishers, behind whom the Pennsylvanians' capture had just unfolded. The Federal probably was Brig. Gen. Joseph F. Knipe, until recently colonel of the 46th Pennsylvania. Knipe had approached his old regiment, rejected its intelligence about rebels nearby in front, "raved . . . in language more forcible than polite," and then dashed forward alone. "He did not go far, or stay long when he got there," the 46th's historian gloated, noting that Knipe lost his hat in his undignified scramble to escape.[22]

During his brief foray, Knipe, or a fellow officer in the vicinity, called out loudly for "General Williams," referring to Alpheus S. Williams of the Federal Twelfth Corps. Capt. Joseph A. Saunders, whose Company A of the 33rd North Carolina held down the far right of the skirmish line, meanwhile had gone with Lt. Col. Robert V. Cowan toward the Plank Road to check for further orders. Nineteen-year-old Sgt. Thomas A. Cowan was therefore left in charge opposite the inquisitive Yankee. Young Cowan challenged the Federal, who responded that he and his party were "friends." "To which side?" "To the Union." Cowan stepped back to his company and ordered them to fire toward the sounds. Men across an arc of hundreds of yards distinctly heard a single shot ring out, quickly picked up by the rest of Company A and then the remaining skirmishers in the area. The musketry became sharper and rolled northward in ever-heavier volume from both the picket line and the startled Confederates in the main line (who, of course, were firing toward the rear of their own skirmishers!).[23]

Stonewall Jackson had not ridden far on his return trip toward the lines of the 18th North Carolina when Sergeant Cowan's encounter triggered fire hundreds of yards away to the southwest. The deadly volleys scything through the Wilderness brush had nothing to do with Jackson, having been initiated far away in an unrelated episode. Despite the conventional wisdom about Jackson's wounding, no Confederate opened fire directly on the general's party by mistake. Cowan and his men were shooting at a real threat in a reasonable manner. The other Carolinians who volleyed into the darkness far to Cowan's north were firing at absolutely nothing at first. Then, when Jackson and Hill and their escorts stumbled noisily into the confused tableau, the Confederate line continued its fire toward the frightening specter of what seemed like approaching enemy troops.

Captain Wilbourn's memory of those frantic moments sifted through the complexities and focused on the simple facts. He recalled that the general had ridden eastward and that fire had suddenly burst from the Confederate line. Wilbourn remembered that Jackson turned toward the rear to avoid the fire that started far off near the 7th North Carolina. According to Wilbourn's account, Stonewall swerved north away from the initial firing at about the same time that he spun back toward the east. Two other contemporary witnesses not far from the scene echoed this simplistic construction of events.[24]

As the only man on the reconnaissance who knew where he was, David Kyle was able to track Jackson's movements with considerable precision. When the general had his fill of listening to Federal noise and started back whence he came, Kyle rode directly behind him. Within about seventy-five yards, however, four or five mounted men filtered into the gap between Kyle and Jackson and the youngster "sorter reigned my horse in a little" and kept pace about ten yards behind. As the party came opposite the Van Wert house, Stonewall turned Little Sorrel's head to the left and started to leave the Mountain Road, changing his direction from west to south. "Just as his horse[']s front feet had cleared the edge of the road whilste his hind feet was still on the edge of the bank," Kyle wrote, the widely heard single shot rang out far to the south. "In an instant it was taken up, and nearer there were five or six shots . . . and then suddenly a large volley, as if from a Regiment."[25] Sgt. Tom Cowan's shot at the inquisitive Yankee had unleashed a rolling barrage that inexorably spread toward Jackson's vicinity and quickly struck him down.

Stonewall Jackson's location vis-à-vis A. P. Hill's party is instructive in determining precisely where the general suffered his deadly wounds. Major Palmer estimated that he and Hill and Boswell were about sixty yards in front of the 18th North Carolina. Jackson was about sixty yards beyond Hill. Because Hill was at the edge of the Plank Road and Jackson was deeper in the woods on the Mountain Road, the sixty-yard gap between the two generals ran diagonally northeast rather than due east down the main road. Jackson's distance eastward from the 18th North Carolina, therefore, was a bit less than 100 yards. The next morning Murray Forbes Taylor drove A. P. Hill to the scene in an ambulance. The two men saw a cluster of familiar horses, dead in heaps where Hill's party had been struck the night before. Hill directed Taylor to proceed about 75–100 yards farther east, then stopped the ambulance and pointed out the place where he had found Jackson after he was wounded. This location was not, of course, the exact site where Stonewall had been hit, but it helps to confirm the considerable distance eastward from Hill's party to Jackson's.[26]

The monument erected in 1888 to commemorate Jackson's wounding was designed to mark the spot where he was tended, not where the volley struck him. Even for that event, the monument is located a bit too far west. Surgeon Benjamin P. Wright of the 55th Virginia went forward to aid Jackson when beckoned by A. P. Hill. He recalled going past "Van Worts Shop" for "about twenty steps further" before reaching the knot of worried Confederates "on the left of the road." Van Wert's house stood directly across the road from the 1888 monument, however.[27]

James Power Smith reached his chief just before the wounded general began the difficult trek rearward. Smith later participated in the erection of the crude 1887 marker and the final 1888 monument and concluded that Jackson actually was "a few rods . . . farther to the front than where the . . . monument now stand[s]." This view conforms precisely with Wright's recollection. At the time of the 1880s commemoration, dispute arose about whether the wounding site was along Plank Road or Mountain Road. One of the Talleys who farmed just west of Chancellorsville had marked a stump on the Mountain Road as the location, but that identification had vanished long ago without permanent record.[28]

David Kyle's account makes the Mountain Road the almost inarguable site of Jackson's wounding. A. C. Hamlin concluded aptly that the general's position when hit "was about 60 or 70 paces north of the plank road [from] where the monument now stands." If Hamlin had factored in a few more yards of easterly distance, he would have been exactly right. The Mountain Road trace that Hamlin examined in the 1890s survived into the 1920s, when a government survey team drew the trace about sixty yards north of the main road. The Mountain Road can no longer be discerned in the vicinity with any clarity because the National Park Service thoroughly destroyed the area by constructing a modern building and a parking lot in 1963 and a series of water and sewer treatment facilities in the 1970s. The location of the 1963 building, however, somehow ended up missing the best estimate of where Jackson was hit by a tiny margin; the site lies a few yards off its southeast corner and just below the southwest corner of the parking lot.[29]

Within moments after the fatal bullets sped through the Wilderness, men began to speculate on their origins with a mixture of guilt, concern, and abject curiosity. Lane's North Carolinians unquestionably fired most—and probably all—of the deadly rounds that decimated Hill's and Jackson's parties. The 18th North Carolina stood opposite both impact zones and received the most blame, no doubt correctly. The two bullets that shattered Stonewall Jackson's left arm disappeared after they accomplished their deadly harm, probably passing through the limb after impact or else falling out of the sleeve that was ripped open to tend the wounds. A third ball, however, remained in the general's right hand. When surgeon Hunter Holmes McGuire removed it, he found it to be "the round ball, (such as is used for the smooth-bore)."[30]

By May 1863, the well-supplied Federal armies had virtually eliminated the use of obsolete smoothbore muskets. Ordnance-poor Confederates did not enjoy that luxury. The dichotomy is useful for historical purposes—a round ball means Confederate origin. Ordnance returns taken not long before Chancellorsville, however, show that the 18th had only one-third as many smoothbores as the 28th to its left (in Jackson's general direction). The 37th North Carolina, just beyond the Plank Road, carried four times as many smoothbores as the 18th. A single muzzle delivered the single round ball that hit Jackson's right palm, of course, but the statistics raise the possibility that oblique fire from either side of the 18th must be considered. On the other hand, the colonel of the 28th was so little affected by the incident that his lengthy official report does not even mention the night of May 2. One North Carolina source placed the 50th Virginia Infantry to the left of the 18th North Carolina, but the 50th must have been a bit to the rear as well, judging from Lane's failure to mention it as he shook out his line.[31]

The view from the deadly end of the muzzles, as seen by Hill's detachment at very short range from the 18th, was unequivocal. Every survivor of the group attributed the fire to Lane's brigade and the 18th regiment. In Lane's words,

"Gen. Hill always told me that he thought . . . the 18th regiment" had hit Jackson. As Murray Forbes Taylor lay trapped under his horse, he heard Hill shouting at the 18th, "You have shot your friends. You have destroyed my staff." The general often discussed with Lieutenant Taylor what had happened: "He saw the troops fire; saw his staff destroyed," and the fire came from the 18th. Some of the troops also saw Hill under startling circumstances. A captain in the regiment recalled Hill's familiar figure dashing toward them, lit up by the flickering muzzle blasts.[32]

Jackson and his escort could see less well, having much more brush between them and the Carolinians, but they too harbored no doubts about the source of the gunfire. The general himself said, as if in bewilderment, "All my wounds are by my own men." When Wilbourn remarked that "they certainly must be our troops," he saw Jackson looking toward his lines "with apparent astonishment . . . as if at a loss to understand." Wilbourn noticed that the fire came from near ground level and presumed that the Tar Heels had been "stooping down or on their knees." Lieutenant Morrison, who soon dashed in among the troops, found them "all lying down . . . owing to the thick underbrush & the habit of the men to shelter themselves." No one with Jackson doubted that the fire came from the 18th North Carolina; Wilbourn even insisted, inaccurately, that "not a gun was fired by the enemy" during the uproar.[33]

The North Carolinians behind the guilty muskets also knew at once what they had done. An officer in the 18th wrote, "Our regiment was fully aware of the terrible mistake . . . within 10 minutes after it happened." The first shots from the 18th erupted inexorably as the fire swept up the line from the south. The troops continued to fire, however, due to uncertainty over who was thrashing about on horseback just to the regiment's front. That perceived threat came from Hill and his friends, not the more distant and probably invisible Jackson. Lt. Col. Forney George of the 18th summarized the matter succinctly: "General A. P. Hill and staff . . . rushed upon our line . . . when our men, thinking it was a cavalry charge from the enemy, fired several rounds at them." The effect of Hill's party was magnified when the 18th's own commander, Col. Thomas J. Purdie, dashed back on the Plank Road toward his regiment from a foray out front, shouting to the 18th to fix bayonets (which only 63 percent of the regiment had).[34]

The cavalry charge motif runs deep through most Carolinian accounts and understandably so, even if the original flurry of fire came as an instinctive extension of the volleys south of the Plank Road. The horsemen in the thick brush to the front could hardly be Confederate skirmishers since those friends were afoot. Hill's cavalcade's "appearance in the gloom . . . was well calculated to create the impression that the enemy's cavalry were advancing." "The rattle as if a squadron of horsemen was bearing down . . . at a rapid speed," an intelligent officer remembered, left as "the only reasonable conclusion . . . that it was a cavalry charge." Maj. John Decatur Barry, whose direct orders to fire made him most responsible, told General Lane that he heard the skirmish fire and then horsemen and presumed that enemy riders had penetrated the 33rd North Carolina's screen. Dozens of men cried "cavalry charge!" The recent surprising—to both sides—eruption of the 8th Pennsylvania Cavalry into the midst of Jackson's corps nearby probably contributed to the mindset.[35]

Honest but confused Carolinians had to confess uncertainty about the circumstances in the smoking woods. One soldier admitted, "I do not know whether I fired or not so great was the excitement." None could say with even remote certainty where his missiles went. Some veterans refused for years to talk about the event, eventually confessing late in life, even on their deathbeds, that they had harbored guilty worries. Members of the 33rd, far to the front and between two fires, faced the most difficult situation. The fire into their backs from Lane's main line forced them forward into the Yankees, who, of course, fired on them as well. The regiment lost a number of men who became Federal prisoners in the melee, and its lieutenant colonel fell hard hit.[36]

Some grieving Confederates inevitably placed the blame for Stonewall's loss on the 18th North Carolina and the aggressive Major Barry. One Second Corps staff officer stated bluntly in an official report written the day before Jackson's death: "General Lane got scared, fired into our own men, and achieved the unenviable reputation of wounding severely . . . Jackson." A Virginia artillery captain whose guns were threatened by the ill-conceived fire also derided Barry's behavior and reasoning. Near the turn of the century, a historian wrote that Lane's "whole brigade has been blended in the severe denunciations hurled upon them in this unfortunate affair." General Lane wrote with pride of A. P. Hill's reaction: "In all my intercourse with [Hill] I never heard him . . . censure the 18th." Lane defended Barry as "one of those fearless, dashing officers who was especially cool under fire."[37]

James H. Lane remained a brigadier general for the rest of the war, despite apparently successful performances in all of the army's major battles. Even when untried youngsters pushed into brigade command and Lee faced a desperate shortage of leadership, Lane stayed in his 1862 rank as one of the senior brigadiers in Confederate service. It is impossible to attribute his stagnation to stigmata accumulated on May 2, 1863; but it is equally impossible to ignore the possibility. No one could blame Lane in person for what happened, but the odor of the catastrophe remained in southern nostrils as events made Jackson's absence loom ever more dire.

Major Barry certainly suffered no retardation of advancement, moving upward through three ranks to brigadier general in just more than a year after Chancellorsville. Even so, family lore holds that Barry carried Jackson's fate on his soul and ended the war a heartbroken man. That tradition suggests that Barry succumbed to melancholia when he died in 1867 at the age of twenty-seven, less than two years after the war's end.[38]

Given Stonewall Jackson's immense fame, it is hardly surprising that a wide range of Federals sought credit for having fired the fatal bullets. Some of them are ingenuous and credible, though errant; others are palpable hoaxes of varying caliber. One of many apt rejections of the notion of Federal responsibility came from a Confederate surgeon close to the front who saw the muzzle flashes of the fatal volleys. "Our men jumped up and seized their arms," he recalled, but the regimental commander steadied them by saying logically: "Those are our men firing, you did not hear any bullets pass our way." Among the reasonably modulated, but mistaken, Federal claims are those from the 46th Pennsylvania, 124th New York, 20th Massachusetts, and 1st Massachusetts.[39]

The most widely repeated Federal claim is also the most ludicrous. Gen. Joseph W. Revere, a grandson of the 1775 horseman, concocted soon after the war a fantastic fable worthy of Baron von Münchhausen. Revere insisted that in the spring of 1852 he had met Maj. Thomas J. Jackson on a Mississippi riverboat. The major, suddenly both irreligious and garrulous for the only time in his adult life, forced upon Revere his notions of astrology. Sometime later, Jackson the star gazer forwarded an elaborate chart showing that Saturn, Mars, and Jupiter would be aligned in a manner "quite dangerous and malign" in the first days of (mirabile dictu) May 1863. "It is clear to me," Jackson supposedly told Revere, "that we shall both be exposed to a common danger at the time indicated."

The northern general was positioned opposite the Second Corps on the night of May 2. He claimed to have ridden upon a knot of shadowy figures tending a wounded officer—Stonewall Jackson, of course. Most of Revere's fable is susceptible to thorough debunking from available documents. The notion of a mysterious "dark rider" observing through the bushes, however, got a boost from an early Jackson biography that recorded such an event with eager relish. The "silent personage," his identity "left to conjecture" by the biographer—reminiscent of der grau Fremde of Mozart's last days—appealed to mid-nineteenth-century tastes. In consequence, Revere's chimerical nonsense received wide play.[40]

More than a few Confederates also launched whoppers about Jackson's death, some of them genuinely convinced in their dotage that fading memories placed them in the spotlight. Others employed uncomplicated lying. A long-time colleague of evangelist Dwight L. Moody announced in 1914 that he had shot Stonewall by accident (then supported the wounded hero's head on an overcoat from his pack—"the same one that Gen McPherson had died on at Atlanta"). A member of the distant 1st Louisiana admitted late in life that he really fired the shot. A Virginia officer announced that he drove Jackson's ambulance to the rear—well before sundown on May 2! A kinswoman of the general's widow spun a delicious tale, tongue firmly in cheek, about Jackson's escape and reappearance at his wife's door in 1888 (she sequestered the prodigal in a closet and supplied him with Gideon Bibles and lemons). The most outlandish of the fables depicts Jackson changing places with a Yankee, going west to become prominent as the scout "California Joe," and dying under the guns of Swiss assassins hired by a thorough and vengeful U. S. Grant in 1876.[41]

None of these digressions from the truth has any intrinsic historical significance. Taken together, however, they and many others like them illustrate anew the tremendous stature of Jackson. Such figures, grown immeasurably larger than life, always attract quaintly American nonsense. The Jackson of legend looms as large on the nation's historical landscape as any figure of any era and therefore inevitably receives his share of the foolishness.

Three balls hit Jackson, even though he was among the farthest from the offending muskets of any of the nineteen Confederates in the two scouting parties. A. P. Hill's detachment, much closer and less screened by woods, suffered dreadfully. The general himself, unlike his nine companions, responded to an instinctive voice and "lay down on his face in the road" rather than dashing into the woods. That reaction saved him. Just to his right, Captain Boswell instantly fell dead, two bullets (rifled, not smoothbore) through his heart. Two men in Jackson's party saw Boswell's famous black stallion dash toward the enemy, loose chain halter rattling furiously, and rightly feared the worst for their comrade.[42]

Major Palmer's horse was killed and his shoulder was broken in the melee. Capt. Conway R. Howard's horse took a bullet, panicked, and carried his helpless rider through most of the Federal army to the Chancellorsville clearing; along the way, fire that was poured at him cut away the reins and the stirrups but left Howard untouched, albeit a prisoner. Sgt. George W. Tucker underwent an almost identical ordeal and found himself being interrogated by General Hooker's staff at Chancellorsville Inn. Bullets killed courier Eugene L. Saunders, hit courier Richard J. Muse in the face twice (he survived), and killed Muse's horse. James F. Forbes was mortally wounded and died during the night at Melzi Chancellor's house. The only two staff members not killed, injured, or captured were Benjamin Watkins Leigh and Murray Forbes Taylor, each of whose horses were killed. Only A. P. Hill among his ten-man party escaped unscathed together with his mount. Hill was trying to pry the helpless Lieutenant Taylor out from under his horse, dead from five bullet wounds, when word came that Jackson lay wounded to the front. "Help yourself," Hill muttered to Taylor, "I must go to Gen. Jackson."[43]

Jackson's party suffered less drastically than Hill's, at least in quantity, as would be expected because of its distance from the flashpoint. Bullets killed signal corps courier William E. Cunliffe and wounded courier Joshua O. Johns. The latter's horse carried him into enemy hands to join Tucker and Howard. Morrison's and courier Lloyd T. Smith's horses were killed, but seven animals escaped harm. Jackson's other four companions—Wilbourn, Randolph, Wynn, and Kyle—remained untouched, man and horse. Wilbourn correctly attributed the escape of most of the party to "the thickness of the woods [which] afforded some shield." To that physical factor Wilbourn insistently appended his conviction that "nothing but the gracious interposition of divine Providence saved any of us . . . [or] none of the party would have survived to give an account of this melancholy event." A less relentlessly devout mind would have wondered whether Providence cared—or whether it had perhaps rejected Thomas Jackson as a ward. Six of the nine men in the group were untouched by bullets. Since five bullets found their mark in the nine-man cavalcade, Jackson's odds of being hit at all were only 1 in 2. For three of the five bullets to hit one man—the devout and invaluable Jackson—defied the odds by a staggering ratio and surely must have prompted even hardened pietistic zealots to reconsider some dearly held tenets.[44]

By the time A. P. Hill reached Stonewall, aides had lifted their stricken chief from his horse and begun initial treatment of his wounds. The general suffered from four injuries—three bullet wounds and a scratched face. The scratches, ugly but inconsequential in the struggle for life that lay ahead, came from a post oak on the southern side of the Mountain Road with a limb that extended northward to the road's edge. Little Sorrel had wheeled violently away from the muzzle blasts along the 18th North Carolina's line and passed under the limb, which had "come near pulling" the wounded rider out of the saddle. Wilbourn's horse followed with like results. Both men lost their hats but managed to stay mounted. Jackson somehow caught the bridle in his right hand, which was mangled by a bullet, and by agonizing exertion turned the animal back toward the Confederate line. He was unable to stop Little Sorrel completely. Jackson's "terribly" lacerated face would be repaired hours later with isinglass.[45]

One of the three bullets that hit Jackson tore through the inside of his right palm, that arm having been raised either to shield his face from the brush, in instinctive reaction to the fire, or in a typical gesture of prayerful supplication. A soldier in Pender's brigade found Jackson's gloves the next day (with "T. J. JACKSON, Virginia . . . printed neatly on the wrist of each") and eventually sent them to the general's widow. Mary Anna Jackson kept them as "a harrowing relic indeed, but . . . I could not bear that *anyone else* should have them." The right gauntlet showed an entry wound "just above the base of the thumb." The missile broke two fingers and caused enough damage to fill the glove with blood by the time A. P. Hill gently pulled it from Jackson's hand. The projectile, a round ball and therefore surely Confederate ammunition, lodged just under the skin on the back of the general's hand. Mary Anna Jackson retained the round ball as another terrible memento. "It almost breaks my heart to look at it," she told a friend that July.[46]

The other two bullets did far more damage. Both hit Jackson's left arm. Each caused enough destruction to warrant amputation of the arm according to the current surgical practices. The forearm wound, however, actually escaped attention for hours because a more serious wound near the shoulder made the lower extremity numb. Surgeon McGuire, who performed the amputation, described the lower ball as "having entered the outside of the forearm, an inch below the elbow [and] came out upon the opposite side, just above the wrist." In an earlier account, McGuire placed the exit wound "through the palm of the hand," but the hole in the left glove was "on the wrist, near the top." The rain slicker that was Jackson's outer garment survives and shows a bullet hole low on the forearm, apparently the lower entry point. No visible exit hole for the wound exists high on the left arm, but there are ample alternative explanations for that fact.[47]

Jackson suffered most from the bullet that shattered his upper left arm. It struck, McGuire wrote, "about three inches below the shoulder-joint, the ball dividing the main artery, and fracturing the bone." The bullet-torn slicker bears a hole precisely three inches down the sleeve, and Jackson's arm certainly was fractured. McGuire may have been mistaken in his presumption that the ball severed the main artery, however, in light of evidence explained below.[48]

Captain Wilbourn and General Hill performed most of the first aid that Jackson received while still beyond the Confederate front line. Getting Jackson dismounted had been difficult for both the general and Wilbourn, one of whose arms was essentially useless because of an old wound not yet fully healed. Fortunately Jackson had fallen against his aide's good side as he collapsed off of Little Sorrel's back. Soon thereafter, A. P. Hill had arrived. Hill's expressions of sorrow have often been represented as a sort of deathbed rapprochement with Jackson, the generals having been starkly at odds for many months theretofore. In fact, recently uncovered evidence shows that the two men had somehow worked their way to good terms by the eve of the Chancellorsville campaign.[49]

Between them, Hill and Wilbourn ripped open the layers of sleeves conceal-

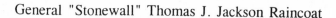

General "Stonewall" Thomas J. Jackson Raincoat

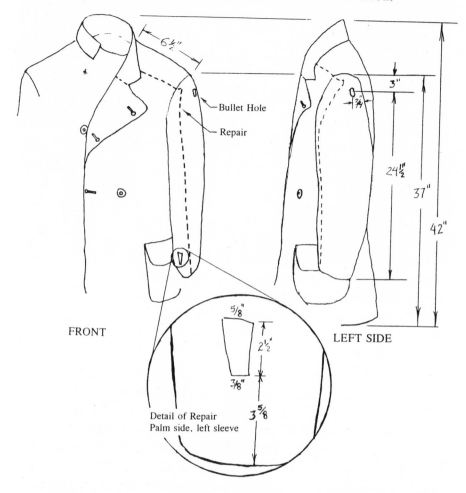

FRONT

LEFT SIDE

Detail of Repair
Palm side, left sleeve

Diagram indicating location of bullet hole in the raincoat Jackson wore on the night of May 2, 1863 (sketch by Keith E. Gibson). Virginia Military Institute Museum Collection

ing Jackson's damaged arm, pulled off his blood-filled gauntlets, and applied primitive bandages. They tied handkerchiefs above and below the upper-arm wound and fashioned a third handkerchief into a sling. Although Jackson had of course bled considerably from his torn and broken arm, it seems likely that the artery had not yet ruptured. Wilbourn wrote not long after the event that the wound "had apparently ceased bleeding and we indulged the hope that the artery was not cut." When surgeon Benjamin P. Wright of the 55th Virginia reached the general and examined the arm, he found that the ersatz bandaging had already been done and noted that "the hemorrhage had been slight." A

"You must hold your ground, General Pender; you must hold your ground, sir!" This early engraving correctly depicts Jackson (third from left) walking with assistance shortly after his wounding. Sarah Nicholas Randolph, The Life of Gen. Thomas J. Jackson ("Stonewall" Jackson) *(Philadelphia: J. B. Lippincott, 1876), 322*

tourniquet soon arrived and Hill suggested that Wright put it on Jackson, but the lack of bleeding seemed to make the appliance superfluous.[50]

Surviving physical evidence supports the notion that Stonewall Jackson's bleeding had been controlled and was therefore presumably only venous. The general's daughter gave one of the handkerchiefs that had bound the wound to the Virginia Military Institute after the war. Too small to have been the sling, it must have been used to bandage the wound, yet the linen material is blood-spotted rather than drenched or heavily stained. No more than 10 percent of the material is affected.[51]

More than a dozen officers and men tended Stonewall Jackson as his aides moved him in agonizing stages toward the rear. The journey proceeded by mixed means, all of them interdicted by savage artillery fire. He was carried awkwardly by three aides, who took laborious steps while supporting him, and transported in three or four spells on a litter. Most of the men who took part in this phase of what would become the Confederacy's Passion Play left accounts of their involvement—some confused or exaggerated but most reasonably reliable. That halting hegira, leading inexorably toward an amputation table, lies beyond the scope of this essay about the fatal volley. Two painful falls along the route, however, must be examined in order to weigh the impact of the volley.

Jackson fell from the litter a first time when an enlisted man bearing the front left corner was shot down with serious wounds to both arms. Pvt. John James Johnson, Company H, 22nd Virginia Battalion, lost his right arm at the shoulder socket and his left arm was "so completely paralysed as to be useless." A contemporary source reported that the litter bearers had been carrying Jackson at shoulder height, and Joe Morrison estimated that "the General fell about 3 feet." With jagged bone ends adjacent to the delicate surface of the artery, a consequence of the fall must have been tearing of the vessel and resultant profuse bleeding. The party at the time had been cutting "obliquely across the . . . Plank road for the road that led to stoney ford . . . which is about two hundred yards from where he was put on the litter."[52]

Everyone agreed that this first fall caused Jackson incredible suffering. His brother-in-law Joe Morrison marveled that the general "did not even groan," but others heard Jackson moan "frequently and piteously." One account, late and with hearsay ancestry, declared that the general's left arm landed squarely on a roadside stump.[53] Since Jackson apparently fell from near shoulder height, and certainly must have been lying face up on the litter, the sudden collapse of the left front corner of the litter would have put his right shoulder at immediate risk. From that height, however, and considering the credible reports of the damage and suffering inflicted on the battered arm, it is evident that the fall spun Jackson in an arc that landed his excruciatingly painful left side on the ground.

A second fall from the litter ensured the final destruction of Jackson's left arm. Three enlisted men and one officer carried the general through dense woods just south of the Plank Road, the officer supporting the front right corner. One of the soldiers "got his foot entangled in a grape vine and fell," Maj. Benjamin Watkins Leigh recalled, "letting General Jackson fall on his broken arm. . . . He must have suffered agonies." Leigh reported that this fall elicited the first audible indication of suffering from Jackson, but Morrison considered it "very light" in contrast with the first fall. A North Carolinian helping with the litter attributed the stumble to tripping over one of the bodies of Confederates strewn thickly throughout the woods. Whatever the obstacle that caused the second drop, the consequences of the two incidents were damaging and perhaps fatal.[54]

The solid evidence from multiple sources that Jackson's arm was not bleeding at all when his trip to the rear began suggests that the artery remained intact at that point. When the general reached McGuire after the two falls, however, he had "lost a large amount of blood . . . and would have bled to death, but a tourniquet was immediately applied. For two hours he was nearly pulseless." Jackson calmly informed McGuire, "I fear I am dying." In sharp contrast to his normal habits, the suffering man asked repeatedly and urgently for spirits. McGuire found his patient's "skin clammy, his face pale, and his lips compressed and bloodless . . . and the thin lips so tightly compressed that the impression of his teeth could be seen through them."[55]

Pneumonia killed Stonewall Jackson on May 10. The fatal malady's etiology likely lay in an upper-respiratory infection that predated the wounds. Jackson's severe hurts, of course, impaired his body's ability to fight its battle against pneumonia, which almost certainly would not have developed, or at least not proved fatal, without the injuries. Was the trauma from the bullets' impact or the nearly fatal loss of blood from the subsequent litter accidents the decisive blow? Although the answer to this question can only be speculated, it is difficult to avoid the conclusion that the arterial bleeding constituted the greatest problem; the two falls therefore must be considered the fatal events. Jackson felt certain that he was dying at the time. Ten days after his death, a Virginia newspaper wrote that Jackson "himself attributed [the pneumonia] to the fall from the litter." The word throughout the army was that McGuire felt similarly, having commented "that the Genl's death was caused by the fall which he got when being carried off of the field . . . injuring the Gen's side so severely that he caught cold in it, and consequently could not get over so many diseases."[56]

The effect of Jackson's demise is incalculable, falling as it does into the realm of hypothesis. That it would affect Confederate morale immediately and harshly was so evident to all concerned that they made strenuous—but unavailing—efforts to conceal the fact of the wounding. As more than one contemporary noted, "In a very short time everybody knew it." Maj. W. G. Morris of the 37th North Carolina had rolled into a roadside ditch to nurse a wounded foot when Jackson's litter party halted within a few feet of him. Morris until then had been "feeling cheerfull and comparatively happy" despite his pain. "You cant imagine what a change the thought of . . . Jackson being wounded made in my feelings," he wrote years later.[57]

Confederates yearned in vain for Stonewall's recovery, sensing the impact his absence would have. Not a few northerners greeted the general's death with mixed feelings. Gen. Gouverneur K. Warren, soon to be a great northern hero at Gettysburg, wrote: "I rejoice at Stonewall Jackson's death as a gain to our cause, and yet in my soldier's heart I cannot but see him the best soldier of all this war, and grieve at his untimely end." An observant Englishman admitted that the dead leader "was not a great strategist" but marveled at Jackson's capacity for "triumphing over difficulties which stood in his way with a facility unknown to any other General." Because Jackson was the most famous American in Europe, his death made stunning headline news there.[58]

Southern patriots of pious bent filled their letters during May and June 1863 with resigned declarations about God's will and his obvious intention to raise up another Jackson to defend the cause. Such eager expectations constituted a classic case of whistling in the cemetery—the Lexington Cemetery, in this instance. Less naive soldiers, facing combat that now seemed more dangerous and less likely to succeed in the absence of their indomitable leader, sadly accepted the probability that their side had lost an irreplaceable asset. A member of the 26th Georgia wrote dolefully on May 15 that "all hopes of Peace and Independence had forever vanished." Two members of Lane's brigade reacted in a similar vein. Wesley Lewis Battle of the 37th North Carolina declared, "I don't think his place can ever be filled." Ross Marcius Gaston of the 28th North Carolina, in a postwar reminiscence, reflected: "We never got over Jackson's death, for all the men lost all hopes of success after he was gone." Joshua Howell of the 47th Alabama minced no words in describing the prospects to his wife in a letter dated May 14: "Stonewall Jackson was kild. . . . I think this will have a gradeal to due with this war. I think the north will whip us soon."[59] And so it came to pass, perhaps in some degree as the result of self-fulfilling prophecies like Howell's but primarily because Stonewall Jackson was no more.

A tangled skein of tactical developments led a teenaged sergeant to order a shot against a lost Yankee in the woods near Chancellorsville that dark night of May 2, 1863. The spark inevitably flared into fire from nearby lines. The firing spread northward, instinctive and unreasoning. It eventually resulted in the discharge of several hundred musket balls and rifled bullets eastward from the front of the 18th North Carolina toward the backs of friendly skirmishers—and through A. P. Hill's and Thomas J. Jackson's parties in the intervening ground. Most of the several dozen projectiles spinning toward Stonewall's precise location buried themselves in, or were deflected by, the dense growth that crowded the fire zone. The five that tore human flesh in Jackson's group were fiendishly effective. Six of Jackson's eight escorts escaped untouched. The relatively immense target that the general bestrode, Little Sorrel, remained unhit. As though vectored specially toward Jackson, three bullets missed every impediment and every other target, dodged precipitous laws of averages, and mortally wounded Lee's right arm. Nothing could have done more harm to the Army of Northern Virginia and to the nascent nation for which that army was the sturdiest underpinning.

NOTES

1. Richard W. Freeman, "Stonewall Jackson's Death," *Sunny South* (Atlanta), December 19, 1896; Van Valentine Richardson, "The Death of Stonewall Jackson," Fayetteville (N.C.) *Observer*, February 20, 1884. Freeman was a sergeant in the 44th Georgia who became regimental adjutant in 1863. Captain Richardson commanded Company C of the 18th North Carolina.

2. W. G. Morris (major and later lieutenant colonel of the 37th North Carolina) to James H. Lane, January 3, 1895, folder 113, and James H. Lane to A. C. Hamlin, [1892], James H. Lane Papers, Ralph Brown Draughon Library, Auburn University, Auburn, Ala. (repository hereafter cited as AU); U.S. War Department, *The War of the Rebellion: A Compilation of the Official Records of the Union and Confederate Armies*, 127 vols., index, and atlas (Washington, D.C.: GPO, 1880–1901), 25(1):916 (hereafter cited as *OR*; all references are to series 1). Of Hill's six brigades, only those commanded by Henry Heth and W. Dorsey Pender initially formed into line. E. L. Thomas's and J. J. Archer's brigades had turned around to protect the column's rear and remained far from the attack zone. Lane's and Samuel McGowan's brigades followed the assault while still in column. The road was a commercial highway of early 1850s vintage, the Orange Plank Road, on the same right-of-way at this point as the century-old Orange Turnpike. Elsewhere on both the Chancellorsville and Wilderness battlefields, the two roads took divergent paths and would play important separate roles.

3. W. G. Morris to James H. Lane, January 3, 1895, and James H. Lane to A. C. Hamlin, [1892], Lane Papers, AU; Octavius A. Wiggins speech on Chancellorsville, 1895, box 75, folder 1, Military Collection, North Carolina Department of Archives and History, Raleigh, N.C. (repository hereafter cited as NCDAH).

4. James H. Lane, "The Death of Stonewall Jackson," Fayetteville (N.C.) *Observer*, January 23, 1884; William Fitzhugh Randolph, *With Stonewall Jackson at Chancellorsville* (n.p., n.d.), 7–8; Mary Anna Jackson, *Memoirs of Stonewall Jackson by his Widow, Mary Anna Jackson* (Louisville, Ky.: Prentice, 1895), 545–46; James H. Lane to A. C. Hamlin, [1892], Lane Papers, AU. Randolph was a captain in the 39th Virginia Cavalry Battalion and played a role in the deadly drama about to unfold. His turn-of-the-century pamphlet on the affair is full of anomalies and even outright errors, but some of the color warrants its use.

5. Walter Clark, ed., *Histories of the Several Regiments and Battalions from North Carolina in the Great War, 1861–'65*, 5 vols. (Raleigh, N.C.: E. M. Uzzell, 1901), 1:376, 2:659; *OR* 25(1):916, 920.

6. William H. Palmer, "Another Account of It," *Confederate Veteran* 13 (May 1905): 232–33; John J. Shoemaker, *Shoemaker's Battery, Stuart Horse Artillery, Pelham's Battalion, Afterwards Commanded by Col. R. P. Chew, Army of Northern Virginia* (Memphis, Tenn.: S. C. Toof, 1908), 34; Marcellus N. Moorman, "Narrative of Events and Observations Connected with the Wounding of General T. J. (Stonewall) Jackson," in *Southern Historical Society Papers*, ed. J. William Jones and others, 52 vols. (Richmond: Southern Historical Society, 1876–1959), 30:111–13 (hereafter cited as *SHSP*). Shoemaker described the officer commanding the piece as "Lt. Birl," which after some deciphering in official records was identified as "Burwell" rendered with a Virginian accent. Moorman's intermittently useful account is marred by his egocentric view, which includes the assumption that all three pieces belonged to his battery and ignores the presence of his superior, Major Beckham.

7. Clark, *Histories of the Several Regiments and Battalions from North Carolina*, 1:376, 2:559, 659; R. E. Wilbourn to R. L. Dabney, December 12, 1863, Charles William Dabney Papers, Southern Historical Collection, Wilson Library, University of North Carolina, Chapel Hill, N.C. (repository hereafter cited as SHC); *OR* 25(1):922.

8. R. E. Wilbourn to R. L. Dabney, December 12, 1863, Charles William Dabney Papers, SHC; *OR* 25(1):1010; Lane, "Death of Stonewall Jackson"; Randolph, *With Stonewall Jackson*, 7; James H. Lane to A. C. Hamlin, [1892], Lane Papers, AU; James Power Smith, "Stonewall Jackson's Last Battle," in *Battles and Leaders of the Civil War*, ed. Robert

Underwood Johnson and Clarence Clough Buel, 4 vols. (New York: Century, 1887–88), 3:209; "Who Fired the Bullet That Killed Gen. Stonewall Jackson?," *Rockbridge County News*, January 12, 1951 (quoting 1901 Memphis paper); *Richardson's Virginia & North Carolina Almanac* (Richmond: J. W. Randolph, [1862]).

9. David J. Kyle, "Jackson's Guide When Shot," *Confederate Veteran* 4 (September 1896): 308–9; R. E. Wilbourn to R. L. Dabney, December 12, 1863, Charles William Dabney Papers, SHC; Palmer, "Another Account," 232; Murray Forbes Taylor, "Stonewall Jackson's Death," *Confederate Veteran* 12 (October 1904): 493; Mary Anna Jackson, *Memoirs*, 547; Lane, "Death of Stonewall Jackson"; James H. Lane to A. C. Hamlin, [1892], Lane Papers, AU; "Stonewall Jackson!," Richmond *Dispatch*, October 26, 1875. The latter source includes accounts by several officers, including one of many by Dr. H. H. McGuire. The most important account is a detailed narrative by an anonymous staff member under A. P. Hill. The Murray Forbes Taylor account also appeared in substantially the same form in the Fredericksburg *Journal*, October 22, 1904. The original typescript of Taylor's account, in the author's possession, includes some material excluded from the *Confederate Veteran* version.

10. Palmer, "Another Account," 232; Murray Forbes Taylor, "Stonewall Jackson's Death," 493; anonymous Hill staff member, in "Stonewall Jackson!," Richmond *Dispatch*, October 26, 1875. In R. E. Wilbourn to Jubal A. Early, March 3, 1873, vol. 6, Jubal A. Early Papers, Library of Congress, Washington, D.C. (repository hereafter cited as LC), Wilbourn also specified a gap of "fifty or sixty yds." between Hill and Jackson.

11. R. E. Wilbourn to R. L. Dabney, December 12, 1863, Charles William Dabney Papers, SHC; Palmer, "Another Account," 232; James H. Lane to A. C. Hamlin, [1892], Lane Papers, AU; Robert K. Krick, *9th Virginia Cavalry* (Lynchburg, Va.: H. E. Howard, 1988), 72; Richard O'Sullivan, *55th Virginia Infantry* (Lynchburg, Va.: H. E. Howard, 1989), 142, 149; Mary Anna Jackson, *Memoirs*, 427.

12. J. G. Morrison to Jubal A. Early, February 20, 1879, vol. 10, Early Papers, LC; Alfred H. H. Tolar, "Stonewall Jackson," Wilmington (N.C.) *Daily Review*, December 15, 1883; R. E. Wilbourn to R. L. Dabney, December 12, 1863, Charles William Dabney Papers, SHC; Randolph, *With Stonewall Jackson*, 8; R. E. Wilbourn to Jubal A. Early, February 12, 1873, in Jubal A. Early, *Lieutenant General Jubal Anderson Early, C.S.A.: Autobiographical Sketch and Narrative of the War Between the States* (Philadelphia: J. B. Lippincott, 1912), 214. The only person claiming to have been a member of the cavalcade not identified by someone else was Lloyd T. Smith, a seventeen-year-old member of the 39th Virginia Cavalry Battalion. Smith's claim is in Philip A. Bruce, ed., *History of Virginia*, 6 vols. (Chicago: American Historical Society, 1924), 5:286. Smith's story seems to be valid. He made no extravagant claims of positioning at center stage, and his unit unquestionably supplied the couriers. An important anonymous account in *Land We Love* 1 (July 1866): 179–82 has previously been attributed to Joe Morrison because internal evidence suggests his authorship and the periodical was edited by his brother-in-law, D. H. Hill. Morrison in his letter to Jubal A. Early, February 20, 1879, vol. 10, Early Papers, LC, however, states: "I have never written anything connected with [Jackson's wounding] for the press or contributed my testimony to the establishment of truth." This apparently emphatic declaration by Morrison, thirteen years after the *Land We Love* article appeared, seems to abolish earlier assumptions. Morrison remains a possible author of the 1866 article, however, if his 1879 pronouncement is viewed as having a central caveat about "for the press. . . ." For present purposes, note that the article wrongly identifies Boswell as with the group but mentions Wilbourn, Morrison, and "five or six couriers," further validating the eight-man register of participants listed in the text.

13. Krick, *9th Virginia Cavalry*, 84, 123; Douglas Southall Freeman, *Lee's Lieutenants: A Study in Command*, 3 vols. (New York: Charles Scribner's Sons, 1942–44), 2:563n; U.S. Eighth Census, 1860, Schedule 1, "Free Inhabitants, Spotsylvania County, Virginia," p. 72, M653, National Archives, Washington, D.C. (repository hereafter cited as NA). The 1860 census showed Kyle as a native of Maryland, age sixteen (he was born on December 17, 1843). Catharine Bullock, age eighteen, was the only other member of the household born in Maryland. She and Oscar Bullock, age thirty-five, already had two children. David evidently was living with his sister and brother-in-law.

14. The preceding account is based entirely on Kyle's own recollection of the afternoon and evening. Kyle's invaluable narrative in *Confederate Veteran* ("Jackson's Guide") includes some of these details but not nearly as many as the ten-page penciled original, in the possession of Steve R. Jones of Oxford, N.C., which runs fully one-third longer than the edited (and somewhat revised) published version. A typescript is at the Fredericksburg and Spotsylvania National Military Park Library, Fredericksburg, Va. (repository hereafter cited as FSNMP). Hereafter, the published version will be cited whenever possible because it is more readily available to students, and the manuscript account at FSNMP will be cited only when it offers elaboration or (less often) variant language or details. In at least two places, the editorial pen at *Confederate Veteran* obscured as it attempted to smooth.

15. James C. Bosserman, "Bullets Didn't Kill 'Stonewall' Jackson," Richmond *Times-Dispatch*, October 12, 1930; anonymous Hill staff member, in "Stonewall Jackson!," Richmond *Dispatch*, October 26, 1875; Murray Forbes Taylor, "Stonewall Jackson's Death," 493; R. E. Wilbourn to Jubal A. Early, March 3, 1873, vol. 6, Early Papers, LC.

16. R. E. Wilbourn to R. L. Dabney, December 12, 1863, Charles William Dabney Papers, SHC; *Land We Love* 1 (July 1866): 181; J. G. Morrison to R. L. Dabney, October 29, 1863, Charles William Dabney Papers, SHC.

17. Kyle, "Jackson's Guide," 308; Kyle manuscript account, FSNMP.

18. Palmer, "Another Account," 232.

19. A. C. Hamlin, in Mary Anna Jackson, *Memoirs*, 549–51; Augustus Choate Hamlin, *The Battle of Chancellorsville: The Attack of Stonewall Jackson and His Army upon the Right Flank of the Army of the Potomac at Chancellorsville, Virginia, on Saturday Afternoon, May 2, 1863* (Bangor, Maine: Published by the author, 1896), 108.

20. Jedediah Hotchkiss, *Virginia*, vol. 3 of *Confederate Military History*, ed. Clement A. Evans, 12 vols. (Atlanta: Confederate Publishing Company, 1899), 386; Smith, "Stonewall Jackson's Last Battle," 211; Kyle, "Jackson's Guide," 308; Kyle manuscript account, FSNMP; A. C. Hamlin, in Mary Anna Jackson, *Memoirs*, 551–52.

21. Moorman, "Narrative of Events," 113; James H. Lane to A. C. Hamlin, [1892], Lane Papers, AU; James H. Lane, "How Stonewall Jackson Met His Death," in *SHSP*, 8:494 (also published in *Our Living and Our Dead* 3 [July 1875]: 33–36); Clark, *Histories of the Several Regiments and Battalions from North Carolina*, 1:377, 2:559; James S. Harris, *Historical Sketches of the Seventh Regiment North Carolina Troops* (Mooresville, N.C.: Mooresville Printing Company, [1893]), 28–29; *OR* 25(1):184, 916.

22. Alexander W. Selfridge, "Who Shot Stonewall Jackson?," in *Camp-Fire Sketches and Battle-Field Echoes*, comp. W. C. King and W. P. Berry (Springfield, Mass.: W. C. King, 1889), 377–79.

23. Joseph H. Saunders, "Stonewall Jackson—His Wounds, &c.," Fayetteville (N.C.) *Observer*, February 6, 1884; A. C. Hamlin, in Mary Anna Jackson, *Memoirs*, 548; James H. Lane to A. C. Hamlin, [1892], Lane Papers, AU. J. G. Morrison to Jubal A. Early, February

20, 1879, vol. 10, Early Papers, LC, never heretofore published or used, confirms the evidence that the opening rounds came from the skirmish line, not the main line: "My recollection is that it was in advance of where our line was supposed to [have] been."

24. R. E. Wilbourn to R. L. Dabney, December 12, 1863, Charles William Dabney Papers, SHC; R. E. Wilbourn to Jubal A. Early, February 12, 1873, in Early, *Autobiographical Sketch and Narrative*, 214; Jedediah Hotchkiss to his wife, May 19, 1863, Hotchkiss Papers, LC (microfilm roll 4, frames 515–16); *Land We Love* 1 (July 1866): 181. Neither Wilbourn nor whoever wrote the *Land We Love* article ever did figure out that the 33rd North Carolina was picketing to their front. Hotchkiss implies the same misconception, which, of course, contributed mightily to the staff's disorientation.

25. Kyle manuscript account, FSNMP; Kyle, "Jackson's Guide," 308.

26. Palmer, "Another Account," 232–33; Murray Forbes Taylor, "Stonewall Jackson's Death," 494; R. E. Wilbourn to Jubal A. Early, March 3, 1873, vol. 6, Early Papers, LC.

27. Benjamin P. Wright, "Recollections of the Battle of Chancellorsville and the Wounding of General Jackson," typescript, bound vol. 176, FSNMP. The foundation of the Van Wert house was destroyed in 1972 by the Virginia Department of Highways despite being situated on property of the National Park Service.

28. James Power Smith to George H. Stuart, April 27, 1905, FSNMP. A rod—also called a pole or a perch—measures 16.5 feet. A newspaper account of the monument's dedication declared frankly that Jackson actually was struck "about 150 yards further down in the woods" but that the monument had been sited with visibility from the road in mind ("Monument to 'Stonewall' Jackson," *Sunny South* [Atlanta], July 7, 1888). John W. Thomason's account of the placement of the first, unmarked stone in 1887 is badly garbled (*Jeb Stuart* [New York: Charles Scribner's Sons, 1934], 389). The best report of the earlier stone is in Sallie M. Lacy, "Jackson Marker Placing Recalled," Fredericksburg *Free Lance–Star*, May 16, 1938. Sallie was the daughter and sister-in-law of the two men who put up the first stone.

29. A. C. Hamlin, in Mary Anna Jackson, *Memoirs*, 549, 552; War Department survey transit books, book 2, [1927] (no later than 1933), FSNMP. The northern (westbound) lanes of the modern highway that bisects the battlefield follow the original route of the Orange Plank Road. The distance is 95 yards from the road to the southern edge of the parking lot and 95 yards from the east edge of Bullock Road to the 1888 monument. A comparison of the Van Wert site, the 1888 monument, the Orange Plank and Bullock roads, and the documentary evidence places Jackson's wounding two-thirds of the way from the modern road to the parking lot and 30 to 50 yards east of the longitude of the 1888 monument.

30. Hunter Holmes McGuire, *The Confederate Cause and Conduct in the War Between the States* (Richmond: L. H. Jenkins, 1907), 222. McGuire's several other accounts of treating Jackson confirm the ordnance identity.

31. The ordnance returns, for which I thank Bill McDaid, historian of Lane's brigade, were recorded by James A. W. Bryan on April 3 and 4, 1863, and are in vol. 59, Bryan Family Papers, SHC. The actual numbers of .69 and higher caliber (thus smoothbore) shoulder arms in the brigade were 64 in the 7th, 67 in the 18th, 184 in the 28th, 86 in the 33rd, and 271 in the 37th. The report of the 28th is in *OR* 25(1):921. The historian of the 18th in Clark, *Histories of the Several Regiments and Battalions from North Carolina*, 2:72–73, is the sole source mentioning the 50th Virginia (for which there are no known ordnance returns).

32. Palmer, "Another Account," 233; anonymous Hill staff member, in "Stonewall Jackson!," Richmond *Dispatch*, October 26, 1875; Lane, "Death of Stonewall Jackson"; typescript of Murray Forbes Taylor account, in the author's possession; Richardson, "Death of

Stonewall Jackson." Richardson also reported that Hill promptly cornered Colonel Purdie and "had a conversation" with him that must have been heated. Tolar in "Stonewall Jackson" wrote that Hill gave Purdie "a severe reprimand, then and there," but subsequently retracted the comments once the circumstances became clear.

33. Richmond *Enquirer*, May 13, 1863; *Land We Love* 1 (July 1866): 181; J. G. Morrison to Jubal A. Early, February 20, 1879, vol. 10, Early Papers, LC; J. G. Morrison to R. L. Dabney, October 29, 1863, and R. E. Wilbourn to R. L. Dabney, December 12, 1863, Charles William Dabney Papers, SHC; R. E. Wilbourn to Jubal A. Early, February 12, 1873, in Early, *Autobiographical Sketch and Narrative*, 214–15. The less reliable Randolph reported that Jackson said to him, " 'Wild fire, that, sir; wild fire' . . . in his usual rapid way" (*With Stonewall Jackson*, 10).

34. Tolar, "Stonewall Jackson"; *OR* 25(1):920; A. C. Hamlin, in Mary Anna Jackson, *Memoirs*, 553. The percentage of bayonets on hand is from the ordnance returns in vol. 59, Bryan Family Papers, SHC. George filed the regiment's official report because Colonel Purdie was killed within a few hours.

35. Clark, *Histories of the Several Regiments and Battalions from North Carolina*, 2:72–73; Lane, "How Stonewall Jackson Met His Death," 494; Tolar, "Stonewall Jackson"; James H. Lane to Charles E. Jones, October 26, 1898, Lane Papers, AU; Lane, "Death of Stonewall Jackson"; Richmond *Enquirer*, May 13, 1863; Randolph Barton, aide to Brig. Gen. E. F. Paxton of the Stonewall Brigade, in John Bigelow, Jr., *The Campaign of Chancellorsville: A Strategic and Tactical Study* (New Haven, Conn.: Yale University Press, 1910), 317n.

36. Richard M. V. B. Reeves memoir, Confederate Veteran Papers, Perkins Library, Duke University, Durham, N.C.; George W. Corbett manuscript account, FSNMP; *OR* 25(1):922.

37. *OR* 25(1):1010; Moorman, "Narrative of Events," 113–14; James H. Lane to A. C. Hamlin, [1892], Lane Papers, AU; James H. Lane to A. C. Hamlin, n.d., in Mary Anna Jackson, *Memoirs*, 557.

38. Conversation of the author with E. M. "Tiny" Hutton, aide to U.S. congressman Thomas N. Downing of Virginia, in 1975. Hutton, who died in 1979, had familial connections with the Barry clan and had always heard the story told in this fashion.

39. Wright, "Recollections"; Selfridge, "Who Shot Stonewall Jackson?" (for 46th Pennsylvania claims); Charles H. Weygant, *History of the One Hundred and Twenty-fourth Regiment, N.Y.S.V.* (Newburgh, N.Y.: Journal Printing House, 1877), 110–13; John L. Parker, *History of the Twenty-second Massachusetts Infantry, the Second Company Sharpshooters, and the Third Light Battery, in the War of the Rebellion* (Boston: Press of Rand Avery Company, 1887), 301 (for 20th Massachusetts claims); J. H. Stine, *History of the Army of the Potomac* (Philadelphia: J. B. Rodgers, 1892), 358–61. Selfridge's account is the most probable of the northern claims. Henry Kyd Douglas, a quondam member of Jackson's staff but not a paragon of reliability, wrote years later, "I heard then & believe the shot in the right hand was from the enemy" (Douglas marginalia on his copy of G. F. R. Henderson, *Stonewall Jackson and the American Civil War*, 2 vols. [London: Longman, Green, 1898], 2:555, Antietam National Battlefield, Sharpsburg, Md.). The right hand wound, of course, was the one most unequivocally demonstrable as of Confederate origin.

40. Joseph W. Revere, *Keel and Saddle: A Retrospect of Forty Years of Military and Naval Service* (Boston: James R. Osgood, 1872), 254–57, 276–77; John Esten Cooke, *Stonewall Jackson: A Military Biography* (New York: D. Appleton, 1866), 422. Revere's imaginary construction is thoroughly demolished in Jubal A. Early, "Stonewall Jackson—The Story of His Being an Astrologer Refuted—An Eye-witness Describes How He Was Wounded," in *SHSP*, 6:261–82 (published earlier in *Southern Magazine* 12 [1873]: 537–55).

41. J. S. F. Saul account, 1914, in E. M. Douglas to Librarian of Congress, May 20, 1941, Ms. AC65077, LC; "Who Fired the Bullet That Killed Stonewall Jackson?," *Rockbridge County News*, January 12, 1951; James H. Lane to A. C. Hamlin, [1892], Lane Papers, AU; Augusta Eugenia Barringer, "A Definitive Account of the 'Wounding' and Death of Thos. J. ('Stonewall') Jackson," typescript, in the author's possession; John Murphy accounts, in letters of Roy A. Wykoff to Fredericksburg-area newspaper editors, October 10, 27, 1958, FSNMP. Three earnest but unreliable claims are in *Blackwood's Magazine*, October 1930; A. C. Atkins manuscript account, NCDAH; and Randolph, *With Stonewall Jackson*. The Barringer burlesque on the subject is very cleverly done but was rejected by conservative newspaper editors early in this century.

42. Palmer, "Another Account," 233; Randolph, *With Stonewall Jackson*, 9; R. E. Wilbourn to Jubal A. Early, March 3, 1873, vol. 6, Early Papers, LC; Jedediah Hotchkiss to his wife, May 19, 1863, Hotchkiss Papers, LC. A sketchbook that was in Boswell's shirt pocket survives at the Museum of the Confederacy, Richmond, Virginia, showing the clear imprint of a rifled minié ball that passed through it.

43. Murray Forbes Taylor, "Stonewall Jackson's Death," 493–94; James H. Lane to A. C. Hamlin, [1892], Lane Papers, AU; Palmer, "Another Account," 233; anonymous Hill staff member, in "Stonewall Jackson!," Richmond *Dispatch*, October 26, 1875; R. E. Wilbourn to R. L. Dabney, December 12, 1863, Charles William Dabney Papers, SHC; typescript of Murray Forbes Taylor account, in the author's possession; Lane, "Death of Stonewall Jackson"; B. W. Leigh, "The Wounding of Stonewall Jackson," in *SHSP*, 6:232; O'Sullivan, *55th Virginia Infantry*, 142, 149; Eugene L. Saunders and Richard J. Muse Compiled Service Records, M324, microfilm rolls 967, 969, NA. Tucker survived to be the sole companion of his chief, A. P. Hill, under similar melancholy circumstances in April 1865. Leigh's account mentions that he shared Hill's instinct to dismount and lie down, but his horse "was rearing and plunging so violently that I could not do so." Just then a bullet hit the animal, which made a "frantic leap—and whether he threw me or I managed to get off myself, I am unable to say," Leigh admitted.

44. J. G. Morrison to R. L. Dabney, October 29, 1863, and R. E. Wilbourn to R. L. Dabney, December 12, 1863, Charles William Dabney Papers, SHC; Bruce, *History of Virginia*, 5:286.

45. Kyle manuscript account, FSNMP; R. E. Wilbourn to R. L. Dabney, December 12, 1863, Charles William Dabney Papers, SHC; Kyle, "Jackson's Guide," 308; anonymous Hill staff member, in "Stonewall Jackson!," Richmond *Dispatch*, October 26, 1875. A soldier later found Jackson's cap and gave it to General Pender (Wm. D. H. Covington [38th North Carolina] to Mary Anna Jackson, June 26, 1863, West Virginia University Library, Morgantown, W.Va. [repository hereafter cited as WVU]; two unidentified newspaper clippings on the same topic accompany the original letter).

46. McGuire, *Confederate Cause and Conduct*, 222; Wm. D. H. Covington to Mary Anna Jackson, June 26, 1863 (and two accompanying newspaper clippings), WVU; R. E. Wilbourn to R. L. Dabney, December 12, 1863, Charles William Dabney Papers, SHC; Mary Anna Jackson to Mrs. Brown, July 9, 1863, Wimberley Library, Florida Atlantic University, Boca Raton, Fla.

47. In R. E. Wilbourn to R. L. Dabney, December 12, 1863, Charles William Dabney Papers, SHC, Wilbourn says of the wound in Jackson's lower left arm that "no one knew of it till the surgeon got ready to amputate" (and he says he had provided initial first aid). McGuire's more formal, but later, account is in *Confederate Cause and Conduct*, 222; an

earlier, sketchier version obviously by him is in the Richmond *Enquirer*, May 13, 1863. The physical evidence from the glove is recorded in the newspaper clippings accompanying Wm. D. H. Covington to Mary Anna Jackson, June 26, 1863, WVU. The rain slicker is at the Virginia Military Institute, Lexington, Va. It is possible that the evidence from the gauntlet (no doubt pulled very high up the wrist) and rain slicker shows an exit point for the lower wound, with entry through a now-repaired segment of the coat. McGuire's evidence for the entry point from the damaged arm seems immutable. The author is grateful to the efficient and cordial Col. Keith E. Gibson of the institute for measuring and drawing both the raincoat and Jackson's handkerchief (see n. 51).

48. McGuire, *Confederate Cause and Conduct*, 222; Richmond *Enquirer*, May 13, 1863. For a fascinating review of the remarkable career of Jackson's rain slicker, which traveled across Virginia and around the world, sometimes in anonymity, see David F. Riggs, "Stonewall Jackson's Raincoat," *Civil War Times Illustrated* 16 (July 1977): 36–41. Other relics of the event gathered by participants included Jackson's field glass and haversack (which contained papers, envelopes, and two religious tracts), picked up by Wilbourn (R. E. Wilbourn to R. L. Dabney, December 12, 1863, Charles William Dabney Papers, SHC); a book of Napoleon's maxims that had been a gift from J. E. B. Stuart (Douglas Southall Freeman, *A Calendar of Confederate Papers* [Richmond: Confederate Museum, 1908], 519n); and a medicine case ("Has Relic of 'Stonewall,'" Fredericksburg *Free Lance*, December 8, 1914).

49. R. E. Wilbourn to R. L. Dabney, December 12, 1863, Charles William Dabney Papers, SHC. Hill's expressions of dismay are reported in much of the primary material on the event. The solid evidence of an earlier accommodation between the generals is in an account reported by Conway R. Howard to Jedediah Hotchkiss that was recorded in Hotchkiss's notes on blank pages of an 1857 Mossy Creek Academy catalog under the title "Incidents Relating to the Life of Gen. Jackson Compiled by Jed. Hotchkiss Capt. & Top. Engr. 2nd Corps A.N.Va.," University of Virginia, Charlottesville, Va. Howard's matter-of-fact, detailed account rings true and seems entirely reliable. I thank Steve Ritchie of Indiana for the discovery of this rich source of Jackson material.

50. R. E. Wilbourn to Jubal A. Early, February 12, 1873, in Early, *Autobiographical Sketch and Narrative*, 215–16; R. E. Wilbourn to R. L. Dabney, December 12, 1863, Charles William Dabney Papers, SHC; Wright, "Recollections."

51. Information and a measured drawing of the handkerchief from Virginia Military Institute, Lexington, Va. The linen bears Jackson's name and came directly from his daughter Julia. It measures 40.5 by 50.5 centimeters and is therefore far too small to have supported an arm as a sling. The deadly hemorrhaging that occurred after Jackson's two falls from the litter presumably flowed away (down the arm) from this handkerchief; but the initial frantic treatment—in pitch darkness—of a shattered arm with a severed artery would hardly have left the modest stains this linen piece bears.

52. Kyle, "Jackson's Guide," 308–9; Richmond *Enquirer*, May 13, 1863; R. E. Wilbourn to R. L. Dabney, December 12, 1863, Charles William Dabney Papers, SHC; "Stonewall Jackson's Death," in *SHSP*, 10:143; J. G. Morrison to Jubal A. Early, February 20, 1879, vol. 10, Early Papers, LC; Kyle manuscript account, FSNMP. The good people of Fluvanna County, whence Private Johnson came, raised money to buy him "a little place and house, where he can be comfortably situated," although he was so badly injured that he could not even feed himself. Johnson was living there in 1882, a solid but "very poor" citizen.

53. J. G. Morrison to R. L. Dabney, October 29, 1863, Charles William Dabney Papers,

SHC; R. E. Wilbourn to Jubal A. Early, February 12, 1873, in Early, *Autobiographical Sketch and Narrative*, 217; R. E. Wilbourn to R. L. Dabney, December 12, 1863, Charles William Dabney Papers, SHC; H. H. McGuire, "Jackson's Death," Fredericksburg *Star*, March 24, 1886; W. L. Goldsmith, in *Tales of the Civil War*, ed. C. R. Graham (Boston: Perry Mason, 1896), 519–20. The account of landing on a stump is from a veteran of the 5th Virginia of the Stonewall Brigade, in Bosserman, "Bullets Didn't Kill 'Stonewall' Jackson." Bosserman's late-life rambling deserves little credence.

54. Kyle manuscript account, FSNMP; Leigh, "Wounding of Stonewall Jackson," 233–34; J. G. Morrison to Jubal A. Early, February 20, 1879, vol. 10, Early Papers, LC; "Stonewall Jackson's Death," 143.

55. Richmond *Enquirer*, May 13, 1863; H. H. McGuire, in Mary Anna Jackson, *Memoirs*, 433; R. E. Wilbourn to R. L. Dabney, December 12, 1863, Charles William Dabney Papers, SHC; H. H. McGuire, in "Stonewall Jackson!," Richmond *Dispatch*, October 26, 1875.

56. Lexington (Va.) *Gazette*, May 20, 1863; "The Civil War Diary of Peter W. Hairston," *North Carolina Historical Review* 67 (January 1990): 77; Daniel Perrin Bestor to "Dear Sister," June 1, 1863, Lida B. Robertson Papers, Alabama Department of Archives and History, Montgomery, Ala.

57. W. L. Goldsmith, in Graham, *Tales of the Civil War*, 519–20; W. G. Morris to James H. Lane, January 3, 1895, folder 113, Lane Papers, AU.

58. Emerson G. Taylor, *Gouverneur Kemble Warren: The Life and Letters of an American Soldier* (Boston: Houghton Mifflin, 1932), 112; "The Memory of Stonewall Jackson in England," *Daily Southern Guardian* (Columbia, S.C.), June 23, 1863; London *Times*, June 17, 1863; Anna J. P. Shaff[n]er, *Stonewall Jackson* (Washington, D.C., 1936), 3.

59. Joseph Hilton to "Dear Cousin," May 15, 1863, Joseph Hilton Papers, Georgia Historical Society, Savannah, Ga.; Wesley Lewis Battle to his father, May 16, 1863, Battle Family Papers, SHC; Ross Marcius Gaston reminiscence, box 70, folder 52, Military Collection, NCDAH; Joshua Howell to his wife, typescript, May 14, 1863, FSNMP.

The Valiant Rearguard

HANCOCK'S DIVISION
AT CHANCELLORSVILLE

Carol Reardon

"IT WAS A delightful spring morning. The sun shone bright
and warm, the trees were just beginning to put forth their
green leaves and the grass and early flowers had already
changed the grayish sandy soil to brighter and more attractive
hues."[1] So seemed the early hours of May 1, 1863, to one
member of the 148th Pennsylvania, a regiment as green as the
grass he described. In the next seventy-two hours, he would
undergo a baptism of fire at Chancellorsville. As part of Brig.
Gen. Winfield Scott Hancock's First Division of Maj. Gen.
Darius Couch's Second Corps in the Army of the Potomac,
he and his comrades helped to provide a rare bright spot in
the dark news of yet another Union defeat. Posted to the
Union left flank—the end that Stonewall Jackson did not
crush—Hancock's men gave a performance at Chancellorsville that remains as noteworthy as it is underappreciated.

In the spring of 1863, the First Division of the Second
Corps already held a distinguished combat record. On the

Peninsula, at Antietam's Bloody Lane, and at Marye's Heights at Fredericksburg, it had won great fame at high cost. Just before Chancellorsville, Sgt. Frank Higby of the 57th New York hoped that the division might be assigned some easier duty and "get some place or Fort to garrison." He knew, however, that the high command appreciated the men's fighting abilities, "& I presume that they will keep us at that business as long as there is a man left."[2]

Division commander Winfield Scott Hancock, a Pennsylvanian and West Point graduate, was worthy of such men. In their eyes, he had already won the title "Hancock the Superb." His division included four brigades. The First Brigade—the famous 5th New Hampshire, the 61st New York, the 81st Pennsylvania, and the rookie 148th Pennsylvania—served under Brig. Gen. John C. Caldwell. The Second Brigade was the renowned Irish Brigade; on detached service for most of the battle, it played only a small part in the division's experiences at Chancellorsville. Brig. Gen. Samuel K. Zook's Third Brigade included Sergeant Higby's 57th New York, the veteran 52nd and 66th New York, and the new 140th Pennsylvania. The Fourth Brigade under Col. John R. Brooke included the veteran 2nd Delaware, 53rd Pennsylvania, 64th New York, and 145th Pennsylvania, along with the nine-month men of the 27th Connecticut. At Chancellorsville, however, formal tables of organization meant little to Hancock. Indeed, as it happened, he created a fifth, or provisional, brigade when he thought it necessary.

Hancock's men played no major role in Hooker's initial plans for May 1. Other elements of the army took the lead in an advance along three roads that would take the Union forces out of the Wilderness to turn Lee's lines at Fredericksburg. Brig. Gen. Charles Griffin's division of Maj. Gen. George G. Meade's Fifth Corps marched along the River Road to uncover Banks Ford. In the center, Brig. Gen. George Sykes led his Fifth Corps division, mostly U.S. regulars, east along the Orange Turnpike. To the southeast, along the Orange Plank Road, Maj. Gen. Henry W. Slocum led the Twelfth Corps. The three commands expected to extend their lines to link up with each other once they emerged from the Wilderness into open ground east of Chancellorsville. Sykes's men, however, moved more quickly than the others, and the cavalry screen that preceded the head of the Union infantry encountered skirmishers of the 12th Virginia Infantry on the Orange Turnpike at about 11:00 A.M.

The Virginians, from Brig. Gen. William Mahone's brigade, served as the advance guard of Maj. Gen. Richard H. Anderson's division, which, with Maj. Gen. Lafayette McLaws's division close behind, had begun to deploy along the Orange Turnpike to intercept Hooker's turning force.[3] They had begun to push back the Union cavalry when Sykes's infantrymen arrived on the double-quick. Very quickly, the regulars made their presence felt. The Confederates began to

Maj. Gen. Winfield Scott Hancock. Library of Congress

fall back, but McLaws, having just arrived on the scene, did not appear worried. The Virginians, he believed, were merely doing as expected, "running to the rear, as all skirmishers are ordered to do, when the main line of the enemy advanced" on them. As the regulars pressed on toward the southern line, Capt. Tyler C. Jordan of the Bedford Artillery disobeyed his orders to "do nothing that will bring on a fight, and act strictly on the defensive." He would always be proud that his were *"the first guns fired in this great battle."* McLaws himself brought up troops from Brig. Gen. Paul Semmes's brigade. He asked Semmes if his Georgians could hold the Union troops until reinforcements arrived. "No fear of this Brigade, Sir," Semmes replied, "it will not give way!"[4] Semmes remained true to his promise. Soon his own Georgia troops, along with those of Brig. Gen. William T. Wofford and some of Mahone's Virginians, lapped both flanks of Sykes's line and began to push back the Union troops.

As the southern pressure mounted, about 1:00 P.M., Hancock's men, along with elements of Capt. William A. Arnold's Battery A, 1st Rhode Island Artillery, and one section of Lt. Alonzo H. Cushing's Battery A, 4th U.S. Artillery, answered Sykes's call for help.[5] The trees muffled the sounds of imminent battle, and the men could still joke and laugh. "Notwithstanding the seriousness of the occasion, we could not refrain from smiling at the sight of the myriads of cards strewn all along the whole breadth of the road, and among the bushes along the sides, lying thick as autumnal leaves," one later recalled. Caldwell took the lead. Breaking out of the woods onto a ridge near two buildings—the Absalom McGee house and the Newton house—he immediately deployed the 61st New York as skirmishers on the right of the road. The unit's colonel, an up-and-coming officer named Nelson A. Miles, placed his men about 200 yards in front of Hancock's main battle line and advanced to assist the regulars.[6]

Behind the 61st New York deployed the untried 148th Pennsylvania. As the men moved into their initial line of battle, the officers tried to calm them. When the first artillery shells crashed overhead, Maj. George A. Fairlamb asked Pvt. William Perry how he liked it: "Perry said, 'Well, Maj., to stand here and be shot at and darsent shoot back I be d——d if I like it,' " his eyes fixed to the front all the while as if "standing on the banks of the Susquehanna waiting for a deer to come down." Col. James A. Beaver reassured his men that he would tell them when to fire so that they could show the division's veterans, who had harassed them unmercifully, "that Sunday soldiers are good soldiers." Some enlisted men found their own way to lessen the tension. As one of the Pennsylvanians recalled, a comrade "got up and took hold of one of my chums and chucked him against his neighbor. At once the company was on its feet sparring and the horrid feeling was gone."[7]

To add greater strength to Miles's thin skirmish line, Hancock called for the veteran 64th New York of Brooke's brigade. While the New Yorkers deployed on the left of the 61st New York, Brooke placed the rest of his men on the high ground on the Newton house ridge. Zook aligned his command behind the 148th Pennsylvania south of the turnpike. All the while, the Pennsylvanians watched the skirmishers ascend the next hill. "This was our first view of a battle," remembered one man, "and to inexperienced soldiers it was magnificent." For the skirmishers, however, it was confounding. The 64th New York searched in vain through the woods and ravines for the 61st New York until one of its sergeants spotted the men of the 61st in a place where they were not supposed to be. With his troops' alignment so confused, it was probably fortunate that the first combatants Hancock met were the retiring soldiers of the 6th U.S. Infantry and not the Confederate battle line.[8]

The arrival of Hancock's men was nonetheless timely. Sykes's regulars and the troopers of their cavalry screen had used up much of their ammunition and had begun to fall back. Moreover, although the clash had been brief, they had become disorganized and suffered moderately heavy casualties, including the loss of some men who were taken prisoner. As McLaws recalled it, several regulars who had been captured came running up to him, and "as they came near I recognized them as members of my old Company in the U.S. Army." They told the general that "they had deserted to come to me." As Hancock's men advanced beyond the retiring regulars, they took their first fire and saw evidence that hard work lay ahead. Col. Daniel G. Bingham of the 64th New York observed that "several of the dead lay in the woods, and the ground was strewn with knapsacks of friends and foes."[9]

While the skirmishers held the advance, Hancock's main battle line occupied the Newton house ridge to allow Sykes's men to re-form behind them. Increasingly heavy Confederate artillery fire made their position uncomfortable. New troops continued to find this a learning experience: "Shells crashing in tops of trees behind us. Balls occasionally zipping nearby, and enemy coming nearer, but could not be seen. In those moments of trial, what a study in human nature!" An untested soldier in the 148th Pennsylvania found that "our military ardor which had been raised to a high pitch by the carnival of war around us, cooled very rapidly under the potent influence of the bursting shells," which, to a veteran from Connecticut, went "bang-whiz a wiz a wiz bang."[10]

About 2:00 P.M., Couch received orders to pull Hancock back to the clearing around the Chancellor house. He delayed the execution of the order, sharing the opinion of other officers on the field that it was ludicrous to give up a good position on the Newton house ridge for lower wooded ground near Chancellorsville. Hooker relented enough to order the division to hold its position until 5:00 P.M. Soon after Hancock received these orders, however, Slocum's Twelfth Corps on the Orange Plank Road pulled back quickly before a fierce Confederate onslaught. Up on Hancock's skirmish line, Colonel Miles saw departing from the field "a brigade belonging to the Twelfth corps, which was retreating double-quick, without rear guards or flankers." Except for the skirmishers from

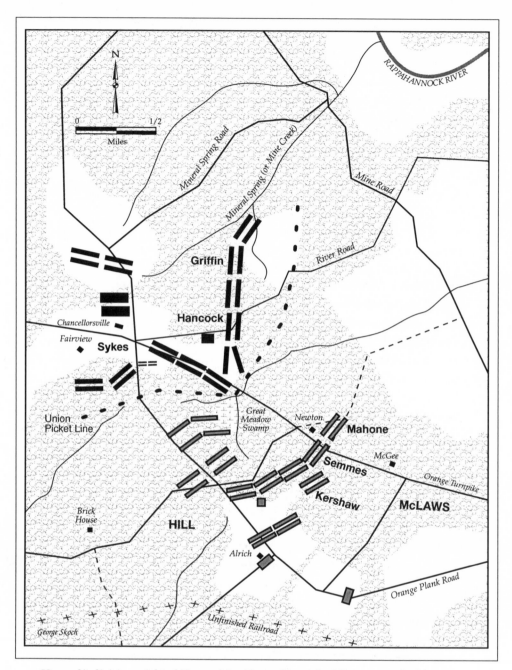

Hancock's division, night of May 1, 1863. Hancock's original line was on the Newton house ridge facing east. Mahone and Semmes occupied this position by nightfall.

Miles's 61st New York, now reinforced by men from the 52nd New York who had formed on the right of and nearly perpendicular to his line, Hancock's right flank was unprotected.[11]

If that were not enough of a problem, the Confederate infantry fire in Hancock's immediate front increased dramatically. McLaws had called for reinforcements as soon as he spotted Hancock's large force deploying along the heights behind Sykes's men. Brig. Gen. Joseph B. Kershaw's South Carolina brigade fell into line south of the Orange Turnpike, a captain recalling it as "the proudest moment of his life" when his men cheered at his approach: "Hurrah! for the Dutch; the Dutch has come; make way to the left for Dutch."[12] This salute to a man from a part of South Carolina settled by German immigrants may be the only time in the various accounts of Chancellorsville when "Dutch" appears as a compliment. More artillery arrived along with additional infantry, and late in the afternoon, McLaws attacked in force.

Hancock's men saw it coming. Colonel Morris of the 66th New York spotted a "line of battle, with a heavy line of skirmishers in front." Colonel Miles noted that the southern formation "was different from any I had ever seen, being much stronger and in four ranks. Part filed to the front, keeping up a continuous fire."[13] Hancock found it impossible to hold on. He sent word to fall back behind Sykes's redeployed division and, most important, to continue fighting all the way.

As the generals described it, the withdrawal went smoothly and concluded successfully. The soldiers did not recall it quite the same way. Colonel Brooke discovered that some of the men of the 27th Connecticut "had thrown away everything. He reprimanded them and ordered them to march back from where they started and pick up everything" before withdrawing farther. The woods confused everybody. The 140th Pennsylvania "could only guess at the general direction" to the rear, "happily unconscious of the fact" that the southerners were closing in rapidly. Still another soldier in the 140th saw Zook tell Col. R. P. Roberts, " 'There is only one chance for you and that is to fight as long as you have a man, or surrender.' " When they broke out of the woods, they found themselves at the edge of a "broad but comparatively shallow swamp." They tried to skirt it, but "General Hancock suddenly appeared on horseback, his face blazing with the heat and excitement, and with expletives and gestures, which, at times, were characteristic of the man, emphasized his short, curt command: 'Dash through that swamp or you will all be taken by the enemy.' At that moment he was 'Hancock, the Superb.' . . . For the first time we realized that the enemy in strong force was close behind us."[14]

Brigadier General Semmes, his Georgians among those following Hancock's men most closely, watched with wonder as the northern troops departed: "The road, the woods, and fields on either side, over which the enemy retired, was strewn with knapsacks, blankets, overcoats, and many other valuable articles." "Valuable," of course, is in the eye of the beholder. To Lt. Col. Willis C. Holt of the 10th Georgia, the capture of thirteen Springfield rifles and two cartridge boxes warranted comment in his postbattle report.[15]

As Union artillery near the Chancellor house and Sykes's re-formed troops finally broke the Confederate attack, Hancock's men redeployed near the crossroads at Chancellorsville. For now, as ordered, they massed in the clearing in front of the Chancellor house and faced south, linking up with the right flank of Sykes's division and facing the growing threat along the Orange Plank Road. They stayed in this position only briefly but long enough for the 148th Pennsylvania to suffer its first battle-related death. Ironically, Pvt. Samuel Holloway was killed by the "friendly fire" of Union batteries shooting over their own infantry, an inadvisable practice because of the unreliability of shell fuses and the frequency of short rounds. That first death left a lasting mark in the memory of his comrades. Pvt. Henry C. Campbell recalled that "one year to the day on our way to the wilderness we put a marker to his grave."[16]

After only a "few moments" in that deadly clearing, as a soldier in the 27th Connecticut explained it, Hancock's men again marched east "down the road a short distance" and "deployed through the thick and tangled woods on the left" of the Orange Turnpike.[17] On their way out to the road, exploding artillery shells stampeded a herd of cattle brought along to provide fresh meat for the troops. They "charged madly, with heads down and tails up, across the open space in which we were moving," recalled a man in the 140th Pennsylvania, noting that the "encounter was designated by 'the boys' who were immediately concerned, as the 'charge of the Texas steers.' "[18]

Hancock's new east-facing line introduced an element of Second Corps troops into what was ostensibly the Fifth Corps position. Caldwell's brigade found Griffin's Fifth Corps division on its left, while Brooke's command, on Caldwell's right, found some of Sykes's troops on its right. Zook's men lay in reserve behind Caldwell and Brooke. As they settled into the new position, they waited nervously because "appearances indicated the rebels were about to charge down from the [Newton house] ridge from which we had just retired." In many places, probing attacks by southern troops were quite real, not merely appearances.[19]

As darkness fell, Hancock took steps to strengthen his line when several of his regiments returned from detached duty. He combined the 5th New Hampshire and 81st Pennsylvania from Caldwell's brigade and the 88th New York of the Irish Brigade into a single so-called provisional brigade under Col. E. E. Cross and placed them in reserve along the Orange Turnpike. Their tired comrades hardly noticed their arrival. Distracted by the fire of Confederate artillery from the Newton house ridge, they remembered for years that the "rebel guns woke the sleeping forest echoes, and shells careened wildly through the air, and crashed among the trees." Union guns answered in kind, still firing over their own infantry. Some new soldiers passed around a shell fragment, one noting afterward that "it was more of a curiosity then than it would have been a few days later."[20]

When pauses in the artillery fire permitted, nearly all of the soldiers worked hard to dig rifle pits or erect breastworks. Soldiers of the 27th Connecticut recalled the "rapid strokes of axemen, followed by the dull sound of falling trees," that "rang through the woods in every direction." Southerners did the same. The men of Kershaw's brigade found themselves so close to the Union line that they slept on their arms in case of night attacks, and they grumbled about the restriction against fires.[21]

Probably the only men not digging on either side were the pickets, whose duty on the advance line this night was not easy work. Major Bradley of the 64th New York reported that Confederates in front of Brooke's brigade were "moving at first to our left and afterward back to the right." Picket and artillery fire continued well after nightfall. The combined effect of this confusion, plus sheer exhaustion, finally wore on some of the 148th Pennsylvania's pickets, who fell back in disorder behind the 64th New York and fired at least two volleys to the front, more likely hitting friend than foe.[22]

Finally, the long day was over. Great numbers of Hancock's men, though very close to the action, had actually seen very little of it. The density of the Wilderness had hidden many horrible sights during the day. Now darkness obscured everything. Veteran soldiers wondered why they had been withdrawn from good high ground. One of Arnold's artillerymen later wrote, "After marching up the hill our troops met the enemy on top where we could doubtless have driven them from their position, but for some reason unknown to the soldiers in the ranks we were ordered back, fighting every inch of the way, in the same manner as we did from Fair Oaks to Malvern Hill, only with heavier losses. Our troops continued to come in . . . very much discouraged." New soldiers understood it even less. Sgt. Benjamin Powelson of the 140th Pennsylvania concluded, "We had been initiated, practically blindfolded."[23] The blindfolds would soon come off.

Uncomfortable with his troop dispositions early on the morning of May 2, Hooker withdrew Sykes's men from their position parallel to the Orange Turnpike and reunited them with the rest of the Fifth Corps on the Union left. Shortly afterward, between 2:00 and 3:00 A.M., Hancock began to realign his command to fill the gap between his right and the left of the Twelfth Corps that

Typical Federal breastworks at Chancellorsville. Francis Trevelyan Miller, ed., The Photographic History of the Civil War, *10 vols. (New York: Review of Reviews, 1911), 2:119*

Sykes's departure had created. Reconstituting the Union line required Hancock to pull back his entire command from the entrenchments his men had built during the night of May 1. The men's labors were not wasted, however, because the trenches that marked Hancock's main line late on May 1 would protect his advance line on May 2–3.

To create his new division line, Hancock had deployed Cross's provisional brigade on the right facing southeast, the 5th New Hampshire loosely linked up with the Twelfth Corps near the Orange Plank Road. Next, running north from Cross, came the 66th New York of Zook's brigade. For now, the 66th took orders from Caldwell, whose 61st New York and 148th Pennsylvania continued the line northward. Brooke took position on Caldwell's left. Zook extended the division line almost to the Chandler house, where it connected to Brig. Gen. William H. French's division of the Second Corps.[24]

Once again Hancock's men used shovels, picks, and axes to build rifle pits and an abatis on their front. Hancock again posted pickets at three-pace intervals—many in his former first line facing east, others in the abatis that Sykes's men had built paralleling the turnpike facing south. He named Colonel Miles of the 61st New York to command the advance line. The pickets were ordered to stay awake—a "precaution [that] seemed to us quite necessary," recalled one, because fatigue made it "difficult to keep the eyes open." But then they heard southern voices yell, "Forward." The "rustling of the leaves on the ground and the snapping of twigs" revealed the nearness of Confederate troops. Years later, with a bravado that surely resulted from the passage of time, some boasted they were sorry no attack came: "It was a beautiful moonlight night and our boys being concealed behind trees and logs would have had the advantage of the first volley at close range."[25]

Hancock's men enjoyed little peace and quiet throughout the morning and afternoon of May 2. They took artillery fire most of the day from the Newton house ridge and from southern guns on high ground along the Orange Plank Road. The men of the 27th Connecticut became convinced that southern gunners had located their position by the smoke from their campfires. The shelling appeared to increase dramatically every time supply wagons ventured toward the front, causing some of the Union troops to suspect that the rebels were "determined to involve commissaries and rations in one common ruin." Some of the 148th Pennsylvania still feared the cannonading, "but we couldn't let our meat and coffee go for a trifle like that."[26]

Confederate infantry probed Hancock's forward line much of the day, keeping the Union soldiers on edge. The southern commander on this part of the line, Lafayette McLaws, explained that General Lee had asked him to perform "a duty which would call for a sacrifice on my part." While Stonewall Jackson's

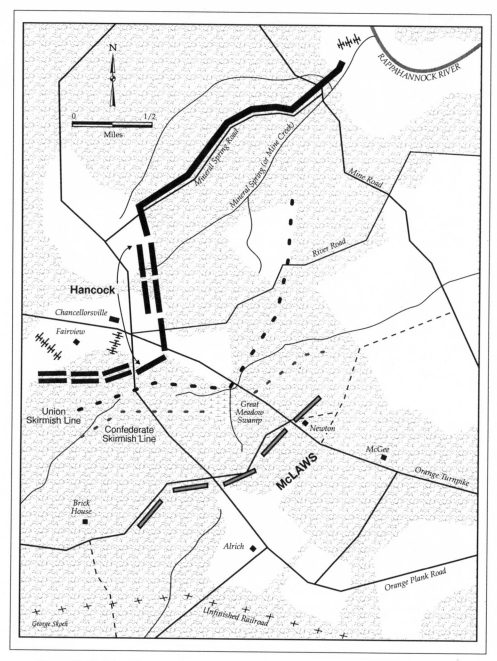

Hancock's division, May 2, 1863

Maj. Gen. Lafayette McLaws. Robert Underwood Johnson and Clarence Clough Buel,
eds., Battles and Leaders of the Civil War, *4 vols. (New York: Century, 1887–88), 3:333*

column began its flank march around the Union right, McLaws later wrote, Lee ordered that McLaws's skirmish line, in concert with the skirmishers of Anderson's division, "make frequent demonstrations against the enemy in my front so as to create the impression that an assault was intended, but he did not wish me to really engage seriously, but rather to avoid doing so." It would do the southern forces no good if aggressiveness on McLaws's part caused Hooker to

Col. Nelson Appleton Miles (shown later in the war as a major general). Francis Trevelyan Miller, ed., The Photographic History of the Civil War, *10 vols. (New York: Review of Reviews, 1911), 10:213*

advance in force against him and discover that the Confederate right flank had become "a mere shell."[27]

McLaws's men followed their orders well. About 1:00 P.M., the pickets of the 2nd Delaware believed they had taken on "a strong force of the enemy" yet somehow repulsed them with the miraculously small loss of one wounded. Their fire must have been remarkably accurate, because when men from the 27th Connecticut relieved the 2nd Delaware later that day, one soldier noticed that the rebels lay "in heaps outside of the works."[28] Skirmishers of the 11th Massachusetts, a Third Corps regiment sent to Hancock's front between the Orange Plank Road and the Orange Turnpike for duty as sharpshooters, lost and then regained their advanced position twice during the late afternoon, but they did not perceive a sufficient threat from that front to push for a more concerted attack.[29]

About 3:00 P.M. the part of the Union skirmish line closest to the Orange Turnpike stiffened in anticipation of an apparently substantial Confederate assault. Some 800 yards away, in the woods to their front, northern troops saw men from Wofford's and Semmes's Georgian brigades massing. McLaws admitted that about this time he had increased the number of men in active contact with the enemy to three regiments and four companies "to prevent a concentration against Jackson." Pickets of the 11th Massachusetts heard a southern officer remind his soldiers "that the 'Yanks' had plenty of rations." Colonel Miles also recalled that the orders of the southern commanders "could be distinctly heard." Then, according to Miles, the Confederates advanced "in two columns, one on each side of the road, flanked by a line of battle." They advanced with a tremendous yell and "were met with a sure and deadly fire of one simple line." The impetuous charge advanced "to within 20 yards of my abatis," the colonel wrote, but it was "hurled back with fearful loss."[30] McLaws had to be pleased, however, that even now no Union counterattack followed.

Miles drew the admiration of his superiors for his work. Caldwell credited the colonel's skill and gallantry for repelling "a determined attack of the enemy made in column, a feat rarely paralleled." Hancock observed the whole scene and said to his aide: "Capt. Parker, ride down and tell Col. Miles he is worth his weight in gold." Corps commander Couch announced to Hancock and French, "I tell you what it is, gentlemen, I shall not be surprised to find myself, some day, serving under that young man."[31] Rarely, it seems, had so thin a picket line done such good work.

Or had it? McLaws could not hide his amusement at such hyperbole. Writing years later, he played down the seriousness of the Confederate assaults on Hancock's line on May 2: "When one considers that this advance of the Confederate skirmishers, *was intended as* a mere bluff and that the 'tremendous yell' was but a part of the show arranged beforehand, and that it was never intended to assault the superior forces of the enemy in their entrenchments *behind abatis*, one can realize the ridiculousness" of the bombastic statements of the Union commanders. Indeed, such claims added to "the burlesqueness" of the Union perspective of the whole battle. McLaws argued that any description of an "advance in two columns flanked by a line of battle, is only an imaginary incident put in to give some color to the gallantry that is claimed—an idyl manufactured to promote promotion of the hero."[32] Never known for his aggressiveness, McLaws had been assigned a mission ideal for his temperament and skills. For once, the often-maligned Georgian had executed his orders to perfection.

The memories of some of McLaws's men reinforced his description of the fighting on May 2. To Fred H. West of the 51st Georgia of Semmes's brigade, the most notable occurrence of the afternoon of May 2 "while the battle of Chancellorsville was raging on our left not far from us" was a mail call that came "amid the roar of battle." A skirmisher from the 2nd South Carolina later described his comrades' primary effort on this day as making "music for Mr. Hooker's benefit." Union bullets "came among us singing as they came 'where are you.' Our men would sing out, 'here I am.'"[33]

Late in the afternoon, Hancock's men heard loud firing and commotion in their rear, toward the army's right flank. They quickly discovered that Stonewall Jackson's men had smashed into the Eleventh Corps like "striking a cambric needle on the Point with a sledge," as a man in the 27th Connecticut described it. The 140th Pennsylvania tried to stop hundreds of men who were running "pell-mell to our rifle pits" and "would have dashed through them, if they had not been opposed, into the enemy's line." Colonel Cross's command fixed bayonets and turned back "more than one thousand officers and men. . . . The cowardice of the German troops was ludicrous."[34]

Hancock's primary concerns now rested with stopping the rout and preventing the collapse of the entire Union line. His prepared line faced east. Now on the reverse side of the trenches, his soldiers stacked knapsacks, logs, and anything else they could find to allow them to fire under cover toward the west. Tension ran high. One of Hancock's Connecticut soldiers noticed his general's "flushed cheek and wilted shirt collar which indicated trouble in the camp." If the soldier's observation was true, it is quite a revealing comment about Hancock, whose reputation for meticulous dress was well known.

Around them, the forest shook "with the terrific cannonade, vying with the thunders of heaven in the compass of its sound." Some soldiers insisted they could hear "the deep, prolonged boom of a hundred-pounder" among the southern artillery that "swells the bass notes of the chorus." Still, in the chaos, the northerners watched a brass band take up a position in the open and play "the stirring strains of the grand old song, born amid battle scene:—'The Star Spangled Banner.'" The effect was electric: "Spontaneously, the men who were yet standing by the flag broke out into cheers and took heart again." "I mean to hold my ground right here," shouted General Zook to his men. "Will you stand by me?" Amid a din of affirmative cries, one young soldier answered, "Yes, we will stand by you as long as there is a button left on our breeches." Hancock told the 64th New York, "'Now, boys, you are going to put backbone into the 11th Corps,—and they need it badly enough!'" The men gave him a "vociferous cheer" and eagerly embraced "specific orders to bayonet any of the Teutonic division who might attempt to run away." Cross rode up and down his line, his red silk handkerchief tied around his head, "exhorting every man to stand firm, and the men answered with loud cheers, which had the effect to shame some of the fugitives, and they halted."[35]

As the Union position stabilized, Hancock took pride in his men's accomplishments. His main line facing west and advance line facing east had operated for a time back-to-back, and they had done so quite effectively. He especially appreciated the actions of his thin picket line: "The enemy was never able to reach my principal line of battle, so stoutly and successfully did Col. Miles contest the ground." Still, perhaps he did not understand just how lucky he had been. Robert E. Lee had not changed McLaws's orders even after Jackson's advance diverted the Union high command's attention away from its left flank. Indeed, some of McLaws's infantrymen had so little to do that they climbed tall trees to see what they could of Jackson's attack. Finding few good observation points, however, the South Carolinians amused themselves on the evening of May 2 by watching the "improvised aurora borealis" given off by the fire on the other flank of the armies.[36] Fortunately for Hancock's men, Lee had spared them a two-front fight.

To his credit, Hancock understood that fatigue, fear, and isolation could wear on pickets, and he ordered the exhausted men to be relieved by fresh troops during the night of May 2. The 66th New York established its line roughly "parallel with and a few paces beyond the road, fronting a woods occupied by the enemy's pickets," its left "connecting and forming right angles with the Sixty-fourth" and its right "extending, in conjunction with two companies of the One hundred and fortieth Pennsylvania . . . to the open field in front of the breastworks, where it connected at right angles with the Fifth New Hampshire."[37]

The soldiers again worked most of the night to strengthen their works. This effort was inspired in part by continuous firing in Hancock's rear and off his right flank, where the Twelfth Corps had fought hard during much of the day. The men also listened to disconcerting noises on their own front. The soldiers of the 64th New York heard the Confederates working all night: "Orders to troops were plainly heard, and sounds of chopping and falling trees and owl signals were passed along their line in our front." But finally "the quiet moon rose over the bloody field, and Nature sank into a silence fairly oppressive."[38]

The battle opened abruptly at 5:00 A.M. on May 3 with artillery crashing in on Hancock from front, right, and rear. Expecting to conduct any serious fight against the enemy from his main line of battle, Hancock had kept his skirmish line thin, but now, "knowing the danger and confusion that would arise from the musket-balls of the enemy crossing our line of communication at Chancellorsville from [the Union left and rear], I strengthened the advanced position, believing, from the experience of the previous day and the well-known ability and gallantry of Colonel Miles, that it could be held."[39] Joining the 66th and 64th New York and others assigned to the picket line the night before came a large detail of officers and men from the 53rd and 145th Pennsylvania and the 2nd Delaware of Brooke's brigade.

The reinforcements arrived just when they were most needed. The Confederates assaulted the Union advance line shortly after the artillery fire began, and the southern infantry had nearly reached the northerners' defenses. On the 64th

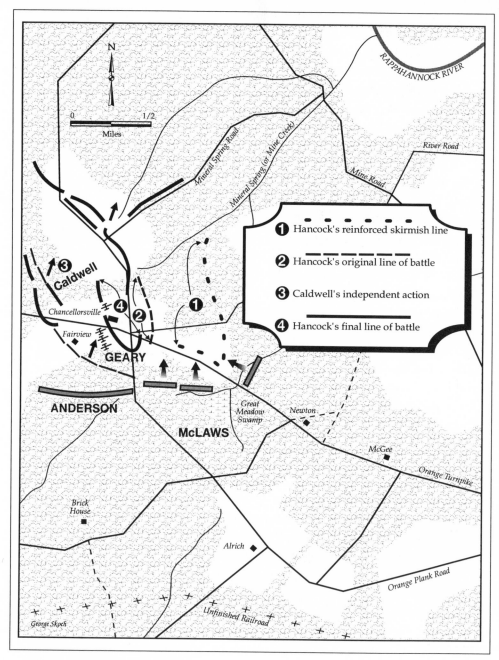

Hancock's division, May 3, 1863

New York's front, soldiers "heard the order from the enemy, 'Prepare for an advance,' and immediately after a line of skirmishers appeared in our front, and advancing with their peculiar yell, commenced the attack, and, after a sharp struggle of about half an hour, retired." A second, better-organized assault began a short time later. This time the Confederates "held their ground with the greatest stubbornness, advancing to within 5 or 6 rods of our breastworks," where they remained for about an hour. Then, a defender wrote, "the enemy gave way and retired in confusion, followed by the cheers of our men."[40]

The undaunted Confederates launched a third attack on the Union advance line. By now, Colonel Bingham's beleaguered 64th New York was running out of ammunition: "My men began to fall, killed and wounded, and it became quite hazardous for a man to show his head above the parapet long enough to aim with certainty." They managed to break that third attack, only to watch the Confederates approach yet again. This time they advanced "in double column, closed in mass (for the colors were in the first sub-division of the masses). One of the regiments in this line was the Sixteenth Georgia, whose battle-flag was brought up to within 2 rods of our breastwork." The Georgians may have discovered a weak point in the Union line; back when they built it on May 1, the northerners had left an opening in their trenches for their skirmishers to use when they were falling back. Of this fight, Eli Landers of the 16th Georgia wrote: "The 3rd of May our Brigade got into it heels over head and our regiment lost more men than we ever have in any fight yet. We had to fight them behind their entrenchments. There was some of our company killed within fifteen steps of their trench. Our company is nearly ruined." Colonel Bingham had stopped them by ordering the two companies on the right and left of the gap to oblique their fire and cover the opening.[41] The colors of the 16th Georgia fell twice. Private Landers and his comrades ran. A friend of Landers's took a bullet, and the Georgian never forgot how he "looked very pitiful at me when he was shot and begged me to help him but I had no time to lose. It was everyman for himself."[42]

The fight on the skirmish line grew more costly as the morning progressed. At about 9:00 A.M., Colonel Morris of the 66th New York discovered that the enemy was massing troops in front of his left flank, posted at a bend in the line where the troops were vulnerable to enfilade fire. At this moment, Colonel Miles rode by, and just as Morris was requesting reinforcements, Miles—only a few feet away—took a bullet in the abdomen. Morris was certain Miles had been hit by one of the southern sharpshooters who had been harassing his men. The injured officer left the field under his own power, and although initially reported mortally wounded, he lived to wear a general's stars, marry William Tecumseh Sherman's daughter, and become commanding general of the U.S. Army in

1895. He died attending a circus performance in 1925. For his efforts at Chancellorsville, he received the Medal of Honor.[43]

With Miles down, Morris took charge of the advance line. He contended with "repeated and determined assaults upon our lines," but they were "each time gallantly repulsed by our men, with severe loss." Still, things got hotter by the moment. About the time Miles was hit, enemy gunners again opened up "a terrific fire of artillery." Southern losses also mounted. Morris claimed that every volley of Confederate musketry and every discharge from Confederate cannon seemed to "give renewed energy to our brave men and to increase their determination to maintain their position." Each man "fired with the utmost coolness and deliberation, taking careful and steady aim at his object, as if firing at a target for a prize." Charging through the same swamp that had confused Hancock's men on the first day of the fight, Lt. A. G. Grier of Cobb's Legion received a wound that cost him a leg. He could attest to the stoutness of the Union defense. From the hospital, he wrote: "I carried 62 men into the fight and I learn that only 22 or 23 escaped unhurt." Nearby, Fred West and his comrades of the 51st Georgia advanced nearly to the muzzles of the Union muskets before they were permitted to return the fire. In so doing, West wrote home, "we had 35 men and officers killed and wounded for nothing but the Regt stood the fire not a man quitting his place til shot."[44] Hancock's advance line would hold a while longer. Its support was never more necessary.

As southern infantry assaulted Hancock's picket line from the south and east, the general received orders for his main line to face about to the west. Except for Colonel Cross's command, Hancock's men left their trenches and marched a short distance to the road running north from the Chancellor house. Hancock met Hooker himself, who immediately ordered him to detach one brigade to support the weakening Third Corps front to the west. Hancock sent for Caldwell's brigade, but the terrain, the confused fighting, and the constant turnover of the picket line had disrupted his division's organization. What appears on most battle maps as Caldwell's brigade included four companies of his 148th Pennsylvania and 61st New York but also the 52nd and 57th New York of Zook's brigade.[45] These 500 to 600 men, supported on their left by the newly arrived Irish Brigade, deployed left of the road, facing west.

Hooker himself, according to regimental legend, turned to Col. James A. Beaver of the 148th Pennsylvania, pointed westward, and said, "There is your work, Col.: occupy that wood." "Hadn't I better throw out a skirmish line, General?" asked Beaver. "Wait for nothing," replied Hooker. "Everything depends on holding those woods." As Caldwell's men advanced, they became aware of the presence of the enemy when the first crashing volley hit them. Some Union soldiers believed that the Confederates had posted sharpshooters in the treetops. Soon, Pvt. Thomas Myton of the 148th Pennsylvania discovered that "I was losing faith in myself because of a certain nervousness and a disposition of my knees to knock together." His regiment, on the right flank of Caldwell's line, took the brunt of the southern volleys. Myton was wounded, becoming one of six men in his company to lose an arm at Chancellorsville. Nearby, Pvt. Henry Campbell was hit twice; as he began to move to the rear, "the bottom was knocked out of the cook pan that hung on my back[,] the ball lodging in the last ply" of his blanket. A bullet struck Colonel Beaver in the abdomen. Deciding that he had been wounded mortally, he refused proffered help: " 'Go to your places, it will be time enough to bury the dead when the battle is over.' " Fortunately for the colonel, the bullet had hit a gutta-percha pencil in his trouser pocket, deflecting it enough to save his life. But his green soldiers did not know that and wavered briefly, then steadied and pushed the Confederates back. The timely arrival of more Confederate artillery, the approach of a sizable column of enemy infantry on their left flank, an acute ammunition shortage, and Caldwell's inability to find reinforcements ended their opportunity to accomplish more.[46]

As Caldwell's men pulled back, the horrors facing the wounded men left behind increased dramatically. One injured soldier, hit twice in the right hip, found that the woods were on fire all around him. To save himself, "I lit a match as best I could, burned a space large enough to lie upon and thus escaped the flames." Two other hurt soldiers found their way to the spot and survived, all the while helplessly watching other "poor wounded comrades burning to death." Few later forgot their efforts to identify dead comrades beyond their lines, regretting exceedingly that they often failed "owing to the distance from them and the charred condition of their bodies."[47]

While Caldwell's men fought their battle, Hancock returned the rest of his division to his original lines facing east down the Orange Turnpike and spread out to fill Caldwell's empty front.[48] By 9:00 A.M., as the Union right and center threatened to collapse, possession of the Chancellorsville clearing itself remained the sole major point of contention. When pressure on the Twelfth Corps line increased from the south, Cross's men faced about from east to west and deployed in a position that would allow them to flank any Confederates that penetrated the Union line.

While Cross kept his eye on the action to his south, the Third Corps line west of Chancellorsville slowly gave way. "Seeing the enemy advancing in line of battle in the open plain toward the Chancellor house," Hancock again left his east-facing trenches, redeployed to the west, and fell into line with Cross and in support of several batteries in the clearing around the Chancellor house. As long as his advance line held off the Confederates to the east, he could risk turning his back on McLaws's forces. Although Union artillery held Confederate infantry at bay, more southern batteries wheeled into line. Those to the west in the open plain at Fairview were only "about 900 yards to my front," Hancock reported. Union gunners gave the Twelfth Corps time to begin its withdrawal, which left Hancock's men increasingly alone and vulnerable. "I was now fighting in opposite directions, one line faced [east] toward Fredericksburg, the other [west] toward Gordonsville, these two lines being about half a mile apart. Projectiles from the enemy's artillery, from the front and rear, passed over both lines, while other pieces, in different positions, enfiladed both."[49]

It was pure hell for Union troops at the Chancellor house. The 140th Pennsylvania watched "a little group of powder-begrimed men" pause to catch their breath, at which time a well-aimed shell burst among the squad, dismembering several on the spot. "What wild eyes and blanched faces there were when the shells and solid shot came in from the right front and rear of us," wrote one lieutenant years later. Artillery fire from at least fourteen guns kept Confederate infantry from reaching Hancock's lines, "although [their] battleflags were within a few hundred yards of us." Southern gunners kept up their hot fire, however, and the troops suffered severely from it. Men in the 140th Pennsylvania watched in horror as "Lieut. [Joseph] McCune [Ewen], Co. G had his head blowed off." A soldier of the 148th Pennsylvania, who found himself separated from his unit, fell in with the 140th Pennsylvania as it advanced into the Chancellor house clearing to support the batteries. Soon thereafter, he was killed instantly by a shell. As the unit's historian recorded, "No one present seemed to know his name or company, and his body, which was mangled beyond recognition, doubtless fills an unknown grave somewhere on that bloody field." As if the artillery fire were not bad enough, "the morning was hot and sultry, and so intolerable was the thirst which parched throat and lips in this terrible place that some of the men . . . took the risk of losing life or limb in order to get a mouthful of tepid water from the canteens by their sides." Five days later, Capt. David Acheson wrote of the artillery fire: "Old soldiers say that the firing . . . was heavier than any they ever heard. Antietam was surpassed. Malvern Hill was cast into the shade."[50]

The Chancellor house, now a hospital, caught fire from southern projectiles. Surgeon Calvin Fisher of the 148th Pennsylvania remembered that "at one time whilst dressing a wounded Rebel leg a shell struck the chimney, when the whole thing came in with a tremendous crash nearly falling in on me." Rescuers from the 2nd Delaware followed one of Hancock's aides into the building to move the wounded away from the flames, losing two officers in the effort. Company F of the 140th Pennsylvania, under Capt. Thomas Henry, sprinted to the rescue as well. Even in the midst of chaos, the randomness of death amazed the soldiers.

Pvt. James A. Carson, "the first man to rise in response to his captain's command" to save the wounded, was killed instantly by a piece of shell. The man next to him marveled that he only had his "little finger nipped but it doesnt hurt."[51]

As the house was emptied, Fisher discovered "about a dozen or more women in the cellar." When he insisted they leave, "there commenced a scene I pray God I may never again witness." Captain Henry left the building with one woman on each arm and another holding his coattail. Others walked alone because "there were not any dudes there to escort them in our lines." Despite the troops' best efforts, the women's safety was not secured. Fisher recalled that "one had her leg shot away, another the side of her face. Another was killed and of the others I know not." The soldiers watched one black woman run directly into the Confederate lines. A particularly unsympathetic observer later sneered: "I thought it was a poor place for hoops."[52]

Sometime about 10:00 A.M., Hancock received orders to withdraw from the Chancellor house plateau. There was no time to lose. As Colonel Cross remembered it, "Had we delayed *five* minutes more we should have been taken prisoners or cut to pieces."[53] Hancock first sent orders to the batteries to retire, but nearly all of the horses and most of the gunners had been killed or wounded. Many of the pieces had to be brought off by hand by volunteers from the infantry. Capt. David Acheson of the 140th Pennsylvania wrote his father that "Lieut. Linton took a squad of men from Parker's Co. and mine and dragged the pieces off the field." Acheson "never expected to see [Linton] return alive, but he not only escaped unhurt himself but brought his men back also." The lieutenant apparently had questioned his own chances for survival as well. He recalled years later that "the shot and shell were coming so thick and fast that it seemed one could not take his nose out of the dirt lest he would have his head blown off."[54]

Credit for rescuing the guns became a point of honor for soldiers in Zook's brigade, and they resented the men of the Irish Brigade who claimed that honor. This "organization was—in the estimation of some . . . imaginative writers, like the 'Black Horse Cavalry,' or the 'Louisiana Tigers'—supposed to be everywhere present and to perform all the deeds of heroism, which were done in the command to which they belonged," complained one soldier. The Pennsylvanians made clear that while they were not the only ones to help save the guns, they—and not the Irish Brigade—"*took the initiative in this act*." The squabble continued well into the twentieth century. In 1909, ex-corporal John Kelley of the 140th Pennsylvania still insisted that he and his comrades deserved credit for their acts of bravery: "Gen. Zook was there, Col. R. P. Roberts was there and don't try to make me believe that I was not there."[55]

After the Union guns were gone, nothing could stop the onrushing Confederate infantry or neutralize the enemy's artillery. Hancock marched his men nearly a half-mile to the rear toward a new line of entrenchments that protected the Union escape route to United States Ford. As they withdrew with the Confederates on their heels, Hancock's men shared a common opinion about the ferocity of the southern infantry assaults: "The rebs say we may kill them but we cant conquer them and I believe it. I saw whole regiments cut down and still they came on." The withdrawal was not quite orderly yet nowhere near a rout. Some of the men even stopped under fire to pick up their knapsacks, which had been rifled, getting "the most & best" they could out of them before moving to their new position. As Captain Acheson told his mother, "We came off better than I expected."[56]

As his main line began to fall back, Hancock finally ordered his stalwart picket line to retire. For a number of reasons, many of the valiant skirmishers would not reach safety. About the time Hancock issued his withdrawal order, Colonel Morris again reorganized his thin line. The 64th New York, after fighting all morning, had exhausted its ammunition. Short-term expedients no longer worked. When part of the 145th Pennsylvania showed up earlier that morning, they were ordered to share their ammunition with the New Yorkers. Unfortunately, the Pennsylvanians had old "buck and ball" .69 caliber ammunition that was of no use in the Austrian rifles carried by the New Yorkers. The latter were told "to tear off the ball and use the buckshot, which was efficient for such short range" work.[57] By now, the ammunition shortage had grown so desperate along most of the Union advance line that men were seen reaching for their bayonets. They did not have to use them, however, because the Confederates suddenly fell back.

Before the southerners returned, the Union skirmish line was strengthened by eight companies of the 27th Connecticut from Brooke's brigade. Sent over when the rest of Hancock's men first headed west to answer Hooker's call for reinforcements for the Third Corps front, the 27th understood the danger inherent in their assignment: "As is usual in such cases, when a picket in force is ordered, the colors did not accompany the column." Double-quicking out the turnpike, "we received a heavy cross fire from the Rebs," a sergeant recalled. "I noticed the very unpleasant Hum of Bullets about my ears. . . . I must confess that the Horrid screaming of those Infernal shells came near lowering my heart into the seat of my pants."[58]

The exhausted 64th New York finally could retire from the line. Colonel Bingham was proud of their work: "Not a man flinched; none passed to the rear unless wounded or sent on a message. The officers kept themselves continually on the alert, cheering and directing the men, very many tearing cartridges to expedite the firing." The New Yorkers' relief came at a fortuitous time; disaster awaited the men who took their place. The sergeant from Connecticut saw it coming: "Now I for one begin to smell a small Rat."[59]

Even before the deployment of the fresh units was completed, Hancock's aide arrived with a warning order for Colonel Morris to be ready to withdraw at any time. Morris spread the word to his subordinates. To Colonel Bostwick of the 27th Connecticut, he "pointed out . . . the direction in which we would retire . . . indicating to him with my hand the exact direction." When they moved, they were to "oblique gradually . . . to move back steadily, not too fast, keeping [the] line well closed" to "preserve an unbroken front" so "we might be able to retire, firing."[60]

Just then, heavy firing broke out on the right of the picket line as the Confederates who had ousted the Twelfth Corps now turned on it. Morris headed for the new trouble spot. Hancock's aide arrived again, this time with orders to withdraw the skirmishers after the main line to their right and rear began to fall back.[61] After Hancock's main line moved, Morris pulled back his pickets, beginning with his threatened right. He watched his own 66th New York move out handsomely, and he believed each successive unit was prepared to move to the rear as ordered.

But Morris was mistaken. Fearing that his first aide might not get through, Hancock had also sent Capt. Henry H. Bingham to the picket line with identical withdrawal orders. Bingham could not find Morris, so he "informed several [other] officers who had command of portions of the picket" to fall back. The rearward movement quickly gained too many leaders. Complicating matters considerably, pressure mounted simultaneously from the direction of the broken Twelfth Corps line, from the Orange Plank Road, and from the Orange Turnpike. Soldiers from the 148th Pennsylvania discovered they were trapped on three sides—right, rear, and front—and ran into troops from another Union unit as they tried to cross an open field. The two senior officers could not agree on the direction to safety, so each took his own course. "Our six companies following Captain Marlin came out all right, but what became of the other troops I don't know," wrote R. M. Wadding of the 148th.[62]

Confederate troops sensed the Union line's imminent collapse and pressed their advantage. The 27th Connecticut, facing east, watched a large body of southern infantry in their front moving to the right. A sergeant saw similar movement to the left: " 'Look out on the right!' 'Look out on the left!' passed up and down the line, and every man was on the alert, ready to meet them should they attempt to carry our entrenchments." Along the whole line, men were caught in a terrific fire of shrapnel that poured in from the direction of the Chancellor house and "caused considerable confusion." Many of them, "in order to avoid the shelling moved off in the opposite direction, directly toward the enemy's line."[63] Officers achieved mixed results in trying to keep the line going in the right direction.

Also caught in the deadly fire from front, rear, and right were many men of the 2nd Delaware and 145th Pennsylvania. The 2nd Delaware detail, believed Colonel Brooke, "with few exceptions, was either killed, wounded, or taken prisoners on the outposts." Four days after the battle, Brooke admitted that "I have no knowledge of them, nor can I ascertain the true facts of the case from those who came off in safety." Colonel Brown of the 145th Pennsylvania had sent 166 men and 10 officers to the picket line early on May 3, but "in the evening of the same day, [only] 61 men and 4 officers of this detail reported back." As Pvt. W. S. Trimble, a Pennsylvanian who escaped, explained, "The boys stood their ground and fought till they were surrounded and had to give up." He felt badly that some of his comrades had been captured: "There are 25 of our Co. taken prisoner. . . . There are only 6 of our Co. with the Regt. . . . It is hard to hear of our boys being taken Prisoner; but it is better than to hear of them being dead."[64]

Fate saved its cruelest twists for the recently arrived 27th Connecticut. The Nutmeggers, too, were "driven into the enemy's lines by the shelling while retiring through the woods." When the artillery fire slowed, they noticed a rebel officer in their front waving a flag of truce. At first they disregarded the white flag and continued to fire, but as the southern officer approached the Union works, Colonel Bostwick received him. "The rebel—a tall, rough specimen— announced himself as Lt. Bailey, of a Georgia regiment." He had been sent to inform us that we were entirely surrounded and "summoned us to surrender, and thus avoid the loss of life which would inevitably follow." According to McLaws, Colonel Holt, commander of the 10th Georgia, made that demand "of his own volition and to save the assault which would have followed a refusal to surrender." In any case, Bostwick was not interested. The southern officer replied, "Very well . . . give me time to get away." Bostwick had sent several officers to investigate his regiment's dilemma who had reported that they were indeed trapped, expressing a desire "to attempt to force our way through." Bostwick reconsidered the Confederate's offer, however, and called after him, "Wait one moment." After conferring with his subordinates, Bostwick asked a nearby soldier for a white handkerchief to tie to his sword. No sooner were the formalities concluded than a heavy line of rebel skirmishers swept out of the woods to the Union rear with McLaws himself close behind. "Only five minutes before, the men stood at their posts undisturbed by even a doubt of their security," one Connecticut soldier recalled, and "now, astonished at the sudden *denouement*, we found ourselves about to enter upon the terrible uncertainties of rebel captivity."[65]

Among the captors was an exultant Private Landers of the 16th Georgia: "We fought desperately to gain the day but after all our destruction we captured the whole passel of the line that was fighting us. They raised from their trench with a white flag and surrendered to us like lambs."[66] Indeed, not just the 27th Connecticut but several hundred of Hancock's men were now on their way to Richmond. Most would be exchanged soon enough to escape the horrors of southern prisons.

The handsome holding action along Hancock's picket line slowed the completion of the Confederate concentration at the crossroads of Chancellorsville. The Union army thus obtained the time needed to complete a withdrawal to its new defensive line behind the charred ruins of the Chancellor house. It should come as no surprise that some members of the advance line felt they had been sold out. The Connecticut sergeant who had provided the white handkerchief mused later, "In my opinion we were placed there to be sacrificed in order to keep the whole Army from being captured." It took years for the veterans of the 148th Pennsylvania to become a bit more philosophical about their fate. They understood that their contributions on the picket line, if remembered at all, would be little more than "a history within a history" of the battle. Nonetheless, they resented mightily that their "acts of bravery, skill and endurance, of pure heroism and patriotism," were doomed to "individually pass, 'unhonored and unsung,' swallowed up in the collected mass" of events that led ultimately to a Union defeat.[67]

Hancock's survivors were reunited by May 4 and enjoying an uneasy but well-deserved respite in Hooker's new defensive position. They stayed there two days, often under the harassing fire of Confederate artillery. Lt. Wilson Paxton of the 140th Pennsylvania summed up the troops' feelings succinctly: "Can't hold our eyes open." "I was never nearer worn out in my life," agreed surgeon Calvin Fisher, "than after that battle." Not surprisingly, the newly blooded veterans now also understood something else. As Pvt. J. S. Graham wrote, "There is no fun in fiting I do asshure you." In a letter to his wife written early on May 4, Hancock said much in a few words describing the conduct of his men in the three days of battle: "My division did well." His men viewed their commander in much the same way. As one of his soldiers wrote home with pride: "Old Hancock is ball proof and a brave man."[68]

The accomplishments of Hancock's division exacted a substantial cost. Seventy-seven men were killed, 444 wounded, and 601 missing or captured, for a total of 1,122. Excluding the light casualties of the late-arriving Irish Brigade, Hancock's men suffered a 28 percent loss. Remarkably, except for Caldwell's brief fight on May 3 and the rescuing of the cannon in the Chancellor house clearing, most of these casualties occurred at artillery range, while moving between positions, or on the picket line. Indeed, Hancock's men had done little traditional, close-range infantry fighting over the course of their three-day battle.

What can the performance of Hancock's men add to our understanding of the battle of Chancellorsville? What had they accomplished? On May 1, they provided a strong bulwark behind which the regulars could rally to help stop the southern advance west along the Orange Turnpike. From his position on the Orange Plank Road, Confederate artilleryman E. Porter Alexander noticed that the southern troops on the Orange Turnpike had "struck strong forces in good positions," and detailed accounts of the fight, "which we afterward received, convinced me that the force which we had on that road would not have been adequate for the work, had not Hooker called back his men."[69] The stout defense of Hancock's men along the Orange Turnpike may well have made Jackson's suggestion to flank that position sound like the most promising alternative for May 2.

Hancock's defensive efforts on May 2 certainly won the plaudits of the army's senior leadership. Although we know now that McLaws's men were ordered only to fix the northerners in place while Jackson marched around their flank, Hancock's men did not know that. They sustained an aggressive fight all day that kept McLaws—despite his postwar literary boasting—worrying about a possible attack from that quarter just as the Union soldiers remained concerned about a potential southern assault. Moreover, Hancock managed to aid his own army in a manner the Confederates did not foresee: while the advance troops facing east kept up their sharp fire, he—with near complete security—was able to turn his main body to face west and help stabilize the Union line after the collapse of the Eleventh Corps. Veterans of the 148th Pennsylvania's contingent on the picket line always believed that "had McLaws been able to produce any impression however slight upon the turnpike he would have fearfully complicated the problem for the Union army" on May 2.[70] The Pennsylvanians could not have known that Lee's line opposing them on May 2 had stretched and become so thin, even discontinuous, that McLaws could not have risked doing any more than he did, even if his orders had not cast him in an essentially defensive role. However one views the circumstances, Hancock's actions had paid off handsomely for the Union.

On May 2 and especially on May 3, Hancock's main line served as an active, mobile reserve, plugging holes, changing fronts, supporting and retrieving artillery, and covering the army's retirement. Many of these actions were possible only because the stalwart picket line provided security. As an example of an economy-of-force action for students of military art, Hancock's men at Chancellorsville—both the main line facing west and the advance line facing east—provide superb illustrations.

Could Hancock's men have done more? Perhaps, but only if someone other than Joseph Hooker had commanded the Army of the Potomac. Capt. Matthew Forney Steele, one of the U.S. Army's most influential military thinkers in the years between Appomattox and World War I, argued that on May 2, near the Orange Turnpike, Lee had fixed 50,000 Union troops—including those of Hancock—with only about 12,000 troops of his own, while "not a motion of offense was made by Hooker." He asserted further that "there was not a time, when by a vigorous, combined assault," Hooker "might not have defeated Lee's army."[71] Steele was correct in observing that Hancock's men stood on the Union's most direct line of advance toward Fredericksburg and the rear of Lee's lines. But Hooker did not order them to attack, and it was not Hancock's responsibility as a mere division commander to do more than suggest such a move as a possible course of action.

Satisfied that they had done their duty and proud of their accomplishments, Hancock's men found that the longer they reflected on the battle of Chancellorsville, the less it seemed a Union defeat. One soldier, who initially had believed that the army was "whipped fair and had to recross the river," wrote a few days later: "I don't call it a defeat, for they were too badly whipped to follow us." That notion soon became an article of faith for Hancock's men. "I suppose you think we are discouraged," a Pennsylvania sergeant wrote home. "Well we aren't and I still believe we can whip the rebs."[72]

Hancock's men—like many in the army—pointed the finger of blame directly at their commanding general. Capt. David Acheson of the 140th Pennsylvania observed that his men had fought desperately, "but the rebels outgeneraled us." Surgeon Fisher agreed "that Genrl. Hooker did not manage the battle rightly." Henry Crofoot of the 57th New York insisted that "the army was very poorly managed in this last fight." Hooker "was completely out Generalled." To a friend who had considered Hooker a breath of fresh air after McClellan, Crofoot wrote, "I have seen [Little Mac] and been under his command and would like to be under his command and now I think he is the only man to command this army."[73] Joe Hooker manifestly was not the only one to lose faith in Joe Hooker, and Hancock's men bore him an extra grudge. When he tried to apportion blame for the defeat among several generals, including Second Corps commander Darius Couch, one cheap shot particularly rankled. Hooker allegedly had said that "the 2nd Corps isn't worth a d—n."[74] Hancock's men surely did not deserve that comment.

The story of Hancock's division and the southerners they fought at Chancellorsville does not end here, of course. Less than two months later, many of these same soldiers (as Caldwell's division) would meet McLaws's men again. History would record that fight on a far more prominent page. It occurred on a nondescript wheatfield south of a little Pennsylvania town named Gettysburg.

1. Joseph W. Muffly, ed., *The Story of Our Regiment: A History of the 148th Pennsylvania Vols., Written by the Comrades* (Des Moines, Iowa: Kenyon, 1904), 523.

2. B. Frank Higby to Perry R. Smith, April 6, 1863, Perry R. Smith Papers, *Civil War Times Illustrated* Collection, U.S. Army Military History Institute, Carlisle Barracks, Pa. (repository hereafter cited as USAMHI).

3. U.S. War Department, *The War of the Rebellion: A Compilation of the Official Records of the Union and Confederate Armies*, 127 vols., index, and atlas (Washington, D.C.: GPO, 1880–1901), 25(1):825 (hereafter cited as *OR*; all references are to series 1).

4. Rev. Joseph A. Graves, *The History of the Bedford Light Artillery* (Bedford City, Va.: Press of the Bedford Democrat, 1903), 29; Lafayette McLaws, "The Battle of Chancellorsville: The Most Remarkable One of the War," p. 8, undated typescript, folder 31, Lafayette McLaws Papers, #472, Southern Historical Collection, Wilson Library, University of North Carolina, Chapel Hill, N.C.

5. *OR* 25(1):318. Hancock's artillery was placed under the tactical direction of Capt. Stephen H. Weed of the Fifth Corps artillery with Sykes.

6. Muffly, *148th Pennsylvania*, 524; *OR* 25(1):318.

7. Muffly, *148th Pennsylvania*, 680, 772, 631.

8. *OR* 25(1):340–41; Muffly, *148th Pennsylvania*, 524.

9. McLaws, "Battle of Chancellorsville," 9; *OR* 25(1):341.

10. Benjamin F. Powelson, *History of Company K of the 140th Regiment Pennsylvania Volunteers* (Steubenville, Ohio: Carnahan, 1906), 22; Muffly, *148th Pennsylvania*, 524; unknown sergeant to "Friend Bigelow," May 29, 1863, 27th Connecticut file, Wiley Sword Collection, USAMHI.

11. *OR* 25(1):322, 311, 329.

12. Ibid., 825; D. Augustus Dickert, *History of Kershaw's Brigade, with Complete Roll of Companies, Biographical Sketches, Incidents, Anecdotes, etc.* (1899; reprint, Dayton, Ohio: Morningside, 1973), 210–11.

13. *OR* 25(1):331, 322.

14. Unknown sergeant to "Friend Bigelow," May 29, 1863, 27th Connecticut file, Wiley Sword Collection, USAMHI; diary of unknown member of 140th Pennsylvania, May 8, 1863, Timothy Brooks Collection, USAMHI; Robert Laird Stewart, *History of the One Hundred and Fortieth Regiment, Pennsylvania Volunteers* (Philadelphia: Regimental Association, 1912), 53.

15. *OR* 25(1):834, 837.

16. Ibid., 311, 318; Henry C. Campbell memoir, Henry C. Campbell Papers, Civil War Miscellaneous Collection, USAMHI.

17. Winthrop D. Sheldon, *The "Twenty-Seventh [Connecticut]": A Regimental History* (New Haven, Conn.: Morris & Benham, 1866), 47. See also *OR* 25(1):311.

18. Stewart, *One Hundred and Fortieth Regiment, Pennsylvania Volunteers*, 57.

19. Sheldon, *The "Twenty-Seventh,"* 47.

20. *OR* 25(1):312; Sheldon, *The "Twenty-Seventh,"* 48; Stewart, *One Hundred and Fortieth Regiment, Pennsylvania Volunteers*, 57.

21. Sheldon, *The "Twenty-Seventh,"* 48; Dickert, *Kershaw's Brigade*, 211.

22. *OR* 25(1):341–42.

23. Thomas M. Aldrich, *The History of Battery A, First Regiment Rhode Island Light*

Artillery, in the War to Preserve the Union, 1861–1865 (Providence, R.I.: Snow & Farnham, 1904), 175; Powelson, *Company K of the 140th Regiment Pennsylvania Volunteers*, 22.

24. *OR* 25(1):312.

25. Ibid.; Muffly, *148th Pennsylvania*, 525.

26. *OR* 25(1):312; Sheldon, *The "Twenty-Seventh,"* 48–49; Muffly, *148th Pennsylvania*, 632.

27. McLaws, "Battle of Chancellorsville," 12.

28. *OR* 25(1):338.

29. Unknown sergeant to "Friend Bigelow," May 29, 1863, 27th Connecticut file, Wiley Sword Collection, USAMHI; *OR* 25(1):313, 454–55.

30. McLaws, "Battle of Chancellorsville," 12; Henry N. Blake, *Three Years in the Army of the Potomac* (Boston: Lee and Shepard, 1866), 173; *OR* 25(1):323.

31. *OR* 25(1):319; Francis A. Walker, *General Hancock* (New York: D. Appleton, 1894), 82.

32. McLaws, "Battle of Chancellorsville," 15–16.

33. Fred H. West to "Maggie," May 18, 1863, copy, bound vol. 128, Fredericksburg and Spotsylvania National Military Park Library, Fredericksburg, Va. (repository hereafter cited as FSNMP); W. A. Johnson, "Battle of Chancellorsville," Atlanta *Journal*, January 4, 1902.

34. Unknown sergeant to "Friend Bigelow," May 29, 1863, 27th Connecticut file, Wiley Sword Collection, USAMHI; Stewart, *One Hundred and Fortieth Regiment, Pennsylvania Volunteers*, 60; William Child, *A History of the Fifth Regiment New Hampshire Volunteers in the American Civil War, 1861–1865* (Bristol, N.H.: R. W. Musgrove, 1893), 184.

35. Sheldon, *The "Twenty-Seventh,"* 50; Stewart, *One Hundred and Fortieth Regiment, Pennsylvania Volunteers*, 61, 63; Franklin P. Ellis, ed., *History of Cattaraugus County, New York* (Philadelphia, 1879), 105; Child, *Fifth Regiment New Hampshire Volunteers*, 184.

36. Johnson, "Battle of Chancellorsville."

37. *OR* 25(1):331.

38. Ibid., 343.

39. Ibid., 313.

40. Ibid., 343.

41. Ibid., 344; Elizabeth Whitley Roberson, *Weep Not for Me Dear Mother* (Washington, N.C.: Venture, 1991), 102.

42. Roberson, *Weep Not for Me*, 102.

43. *OR* 25(1):333; Ezra J. Warner, *Generals in Blue: Lives of the Union Commanders* (Baton Rouge: Louisiana State University Press, 1964), 322–24.

44. *OR* 25(1):331–32; "Private Letter from Lieut. A. G. Grier," *Southern Confederacy* (Atlanta), May 19, 1863; Fred H. West to "Maggie," May 18, 1863, copy, bound vol. 128, FSNMP.

45. *OR* 25(1):313, 319.

46. Frank A. Burr, *Life and Achievements of James Addams Beaver: Early Life, Military Services, and Public Career* (Philadelphia: Ferguson Brothers, 1882), 60–61; Muffly, *148th Pennsylvania*, 632, 835, 841; Henry C. Campbell memoir, Campbell Papers, Civil War Miscellaneous Collection, USAMHI; *OR* 25(1):320.

47. Muffly, *148th Pennsylvania*, 652–53.

48. *OR* 25(1):313.

49. Ibid., 313–14.

50. Stewart, *One Hundred and Fortieth Regiment, Pennsylvania Volunteers*, 66, 71, 69;

"Saving the Guns," *National Tribune* (Philadelphia), December 23, 1886; *OR* 25(1):314; Alexander W. Acheson to his mother, May 4, 1863, Alexander W. Acheson Papers, Pennsylvania Save the Flags Collection, USAMHI.

51. Dr. Calvin Fisher to Dr. Alfred Fisher, May 19, 1863, Benjamin Fisher Papers, USAMHI; *OR* 25(1):337; Stewart, *One Hundred and Fortieth Regiment, Pennsylvania Volunteers*, 70; diary of unknown member of 140th Pennsylvania, May 8, 1863, Brooks Collection, USAMHI.

52. Dr. Calvin Fisher to Dr. Alfred Fisher, May 19, 1863, Benjamin Fisher Papers, USAMHI; Stewart, *One Hundred and Fortieth Regiment, Pennsylvania Volunteers*, 71; "The Burned Chancellors House," *National Tribune* (Philadelphia), January 28, 1909; diary of unknown member of 140th Pennsylvania, May 28, 1863, Brooks Collection, USAMHI.

53. *OR* 25(1):314; Child, *Fifth Regiment New Hampshire Volunteers*, 185.

54. David Acheson to his father, May 4, 8, 1863, Alexander W. Acheson Papers, Pennsylvania Save the Flags Collection, USAMHI; "Saving the Guns."

55. Stewart, *One Hundred and Fortieth Regiment, Pennsylvania Volunteers*, 71, 74; "Burning of Chancellor House," *National Tribune* (Philadelphia), July 8, 1909.

56. Diary of unknown member of 140th Pennsylvania, May 8, 1863, Brooks Collection, USAMHI; John Mitchell diary, May 4, 1863, John Mitchell Papers, USAMHI; David Acheson to his mother, May 8, 1863, Alexander W. Acheson Papers, Pennsylvania Save the Flags Collection, USAMHI.

57. *OR* 25(1):344.

58. Sheldon, *The "Twenty-Seventh,"* 51; unknown sergeant to "Friend Bigelow," May 29, 1863, 27th Connecticut file, Wiley Sword Collection, USAMHI.

59. *OR* 25(1):345; unknown sergeant to "Friend Bigelow," May 29, 1863, 27th Connecticut file, Wiley Sword Collection, USAMHI.

60. *OR* 25(1):317, 334.

61. Ibid., 318, 334.

62. Ibid., 317; Muffly, *148th Pennsylvania*, 778.

63. Sheldon, *The "Twenty-Seventh,"* 52; *OR* 25(1):335.

64. *OR* 25(1):336, 348; W. S. Trimble to "Friend Nan Bowden," May 9, 1863, Nancy Bowden Ellis Papers, Civil War Miscellaneous Collection, USAMHI.

65. Sheldon, *The "Twenty-Seventh,"* 53–54; McLaws, "Battle of Chancellorsville," 17; unknown sergeant to "Friend Bigelow," May 29, 1863, 27th Connecticut file, Wiley Sword Collection, USAMHI.

66. Roberson, *Weep Not for Me*, 102–3.

67. Unknown sergeant to "Friend Bigelow," May 29, 1863, 27th Connecticut file, Wiley Sword Collection, USAMHI; Muffly, *148th Pennsylvania*, 700.

68. Wilson Paxton journal, May 4, 1863, Wilson Paxton Papers, Civil War Miscellaneous Collection, USAMHI; Dr. Calvin Fisher to Dr. Alfred Fisher, May 19, 1863, Benjamin Fisher Papers, USAMHI; J. Smith Gordon to Miss Mary Graham, May 26, 1863, in *Aunt and Soldier Boys from Cross Creek Village, Pennsylvania, 1856–1866*, ed. William H. Bartlett (Santa Cruz, Calif.: Moore Graphic Arts, 1973), unpaginated; [Almira Russell Hancock], *Reminiscences of Winfield Scott Hancock by His Wife* (New York: Charles Webster, 1887), 94; diary of unknown member of 140th Pennsylvania, May 16, 1863, Brooks Collection, USAMHI.

69. Edward Porter Alexander, *Fighting for the Confederacy: The Personal Recollections of General Edward Porter Alexander*, ed. Gary W. Gallagher (Chapel Hill: University of North Carolina Press, 1989), 198.

70. Muffly, *148th Pennsylvania*, 791.

71. Matthew F. Steele, *Strategy and Military Geography and History: Lecture No. XVI, The Battle of Chancellorsville* ([Fort Leavenworth, Kans.]: Infantry and Cavalry School, 1907), 28. This lecture became part of Steele's more famous work, *American Campaigns*, 2 vols. (Washington, D.C.: Byron S. Adams, 1909), used as a text in army classrooms until the 1950s.

72. Diary of unknown member of 140th Pennsylvania, May 7, 10, 1863, Brooks Collection, USAMHI; David Acheson to his mother, May 8, 1863, Alexander W. Acheson Papers, Pennsylvania Save the Flags Collection, USAMHI.

73. David Acheson to his mother, May 8, 1863, Alexander W. Acheson Papers, Pennsylvania Save the Flags Collection, USAMHI; Dr. Calvin Fisher to Dr. Alfred Fisher, May 9, 1863, Benjamin Fisher Papers, USAMHI; Henry Crofoot to unknown, May 10, 1863, Perry R. Smith Papers, *Civil War Times Illustrated* Collection, USAMHI.

74. Alexander W. Acheson to his mother, May 25, 1863, Alexander W. Acheson Papers, Pennsylvania Save the Flags Collection, USAMHI.

Medical Treatment at Chancellorsville

James I. Robertson, Jr.

TWO WEEKS after the battle of Chancellorsville, a Union surgeon used a rare quiet period to make an entry in his diary. "As I write this after all is past . . . I thank God for his goodness to me," he recorded, adding, "I consider war as a dire calamity and a visitation from the Almighty and especially such is this national war." A medical colleague in an Illinois regiment agreed in even more forceful terms. "There is no God in war," he stated. Battle "is merciless, cruel, vindictive, un-christian, savage, relentless. It is all that devils could wish for."[1]

Many Civil War surgeons shared these sentiments, and for good cause. Jonathan Letterman, medical director for the Army of the Potomac, took the high road when he observed: "It is the interest of the Government, aside from all motives of humanity, to bestow the greatest possible care upon its wounded and sick, and to use every means to preserve the health of those who are well, since the greater the labor given to the preservation of health, the greater will be the number for duty, and the more attention bestowed upon the sick and wounded, the more speedily will they perform the duties for which they were employed."[2]

Several obstacles blocked this idealistic viewpoint from becoming reality in the 1860s. Senility and shortsightedness in the army medical department, ignorance in both North and South about how to cope with large-scale medical needs, shortages of supplies, and limitations in medical knowledge were the primary factors that hampered military medicine and heightened soldier suffering. A number of generals (the hapless Don Carlos Buell among them) did not even believe the army should have a medical corps. They subscribed to the idea that the purpose of war was to tear the body, not to mend it. This explains why one authority termed the Civil War, especially its early stages, "one vast experiment in the determination of how much injury the human body can endure."

Understandably, frustration marks most of the memoirs of Civil War surgeons. Typical was this statement by an army physician in the immediate aftermath of the 1862 battle of Antietam: "I am tired of this inhuman incompetence, this neglect and folly, which leave me alone with all these soldiers on my hands, five hundred of whom will die before daybreak unless they have attention and I with no light but a five-inch candle."[3]

The development of the Union and Confederate army medical departments had much to do with what was—and was not—done in medical treatment at the battle of Chancellorsville. Suffice it to say that by 1863 both sides were making slow progress through equal amounts of trial and error. The journey, though long, could only be upward. A year before the war began, the illustrious Dr. Oliver Wendell Holmes told a gathering of physicians that if all medical techniques then known "could sink to the bottom of the sea, it would be all the better for mankind—and all the worse for the fishes."[4]

Urgency, oftentimes bordering on desperation, marked medical efforts in the first two years of the Civil War. An Indiana soldier during the first autumn of the war offered what he thought was the supreme criticism when he stated that "the docterking [was] about in keeping [with] the Cooking." A few months later, Illinois artillerist Timothy Blaisdell became incensed at what he considered the autocracy of army surgeons. "Because a man has enlisted to serve his country," Blaisdell wrote, "it is no reason he should be treated like a dog by one-horse country doctors, who once they mount shoulder straps, think they are very near Almighty."[5]

Advances soon began to appear in Civil War medicine. For example, Dr. Edward Squibb perfected a large-scale production method for manufacturing ether and chloroform, and his firm turned out enormous quantities of the painkillers during the war. Surgeon Julian Chisholm achieved pathbreaking success with his technique of sealing gunshot wounds and thereby reducing infection. Another Confederate surgeon, Joseph Jones, encouraged increased use of maggots in open wounds by demonstrating conclusively that they destroy only diseased tissue, otherwise leaving wounds in a healthy condition.

The introduction of female nurses was a godsend for many sick and wounded soldiers—although the Union stipulations imposed on nursing applicants were unusually stringent. One circular noted: "No woman under 30 years of age need apply to serve in government hospitals. All nurses are required to be very plain looking women. Their dresses must be brown or black, with no bows, no curls, no jewelry, and no hoop skirts." One of the first responses stated in part: "I . . . will comply with all of your requirements. I am plain looking enough to suit you, and old enough. I have no near relatives in the war; no lover there. I never had a husband and am not looking for one. Will you take me?" Fortunately the medical department accepted the woman for nursing duty.[6]

These forward steps notwithstanding, casualty figures in Civil War battles remained high from start to end. Also, such statistics are conservative to the point of being flagrantly misleading. Most casualty charts show six to eight men wounded for every man killed. Yet among the wounded, two would die of sickness and disease for every man lost in action. In addition, two more of the wounded would be permanently disabled. Further, a tragically high number of those listed under the "missing" columns were in fact dead. They had been blown to bits or else had crawled wounded to some inconspicuous place and died without ever being found.

One historian worked out a simple table that could apply to any Civil War battle, including Chancellorsville. In a major action in which 100 men were killed and 900 wounded, 65 of the injured would die and 400 would be too maimed to return to duty. Hence, what appeared to be a temporary loss of 900 soldiers was in fact a permanent loss of close to 500 men.

Unsophisticated field care made these figures so large. Before 1863, receiving prompt and proper attention to battle wounds was the exception rather than the rule. One authority commented on this doubly crippling problem: "During the progress of a great battle, no duty is more imperative, both for preserving the integrity of an army, and for humanity's sake, than the care for the wounded. Indeed, on the medical direction of an army largely depends its efficiency."[7]

The system of handling the wounded in battle was primitive. Before the action began, medical directors designated homes, outbuildings, and other shelters as field hospitals. If the weather was clear, many surgeons preferred to work in the open for better ventilation. These sites were usually one to two miles behind the battle lines in order to be out of artillery range. Field hospitals became increasingly overcrowded as the day passed. Small squads of men

Union soldiers performing an ambulance drill in the field, fall 1862. Francis Trevelyan Miller, ed., The Photographic History of the Civil War, *10 vols. (New York: Review of Reviews, 1911), 7:305*

(usually convalescents, musicians, and others considered unfit for battle) were assigned as transporters. Many of these aides carried knapsacks containing dressings, tourniquets, and stimulants when available. Once battle exploded, assistant surgeons on the field administered preliminary treatment. Regimental surgeons at hospitals in the rear did the major work when the wounded arrived by stretcher, cart, wagon, or on the back of a friend.

Ambulances were crude and uncomfortable for the wounded. By 1863, ordinary wagons were still used as the basic conveyance. Usually lacking springs, they traveled through rough, wooded country and over roads as rutted as those in a marine obstacle course. Heavy rainfalls left the roads seas of mud. Wagons became mired, while rain dripped through the covers onto the wounded. The wagon drivers often drove the ambulances at breakneck speed or bounced them over obstacles with little thought to their passengers.

One result of this ongoing nightmare was a marked improvement in ambulance service on both sides by the time of the battle of Chancellorsville. Medical director Jonathan Letterman worked miracles securing and organizing Federal ambulances early in 1863. Meanwhile, the Richmond Ambulance Committee, established in late 1862 by more than 100 concerned citizens, purchased scores of wagons and hired responsible teamsters to handle them. The ambulance service at Chancellorsville could have been the best up to that point in the war. It was not, however, because of Hooker's mismanagement discussed below.

Although both sides were making parallel advances in many areas of military medicine, such was not the case concerning the overall quality of medical care or the condition of the opposing forces after two years of combat. The North was improving steadily; the South was deteriorating at the same pace.

In army medicine in the North, the plump and bearded figure of William Alexander Hammond occupies center stage. A native of Maryland and an assistant surgeon in the army for twelve years prior to the war, Hammond was a man of ideas and action. The Civil War was only a year old when authorities promoted the thirty-three-year-old Hammond over a number of senior army physicians as the Union's new surgeon general. (Hammond replaced an aged and senile physician who opposed the purchase of new editions of medical texts as long as the old ones were still in good physical shape.) As one writer aptly noted, to the "strict constructionists, whose heads had been leaped over, [Hammond] was as welcome as a Bolshevik to the Romanoffs."

The young head of the army's medical department promptly transformed an antiquated, rickety, and largely incompetent medical bureaucracy into a vast, well-organized, professional complex. Folklore and outmoded methods were abandoned; Hammond introduced new, streamlined, seemingly unorthodox treatments. At the time of Chancellorsville, the North had 151 general military hospitals, with a total of 58,700 beds. Satterlee Hospital in Philadelphia was the largest, with a capacity of 3,500 patients.

In the first year of the Civil War, the mortality rate from gunshot wounds was a whopping 25.6 percent. The following year it dropped to 15.3 percent; by 1863, thanks largely to Hammond's organizational skills and rigid directives, the death rate from gunshot wounds was down to 9.5 percent. The fact that the mortality figure had been sliced by almost two-thirds in two years was little short of miraculous.[8]

Maj. Jonathan Letterman was medical director of the Army of the Potomac at the time of the battle of Chancellorsville. Like Hammond, this Pennsylvania surgeon had been in the army for twelve years when civil war came. Letterman was conscientious and indefatigable; and if he occasionally exaggerated the positive side of the medical picture, it was only natural for an army's principal physician to do so. The long 1862–63 winter encampment near Fredericksburg gave Letterman the time to work hard at bringing disease under control while elevating hygiene to a higher plane. By spring, the medical director proudly reported a drop of 28 percent in typhoid fever cases and a 32 percent decline in the number of soldiers suffering from diarrhea. Letterman first determined and then emphasized that sickness was most prevalent in corps with the largest numbers of new regiments. As Maj. Gen. Joseph Hooker planned his spring offensive against Robert E. Lee, Letterman announced that only 6.7 percent of

*Maj. Jonathan Letterman (*seated at left*) and staff. Francis Trevelyan Miller, ed.,* The Photographic History of the Civil War, *10 vols. (New York: Review of Reviews, 1911), 7:219*

the nearly 140,000 men in the Army of the Potomac were on the sick list. "Not only was the percentage small," he later boasted, "but those not on the lists of sick were in vigorous health, and in buoyant spirits arising therefrom." No commander "ever had an army in better health or in higher spirits," Letterman declared.[9]

Lee could not say the same about his Army of Northern Virginia. The fault lay not with any individual but with the nature and the shortcomings of the Confederate experiment in nationalism. Presiding over the South's army medical service was fifty-year-old Samuel Preston Moore. This native of Charleston, South Carolina, spent twenty-six years in the old army before becoming the Confederate surgeon general. Moore was a handsome man: tall, erect, with muttonchop whiskers dominating his features. Like his Union counterpart, he was also a rigid disciplinarian who had little patience for excuses.[10]

Moore had to be demanding in order to maintain a makeshift department for armies that became more enfeebled as the war continued. The Confederacy operated about 150 general army hospitals, but that total is deceiving. The facilities for the most part were small. A third of the hospitals were in Richmond, including the 8,000-bed Chimborazo compound. Yet Surgeon General Moore's problems fanned out in every direction.

During the course of the war, it was estimated that 3,000 Confederate military surgeons treated 3 million wounded or diseased patients, which breaks down to one surgeon per 1,000 patients. Basic drugs were more precious than gold throughout the Confederacy. Surgeon Moore was forced to order the use of native remedies and instruments whenever possible. Hunter McGuire, one of the most famous Confederate surgeons, recalled the hardships and improvisations of the typical southern field surgeon: "The pliant bark of a tree made for him a good tourniquet; the juice of the green persimmon, a styptic; a knitting needle, with its point sharply bent, a tenaculum; and a pen-knife in his hand, a scalpel." McGuire watched a surgeon "break off one prong of a common table fork, bend the point of the other prong, and with it elevate the bone in depressed fracture of the skull and save life." Physicians in the beleaguered Confederacy had no choice but to utilize every home-fashioned potion available. One quack sent the surgeon general some medicine that, he claimed, would cure "colick . . . Dierhea . . . Dysenterry." For what it was worth to the soldiers, the elixir was also guaranteed to prevent abortion.[11]

Lafayette Guild was Lee's only medical director. The Tuscaloosa, Alabama, native was in his late thirties when he took charge of the medical wing of the South's principal army. Guild was tall and impressive looking, with black hair and mustache.[12] He too was a tireless worker, although no amount of work could have eliminated the health problems besetting the Army of Northern Virginia as the war's second year began.

Manpower needs were becoming critical. Early in 1863 the War Department in Richmond ordered that no further exemptions be granted to recruits or conscripts suffering from heart disease, the loss of an eye, the loss of two fingers, hemorrhoids, or general debility. Troops then in the field were fighting filth. One Confederate observed: "Every soldier had a brigade of lice on him, and I have seen fellows so busily engaged in cracking them that it reminded me of an old woman knitting." By late winter 1863, 400 of 1,500 Confederates in one brigade were barefooted. Many soldiers had no blankets. Some of the men, one infantryman asserted, were "without a particle of under-clothing, having neither shirts, drawers, nor socks; while overcoats, from their rarity, are objects of curiosity."[13]

Typhoid fever and scurvy had roared almost out of control during the winter encampment south of Fredericksburg. Worst of all for the Confederate army was an outbreak of smallpox that began in October 1862 and did not run its course until the eve of Chancellorsville. The dreaded disease killed and crippled untold numbers of southern men, and at least 5,000 of Lee's soldiers were unfit for duty in May because of severe reactions to smallpox vaccinations administered hastily during the epidemic.[14]

Lee's army began the Chancellorsville campaign with about 61,000 men in the ranks. How many of them were in acceptable physical condition can never

Dr. Samuel Preston Moore. Francis Trevelyan Miller, ed., The Photographic History of the Civil War, *10 vols. (New York: Review of Reviews, 1911), 7:239*

be answered definitively; however, the Confederate army's health was markedly inferior to that of its Union opponent as the two forces moved toward combat at and to the west of Fredericksburg.

Late on Tuesday, April 28, 1863, it began raining. The downpour lasted two days. Through the storm Hooker moved the bulk of his army to the west in order to cross the Rappahannock River and come in on Lee's supposedly vulnerable left flank. Hooker's plan was good; his marching orders, however, displayed a callous disregard of medical needs. The general permitted only two ambulances to accompany each division. No ambulances or hospital wagons were allowed across the Rappahannock.

Thanks to pleas from medical director Letterman, a few medicine wagons followed the Union army into the Wilderness. All other rolling stock was parked at United States and Banks fords, both of which were several miles from the crossroads of Chancellorsville. Medical directors of the various Federal corps quickly made the usual preparations. For example, Federal surgeon Justin Dwinelle, in charge of the Second Corps hospital at Potomac Creek, compiled inventories of supplies ranging from laudanum to potatoes. Dwinelle also reported in the third week of April that he had enough tents on hand to accommodate 900 incapacitated soldiers and expected to receive a shipment of large Sibley tents momentarily. Dr. Thomas Sim of the Third Corps stated: "I at once established the principal depot for the wounded at the large white house, about half a mile in rear of the Plank Road and on the right of the road leading from the ford to Chancellorsville. . . . The house and outhouses were thoroughly cleaned and policed; operating tables were improvised by detaching some of the doors from their hinges, with the addition of a few boards found about the premises."[15]

In the skirmishes of May 1–2, wounded Federals from the First and Fifth corps went initially to the Chancellor house and then proceeded via United States Ford to division hospitals prepared for the injured at Falmouth Heights. Surgeons in the Eleventh Corps far out on Hooker's western flank improvised field stations but gave little thought to using them. Dr. Robert Hubbard of the 17th Connecticut wrote of selecting "an old log hut in an open field directly in the rear of the 1st Division but within gunshot range that the wounded might be readily brought to it."[16]

Near suppertime on Saturday, May 2, thousands of Confederates under Lt. Gen. T. J. "Stonewall" Jackson suddenly slammed into the unsuspecting and dangling Union flank. Where pandemonium did not exist, panic ensued. Federal major general Gouverneur K. Warren, Hooker's chief topographical engineer, noted disgustingly: "The Eleventh Corps infantry . . . made no stand at all behind its breastworks, but ran away while yet the enemy's bullets scarcely reached them. . . . I tried in vain to assist some of the officers in rallying their men, but soon saw it was a waste of precious time." Among the fleeing Federals was Connecticut's surgeon Hubbard. "Before I had time to receive a patient from the field," he allowed, "our men and the rebels were pouring down upon me and the balls and shells falling around like hail & how I escaped without being wounded I can hardly perceive." Hubbard made it to safety by mounting his horse and galloping frantically to the rear. The broken wing of Hooker's army swept to the east so fast and so forcefully that it momentarily overran its own hospitals in the Chancellor house area. Adding to the chaos of the near-rout, one surgeon reported, a large drove of steers "came dashing down the road at full speed, their drivers yelling at the top of their voices. This was enough to scatter the panic stricken soldiers into the woods."[17]

Confederate artillery fire caused the immediate evacuation of the first-aid stations and doubtless killed some of the wounded awaiting treatment. Union medical officials regarded such action as the chaos of war rather than barbarism on the part of the enemy.[18] In the hasty withdrawal from the Chancellor house sector, Federals abandoned four cases of medical instruments. Most of the twenty-one Union surgeons captured at Chancellorsville were taken at this stage of the battle.[19]

While Jackson was driving the Union right flank into the middle of Hooker's position, Confederate surgeon McGuire and his colleagues were tending to wounded men behind the attack. McGuire served as Jackson's personal physician and chief surgeon of the Confederate army's Second Corps. He was then twenty-seven, eleven years younger than Jackson. Born in Winchester, Virginia, McGuire had been practicing medicine only seven years but was an extraordinary surgeon from the outset. The Civil War period was merely an early stage of what became a luminous career.[20]

McGuire had created at least two advance medical stations. One was at the Talley house, a structure of one and a half stories located west of the Wilderness Church and Brock Road. There fence planks were used variously to keep the wounded off the ground, as fuel, and for coffins.[21] A second field hospital was set up at Dowdall's Tavern, the Orange Turnpike home of Baptist cleric Melzi Chancellor just to the east of the Wilderness Church. This site came within range of Union artillery as the battle unfolded. The main Confederate field hospital materialized several miles west near the intersection of the turnpike with the Germanna Plank Road. It was to this hospital, during the night of May 2, that an ambulance bore the wounded Stonewall Jackson.

The battle of Chancellorsville in its fullest violence raged throughout Sunday, May 3. Confederates renewed their assault and shattered the makeshift Union line near the Chancellor house. Fighting was intense for hours. Wounded men began to accumulate in flood proportions.

At corps surgeon Thomas Sim's field hospital, some 700 injured soldiers arrived for care. Sim wrote: "Beds of leaves and pine branches were prepared for the men, covered with arbors made with the branches of trees, forming a shelter from the hot sun." However, "the enemy's shells again found us, causing a stampede among the wounded who were able to get away, and considerable perturbation among those poor fellows who were helpless. . . . Some were wounded for the second time. Three men were killed, two of whom had already suffered amputation at the hands of the surgeon."

The Chancellor house was again serving as a Union field hospital when Confederate artillery set it afire. Several shells exploded in the tavern. One wounded man was killed as he lay on the table undergoing surgery. The physicians stopped their ministrations and bore a number of helpless men to safety from the burning structure. Some Union field hospitals had to move as many as three times in the course of the day.[22]

Scattered first-aid stations could not handle all of the wounded. Hooker's directive forbidding ambulances on the field—surely one of the most short-sighted measures of the entire war—left human debris strewn throughout the Wilderness. As quickly as wounded men could be collected and given initial treatment, they were dispatched by foot and stretcher to the permanent corps hospitals at Potomac Creek, Brooke's Station, and Aquia Creek. The number of injured Federals was so large, however, that it was impossible for all of them to escape. In the course of May 3, some 1,200 of them fell into Confederate hands.[23]

Cpl. Rice C. Bull of the 123rd New York fell in action with gunshot wounds in the jaw and hip. Stretcher-bearers were able to take him about fifty yards behind the front line to a small creek with high banks that offered some protection from stray bullets. "When I reached the stream," the New Yorker recalled, "I found it already lined with many dead and wounded men. Some had been carried there, others had dragged themselves to the place; numbers had died after reaching the run and some of the wounded were then slowly and needlessly bleeding to death." Not a surgeon could be found. Corporal Bull then added a poignant comment: "I noted that the wounded, as a rule, were very quiet and it was exceptional that any made loud cries or appeared demoralised."[24]

Hindering the removal and treatment of wounded Confederates was the fact that Union cavalry had torn up large sections of railroad behind Lee's army. Delays of several days occurred at sidings and road crossings as men awaited trains bound for hospitals in Richmond.

Meanwhile, on May 3, another battle occurred at the war-gutted town of Fredericksburg a dozen miles to the east of Chancellorsville. At Second Fredericksburg, Union surgeons and stewards won commendation for efficiency. Medical director Letterman later declared: "I know of no instance in which such a number of wounded were so speedily removed from the field, and so promptly and well attended."[25]

Early on the morning of May 3, medical personnel in Gen. John Sedgwick's Sixth Corps moved into those Fredericksburg buildings still standing and converted them into aid stations. The wounded began to stream into town almost at once. More than 1,000 casualties appeared during the first hour of combat. Surgeon George Stevens was among the handful of available army physicians. "Churches and private dwellings," Stevens wrote, "swarmed with the unfortunate men, whose mangled forms told of the fearful work of the day. Surgeons were hard at work ministering relief to the suffering, binding up the wounds or removing the mangled limbs which offered no hope of recovery; while nurses administered food and coffee, and prepared beds, such as could be extemporized from blankets spread upon the floors." At St. George's Episcopal Church, hospital steward John H. Hieber of the 139th Pennsylvania was shocked at the number of casualties arriving throughout the day: "Such sites are too much for human eyes to behold. Dying, screaming and groaning in every quarter and the blood almost running on the floor." To Hieber it looked "more like a slotter [sic] house than a hospital."[26]

The fortitude of badly injured soldiers impressed even the most hardened of observers. Pvt. Erskine Branch of the 77th New York had a leg torn to shreds by an exploding shell. He hobbled to one of the improvised hospitals on his good leg and used his musket as a crutch, all the while singing "The Star-Spangled Banner." Cpl. Henry West, another New York soldier, took an ugly wound in the thigh. On the operating table, West smiled at the surgeon and said: "I guess that old Joe West's son has lost a leg." West hemorrhaged to death a few hours later. Others undergoing treatment endured further suffering amid the heat and humidity of the next afternoon. Ambulances removed more than 3,000 men through battered Fredericksburg, across the river, to the field hospitals on Falmouth Heights.[27]

The heavy fighting at Chancellorsville went into its third day. Surgeons and stewards on both sides literally had their hands full. The surgeon of the 154th New York found time to inform his wife that he had performed amputations and ligations on more than 400 men in the last day and a half. "I have had ample opportunity to see the sad side of the picture," he understated. "Thank God I have escaped so far unhurt. I write this in the midst of the wounded. . . . God grant that this may be the last battle I may ever be called upon to witness."[28]

Field hospitals were a nightmare for soldiers and surgeons alike. Operations took place on any available flat surface, a door laid upon barrels being a typical table. Underneath were tubs to catch the blood; nearby were pails of water, rags, and sponges to wash away the crimson slime from the last patient before the next one was put in place. Water was always scarce, heat and flies everpresent. Amid the groans and screams of mangled soldiers awaiting their turn, surgeons wielded scalpels and saws hour after hour, operating on suffering men whose only anesthesia often was a drink of whiskey and sometimes not even that. Lack of linen and cotton material resulted in old bandages (infested with every imaginable microbe) being used again and again. A piece of a shirt, a filthy handkerchief, discarded socks, underdrawers no longer needed, were all used as tourniquets to control bleeding. Whether they accomplished this purpose is irrelevant because such filthy material contaminated wounds with millions of germs. This produced infections such as osteomyelitis, erysipelas, gangrene, and pyemia. These diseases were basically staphylococcus and streptococcus infections in which bacteria cells generated pus, destroyed tissue, and released into the system toxins that were agonizing journeys to death. Of gangrene, a medical authority stated: "One has to actually see it and smell it to believe it." Pyemia was once described as "a hail of chills, sweat, fever, and advancing jaundice [in which] the patient gallops to his death."[29]

Those wounded men unable to reach a field hospital or locate a surgeon encountered unimaginable misery. In one instance, 800 wounded Federals huddled in the yard of an abandoned log cabin. A single surgeon was present. He had neither medicines nor instruments. One of those injured soldiers remembered: "Night came but no surgeons or supplies arrived. The men were now in a deplorable condition. Their wounds had become inflamed, angry and painful beyond description. Their efforts in getting to the rendezvous had opened many wounds and they were bleeding afresh. There was no nursing, no food, and no medicine to alleviate or stupify the pain of those who were enduring torture here, had no tent covering, and many very little in the way of blanket covering, either over or under them, and all so weak they could scarcely move hand or foot." Most of those hundreds of wounded spent eight days awaiting medical attention.[30]

Naturally, the Chancellorsville battlefield had an atmosphere of hell. The odor of death had become an unbearable stench. Ted Barclay of the 4th Virginia gave one of the most vivid descriptions of any battlefield when he wrote of walking over the Chancellorsville ground after the fighting ceased. "Our own dead had been buried and the wounded removed, but the Yankee dead and wounded lay thickly over the field," wrote Barclay. "Many had not yet had their wounds dressed and lay groaning on the wet ground, praying every passerby to change their position or give them a drink of water. . . . Our men did all in their power to alleviate their suffering, thinking not of them as enemies who had come to subjugate us, but as suffering mortals."

Barclay continued: "Some seemed as though they had died without a struggle. . . . Others could hardly be recognized as human bodies. Mangled and torn by the solid shot, shell and grape, and these showed how awful had been their suffering, with teeth clinched and hands deeply buried in the earth, they seemed to have suffered agonies before death released them." Animals shared the misery with their human companions. "And the poor horses were not spared," noted Barclay. "Here laid some literally torn to pieces, others with feet shot off endeavoring in vain to get up. Our men humanely shot them."[31]

The worst was yet to come. Bullets and shells set the woods on fire. Hundreds of badly wounded men, unable to help themselves, watched the flames first approach and then consume them. Confederate brigadier general James H. Lane wrote of moving his North Carolina brigade into a new position at the time. "The woods which we entered were on fire," he stated. "The heat was excessive. . . . The dead and dying of the enemy could be seen on all sides enveloped in flames." John Casler of the 33rd Virginia was in one of the details sent out to bury the dead. Casler stated that the woods "burnt rapidly and roasted the wounded men alive. As we went to bury them we could see where they had tried to keep the fire from them by scratching the leaves away as far as they could reach. But it availed not; they were burnt to a crisp." A Federal officer who saw the charred corpses noted soberly: "Fortunate were those who had to die, that they did so before the holocaust began."[32]

Late in the afternoon of May 5, as the fighting slowly died away, rain started falling as if some kind of divine cleansing was now in order. Thousands of soldiers were in Federal hospitals at Potomac Creek, fifteen miles from the front. Evacuation to Aquia Creek Landing for transfer to Washington, D.C., hospitals began on May 7 and continued for the next week.

Hundreds of wounded Confederates lay on depot platforms and along the railroad tracks at Guinea Station, twenty-seven miles away. Wagons from the Richmond Ambulance Committee arrived on May 7 and began expediting the transfer of injured men to hospitals in the capital. There a special medical office on Broad Street offered the wounded soldiers "soups and other refreshments on their arrival." Confederate surgeon Francis W. Hancock bore the heavy responsibility of distributing the wounded among the more than twenty-five military hospitals then functioning in Richmond.[33] By the middle of the month, at least 7,100 wounded southerners had been transported from the battlefield to Richmond. Another 1,980 suffering from diarrhea, typhoid fever, and other diseases also entered crowded hospitals in the Confederate capital during the first two weeks of May.[34]

Meanwhile, hundreds of maimed soldiers were receiving their first medical treatment at improvised field hospitals on the south side of the Rappahannock. Men lay in a soaking rain as surgeons slowly made their way through them. Pennsylvania surgeon William Stewart, who had graduated from medical school only two months earlier, entered a crude shelter where some of the wounded had been brought. "The men were lying so close together on the floor," he noted, "that it was almost impossible to walk among them. I found that their wounds had had no attention whatever since the first dressing on the battlefield, the limbs in many instances had become so swollen that the stopping of the circulation by the bandages resulted in the most intense pain. I worked until my materials were exhausted."

Among the overlooked soldiers was Corporal Bull of the 123rd New York, who painted a frightful picture of the army physicians playing "catch-up" as they attempted to tend to neglected and badly injured soldiers. "The surgeons went among the wounded looking for those who required amputations—they said they could do nothing for the others. . . . The surgeons began their bloody work at once, in the immediate presence of the wounded, some of them within ten feet of the operating table. As each amputation was completed, the soldier operated upon was . . . laid upon the floor, and the arm or leg thrown upon the ground in the rear of the table, only a few feet away."

As the rain continued, the hospital area became a huge puddle of water and blood. Many soldiers struggled to stay above the rising mixture. "A few men who had the strength to do so sat erect in the muddy pool but the greater portion of the men, who were wounded and mangled in almost every conceivable manner . . . lay sprawled in the mud and filth, with nothing between them and the ground but their soaked woolen blanket, and many even without that." At least two of the wounded men drowned near the operating table.[35]

Salem Church was one day the centerpiece of a battle and the next day a center for the wounded. Col. Robert McMillen of the 24th Georgia went there in search of friends. He drew back in revulsion at what he saw in and around the church. "The spacious yard was literally covered with wounded and dying. The sight inside the building, for horror, was perhaps never equalled within so limited a space. Every available foot of space was crowded with wounded and bleeding soldiers. The floor, the benches, even the chancel and pulpit, were all packed almost to suffocation with them. The amputated limbs were piled up in every corner almost as high as a man could reach; blood flowed in streams along the aisles and out at the doors; screams and groans were heard on all sides, while the surgeons, with their assistants, worked with knives, saws, sutures and bandages to relieve or save all they could from bleeding to death."

The situation was little improved behind the Union lines at Salem Church. A weary surgeon Daniel Holt of the 121st New York made his way to a structure converted into a field hospital for the wounded members of his regiment. "As soon as I opened the door," Holt stated in a letter to his wife, "a score of voices cried out, 'Oh doctor! doctor! God bless you, doctor Holt, have you come to dress my wounds? Have you brought anything to eat?' and a thousand such questions until I fairly broke down, and had to weep like a child."[36]

Union field hospitals in the rear of the Chancellorsville line presented an equally repulsive sight. Poet Walt Whitman served as a nurse at the time of the battle. After riding out to one of the medical stations at Potomac Creek, he exclaimed:

> O heavens, what scene is this? Is this indeed *humanity*—these butcher's shambles? There are several of them. There they lie, in the largest, in an open space in the woods, some 200 to 300 poor fellows—the groans and screams—the odor of blood, mixed with the fresh scent of the night, the grass, the trees—that slaughter-house! O well is it their mothers, their sisters cannot see them—cannot conceive, and never conceiv'd these things. . . . Some have their legs blown off—some bullets through the breast—some indescribably horrid wounds in the face or head, all mutilated, sickening, torn, gouged out—some in the abdomen—some mere boys—many rebels, badly hurt—they take their regular turns with the rest, just the same as any— the surgeons use them just the same.[37]

By May 6, the beaten Union army had withdrawn from the Wilderness and recrossed the Rappahannock. As the Union army retired across the stream, medical director Letterman ordered two wagons loaded with medical supplies to be left behind, "with the hope that our wounded would receive a share of them, which they did."[38]

On Friday, two days later, medical directors Letterman and Guild of the opposing armies worked out details of a truce for collecting the wounded. Twenty-six Union surgeons, along with five wagons laden with blankets, beef, and medical supplies, headed over the river to Chancellorsville. More than 2,000 rations went forth the next day to United States Ford, while 600 rations of beef, bread, coffee, and sugar headed to Banks Ford and the wounded in that area.

The twenty-six Federal surgeons, along with nineteen colleagues who had been taken prisoner or had chosen to stay behind, worked closely with their Confederate counterparts in tending to those soldiers for whom any treatment had a possibility of success.[39] On the morning of May 15, the last wounded Federals on the battlefield—1,160 in number—crossed the Rappahannock into Union lines. They proceeded to the army hospitals at Potomac Creek and Washington, D.C.[40]

Transfer to the northern capital in the spring of 1863 was not a blessing for all of the wounded. The first contingent from Chancellorsville arrived at night on two boats. Rain was pouring through the darkness as the ships drew up to the piers. Volunteer nurse Walt Whitman observed:

United States General Hospital at Georgetown, D.C. (formerly the Union Hotel). This idealized contemporary engraving depicts wounded Federal soldiers surrounded by order, cleanliness, and supportive family. Paul F. Mottelay and T. Campbell-Copeland, eds., The Soldier in Our Civil War, *2 vols. (New York: Stanley Bradley, 1893), 1:108*

The poor, pale, helpless soldiers had been debark'd, and lay around on the wharf and neighborhood anywhere. The rain was, probably, grateful to them; at any rate they were exposed to it. The few torches light up the spectacle. All around—on the wharf, on the ground, out on side places—the men are lying on blankets, old quilts, &c., with bloody rags bound round heads, arms, and legs. The attendants are few, and at night few outsiders also—only a few hard-work'd transportation men and drivers. (The wounded are getting to be common, and people grow callous.) The men, whatever their condition, lie there, and patiently wait till their turn comes to be taken up. . . . The men generally make little or no ado, whatever their sufferings. A few groans that cannot be suppress'd, and occasionally a scream of pain as they lift a man into the ambulance.[41]

One controversy of a personal nature erupted at Campbell General Hospital in Washington, D.C. A number of women had volunteered to serve as nurses in the military hospitals. One of them was Jane Swisshelm of New York City. In a letter to the *New York Tribune,* she told of ministering to dozens of wounded soldiers. She begged readers to contribute whiskey to be used as an antiseptic on injured limbs.[42]

The printing of Swisshelm's account of nursing service and her plea for help brought at least one negative response. An official in Washington, D.C., wrote Surgeon General Hammond: "In behalf of modesty do I beseech you to issue an order prohibiting Feminine Nurses throwing themselves into the arms of sick & wounded soldiers and laciviously [*sic*] exciting their animal passions. Were I a Surgeon in charge of one of your hospitals I would have no Sighing *Grass Widows* & *Amorous Old Maids*. I would send them all harvesting on the strength of their forks."

Surgeon Jedediah Baxter, in charge of the hospital where Swisshelm worked, held an entirely different view of her contributions. "The lady came to this Hospital . . . and asked the privilege of attending to the wounded for a few days, although I do not employ female nurses. Yet the energy, kindness and sympathy shown by her in her attention to the wounded induced me to allow her to remain a short time."[43]

Other women on both sides volunteered their services as nurses during the campaign. Their petitions usually met with lukewarm receptions at best because physicians were not ready to accept females on any level in the medical profession. For example, Dr. Justin Dwinelle of the Federal Second Corps hospital allowed two women to perform some duties at his medical facility, but he was emphatic about limiting the number of women involved. "No more than one female will be allowed in each division," he decreed.[44]

General Hooker's medical director, Jonathan Letterman, would state of Chancellorsville: "I have seen no battle in which the wounded were so well cared for." Letterman was speaking either in generalities or propagandistically. Medical neglect—insufficiency is actually a better word—was very much a part of the battle of Chancellorsville, as it was of other major battles of the Civil War.

Col. Samuel S. Carroll, who commanded an oversized brigade of six regiments, reported that "no surgeons or their assistants, except Asst. Surg. W. F. Hicks . . . and no ambulance men or stretchers, were furnished me from the time I formed line to move forward until we came out of action." The brigade's casualties of 29 killed, 212 wounded, and 57 missing are ample evidence that Carroll's men saw considerable action and fully merited at least basic medical services.[45]

Some slipshod medical administration was unavoidable, but it should not have included mishandling of the dead—and certainly not weeks after the campaign ended. Unfortunately, such bungling occurred. Late in June the U.S. Surgeon General's Office issued a stern circular to hospital surgeons throughout the Army of the Potomac. The cause and the cure in the message were painfully clear: "Grave complaints have been made to this office that Surgeons in charge of Gen. Hospitals are derelict in taking proper measures to secure the identification of Soldiers dying in Hospitals under their charge. They will be instructed in future to cause to be affixed upon the breast of every soldier thus dying a strong card on which will be legibly written the full name of the man and the company & regiment to which he belongs."[46]

No one faulted the performances of Union and Confederate surgeons at Chancellorsville. Federal commanders singled out a number of army physicians for praise.[47] Lee commended medical director Guild and all of his officers for being "untiring in their attention to the wounded." Guild in turn stated that "as a body of professional gentlemen," Confederate surgeons displayed a conduct that "has secured to them an enviable reputation and has elicited praise from all who have witnessed their noble self sacrifice during and after a battle."[48]

More than 3,150 soldiers North and South were killed at Chancellorsville. Another 8,700 were officially listed as missing. In between those two categories were the near-dead: the injured, the crippled, the sufferers. At Chancellorsville, the wounded numbered more than 18,200 men.[49]

Too often in the chronicles of war, the wounded are ignored. Stories of victory or defeat, death or the heroism of an unknown soldier, have more appeal than those of soldiers mutilated while performing their duty. Few survivors of the Civil War went to lengths to describe injuries they received. Yet Rice Bull did, and he explained why: "These details . . . should be told, so that those who [someday] read this record may know something of the horrors of war—that they may realize in a measure what suffering and privations were endured by our men during the Civil strife, and know something of the price that was paid to insure the peace we now enjoy."[50]

Walt Whitman was extremely moved by what he beheld during the battle of Chancellorsville. At a field hospital in the last stages of the fight, the poet composed a work titled "A Sight in Camp in the Daybreak." It is a little-known work; it ought not to be.

A sight in camp in the daybreak gray and dim,
As from my tent I emerge so early sleepless,
As slow I walk in the cool fresh air the path near by the hospital tent,
Three forms I see on stretchers lying, brought out there untended lying,
Over each the blanket spread, ample brownish woolen blanket,
Gray and heavy blanket, folding, covering all.

Curious I halt and silent stand,
Then with light fingers I from the face of the nearest the first just lift the
     blanket;
Who are you elderly man so gaunt and grim, with well-gray'd hair, and flesh
     all sunken about the eyes?
Who are you my dear comrade?

Then to the second I step—and who are you my child and darling?
Who are you sweet boy with cheeks yet blooming?
Then to the third—a face nor child nor old, very calm, as of beautiful
yellow-white ivory;
Young man I think I know you—I think this face is the face of the Christ
himself,
Dead and divine and brother of all, and here again he lies.[51]

ACKNOWLEDGMENTS

The author expresses special appreciation to Robert K. Krick, chief historian of the Fredericksburg and Spotsylvania National Military Park, Michael Musick of the National Archives Military Reference Branch, and archivist-historian Richard J. Sommers of the U.S. Army Military History Institute for unselfish assistance in providing source material for this essay.

NOTES

1. Cyrus Bacon, "A Michigan Surgeon at Chancellorsville One Hundred Years Ago," *University of Michigan Medical Bulletin* 29 (November/December 1963): 330; Edwin W. Payne, *History of the Thirty-fourth Regiment of Illinois Infantry, September 7, 1861–July 12, 1865* (Clinton, Iowa: Allen, 1902), 173. Any true historical reporting is the product of available source material. Civil War surgeons wrote comparatively little about their wartime experiences. Most of the physicians were too busy to file elaborate reports, resulting in a paucity of sources. Since the bulk of extant material on medical care at Chancellorsville concerns the Union side, the focus of this essay necessarily slants toward Federal medical efforts.

2. Jonathan Letterman, *Medical Recollections of the Army of the Potomac* (New York: D. Appleton, 1866), 100–101.

3. Stewart Brooks, *Civil War Medicine* (Springfield, Ill.: Clark C. Thomas, 1966), 9–10.

4. H. H. Cunningham, *Doctors in Gray: The Confederate Medical Service* (Baton Rouge: Louisiana State University Press, 1958), 16–17. In the 1860s the vast majority of civilian physicians and army "surgeons" were dispensers of medicine unqualified by training and temperament to use a scalpel. In November 1861, a surgeon in a Tennessee regiment confessed from the field: "I am no surgeon. . . . I assisted . . . in several operations and dressed a vast number of wounds but I could not amputate a limb or litigate an artery." He then added: "I should have amputated the other day had it been necessary, but how hazardous it would have been to my patient" (Lunsford P. Yandell to his father, November 18, 1861, Yandell Collection, Filson Club, Louisville, Ky.).

5. Jacob Powers to his mother and daughter, November 10, 1861, Julius and Jacob P. Powers Papers, Indiana State Library, Indianapolis, Ind.; Timothy M. Blaisdell to his sisters, May 15, 1862, Timothy M. Blaisdell Collection, U.S. Army Military History Institute, Carlisle Barracks, Pa. (repository hereafter cited as USAMHI).

6. F. Jackson Stoddard, "Medicine and Surgery in the Civil War," *Lincoln Herald* 55 (March 1953): 25.

7. Bruce Catton, *Mr. Lincoln's Army* (Garden City, N.Y.: Doubleday, 1951), 194–95; Samuel P. Bates, *The Battle of Chancellorsville* (Meadville, Pa.: Edward T. Bates, 1882), 201–2. One early medical director of the Army of the Potomac conceded defeat at the outset. "In my opinion," he stated, "it is impossible to improvise an efficient medical staff" (quoted in Cunningham, *Doctors in Gray*, 253).

8. Lewis C. Duncan, "The Days Gone By: The Strange Case of Surgeon General Hammond," *Military Surgeon* 64 (January 1929): 100; Frank R. Freeman, "Lincoln Finds a Surgeon General: William A. Hammond and the Transformation of the Union Army Medical Bureau," *Civil War History* 33 (March 1987): 14–15. Hammond's continual defiance of tradition, plus his abrasive personality, led to his court-martial and dismissal from the army in August 1864. Nevertheless, a number of writers consider his service a major factor in the North's ultimate victory in the Civil War. For a French visitor's description of Philadelphia's Satterlee Hospital, see General DeChanal, "Good Order and Cleanliness," *Civil War Times Illustrated* 6 (October 1967): 40–44.

9. U.S. War Department, *The War of the Rebellion: A Compilation of the Official Records of the Union and Confederate Armies*, 127 vols., index, and atlas (Washington, D.C.: GPO, 1880–1901), 25(2):239 (hereafter cited as *OR*; unless otherwise noted, all references are to series 1). A few years after the battle, in his memoirs, Letterman reduced the estimate of those on the sick list to 5 percent. See John Bigelow, Jr., *The Campaign of Chancellorsville: A Strategic and Tactical Study* (New Haven, Conn.: Yale University Press, 1910), 493, and Letterman, *Medical Recollections*, 112–13.

10. In 1863 Moore established the Association of Army and Navy Surgeons to improve medical knowledge. Toward that same end, he oversaw the publication in the war's last months of the *Confederate States Medical and Surgical Journal*. Moore established four medical laboratories in the wartime South, obtained medicines illegally through the lines by swapping cotton for opium, calomel, and quinine, and went so far as to seize two distilleries (with a combined capacity of close to 300 gallons of whiskey per day) in order to guarantee medicinal spirits for the army. See Clement Eaton, *A History of the Southern Confederacy* (New York: Macmillan, 1954), 98–99, and *OR*, ser. 4, 3:1074.

11. J. William Jones and others, eds., *Southern Historical Society Papers*, 52 vols. (Richmond: Southern Historical Society, 1876–1959), 17:7–8, 29:273–79 (hereafter cited as *SHSP*); Cunningham, *Doctors in Gray*, 150. For a good overview of Richmond's Chimborazo Hospital, one of the largest military hospitals in world history, see Joseph P. Cullen, "Chimborazo Hospital: 'That Charnel House of Living Sufferers,' " *Civil War Times Illustrated* 19 (January 1981): 36–42.

12. See *Confederate Veteran* 6 (January 1898): 12, and 31 (December 1923): 447.

13. *OR*, ser. 4, 2:408; Cunningham, *Doctors in Gray*, 170, 174.

14. Wyndham B. Blanton, *Medicine in Virginia in the Nineteenth Century* (Richmond: Garrett & Massie, 1933), 293–94; U.S. Surgeon General's Office, *The Medical and Surgical History of the Civil War*, 12 vols., with 3-vol. index (1870–88 [3 vols. in 6 under title *The Medical and Surgical History of the War of the Rebellion (1861–65)*]; reprint, Wilmington, N.C.: Broadfoot, 1990), 6:627–28.

15. Letterman, *Medical Recollections*, 124; *OR* 25(1):399–400, 493; Justin Dwinelle to A. N. Daugherty, April 20, 1863, Dwinelle Collection, bound vol. 157, Fredericksburg and Spotsylvania National Military Park Library, Fredericksburg, Va. (repository hereafter cited as FSNMP).

16. Robert Hubbard to Nellie Hubbard, May 8, 1863, Hubbard Letters, USAMHI.

17. *OR* 25(1):200; William Shaw Stewart, "Experiences of an Army Surgeon in 1863–64," typescript, FSNMP. An early biographer of Gen. Winfield Scott Hancock stated after conversations with veterans that "some of the fugitives were so completely beside themselves with fear that they ran past the Chancellor house, down the Fredericksburg pike, through Hancock's line, and into the hands of the Confederates, without being stopped. One ingenuous German approached Hancock and begged to be directed to the pontoons. The answer he received has been handed down by tradition; but it is best not to put it into cold and unsympathetic type" (Francis A. Walker, *General Hancock* [New York: D. Appleton, 1894], 83).

18. Robert Hubbard to Nellie Hubbard, May 8, 1863, Hubbard Letters, USAMHI; Letterman, *Medical Recollections*, 126–28. Capt. W. M. Norman of the 28th North Carolina was convinced that the Federals around the Chancellor house had placed their wounded in front of their batteries as protection from artillery fire. See W. M. Norman, *A Portion of My Life* (Winston-Salem, N.C.: J. F. Blair, 1959), 176.

19. Jonathan Letterman to William A. Hammond, May 30, 1863, Surgeon General's Office, Letters Received, 1818–70, RG 112, National Archives, Washington, D.C. (repository hereafter cited as NA).

20. A member of Jackson's staff commented that McGuire, besides having "blunt good humor" and being "full of honest life," was "a very smart fellow & gives us entertaining medical prelections at evening sittings" (Jedediah Hotchkiss to Sara Hotchkiss, April 4, 1862, microfilm roll 4, Jedediah Hotchkiss Papers, Library of Congress, Washington, D.C.). For more on McGuire, see John W. Schildt, *Hunter Holmes McGuire: Doctor in Gray* (Chewsville, Md.: Published by the author, 1986), and Maurice F. Shaw, *Stonewall Jackson's Surgeon, Hunter Holmes McGuire: A Biography* (Lynchburg, Va.: H. E. Howard, 1993).

21. Noel G. Harrison, *Chancellorsville Battlefield Sites* (Lynchburg, Va.: H. E. Howard, 1990), 75.

22. *OR* 25(1):401; Robert Hubbard to Nellie Hubbard, May 9, 1863, Hubbard Letters, USAMHI; John W. Storrs, *The "Twentieth Connecticut": A Regimental History* (Naugatuck, Conn.: Press of the *Naugatuck Valley Sentinel*, 1886), 53. Assistant surgeon William Shaw Stewart stated that as he was removing a soldier's leg, a solid shot ripped through the area and beheaded the patient (Stewart, "Experiences," 3).

23. Bigelow, *Campaign of Chancellorsville*, 132; Letterman, *Medical Recollections*, 138.

24. *OR* 25(1):402, 411–12; "Rice Cook Bull Reminiscences," p. 45, typescript, Harrisburg Civil War Round Table Collection, USAMHI.

25. Letterman, *Medical Recollections*, 135.

26. George T. Stevens, *Three Years in the Sixth Corps: A Concise Narrative of Events in the Army of the Potomac from 1861 to the Close of the Rebellion, April, 1865* (New York: D. Van Nostrand, 1870), 200; John H. Hieber diary, May 3, 1863, Soldiers & Sailors Memorial Hall, Pittsburgh, Pa.

27. George T. Stevens, *Sixth Corps*, 206.

28. Henry Van Aernam to his wife, May 4, 1863, Henry Van Aernam Papers, USAMHI. The surgeon did not receive the desired answer to his prayer. He continued in service through November 1864.

29. Infections killed twice as many men in the Civil War as did the enemy. Of 2,818 reported cases of pyemia in the Union army, only 71 of the men survived. See Brooks, *Civil War Medicine*, 83.

30. "Bull Reminiscences," 70, 72.

31. Ted Barclay to his sister, May 12, 1863, Ted Barclay Letters, Virginia State Library, Richmond, Va. See also Friedrich P. Kappelman to his parents, May 10, 1863, *Civil War Times Illustrated* Collection, USAMHI.

32. *OR* 25(1):917; John O. Casler, *Four Years in the Stonewall Brigade* (1893; reprint, Dayton, Ohio: Morningside, 1971), 151; C. A. Stevens, *Berdan's United States Sharpshooters in the Army of the Potomac, 1861–1865* (St. Paul, Minn.: Price-McGill, 1892), 264. For other references to wounded soldiers who were burned to death, see Charles H. Doerflinger, "Personal Reminiscences of the Battle of Chancellorsville," p. 2, typescript, FSNMP, and Bacon, "Michigan Surgeon," 327.

33. "Story of Sergeant George W. Beavers, Forty Fourth Georgia Regiment," p. 2, typescript, FSNMP; Augusta (Ga.) *Daily Constitutionalist*, May 14, 1863, clipping in FSNMP; Richmond *Daily Dispatch*, May 6, 8, 1863. Ambulances departed Richmond on May 5 to collect the wounded from Chancellorsville.

34. Richmond *Daily Dispatch*, May 16, 1863.

35. Stewart, "Experiences," 3–4; "Bull Reminiscences," 76–79.

36. Ernest B. Furguson, *Chancellorsville 1863: The Souls of the Brave* (New York: Alfred A. Knopf, 1992), 310; Daniel M. Holt, *A Surgeon's Civil War: The Letters and Diary of Daniel M. Holt, M.D.*, ed. James M. Greiner, Janet L. Coryell, and James R. Smither (Kent, Ohio: Kent State University Press, 1994), 95.

37. Walt Whitman, *Memoranda during the War* (Camden, N.J.: Published by the author, 1875), 14–15. Many of the battle wounds at Chancellorsville were ghastly almost beyond description. For some of the worst injuries, see U.S. Surgeon General's Office, *Medical and Surgical History*, 7:114–15, 130, 180, 196, 252, 8:294–95, 9:364, 411.

38. Jonathan Letterman to William A. Hammond, May 30, 1863, Surgeon General's Office, Letters Received, 1818–70, RG 112, NA.

39. Most of the Federal surgeons who remained behind Confederate lines with the wounded received polite treatment from the enemy. Medical director George Suckley of the Union Eleventh Corps recrossed the lines a week later wearing the uniform of a Confederate colonel. He had exchanged clothing with an old acquaintance from prewar days. See Augustus Choate Hamlin, *The Battle of Chancellorsville: The Attack of Stonewall Jackson and His Army upon the Right Flank of the Army of the Potomac at Chancellorsville, Virginia, on Saturday Afternoon, May 2, 1863* (Bangor, Maine: Published by the author, 1896), 131. For the recollections of a captured Union surgeon who had a bad experience, see Bacon, "Michigan Surgeon," 323–29.

40. *OR* 25(1):448, 465; Bates, *Chancellorsville*, 206–7; George T. Stevens, *Sixth Corps*, 212–14.

41. Whitman, *Memoranda during the War*, 13.

42. *New York Tribune*, May 18, 1863.

43. A. Boles to William A. Hammond, May 24, 1863, and J. H. Baxter to William A. Hammond, May 28, 1863, Surgeon General's Office, Letters Received, 1818–70, RG 112, NA.

44. Endorsement to letter, A. N. Daugherty to Justin Dwinelle, May 17, 1863, Dwinelle Collection, FSNMP.

45. Letterman, *Medical Recollections*, 129; *OR* 25(1):177, 366–67.

46. U.S. surgeon general to division surgeons, June 29, 1863, Dwinelle Collection, FSNMP.

47. *OR* 25(1):274, 315-16, 503, 620. See also Granville P. Conn, *History of the New Hampshire Surgeons in the War of Rebellion* (Concord: New Hampshire Association of Military Surgeons, 1906), 149, 151, 252.

48. *OR* 25(1):804; Cunningham, *Doctors in Gray*, 261. For further praise of Civil War surgeons, see the statement by Dr. E. Peyre Porcher in *SHSP*, 17:14.

49. *OR* 25(1):185, 191, 809; Letterman, *Medical Recollections*, 144.

50. "Bull Reminiscences," 72.

51. Walt Whitman, *Walt Whitman's Civil War*, ed. Walter Lowenfels (New York: Alfred A. Knopf, 1961), 48.

Disgraced and Ruined by the Decision of the Court

THE COURT-MARTIAL OF EMORY F. BEST, C.S.A.

Keith S. Bohannon

THE FUNERAL OF Emory Fiske Best at Rose Hill Cemetery in Macon, Georgia, on April 29, 1912, was attended by only a few friends and relatives. According to a newspaper obituary, even Best's wife was absent, due to "hindering circumstances." Such a small gathering might seem surprising given the dead man's career as a lawyer, judge, and former Confederate officer.[1]

Unlike the funerals of many ex-Confederates, Best's graveside service did not involve any veterans' organizations. Also unusual was the absence of an inscription on Best's tombstone indicating his Confederate military service. Why would turn-of-the-century southerners, imbued with the sanctity of the Lost Cause, allow an ex-Confederate colonel to go to his final resting place with so little notice?

The answer undoubtedly lies in events that occurred almost fifty years earlier on the bloodstained battlefields of Virginia and Maryland, where Best had commanded for a time the 23rd Georgia Volunteer Infantry. Indicted in June 1863 for displaying cowardice at the battles of South Mountain, Sharpsburg, and Chancellorsville, Best had been found guilty by a court-martial and was cashiered from the army. What events had led to this young officer being, in the words of a family friend, "disgraced [and] *ruined* by the decision of the court"?[2]

Emory Fiske Best was born on March 28, 1840, in Bladensburg, Maryland, the son of Rev. Hezekiah and Adeline Ball Best. Emory spent his early years in Baltimore and various locales throughout Virginia as his father, a Methodist Episcopal minister, moved from one church assignment to another. In 1858 the wealthy reverend relocated his family to Cass County in northwest Georgia, where he paid $30,000 for a large estate called Forrest Home. In addition to preaching "without pay" and building churches, Hezekiah Best erected a gristmill, gin, and sawmill on his property. By 1860 he owned real estate and personal property valued at almost $48,000.

Reverend Best's wealth undoubtedly helped provide his children with fine educations. Although details of Emory Best's earliest schooling are unknown, in 1860 he took a degree in law from Lebanon College in Tennessee. Shortly thereafter, he returned to Cass County, where he read law with prominent attorney Warren Akin. Although family records indicate that Best opened a legal practice in Rome, Georgia, prior to the Civil War, the 1860 census seems to suggest otherwise. His stated occupation, as recorded by the census enumerator, was that of "gentleman."[3]

Upon the outbreak of war in the spring of 1861, Best enlisted as a first lieutenant in a company raised in Floyd County, Georgia, known as the Floyd Springs Guards. That summer, the Guards traveled to Camp McDonald, a large training facility located in Big Shanty, Georgia. On the last day of August, the Guards mustered into Confederate service as Company C, 23rd Georgia Volunteer Infantry, an organization composed of men from "the Cherokee counties" of the northwestern and extreme north-central portions of the state. After mustering into service, the regiment held elections for officers. The office of major went to Best, despite his being known by only a few of the men.[4]

The 23rd Georgia remained at Camp McDonald, drilling without firearms, until it departed on November 10 for Richmond. Arriving in the Confederate capital, the Georgians encamped first at the Old Fair Grounds and later at Chimborazo. On December 10 the regiment left Richmond with orders to proceed down the Peninsula to Yorktown. Within a day or so of the 23rd's arrival in Yorktown, the men received muskets for the first time. Many of them had little chance to drill with the weapons during the following winter due to the detailing of five companies (including Best's) to serve as artillerymen. This assignment, coupled with widespread sickness throughout the 23rd, hampered the efficiency of the regiment during the first winter of the war.

Col. Emory Fiske Best (photograph taken in Baltimore while he was on parole following the battle of Sharpsburg). Published with the kind permission of Fred Shroyer, Annapolis, Md.

Following the siege of Yorktown and the subsequent retreat of the Confederate army up the Peninsula in May 1862, the 23rd saw its first major fighting on May 31 at the battle of Seven Pines. During the engagement, the regiment lost 80 men killed and wounded out of 400.[5] After a month resting in camp along the Williamsburg Road, the regiment came under fire again on June 27, 1862, during the battle of Gaines's Mill. In crossing a dense swamp to attack the Union line, the 23rd, under the command of Major Best, "was surprised and thrown into confusion" along with the other regiments in Col. Alfred Holt Colquitt's Georgia and Alabama brigade. The "indefatigable exertions of Captain [James Howard] Huggins assisted by other officers" eventually restored order within the 23rd, but the regiment remained in the rear during the battle and did not engage the enemy. Despite its inactivity, the regiment lost twenty-nine men killed and wounded, undoubtedly due to northern artillery fire.

Four days after the fighting at Gaines's Mill, Colquitt's brigade participated in the futile Confederate assaults at Malvern Hill. The 23rd, under the command of Captain Huggins since June 27 (the disposition of Best is unknown), lost thirty-one men killed and wounded in these attacks. Colonel Colquitt, accused by his caustic division commander, Maj. Gen. Daniel Harvey Hill, of not keeping his brigade "in hand" at Gaines's Mill, apparently did little better at Malvern Hill. In a private letter to a friend, Colquitt confided that at Malvern Hill he "witnessed acts of cowardice" that were "disgraceful to Southern character." "If the enemy had known," he wrote, "what an unaccountable panic would seize on our men as they came under fire, they would have cut us up."[6]

After the battles around Richmond, Colquitt's brigade camped for several weeks just outside the city on the York River Railroad. During that time, several officers in the 23rd received promotions due to the resignation of the regiment's colonel. Emory Best was appointed lieutenant colonel on August 16, 1862, to rank from June 12, 1862. Only a few weeks after his promotion, Best and his regiment were en route to Maryland as participants in Gen. Robert E. Lee's first invasion of the North.[7]

After entering Maryland, Colquitt's brigade saw very heavy fighting in the battle of South Mountain on September 14, 1862. Ordered by D. H. Hill to protect Turner's Gap, Colquitt placed his regiments astride the National Road with the right of the 23rd resting on that thoroughfare, partially protected by a stone fence. Around 4:00 P.M., three companies of the 23rd, under the command of Lieutenant Colonel Best, went up the side of the mountain to support a section of Capt. John Lane's Georgia battery. "Finding that the artillery could not be effectively used," wrote Best, "and being exposed to the fire of the enemy's sharpshooters covered by a cornfield immediately in front," the guns limbered up and went to the rear. The detachment of infantry received orders from General Hill, according to Best, to return to the rest of the regiment.

Shortly after Best's men returned to their regiment, Federal troops assailed Colquitt's line. The men in the 23rd and 28th Georgia, hotly engaged with the enemy for several hours, held their position until dusk. Their ammunition exhausted, the Georgians then received orders to retire, taking with them all of the wounded they could find in the darkness.[8]

Three days after the engagement at South Mountain, Colquitt's brigade fought again at Sharpsburg. Advancing early in the morning to the northern edge of Miller's cornfield, the Georgians traded volleys with Federal regiments at point-blank range. Searing sheets of musketry tore into Colquitt's brigade. His regiments, Colquitt wrote, were "exposed to a fire from all sides and nearly surrounded." Falling back in disorder, the Georgians left casualties scattered across the cornfield. Among those wounded and captured was Emory Best, whom D. H. Hill characterized in his report of the Maryland campaign as a "gallant and meritorious" officer.[9]

Although he was paroled in Frederick on October 2, Best apparently spent a brief time at Fort McHenry in Baltimore. While he was there, Federal authorities gave the young officer permission to roam around the city he undoubtedly knew from earlier years. Like many other captured Confederates, Best took the opportunity to have his photograph made at the gallery of southern sympathizers Daniel and David Bendann.[10]

Federal officials released Best on November 8 at Aiken's Landing, Virginia, in exchange for a Federal officer of equal rank. Granted a sixty-day furlough on November 15, Best returned to the 23rd sometime in mid-January 1863. He received a promotion to colonel on March 26, 1863, to rank from January 20, to fill the vacancy occasioned by the death of William P. Barclay at Sharpsburg.[11]

A month and three days after Best's promotion to colonel, the 23rd Georgia and Colquitt's brigade left their winter camps south of Fredericksburg and, reacting to news of Federal crossings of the Rappahannock River, marched to the vicinity of Hamilton's Crossing. On April 30 the Georgians occupied a line of unfinished entrenchments, where they remained under sporadic artillery fire until dawn the next day.

Colquitt's Georgians marched with Lt. Gen. T. J. "Stonewall" Jackson's corps on May 1, proceeding six or seven miles west of Fredericksburg along the Orange Plank Road before hearing the sounds of fighting. Formed in line of battle on the right of Brig. Gen. Robert E. Rodes's division, Colquitt's brigade advanced a few hundred yards "before being thrown into some confusion by coming in contact with the troops of General [Lafayette] McLaws' command," which stood at right angles to the Georgians. Officers sorted out the units, after which Colquitt's brigade continued marching forward until ordered to halt. Around dusk, the brigade returned to the Plank Road, marching two or three miles farther west before bivouacking for the night.[12]

At approximately 5:30 A.M. on May 2, Colquitt's brigade moved onto the Orange Plank Road in the vicinity of the Alrich house as the lead unit in a long column beginning one of the most famous marches in American military history. With orders to circle around the Union army and strike its vulnerable right flank, Stonewall Jackson "rode at the head of the column," wrote an officer in the 6th Georgia, "and personally superintended everything." Approximately two hours after sunrise, the Georgians passed near the intersection of the Furnace and Orange Plank roads, where they saw the commanding general of the Army of Northern Virginia. It was here, undoubtedly under the gaze of Colquitt's admiring men, that Robert E. Lee spoke his final words to Jackson.[13]

Around 8:00 A.M., Jackson's infantry, preceded by several regiments of Virginia cavalrymen, marched over high open ground just east of the sluggish waters of Scott's Run. As the footsoldiers descended to the banks of the creek, Jackson ordered Colquitt to detach a regiment "with instructions to guard the flank of the column in motion against a surprise." Jackson also told Colquitt that the regiment's commanding officer could call upon any officer in charge of passing troops for reinforcements if necessary. Colquitt selected Colonel Best and the 23rd for the assignment.[14]

Best marched his regiment to a position one-half mile north of Wellford's (or Catharine) Furnace. As Best conferred with Gen. J. E. B. Stuart and Gen. Robert Rodes, the men of the 23rd lay on the ground watching the flanking column being harassed by sporadic shellfire from Union artillery positioned 600 to 700 yards to the north in the Hazel Grove clearing. Worried about the vulnerability of his regiment's flanks, Best displayed four of his companies as skirmishers to support cavalry vedettes already posted on the 23rd's front. Union skirmishers, the green-coated riflemen of the 1st (Berdan's) U.S. Sharpshooters, began pressing Best's advanced line around 1:00 P.M.[15]

As the 23rd's skirmishers became, in Best's words, "warmly engaged" with the Federals, he heard reports that the enemy threatened to pass around his regiment's right flank. Although numerous witnesses testified that the 23rd scarcely had been engaged and had sustained not a single casualty, Best ordered it to retire to the vicinity of the furnace. A captain commanding two companies of the 14th Tennessee said the Georgians fell back to the furnace "in great confusion." At the same time, Best hastened to the Furnace Road to call for support from passing artillery. Responding to his requests were the artillerists of Capt. J. T. Brooke's Virginia battery. While one of Brooke's guns unlimbered on the north side of the road and fired three canister rounds at the Federals, the battery's remaining cannoneers took their pieces to the open ground around the Wellford house south of the furnace.[16]

After withdrawing to the area of the furnace, Best and Maj. Marcus R. Ballenger re-formed the 23rd, advanced it to the cover of a fence, and ordered the men to lie down. Hard-pressed by fire from the Sharps rifles of Berdan's men as well as skirmishers from several other Union brigades, the Georgians around the furnace began taking casualties, losing at least one man killed and several wounded. At this point, approximately forty-five minutes after the 23rd had first seen action, Best decided to split his command. He left forty-five officers and men under the command of Major Ballenger at the furnace "to check the advance upon the train." Pinned down behind one of the furnace buildings by the rapid fire of the enemy, Ballenger and his men eventually responded to calls from the Yankees to surrender by throwing down their guns and "showing a white rag."[17]

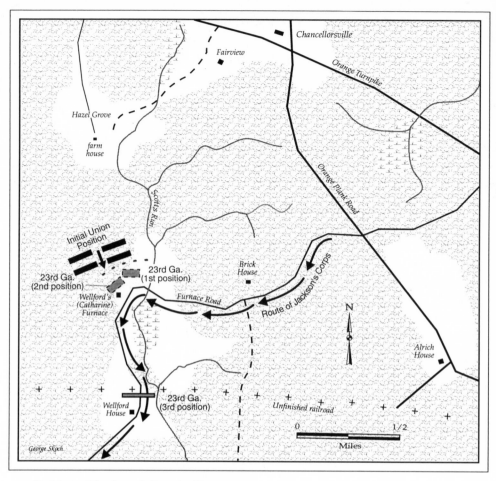

Positions of Best's 23rd Georgia, May 2, 1863

Best took the balance of his regiment and, screened by skirmishers, withdrew a half-mile south to a cut in an unfinished railroad running east-west across the Furnace Road. By this time, Best noted, "the train was virtually saved." The only portion of Jackson's train lost had been a caisson abandoned on the Furnace Road after its tongue had broken and the horses pulling it had all been wounded.[18]

After falling back in disorder to the cut, Best's men began digging toeholds with their bayonets in the steep 7–8-foot-high walls. Some men climbed up the sides of the embankment to fire across the open, marshy ground at the advancing enemy; others remained below, loading guns and passing them up to their comrades. Not surprisingly, the cut provided ample protection even from the fire of sharpshooters, and the 23rd sustained no casualties while in this position.[19]

Shortly after entering the cut, several men saw a courier approach their position, shouting over the gunfire for Colonel Best. The messenger, sent from Gen. James J. Archer, whose brigade had been detached to guard the rear of Jackson's column, brought orders for Best to maintain his position until told to leave. Best replied that he could hold the post only if reinforced on his left. Some thirty minutes later, as the men in the cut watched a "spirited duel" between the Union artillery and the southern cannon near the Wellford house, Archer's skirmishers withdrew from the left of the 23rd's position. At this time, according to the captain in charge of Archer's detachment, the opposing skirmishers were only fifty yards apart.[20]

As Federals began flanking the 23rd's position on the left, Colonel Best, one captain, two lieutenants, and thirty-five or forty men bolted out of the mouth of the cut on the left of the regiment. The regimental color-bearer, carrying the flag rolled up and close to the ground, joined the exodus. The fleeing men came under heavy fire from Union skirmishers within twenty-five to thirty yards. Abruptly changing direction, Best and his followers sprinted through the dense woods for a half mile before regrouping.[21]

The 26 officers and approximately 250 enlisted men of the 23rd remaining in the cut continued firing sporadically for close to half an hour before Capt. John James Augustus Sharp, the senior officer present, decided to surrender. Raising a white flag, the Georgians began leaving the cut in pairs, their guns laid on the ground and their hands in the air. A sergeant in the 2nd U.S. Sharpshooters wrote that the Georgians "were glad to surrender." After relieving the officers of their side arms, the Federals formed the captives into a column and started them rearward at double-quick time.[22]

According to his own testimony, unconfirmed by any other source, Emory Best served throughout the remainder of the Chancellorsville campaign as

Daniel, John, and Pleasant Chitwood (left to right), privates in the Bartow County Yankee Killers, Company A, 23rd Georgia Volunteer Infantry. Pleasant died of chronic diarrhea in Richmond on October 31, 1862. Daniel and John were captured, along with most of their regiment, at Chancellorsville on May 2, 1863. The brothers were exchanged three weeks later and served for the remainder of the war. Courtesy of the Georgia Department of Archives and History

assistant adjutant inspector general on the staff of his division commander, Robert E. Rodes. Best stated that he left the post in late May when his regiment and the balance of Colquitt's brigade received orders to proceed to Kinston, North Carolina.[23]

In early June 1863, Capt. J. J. A. Sharp preferred charges against Best. Along with the other men taken prisoner at Chancellorsville, Sharp had endured several weeks of captivity at Fort Delaware before being paroled and eventually exchanged at Aiken's Landing.[24] The first charge detailed several occasions in which Best supposedly had behaved poorly in the face of the enemy. At South Mountain, stated one specification, Best had acted in "a very cowardly and disgraceful manner, hiding himself behind rocks while under the fire of the enemy." This display had rendered Best useless as an officer and set a poor example for his men. At Sharpsburg, Best also supposedly had hidden behind a pile of rocks until ordered up by a superior officer in an adjacent regiment.

The final specification of the first charge dealt with the battle of Chancellorsville. During the initial fighting north of the furnace, Sharp charged, Best had left his command without authority, remaining absent from his regiment until it had retired several hundred yards. After reappearing and being asked what he planned to do, the colonel supposedly had stated that he was "going to the rear and that by the shortest route possible." After retreating to the cut, Best "shamefully ran away" and abandoned his regiment upon the approach of the enemy.

Sharp's second charge concerned disobedience of orders. The charge's sole specification stated that during the engagement at South Mountain Best had refused to obey a member of Gen. James Longstreet's staff who ordered the Georgian to "move his command to the front."[25]

As soon as Sharp preferred the charges against his colonel, General Colquitt ordered Best placed under arrest (during Best's detention, Major Ballenger assumed command of the 23rd). In a June 22 dispatch to D. H. Hill, Colquitt offered a frank appraisal of the accused man, describing him as "a good drill officer." Best also exercised strict discipline but unfortunately was "without judgment in its exercise." Best's tendency to behave like a martinet, Colquitt added, "may have had some influence in making his officers bitter to him." Colquitt closed with the cryptic statement that Best had "rendered himself liable to distrust." Exactly what Best had said or done to dissipate Colquitt's trust is unknown. Despite this enumeration of flaws, however, Colquitt concluded that he would not have ordered an investigation into Best's behavior "had it not been made necessary by the charges sent forward."[26]

At the request of Colonel Best, Maj. Gen. W. H. C. Whiting, commander of the Military District of Cape Fear, made preparations to convene a trial in Wilmington, North Carolina, around August 1. Before these plans could reach fruition, the 23rd, along with the rest of Colquitt's brigade, had left Wilmington for Charleston, South Carolina. Whiting subsequently informed Best that the charges would be forwarded to the headquarters of Gen. P. G. T. Beauregard, commanding the Department of South Carolina, Georgia, and Florida.

Best remained under arrest for a number of weeks. On September 17 he wrote to General Colquitt requesting a trial. "If the emergency is so great at present as to prevent officers of this Dept from attending a court martial," wrote Best, "may I not be ordered to appear before a military court of this Dept?" Colquitt approved the request, passing it on through military channels until it finally reached Maj. John Francis O'Brien, assistant adjutant general to General Beauregard. O'Brien returned the letter to Colquitt, requesting that the general forward the charges because there was then no copy at headquarters.[27]

Because little wartime correspondence exists from members of the 23rd Georgia, it is impossible to gauge the opinions of men in the regiment concerning the plight of their commanding officer. From the few extant sets of correspondence, it seems clear that at least some of the men supported Best. Lt.

Thomas P. Forrester wrote his sister that the colonel "is a good friend of mine and I shall endeavor to keep him so." Miller Collins, a private who shared a mess with Best and the regimental surgeon, seemed sanguine throughout the fall of 1863 that his chief would be restored to command. Collins's concerns for Best were self-serving, however, because Best had detached him on some type of headquarters duty that undoubtedly exempted him from less pleasant tasks. "It will bee better for mee," scrawled Collins to his wife on September 21, "when he [Best] gits in command."[28]

Emory Best's trial opened in Charleston on November 23, 1863, more than two months after he had requested it from General Colquitt. Present in the courtroom were Col. D. F. Jamison, presiding judge on the military court of General Beauregard; Col. Lucius M. Lamar; Capt. William H. Talley acting as judge advocate (the military equivalent of a prosecuting attorney); a clerk; a provost marshal; and Best. The accused chose to defend himself, undoubtedly because of his legal training.[29]

During the week-long trial, seven witnesses, four for the prosecution and three for the defense, took the stand to describe Best's actions at South Mountain on September 14, 1862. As previously stated, on that afternoon, Best had taken a detachment of three companies of the 23rd up the side of South Mountain to support a section of artillery under the immediate command of Capt. Allen S. Cutts.[30] All of the witnesses agreed that Best's detachment came under heavy enemy infantry fire when it reached a position just in the rear of the cannon. Best ordered the men to lie down, and the entire detachment, including its commander, scattered behind rocks for cover. Several witnesses for the prosecution testified that while in this exposed position Best seemed "highly agitated," one opining that he "did not seem to know what to do." Defense witnesses claimed that during the detachment's stay near the battery, Best conversed for some time with the officer in charge of the guns.[31]

Best's official report of the South Mountain engagement stated that upon "finding that the artillery . . . could not be effectively used, and being exposed to the fire of the enemy's sharpshooters covered by a cornfield," D. H. Hill withdrew the guns and ordered the infantry detachment to return to its regiment.[32] As Best's men started back down the mountain, a column of Confederate troops moving to the front forced them to the side of the road. A mounted staff officer accompanied this column. According to the prosecution's four witnesses, this unidentified horseman ordered Best to fall in with the passing column. None of the defense witnesses mentioned the staff officer. Best disobeyed the officer, the prosecution's witnesses stated, telling him of Hill's orders to return to the 23rd. The detachment subsequently returned to the rest of the regiment.[33]

Six witnesses, three each for the prosecution and defense, testified concerning Best's actions at Sharpsburg. In the words of Pvt. William M. Bishop, the 23rd experienced some "right smart confusion" during its advance across Miller's cornfield. The regiment's left wing under Colonel Barclay made headway, but the right wing under Best fell behind. Seeing this situation, stated the prosecution's witnesses, Col. Levi Beck Smith of the 27th Georgia, advancing just a few paces to the right of the 23rd, told Best "to get out and push up his men." Best then came out from behind a pile of rocks, ordering his wing forward "two or three times" before it finally responded.[34]

When the 23rd and the other regiments in Colquitt's shattered brigade began stumbling back across the cornfield, Capt. William James Boston remembered seeing Best and another officer sprinting toward another rock outcropping. Boston admitted, however, that "all of the regiment was running—including the officers." From that point until the next morning, recalled several witnesses, "no one seemed to be in command." When Boston finally gathered thirty-seven men from the regiment on the morning of September 18, he reported Lieutenant Colonel Best as wounded and missing in action.[35]

Witnesses for the defense denied the assertion that the 27th's Colonel Smith ordered Best to advance. Pvt. Drewry M. Sosebee believed that Best was "as cool as anybody" during the fighting. Sosebee and Capt. William H. Rentfro also remembered that Best remained standing as his men knelt or lay on the ground along the firing line. When the final charge across the field began, they stated, Best marched in front of the regiment.[36]

Best argued in his summation that the prosecution's testimony regarding Sharpsburg was "so baseless that it scarcely deserves notice." Judge Advocate Talley admitted that the testimony describing Best's actions at Sharpsburg and South Mountain was "more or less vague and contradictory" and that the prosecution's evidence perhaps "would not warrant conviction of a charge so grave." Having essentially dropped much of the case against Best, Talley concentrated on the accusation that Best abandoned his regiment in the face of the enemy at Chancellorsville. The evidence in this matter, argued the judge advocate, was "full, clear, and free from discrepancy on all essential points."[37]

Major Ballenger and Capt. William J. Boston testified that Best had seemed determined to retreat from the 23rd's initial position north of Catharine Furnace unless the regiment received support. Both officers told the court they had reminded Best of the importance of protecting Jackson's wagon trains, which were then passing on the Furnace Road to the south. Ballenger further claimed that shortly before the Union advances, Best attempted to leave the regiment in search of support. The major responded by telling Best that if he left and the regiment got into a fight "he would be sorry for it." This threat, Ballenger claimed, kept the colonel on the firing line.[38]

Although Ballenger and Boston certainly raised questions about their colonel's leadership, it was the testimony of witnesses regarding events in the
railroad cut that determined the outcome of the trial. Two captains, six lieutenants, and the regimental sergeant major, all of whom had been in the cut and
several of whom had been near Best, testified that they never heard orders from
the colonel or anyone else to leave the cut. These witnesses had all surrendered
to the Federals.[39]

Among officers of the 23rd, only Capt. W. G. L. Butt and Lt. William Jasper
Keown defended Best's actions in the cut. Both testified that an initial courier
asked Best about the tenability of his position, shortly after which another
messenger approached the cut. Butt did not hear the courier; Keown claimed
that he came from General Archer with orders for Best to "bring his regiment
out." Immediately thereafter, the officers claimed, Best gave orders for the
regiment to deploy as skirmishers and leave the cut. Butt testified that he
repeated the order to the adjacent company but that none of its men responded.
Pvt. James W. Justice, the only other defense witness testifying about events in
the cut, stated that before Best left he walked toward the right of the regiment
and twice gave the order to retreat. Butt, Keown, and Justice all followed Best to
the rear.[40]

Emory Best justified leaving the cut by casting aspersions against those who
remained behind and surrendered. "It was no act of cowardice," he argued, "to
leave a secure place and expose myself for more than two hundred yards to a
heavy fire." Instead of following his orders to retreat, Best claimed, Lt. Benjamin B. Moore, who had the responsibility of passing the order to withdraw
down the line, preferred, along with his company, "to halt behind a large bank
perfectly secure rather than to risk danger from a heavy fire." Best was the
victim, he told the courtroom, of a cabal of officers "prompted by malicious
motives." Since the 23rd's organization, Best insisted, these men had sought
promotion by throwing "darts" at whoever commanded the regiment. After
Chancellorsville, "stung by the mortification of being taken by the insolent foe,"
the malcontents had banded together to "sew the seeds of discord." Chief
among them was Captain Sharp, stated Best, who knew "full well that while I
have the command of the regiment he can never receive my recommendation for
promotion."[41]

In summarizing the prosecution's case, Judge Advocate Talley ignored
Best's claims about a conspiracy, examining instead the actions of the accused
in the cut. If not motivated by cowardice, why had Best run a half mile before
finding that only a portion of his regiment had followed him? Even if the colonel
had told his men to retreat, Talley argued, "an officer's responsibility does not
cease with the issuing of an order." The officer also is "bound to superintend its

execution." Talley ended the prosecution's case by questioning Best's assertions that numerous high-ranking officers, including D. H. Hill and Robert Rodes, held him in high regard. If such were the case, the judge advocate asked, why had the accused not submitted some form of written proof? The absence of such evidence, especially considering Hill's praise of Best in his report of the Maryland campaign, is puzzling.[42]

Having heard the closing statements of both parties, the court cleared for deliberations. Upon reconvening, Col. D. F. Jamison read the findings. The court found Best not guilty of the second charge and the specifications of the first charge relating to South Mountain and Sharpsburg. Of the final specification of the first charge, that Best had shamefully abandoned his regiment in the face of the enemy at Chancellorsville, the court pronounced the accused guilty and ordered him cashiered from the Confederate service.[43]

Within twenty-two days of his dismissal on December 7, 1863, Best applied for a new trial to Thomas Jordan, chief of staff for General Beauregard. He restated his arguments from the trial and added that newly discovered testimony revealed that the officers who stayed in the cut had held a council, deciding "to remain & be taken by the enemy." He further claimed that these officers had ordered men attempting to leave the cut to remain.

Best received a reply to his letter within a week. The newly discovered testimony, Jordan wrote, "might impeach the credibility of certain witnesses" but would not alter the findings of the court. By "seeking his own safety" at such a perilous time and "taking no further thought for his command," Best had proven himself "unqualified for the position he held in the Confederate States Army."[44]

Best apparently remained sanguine about being reinstated in the army despite his failure to procure a retrial. The extent and nature of his activities for the duration of the war are unclear, but references in the personal papers of men serving in the 23rd Georgia suggest that he remained with the regiment for some time. While stationed at Camp Milton, some eight miles north of Baldwin, Florida, Lt. William H. Smith noted in his diary on April 2, 1864, that "Col. E. F. Best came in from Richmond last night." Pvt. Miller Collins, Best's former messmate, wrote on April 15 that "Col Best is hear . . . and he told mee yesterday that he would bee all write soon and if he dose I will be vary glad for he is a good friend of mine."[45]

Best sought to bolster his own efforts with help from others. Confederate congressman Warren Akin, his former legal tutor and family friend, wrote Jefferson Davis on June 24, 1864, asking that the young officer be restored to command. A staunch ally of Davis in Congress, Akin testified to Best's "fine moral character" and requested "that the benefit of the doubt may be given to

Emory Fiske Best after the war. Published with the kind permission of Emory F. Best, El Cajon, Calif.

Col B . . . that a good patriotic and much distressed family may be relieved from the great dishonor which they feel has been cast upon them." Akin's appeal to the president had little immediate effect. In a letter to his wife written on December 14, 1864, Akin noted that "Best has not yet had his case heard by the President."[46] Whether Best ever obtained an audience with Jefferson Davis is unknown.

One piece of evidence in Best's compiled service record indicates a reinstatement. This document, headed "Camp of Instruction, Richmond Feby 24th 1865," instructs a group of Virginia conscripts to report to the post's commanding officer without delay and is signed by E. F. Best (no military rank appears with the name). Perhaps Best's skill as a drillmaster, noted a year and a half earlier by Alfred Colquitt, had led officials to assign him a role processing conscripts into the Confederate army.[47]

After the war, Best lived for a time in Macon, Georgia, where he practiced law for two decades. He moved to Washington, D.C., in 1885 after being appointed chief law clerk in the office of the assistant attorney general for the U.S. Department of the Interior. The former colonel served in that capacity until 1895, when he accepted an appointment as assistant commissioner of the General Land Office. He held the latter position until his death on April 23, 1912.[48]

Several veterans of the 23rd Georgia who had left the railroad cut at Chancellorsville took up pens many years after the war to defend their actions and those of their colonel. In 1901 W. G. L. Butt wrote an account for the Atlanta *Journal* in which he admitted that the findings of the court-martial may have been "in accord with military discipline." He nonetheless believed that "running the gauntlet" had been a better option than "exposing my carcass in such prisons as Rock Island and Fort Delaware in time of war." Seventeen years after the publication of Butt's article, Hiram S. Fuller sent his views on Chancellorsville and Best's trial to *Confederate Veteran* magazine. Fuller blamed "the captains who stood next in line for promotion" for instigating the trial. These men sought to "make it appear that they did their duty in refusing to retreat when ordered to do so by the Colonel." Although Fuller had neither seen nor heard from his old commander since the war, he wanted it known that Best had been made a "martyr."[49]

A solicitation from the editors of *Confederate Veteran* for information on Best's trial, printed at the end of Fuller's piece, elicited only one published response. W. W. Foster, an orderly for Best during the war, replied that the colonel had done his duty at Chancellorsville and that he had remained in the cut "as long as there was any reason for staying." "If the Yankees had not been excited," Foster added, "they could have killed everyone leaving the cut."[50]

Had there really been, as Foster suggested, no reason for Emory Best to remain with his regiment in the cut? By running from the foe, Best had displayed in the eyes of those taken prisoner a conspicuous lack of courage. Indeed, it was Best's capacity to display courage that was on trial for seven days in the winter of 1863. Throughout the court-martial, witnesses spoke at length about the demeanor of the accused while under fire. Was Best "cool" or "agitated" while in battle? Where was he when his men had been fighting? Had he cowered behind rocks and trees, as some witnesses asserted? Or, as others testified, had he marched in front of the line and stood up while his men were on the ground? Finding answers to such questions was extremely important to soldiers fighting in a terrible conflict in which courage provided, in the words of historian Gerald F. Linderman, "the cement of armies."[51]

ACKNOWLEDGMENTS

The author would like to thank Emory F. Best, Noel G. Harrison, Robert E. L. Krick, Robert K. Krick, and Marc Storch for their assistance.

NOTES

1. Macon (Ga.) *News*, April 12, 29, 1912.
2. Warren Akin to Jefferson Davis, June 24, 1864, Emory F. Best Compiled Service

Record, National Archives, Washington, D.C. (item hereafter cited as Best CSR; repository cited as NA).

3. Biographical sketch of Emory F. Best, in possession of Emory F. Best, El Cajon, Calif.; Lucy J. Cunyus, *History of Bartow County, Georgia* (Cartersville, Ga.: Tribune, 1933), 47; U.S. Eighth Census, 1860, Schedule 1, "Free Inhabitants, Cass County, Georgia," p. 848; Warren Akin to Jefferson Davis, June 24, 1864, Best CSR.

4. Best CSR; W. L. Selman reminiscences, Chickamauga-Chattanooga National Military Park, Chattanooga, Tenn.; James Madison Folsom, *Heroes and Martyrs of Georgia* (Macon, Ga.: Burke, Boykin, 1864), 43. Also enlisting in the 23rd Georgia at its inception was Emory Best's twenty-two-year-old brother, Hezekiah Spencer Best (five Best brothers served in the Confederate army).

5. Record of Events Card for December 1861, 23rd Georgia Compiled Service Records, NA; Folsom, *Heroes and Martyrs*, 44.

6. U.S. War Department, *The War of the Rebellion: A Compilation of the Official Records of the Union and Confederate Armies*, 127 vols., index, and atlas (Washington, D.C.: GPO, 1880–1901), 11(2):624–26, 976 (hereafter cited as *OR*; unless otherwise noted, all references are to series 1); Alfred Holt Colquitt to Gen. William M. Tarver, July 11, 1862, original in possession of Jay Northcutt, Atlanta, Ga.; Folsom, *Heroes and Martyrs*, 44. The regimental history of the 23rd Georgia included in Folsom's book was written "in the trenches of Petersburg" by two of the regiment's field officers, James Huggins and Marcus R. Ballenger. The latter officer offered very damning testimony against Emory Best in court. It is hardly surprising that Ballenger showed Best's actions in a poor light.

7. Best CSR; Thomas Hutcherson Compiled Service Record, NA.

8. Account by Col. Emory F. Best of the battle of South Mountain, Md., September 14, 1862, James Longstreet Papers, section A, Special Collections, Perkins Library, Duke University, Durham, N.C. (repository hereafter cited as DU); *OR* 19(1):1052–53; Tully Graybill to his wife, September 26, 1862, 28th Georgia unit file, Antietam National Battlefield Park, Sharpsburg, Md.; Best CSR.

9. *OR* 19(1):1027, 1053. The nature of Best's Sharpsburg wound is unknown.

10. Best CSR; *OR*, ser. 2, 5:46; Eric F. Davis, "The Bendanns of Baltimore," *Incidents of the War* 1 (Winter 1986): 14.

11. Best CSR.

12. *OR* 25(1):974–75.

13. Ibid.; John Bigelow, Jr., *The Campaign of Chancellorsville: A Strategic and Tactical Study* (New Haven, Conn.: Yale University Press, 1910), 274; Folsom, *Heroes and Martyrs*, 27.

14. *OR* 25(1):974–76.

15. *OR* 25(1):979–80; Marcus Ballenger and J. P. Patton testimonies, Best CSR; W. G. L. Butt, "General Jackson's Last Fight," Atlanta *Journal*, October 5, 1901. Capt. W. G. L. Butt, an officer in the 23rd, stated after the war that General Stuart helped place the regiment's skirmish line.

16. *OR* 25(1):934, 979–80; Bigelow, *Campaign of Chancellorsville*, 280.

17. Marcus Ballenger, J. J. A. Sharp, and J. P. Patton testimonies, Best CSR; *OR* 25(1): 502. Ballenger said the 23rd lost one man killed and two wounded at the furnace; Sharp stated that the losses included one man killed and four or five wounded.

18. *OR* 25(1):979–80.

19. Theodore Moss, James E. Covington, and William J. Keown testimonies, Best CSR.

20. *OR* 25(1):934, 980; James W. Justice testimony, Best CSR.

21. William J. Keown, W. G. L. Butt, and James W. Justice testimonies, Best CSR.

22. *OR* 25(1):949, 980. The actual number of men in the 23rd Georgia captured at Chancellorsville is unclear. Emory Best says the regiment lost 26 officers and 250 men on May 2, including those killed, wounded, and captured. The casualty return in the *Official Records* lists the regiment's losses as 3 men wounded and 26 officers and 270 men captured. Federal reports listing the numbers of prisoners taken at the furnace and in the cut vary widely.

23. Best testimony, Best CSR; Folsom, *Heroes and Martyrs*, 46.

24. J. J. A. Sharp testimony, Best CSR; Lillian Henderson, *Roster of the Confederate Soldiers of Georgia*, 6 vols. (Hapeville, Ga.: Longino and Porter, n.d.), 2:1009–82.

25. Best trial minutes, Best CSR.

26. *OR* 27(3):918.

27. Emory F. Best to Alfred H. Colquitt, September 17, 1863, Best CSR.

28. Thomas P. Forrester to his sister, April 2, 1863, Forrester Papers, Georgia Department of Archives and History, Atlanta, Ga. (repository hereafter cited as GDAH); Miller Collins to his wife, September 21, 1863, Miller Collins Letters, Civil War Miscellany, Personal Papers, GDAH.

29. Best CSR. According to Confederate army regulations, every court-martial "shall keep a complete and accurate record of its proceedings, to be authenticated by the signatures of the President and Judge Advocate" (*Regulations of the Army of the Confederate States, Authorized Edition* [Richmond: West and Johnson, 1862], 88). The transcripts of the Best trial conform to these, as well as other, specifications.

30. J. P. Patton testimony, Best CSR; Best account of the battle of South Mountain, Longstreet Papers, DU.

31. Ambrose Worley, Robert N. Groves, and James R. Pritchett testimonies, Best CSR.

32. Best account of the battle of South Mountain, Longstreet Papers, DU.

33. J. P. Patton, Ambrose Worley, and Robert N. Pritchett testimonies, Best CSR.

34. William M. Bishop, Benjamin B. Moore, William James Boston, and Drewry M. Sosebee testimonies, Best CSR.

35. William J. Boston testimony, Best CSR.

36. Drewry M. Sosebee and William H. Rentfro testimonies, Best CSR.

37. Summary arguments of Emory F. Best and William H. Talley, Best CSR.

38. Marcus R. Ballenger and William James Boston testimonies, Best CSR.

39. J. P. Patton, J. J. A. Sharp, Benjamin B. Moore, Tyre B. Davis, Theodore T. Moss, S. G. Burdett, John T. Harris, J. A. Smith, and James E. Covington testimonies, Best CSR.

40. W. G. L. Butt, William J. Keown, and James W. Justice testimonies, Best CSR.

41. Summary argument of Emory F. Best, Best CSR.

42. Summary argument of William H. Talley, Best CSR.

43. Best CSR.

44. Emory F. Best to Gen. Thomas Jordan, December 29, 1863, and Gen. Thomas Jordan to Emory F. Best, January 5, 1864, Best CSR.

45. William H. Smith diary, April 2, 1864, copy in possession of Wayne Lasnick, Gainesville, Fla.; Miller Collins to his wife, April 15, 1864, Collins Letters, GDAH.

46. Warren Akin to Jefferson Davis, June 24, 1864, Best CSR; Warren Akin, *Letters of Warren Akin, Confederate Congressman*, ed. Bell I. Wiley (Athens: University of Georgia Press, 1959), 39.

47. Best CSR.

48. Biographical sketch of Emory F. Best, in possession of Emory F. Best, El Cajon, Calif.

49. Butt, "General Jackson's Last Fight"; Hiram S. Fuller, "Narrowly Escaped Prison," *Confederate Veteran* 26 (November 1918): 473.

50. W. W. Foster, "Not Reprehensible Conduct," *Confederate Veteran* 27 (January 1919): 11.

51. Gerald F. Linderman, *Embattled Courage: The Experience of Combat in the American Civil War* (New York: Free Press, 1987), 36.

Stern Realities

CHILDREN OF CHANCELLORSVILLE AND BEYOND

James Marten

FOURTEEN-YEAR-OLD Sue Chancellor's life collapsed when her ancestral home—the imposing brick house that had at one time served as an inn on the Orange Turnpike between Fredericksburg and up-country Virginia—was caught in the middle of some of the heaviest fighting of the battle of Chancellorsville. On the same battlefield, a young Federal drummer boy named Robert displayed the patriotism, courage, and sheer grit of a grizzled veteran. Sue Chancellor penned her account of this event as a grandmother; it was published first in 1921 and again in the 1960s with little editorial intrusion. Robert's story, as told by Edmund Kirke, appeared as "The Boy of Chancellorsville" in the children's magazine *Our Young Folks* in September 1865.

The Chancellor memoir provides a straightforward account of its author's actual experiences and has all the strengths and weaknesses of thousands of other personal narratives of the war. "The Boy of Chancellorsville," despite its author's assurances that he based it on real-life events, is more representative of the style and themes of northern children's fiction, complete with stilted dialogue, intrusive morality, and a pro-Union political agenda. Whereas Sue Chancellor's account generally can be taken at face value as one child's perceptions of the terrible events she witnessed, "The Boy of Chancellorsville" is less an example of actual experience—although young boys certainly did endure combat in ways similar to those described in Robert's account—than of the perceptions and attitudes expected of young northerners by writers producing wartime juvenile reading material.[1]

Both children were thrown into the vortex of the fighting at Chancellorsville. Robert appeared to be involved in the action against the divisions commanded by Gen. Robert E. Lee to the east of "Stonewall" Jackson's flank attack; after initially "driving" the Confederates, the Union forces fell back and the battle "surged away to the northward"—presumably past the Chancellor house in the Union center. Kirke filled his account of Robert's battlefield experiences with descriptive metaphors of enemy fire much like those found in soldiers' memoirs—bullets created "a leaden storm . . . pouring in torrents"; minié balls fell "like hailstones all about him." Even though the genre of children's literature inhibited the realism of Kirke's story, the battlefield was clearly a very lethal place. Robert witnessed and nursed hundreds of "maimed and bleeding men," knelt on the "blood-dampened ground" to hear the dying words of a man whose wound spouted "a crimson stream" of blood, and worked frantically in an old mill serving as a hospital. The decaying log building had no doors or windows, "but its floor, and nearly every square inch of shaded ground around it, were covered with . . . prostrate and bleeding men."[2] Soon afterward, Robert was captured and continued his adventures far from the Chancellorsville battlefield.

It is much simpler to locate Sue Chancellor on the field. She spent most of the battle's worst hours hiding in the soggy cellar of the Union commanding general's headquarters, past which Robert presumably retreated. Her narrative provided a greater sense of the passage of time than Robert's, as she recounted the presence of both Yankee and rebel soldiers in the neighborhood during the first couple of years of the war as well as rumors regarding Union movements in the spring of 1863. Her account of the battle began with the arrival of Maj. Gen. George G. Meade and his staff, who announced that Maj. Gen. Joseph Hooker would require the use of their house. The Chancellor women and a number of refugees who joined them had little knowledge of what was going on beyond their crossroads clearing, but they did see "couriers coming and going" and sensed that the Yankee officers "were very well satisfied with their position and seemed to be very confident of victory." Indeed they were; witnesses reported a

Susan Margaret ("Sue") Chancellor.
Ralph Happel, "The Chancellors of Chan-
cellorsville," Virginia Magazine of History
and Biography 71 *(July 1963): opposite*
p. 264

jovial, nearly partylike atmosphere at Hooker's headquarters on the eve of the Confederate counterattack.[3]

Sue and her family and friends "got through Thursday and Friday as best we could." When the firing grew nearer on Saturday, the day of Stonewall Jackson's famous march across the Union front, the women were sent to the basement. "There was firing, fighting, and bringing in the wounded all that day," Sue reported, and then all hell broke loose late on Saturday afternoon. "This was Jackson's flank movement, but we did not know it then." Jackson was wounded that evening and an acquaintance of Sue's, Maj. Gen. J. E. B. Stuart, took command of his corps. When he renewed the attack the next morning, the Chancellors were evacuated from their burning house into a holocaust of artillery fire: "Cannons were bombing in every direction, and missiles of death were flying as this terrified band of women and children came stumbling out of the cellar." The chaos to which she testified also appears in dozens of descriptions of the battle at this crucial crossroads.[4] Miraculously surviving their journey through the killing field that had been their front yard, the Chancellors were hurried behind Union lines, where they spent the next ten days under guard.

As Ernest B. Furgurson's recent book amply demonstrates, far better sources are available from which to piece together a detailed and comprehensive account of the battle at Chancellorsville—or as Sue Chancellor labeled it, the "second battle of Fredericksburg"—than the stories of a teenaged girl and a preadolescent boy. These stories resemble the writings left by hundreds of junior officers and enlisted men who could only describe the tiny slices of battles they witnessed personally. Yet the experiences of this southern girl and northern boy provide information about an aspect of the war rarely studied: the effects of the war on the children of the United States and the Confederacy. Chancellorsville tested Sue and Robert and inspired their personal accounts; on other battlefields and in other war zones, a few northern and many southern children shared the same kinds of experiences.

Sue's reminiscences and Kirke's fictionalized account of Robert's view of the great battle belong to two different narrative traditions. Memoirs and autobiographies, the first of these traditions, were produced by women and men whose postwar lives had given them a chance to digest their childhood experiences. The years that passed between the decision to write about their lives and the events they described may have clouded memories in some cases, but they also served "to deepen the insight and heighten the perspective of the writers." They had worked out how the Civil War fit into the larger context of their own lives—what specific events and ideas of the war meant and how these events and ideas had influenced them. Not unlike the unpublished autobiographies of nineteenth-century English men and women compiled by John Burnett, the typical memoir of a Civil War–era child—especially if he or she was a southerner—"enabled the author to give himself identity, to place himself in the context of history, geography and social change, and so to make a kind of sense out of an existence which might otherwise seem meaningless."[5]

The feature articles, editorials, and fiction published in children's magazines, on the other hand, offered more immediate accounts of the war, yet not without a certain degree of detachment. The stories and articles were filtered through traditional moral and literary forms applied, sometimes clumsily, to wartime situations.[6] The ostensible facts recounted in "The Boy of Chancellorsville" are impossible to confirm and, aside from a few striking vignettes, offer a fairly generic description of battle and prison life. The story's value lies in its presentation of themes typical of wartime writing for children, which shares a number of themes with the personal narratives published by Civil War–era children.

Although they shed little light on the campaign that opened fighting in Virginia during the momentous summer of 1863, Sue's and Robert's stories of Chancellorsville introduce some of the elements that characterize Civil War narratives by or about children. Most obviously, they indicate the extent to which this "brother's war" was also a "children's war." Children of all ages were deeply involved in the conflict, taking on romantic and dangerous roles such as that of drummer boy as well as contributing in other ways to the war efforts of the North and the South. The stories also suggest some of the ways the war changed the nature of children's lives—both by freeing them from former restraints and by exposing them to far greater responsibilities and worries previously reserved for adults. Finally, these narratives demonstrate attempts by their authors—an elderly woman recalling her childhood and a professional writer with more than one patriotic axe to grind—to assign meaning to the war by considering issues such as patriotism, slavery, and the nature of the enemy.[7]

Many young Yankees and Confederates must have felt like Robert Martin (not to be confused with Kirke's Robert at Chancellorsville), who was only seven when the war ended but clearly remembered feeling that he was at the center of the action. To him, the main street of his little Shenandoah Valley town led directly to Richmond and the seat of war. The conflict dominated his life, constantly "bar[ring] me from something I wanted, whether food, clothes, or playthings." He began to believe that before the war these things had been plentiful "and that all that was necessary to have those good old times again was for the war to end."[8]

Across the Blue Ridge, Sue Chancellor, her mother, and her six siblings thought they were accustomed to war. Confederate pickets had frequently taken their meals at the Chancellor house, pausing to listen to Sue's sisters play piano and to teach them card games. A number of Confederate generals passed through the house, including J. E. B. Stuart. The plumed cavalier was at the Chancellor house when word—which turned out to be premature—arrived that the Federal army was crossing the Rappahannock at United States Ford; before he dashed off, Stuart presented Sue's sister Fannie with a "tiny gold dollar," which Sue later counted as one of her "most cherished possessions."[9] Other gifts included a pet lamb named Lamar after the South Carolinian who presented it to Sue. Yankees also joined the Chancellor landscape early in the war. When they rode "in a sweeping gallop up the big road with swords and sabres clashing," servants hid meat under the front steps and Sue, despite the fact that the Federals "were kind and polite to us," would "run and hide and pray . . . more and harder than ever in my life, before or since." Completing the wartime scenario in the Chancellor household were several refugees from Fredericksburg. Thus, when the spring campaign of 1863 began, the Chancellors were somewhat familiar with wartime conditions.

But the battle that bore their name changed their lives forever. Soon after fighting erupted on the Rappahannock, Yankees arrived to establish Gen. Joseph Hooker's headquarters, banishing the Chancellors to pallets in a crowded room in the rear of the house. As the fighting swept toward them, they retreated to a

Chancellorsville as Hooker's headquarters, May 2, 1863 (engraving based on a sketch by Edwin Forbes). Robert Underwood Johnson and Clarence Clough Buel, eds., Battles and Leaders of the Civil War, *4 vols. (New York: Century, 1887–88), 3:162*

leaky cellar where water spilled into their shoes. Overhead, the house filled with wounded, whose screams the family could clearly hear, and the piano on which the girls had entertained Confederate officers became an amputating table. As Jackson's corps crashed into the Federal right flank, the situation worsened. "Such cannonading on all sides, such shrieks and groans, such commotion of all kinds!" Sue exclaimed in her postwar memoir of the battle. "We thought that we were frightened before, but this was far beyond everything, and it kept up until long after dark." When the bloodshed resumed the next morning, the Chancellor house caught fire, propelling the Chancellors and their friends into the most harrowing portion of their trial.

A Union general named Joseph Dickinson—a Pennsylvanian serving as Hooker's adjutant—led the frightened women and children through their battered home. Amputated limbs spilled out an open window and "rows and rows of dead bodies covered with canvas" littered the yard. The little band followed Dickinson through the bombardment of the Chancellor house and the "swarming refugees," gleefully described by Confederate artillerist Edward Porter Alexander as "pie"—his term for especially vulnerable targets who cannot fire back. "The woods around the house were a sheet of fire," wrote Sue. "The air was filled with shot and shell; horses were running, rearing, and screaming; the men were amass with confusion, moaning, cursing, and praying." Ducking "missiles of death" and gingerly treading among "the bleeding bodies of the dead and wounded," the Chancellors joined the Union exodus. "At our last look, our old home was completely enveloped in flames," along with virtually all of the family's possessions.[10]

As the hero of "The Boy of Chancellorsville," Robert experienced the same Union disaster from a different point of view. When the shooting started, he discarded his drum in favor of a musket, but as the battle intensified, his captain ordered him to the rear. The boy "lingered" on the battlefield, however, fetching water for dying Confederates and Yankees alike, who rewarded him with "blessings which will be to him a comfort and a consolation when he too shall draw near to death."

At one point, he noticed a young rebel with "a noble countenance . . . a broad, open forehead, and thick, curly hair." Despite a shattered arm, the seventeen-year-old's voice retained "a clear, ringing tone, and his face a calm, cheerful look; for to the brave death has not terrors." Kneeling, Robert comforted the boy and called out to a pair of passing stretcher-bearers. When they hesitated to carry the wounded lad to the hospital—"I don't like the color o' his clothes," declared one—Robert threatened to have them "drummed out of the army for being brutes and cowards." Suitably subdued, the older soldiers carried the young rebel to the hospital, where his life was saved and he promised Robert that he would never forget his kindness. Robert hurried off to help other wounded men, accepted a dog named Ponto from a mortally wounded soldier, and then, as the battle surged past the hospital, found himself a captive of the Confederates.

Robert's and Sue's experiences were more dramatic than those of most Civil War–era children, but many youngsters faced excruciating material and emotional hardships. A future governor of Arkansas, George W. Donaghey, whose father spent part of the war in a Union prison camp, claimed that "starvation is one of the sharpest memories of my childhood." He recalled going barefoot even in winter and wrote that "by the time I was seven or eight years old, I had to work almost like a man, helping mother to keep life in myself and my younger sisters and brothers." For eight-year-old Annie P. Marmion, wartime life in Harpers Ferry was a nightmare in which "the great objects in life were to procure something to eat and to keep yourself out of light by day and your lamps . . . hidden by night" in order to prevent a Union picket from firing into your house. In a town that changed hands numerous times during the war, life was sometimes cheap. During one siege, a shell fragment killed an infant in its mother's arms and a black woman venturing out for water was shot and lay in the street all day.[11]

But it would be misleading to focus solely on the horrors of the children's war, for their experiences were far broader. Even Sue Chancellor emphasized pleasant visits from Confederate officers and equally exciting though decidedly less pleasant experiences with Yankees. Autobiographies and memoirs reveal that children in both sections—including those secure from the sharp edge of war—actually insisted on incorporating the conflict into their everyday lives and, more substantively, on performing vital roles in their sections' war efforts. The war was just as real for such children as it was for victims like Sue Chancellor and heroes like Robert. "The small boy," Andrew James Miller of La Grange, Georgia, recalled as an adult, "soon becomes a politician, as unflinching and uncompromising in his imaginary convictions" as his father. Southern boys, he claimed, were the most important promoters of war songs. "It was common, in those old war-times, to hear every boy whistling or singing some one of the many patriotic airs."[12]

For the first few months of the conflict, Louise Wigfall, the fifteen-year-old daughter of the fire-eating senator from Texas, Louis T. Wigfall, had to demonstrate her patriotism from afar since she was stranded with relatives in Massachusetts. Her absence from the South no doubt intensified her loyalty and confidence in the southern cause. Her letters complained of feeling "like a stranger in a foreign land" and ridiculed the "miserable" attempts to drill by local Zouaves ("If this is a specimen of Northern chivalry, I don't think we have much to fear"). She pleaded for her parents to send her Confederate flags and bragged of surreptitiously buying a photograph of Jefferson Davis. She bravely ignored the bad news from the Confederacy in northern newspapers and reported sitting "down to the piano every day and play[ing] 'Dixie' and think[ing] of you all away in 'the land ob cotton.'" On a more practical level, autobiographers and memoirists commonly recalled "scraping lint" to pack around wounds. Announcing early in the war that "a soldier's children are young soldiers," Celine Fremaux's father put his children to work cutting paper for cartridges that would later be filled with powder and ball.[13]

Children of all ages inevitably got caught up in the pageantry of war, frequently organizing their own companies to mimic the thousands of local men and boys—many as young as Robert—hurriedly learning military drill. Rev. William Ward, an old West Pointer, collected young men in his study at Bladensfield, his family home on Virginia's Northern Neck, to teach them the rudiments of drill. His half dozen children between the ages of four and fourteen joined the eager recruits, using broomsticks and pokers for guns. "We could shoulder arms, carry arms, right-about face, guide right, and guide left, right wheel, left wheel, march, double-quick," and "keep step beautifully," according to one of his daughters. They preferred such activities to their

"The Children's Review." Frank Leslie's Illustrated Newspaper, *June 27, 1863, p. 212*

normal peacetime games. Celine Fremaux and her brothers became such hands at the manual of arms that they gathered at a nearby field to heckle green recruits as they stumbled through their maneuvers.[14]

Yankee children were at least as likely as southerners to catch war fever. A group of Cincinnati boys somehow obtained discarded flintlocks from the local militia armory and promptly formed mock firing squads to shoot "spies" and "deserters"—roles usually given to the smallest boys. They also pounded little mud and wood Fort Sumters to bits with cannon made of old brass pistols and used firecrackers to blow up Jeff Davis effigies made out of potatoes. Little Jeannette L. Gilder longed to follow her brother, who had joined a New York Zouave regiment, into the army. She bought herself a drum with her life's savings, obtained a soldier's cap and a canteen, and drummed up and down the sidewalk in front of her house "until every head in the street must have ached." She avidly followed the war news in the illustrated weeklies and established a museum in her bedroom containing a few photographs of rebel generals and a motley assortment of martial odds and ends. The war provided additional opportunities for pack rats. The future historian John Bach McMaster saved Civil War maps published by New York newspapers; other youngsters collected the hundreds of propaganda envelopes enlivened by political cartoons, patriotic sayings, and martial imagery.[15]

The war assumed a central place in the imaginations of children living far behind the lines. Robert Grant, a ten-year-old Bostonian, raced downstairs every morning to read the war news in the papers before the rest of the family. His reading created a "panorama in my mind of what was going on at the front." Willie Kingsbury created a real panorama, constructing a child's version of these prototypical moving pictures by coloring illustrations from *Harper's Weekly* and pasting them together. As he rolled the series of war scenes from one wooden spool to another, he narrated the events they portrayed to his young audience. Charlie Skinner, a budding theatrical manager, with the help of family members and playmates produced epic tragedies featuring soldiers and sailors, as well as slaves, planters, and overseers, in settings that ranged from Libby Prison to Seminary Ridge to gunboat decks. Even Lincoln's assassination proved to be potent drama for at least one gang of child thespians. Richard Henry Dana's daughter Henrietta recalled her friends, the Longfellow children, acting out Lincoln's entrance into Ford's Theater, his murder, and the chase and death of the assassin Booth.[16]

One of the most elaborate and potentially dangerous examples of boys mimicking their martial elders occurred in tiny Rutherfordton, North Carolina, when a band of boys ranging in age from six to twelve organized a militia company under the command of "Captain" Phip Flaxen. Their target was a watermelon patch, whose owner, Old Sam Canahan, had broken with community tradition and banned poachers, especially young boys. Having absorbed their parents' ideas about states' rights, the boys immediately determined that Canahan had violated their "watermelon rights." The company of just over a dozen boys assembled late one evening—less than two months after the battle of Chancellorsville. Armed with shotguns loaded with peas, they stole a boat and mounted an amphibious attack from Chinquapin Creek. Phip sent a detail to steal the five biggest watermelons and ordered the rest of his men into line of battle at the creek bank. Hearing the boys' rebel yell, Canahan and his son obligingly came charging into the patch armed with shotguns. After Old Sam's gun went off, sounding "like a cannon" to the boys, Phip cried "Fire!" and the stinging but harmless vegetable pellets peppered the Canahans and their dog, sparking an ignominious retreat. Their natural rights successfully defended, the boys retired to feast on the contraband watermelon.[17]

As the watermelon campaign reveals, children clearly sought to fit the war into their lives in meaningful ways. Some, like Sue Chancellor, had no choice; others, like Robert, chose to enter the army or, more commonly, to act out their patriotism through games and activities that mirrored those of their parents and older brothers. Relatively few children experienced the war as intensely as these veterans of Chancellorsville, yet their games and childish partisanship were charged with a sincere urgency.

Part of their enthusiasm no doubt stemmed from the fact that the war opened previously unknown avenues of experience. Due to the absence of fathers or older brothers, for instance, children in both sections—but especially the South—enjoyed freedoms previously unavailable to them and took on responsibilities previously not required of them. Boys and girls explored battlefields—sometimes while fighting still raged—and eagerly sought ideal vantage points from which to watch the action. As soon as army units from either side established campsites, children began to make friends, collect souvenirs, or make a little money by selling items to soldiers. By the same token, both boys and girls found themselves assuming tasks usually reserved for older family members, ranging from caring for younger children or performing heavy farmwork to managing slaves or conducting business negotiations.[18]

Chancellorsville and its aftermath provided experiences that neither Sue nor Robert would ever forget. Not only did the Chancellors lose their home and belongings, but also the intense fighting that engulfed their homestead made Sue an expert on warfare. "If anybody thinks that a battle is an orderly attack of rows of men," she wrote, "I can tell him differently, for I have been there." Robert no doubt made a similar discovery. It is unclear whether or not he had seen combat before May 1863, but his ordeal at Chancellorsville and in the months that followed certainly was unlike anything he had experienced before. After the Federals in his sector were overrun by the Confederates, he continued to nurse both gray- and blue-clad patients at the field hospital. In a scene that projected for its Yankee readers far more antisouthern propaganda than fact, a "tall, broad-shouldered, grave-looking man" with "three dingy stars" on his collar asked him, "What,—my little fellow? What are you doing out here, so far away from your mother?" Robert fearlessly declared, "I came out here, sir, to help fight the wicked men who are trying to destroy their country." His answer, however patriotic, condemned him to share the plight of much older captives, for the officer to whom he had delivered his cheeky retort was none other than Robert E. Lee, who, "placid face flushed with anger," ordered the boy sent "to the Libby with the other prisoners." After surviving the long march to Richmond, Robert endured the torment of cruel captors and even a forty-eight-hour stint in the "dungeon,—a low, close, dismal place, with a floor encrusted with filth, and walls stained and damp with the rain. . . . Its every corner was alive with vermin." Far from his home and family, Robert—frequently and pointedly referred to by the author of the narrative as a "little boy"—experienced horrors daunting to a person of any age.

Although they never spent time in a prison camp, the Fremaux children of Louisiana all took on more work when their father joined the Confederate army. Driven by a harsh mother who sometimes resorted to physical and emotional

The drummer boy Robert's confrontation with Gen. Robert E. Lee. Our Young Folks 1 *(September 1865): 603*

abuse, fourteen-year-old Leon bargained for sugar and completed other tasks previously performed by his father, while for a time Celine worked long, freezing days feeding corn to ornery geese and spent frustrating nights walking the floor with her crying baby brother Henry. Later, after the family had relocated to Jackson, Louisiana, she went to school during the day, gave her two younger brothers reading lessons after school, mended the family's clothes, and made dye from red oak and sweet gum bark. She also had to scrounge for dead animals used for making soap and gather kindling. School provided her sole escape from grinding physical labor.[19]

One northern girl's memoir of pioneering in Michigan resembled the accounts of many southern boys and girls forced to work because of the war. The father and two oldest brothers of Anna Howard, later a feminist colleague of Elizabeth Cady Stanton, joined the Union army soon after the war began, leaving Mrs. Howard and several children—at fourteen, Anna was the oldest— to fend for themselves in the wilderness of the Great Lakes. "I was the principal support of our family," she recalled as an adult, "and life became a strenuous and tragic affair." Little news trickled into this community forty miles from the nearest post office; work was "done by despairing women whose hearts were with their men." As the war dragged on, "the problem of living grew harder. . . . We eked out our little income in every way we could." She and her mother took in boarders from logging camps, sold quilts, sewed, and taught school. "It was an incessant struggle to keep our land, to pay our taxes, and to live."[20]

The enhanced responsibilities placed on children such as Leon Fremaux and Anna Howard may have been trying, but sometimes the children managed to translate their burdens into much greater latitude in other aspects of their lives. Leon's duties foraging for food and minding the farm gave him an excuse to avoid reciting his lessons. He also began chewing gum and "smoking porous vines," activities strictly forbidden in their household. He made the most of one occasion when a skirmish broke out nearby. Hoping to capture a horse in the confusion, he saw a Yankee major shot out of his saddle, dashed into the melee, grabbed the animal's bridle, and retreated to cover. After the firing stopped and the children were ordered to bed, Leon slipped out of a window and back to the battlefield, where he spent most of the night and the next day. Although he came home "looking worn and sad" and refused to answer any questions about his nocturnal activities, it was clear to his little sister that he "was getting out of Ma's jurisdiction."[21]

Younger but just as adventurous as Leon Fremaux was Opie Read, who bribed a Confederate bugler with brandy to let him ride behind him into a skirmish with Union cavalrymen. "On a beautiful morning," with "shouts and songs of discordant loudness we rode forth to battle." As the long lines of horsemen crossed sabers, "it was beauty and not horror" that impressed Opie; he "saw an iron weed bend its purple head beneath the touch of a lark, . . . saw a man with his skull split open, fall to the ground." As the sword fight developed into a decidedly less romantic exchange of gunfire, Opie's bugler-friend stiffened and leaned back against the boy, nearly unseating him. "I moved to one side, reached around and took hold of the horn of the saddle. Blood spurted from the bugler's breast." After the dead Confederate slid to the ground, Opie rode off the battlefield, dismounted, and ran home. Although he was horrified by the turn of events, he feared punishment from his father even more. "My only hope was to thrill him with my story," and for the first time in his life, "I made a clean confession." It worked. His father was thrilled and pleased that Opie's courage had honored the family name. As if his father acknowledged that the war had changed the ground rules for preadolescent behavior, the whipping Opie received for disobeying an order to remain in safety in the cellar "fell upon me with gentleness."[22]

On those few occasions when the shooting war moved into their section, young northerners also got as close to the action as possible. Billy Bayly roamed the battlefield on Gettysburg's first day. After helping his father hide their horses from the Confederates, Billy watched Federal troops arrive and then inexplicably went up Seminary Ridge with his younger brother and a few other friends to pick blackberries. Momentarily forgetting about the imminent blood-letting, the boys were stunned by the concussion of a cannon and a volley of rifle fire, then retreated to a fence rail near a blacksmith shop. Despite his fright, Billy wrote years later, "To me as a boy it was glorious!" When the main body of Confederates advanced to within a few hundred yards of their position, the boys finally withdrew, "not riotously or in confusion, but decorously and in order." During the battle, a group of Gettysburg teenagers forsook their homes, spending a night in a storeroom above a shop, listening to Confederate sentries in an attempt to learn how the battle was going.[23]

Children of both genders and in both sections entertained exciting images of the war, took on increased responsibilities, and exerted greater control over some aspects of their lives. In addition, their interpretations of the war—the lessons they applied as adults to their childhood experiences—provide another point of comparison between northern and southern children's experiences. As children attempted to attach meaning to the war, they often drew on values and assumptions that predated the conflict or were formed by their experiences during it—their attitudes about slavery, for instance, or their contacts with enemy soldiers, or the hardships they personally endured. Although the narra-tives about Robert the drummer boy and by Sue Chancellor vary greatly in approach and literary style, both convey the horrors of the bloody war from which children could not always be shielded. On the other hand, they also reveal that even with a river of blood flowing between North and South, people in both sections remained linked by a bridge of humanity that took many forms.

Despite Sue Chancellor's steadfast loyalty to the South, the hero of her story was the Yankee general Joseph Dickinson. As he led the little group of south-erners out of the burning house and through the chaotic Federal position, Dickinson repeatedly proved his gallantry by obtaining a horse for Sue's sick sister, by angrily refusing to leave the Chancellors when ordered to do so, and by protecting them from less chivalrous Yankees. Other Federals also pro-vided aid. A kind chaplain escorted them across the "wobbly" pontoon bridge that spanned the Rappahannock at United States Ford, and a jovial Yankee guard promised "to write my mother and tell her what a good time I have had with these rebel ladies." On another occasion, a "little drummer boy named Thacker"—who sounded much like the noble Robert—provided ice and a lemon for Sue's faint sister. "If this is 'on to Richmond,'" he declared, "I want none of it. I would not like to see my mother and sister in such a fix." Although Sue's older sisters were "very cool" toward their Federal guards at first, "after a while they relaxed and relieved the irksomeness of our confinement by talking, playing cards, and music." In retrospect, Sue even believed "that there were some flirtations going on." After their release, the family sat out the rest of the war in Charlottesville, where Sue attended school and Mrs. Chancellor worked as a hospital matron. Sue finished her account by revealing that General Dickinson and her mother became fast friends; they corresponded, he visited them whenever he came to Virginia to show companions the battlefield, and he attended her funeral in 1892.

A final example of Sue's unexpectedly benign memories of the war was an "incident of interest" that occurred during a trip to the U.S. Centennial celebration in Philadelphia in 1876. "A distinguished looking gentleman" seated near them on the train heard their name mentioned and introduced himself as Joseph Hooker. "He shared our bountiful luncheon and we had a very pleasant day," which was, of course, quite "a contrast to the three days spent in the same house with him thirteen years before." Sue could not erase the "horrible impression of those days of agony and conflict," and like a good southern matron, she rejected the term "rebel"—"Washington and the Continentals might have been rebels, but we stood for our rights, and under the Constitution, the war was a 'War Between the States'"—and regretted that an otherwise admirable acquaintance had become a Republican after the war. But she ultimately emphasized—at least in her memoirs—the shared humanity of northerners and southerners. Interestingly, her last sentence offered the image of "the courageous and chivalrous" General Dickinson leading them to safety rather than a tribute to the victorious southern soldiers at Chancellorsville.

The meanings Sue Chancellor attached to the war must be gleaned because she does not develop her own ideas about its larger issues and lessons. Other participants were more forthcoming about the ways in which they perceived the war—its causes and results, how it brought out the best or worst in northerners and southerners, and the ramifications of the conflict for themselves and for the country. Many white southerners, for instance, embraced nostalgic images of the peculiar institution that colored their memories of a conflict that not only had interrupted their childhoods but also had emancipated their slaves. Dosia Williams Moore fondly recollected playing with the slave children on her father's Red River plantation, eating "negro" food like collard greens, and accompanying her African American nurse Crecy to a "Negro party." Remarking on the loyalty of slaves before and during the war, Louise Wigfall mused that "those were the good old days and the good old ways," ruined by the war. "The negro in slavery," she insisted, "was lazy and idle—he will always be that—but he was simple, true and faithful. What he has become since his emancipation from servitude is a queer comment on the effect of the liberty bestowed upon him."[24]

Not surprisingly, memoirists who extended their stories into the postwar period and who had spent at least part of their energies defending the social and cultural institutions of the Old South had little good to say about Reconstruction, and they frequently ended their narratives with a very traditional southern version of the postwar years. Dosia Moore, for instance, blamed the "riff-raff of both North and South" for the horrors of Reconstruction. Northerners, she assured her readers, "do not know how" the black race "was made a tool in the hands of unscrupulous wretches, to torture, crush, and humiliate the class of whites who had been in the ascendancy before the War." Her account of Reconstruction in Louisiana focused on the disfranchisement of loyal white southerners, the rise of African Americans to positions far beyond their abilities, and the cynical politics of corrupt carpetbaggers and scalawags. She approvingly recounted the efforts of white supremacists to reclaim their political rights and their place in the society. Although not directly commenting on the race issue, Mrs. W. H. Gregg wrote, "I bear no malice toward the northern soldier until I see their uniform, which carries me back to the Sixties, when the blood was kept at fever heat, the heart made to quiver, the tongue suppressed." Her experiences had hardened her to the point that she could "forgive, but never forget."[25]

Some narrators, however, explicitly or implicitly rejected the bitterness that characterized many descriptions of Reconstruction or of the northerners who won the war. Like Sue Chancellor, they focused instead on reunion and on rediscovered connections between northerners and southerners. Despite her negative view of Reconstruction, Dosia Moore admitted early in her memoirs of the Civil War era that "most of my highlights are rose colored." She told about a wartime Christmas when she received a delightful rag doll as well as ginger cakes and popcorn balls—and when presents were given to the slave children, too. Dosia recalled only positive relationships with the invading Yankees, including a friendly officer who stopped to talk to them every day and sometimes distributed hardtack to children tired of plain cornbread. He even scolded recalcitrant slaves for Dosia's mother and threatened the worst of them with a beheading. On another occasion, a Union colonel who had requisitioned a room in their house invited her to peek into a gold locket attached to his watch chain in return for a kiss. Dosia could not resist, and her reward revealed a miniature of a little girl about her age—the colonel's daughter. "We . . . learned that this Yankee, at least, was just a human being after all." So did Opie Read and his friends after the dreaded Yankees established a camp outside Gallatin, Tennessee. When the boys "ran out to get a better look at them," the well-dressed and orderly Union soldiers "greeted us with good humor, not a frown." Opie enjoyed listening to their jokes. A Wisconsin soldier told him about killing a bear, and the young rebel smuggled him a piece of peach pie. Opie also heard a Yankee sergeant reciting a line he recognized from *McGuffey's Reader* as a Shakespearean quote and gave him an old hen for supper. "Our greatest astonishment," he remarked, "was that removing their head gear they revealed no horns."[26]

Many other southern children of war grew up to have mixed feelings about the outcome and meaning of the conflict. Although he certainly disapproved of northern attempts to reconstruct the South, perhaps Opie Read's entirely pleasant experiences with northern soldiers led him late in his life to decry the South's post-Reconstruction withdrawal "from [the] broad view to narrowness" and to express his disappointment that "the Volunteer State would put a rusty chain about the throat of education and stab at the truth of science." B. H. Wilkins blamed the destruction of his "happy childhood" on the "hated abolitionists," who had sparked "strife between the North and South to free the slaves their fathers had sold to the southern farmers, because the African slaves could not live in bleak and snow-clad 'New England.' " Yet he also seemed to be spreading the blame when he prayed that "every boy and girl . . . could be taught to realize the ruin, the suffering and horrors of war" so that "our quarrels might be settled by arbitration, instead of bloodshed."[27]

Northern children felt less need to try to explain the war, although they certainly expressed fervent patriotism and relief over its outcome. They personally had less at stake—and, of course, their side won the war. Victory apparently demanded less soul-searching and explanation than did defeat. Virtually none of their published reminiscences mentioned Reconstruction. The war ended for northern children with the assassination of Abraham Lincoln, which they often described in great detail. In fact, although a number of southerners published memoirs specifically detailing their childhood experiences during the war, most northerners relegated the conflict to a chapter or two in longer autobiographies.

Whether considered as fact or, probably more usefully, as fiction, "The Boy of Chancellorsville" provided for its readers a conception of what the war was *supposed* to mean and developed a number of the typical themes in wartime stories and articles. It was, first of all, an adventure story, with its young hero exhibiting both physical and moral courage. Although the battle resulted in defeat for the Army of the Potomac, boys and girls could take comfort and inspiration from the bravery and patriotism Robert and his Yankee comrades had shown. In fact, the author began by pointing out the importance of Robert's actions during that terrible battle: "He saved one or two human lives, and lighted the passage of a score of souls through the dark valley; and so did more than any of our great generals on those bloody days. He saved lives, they destroyed them." Dying comrades thought of their mothers first, as "do all brave boys, whether well or wounded." The "stalwart man" from whom Robert inherited the dog Ponto gasped with his penultimate breath, "Tell them that I died—like a man—for my country." Ponto provided an animal interest; he cheated death at Chancellorsville and at Libby and, during the long, hard march to Richmond, kept Robert cheerful "in spite of himself" and draped himself over the sleeping boy, to "cover him, as well as he could, from the cold air, and the unhealthy night dew." In addition, Robert met both good and bad southerners, allowing the narrator to suggest not only that the Union must win the war to put aristocratic as well as white-trash southerners back in their places but also that some southerners deserved to be brought back into the American fold.

Wartime passions heavily influenced Edmund Kirke's portrayal of nasty Confederates, but he, too, managed to convey the natural links between many northerners and southerners. Predictably, the first villain to appear was the vengeful Robert E. Lee. The author provided his own impression of Lee, who must have represented to Kirke all of southern "chivalry." The Confederate chieftain used neither tobacco nor alcohol, having "none of the smaller vices"; however, he had "all of the larger ones; for he deliberately, basely, and under circumstances of unparalleled meanness, betrayed his country and, long after all hope of success was lost, carried on a murderous war against his own race and kindred." Lower-class despicability appeared in the person of Dick Turner, the "inspector" of the guards at Libby. He was "a course [sic], brutal fellow, with breath perfumed with whiskey, and face bloated with drink and smeared with tobacco-juice." Not only did Turner rifle the pockets of the newly arrived prisoners, but he also led a prisonwide chase to capture the elusive Ponto, who nevertheless managed to escape. Turner's brother Thomas, who proudly proclaimed his profession as "Negro-whipper," later joined the search. When Robert accused him of cruelty, he was thrown into the dungeon, where he would have perished if a cellmate had not given up his own blanket and food, nursing "him as if he had been his mother." After nearly two days, Robert was sent to the hospital; when he had completely recovered, he returned to the prison, where he languished for seven months.

At this point, the plot of this supposedly factual story twisted into literary convention: redemption for the general run of no-good Confederates came in the form of the kindness of a few when Robert discovered a friend among the rebels. A handsome young man with an empty left sleeve called to him—it was the "Rebel youth" whose life he had saved on the Chancellorsville battlefield. Other sentries watched the boys' affectionate reunion without interrupting it because "after all," intoned the narrator, "even after the atrocities the Rebels have committed,—it is true that the same humanity beats under a gray coat that beats under a blue one." The next day, a mysterious visitor promised to take Robert to Union lines as a reward for saving the life of the Confederate. The boy returned home to his mother, where he "is now"—just after the close of the war—"fitting himself to acting his part in this great world, in this earnest time in which we are living."[28]

Building on the themes in "The Boy of Chancellorsville," northern magazines such as *The Student and Schoolmate, Our Young Folks, The Little Pilgrim,* and *The Little Corporal* waged a war of words steeled by pro-Republican, prowar, and antislavery attitudes in hundreds of features, pieces of fiction, editorials, and even games and puzzles. "In a word," according to a fatherly Uncle Rodman in a story published just after the end of the war, "slavery was the cause of the war; and God permitted the war in order that slavery might be destroyed."[29] In addition to their moral-political approach to the war, stories in children's magazines revealed their readers' enthusiasm for the forms of warfare. "The Yankee Zouaves" was the story of a company of twenty boys—half claiming officers' titles—who fought over what to name their company and then had to chase away a group of young hecklers. In "The Children's Attic," a family of boys and girls constructed "Camp Brooks" out of a worn-out carpet, drilled in paper hats, and ate "rations" brought upstairs by their mother. In "Nellie's Hospital," a little girl, inspired by the stories of her wounded older brother about the U.S. Sanitary Commission, set up a hospital for wounded animals—among them, a fly trapped in a spider's web ("a black contraband") and a gray squirrel (an injured "Rebel"). In at least two stories, children packed practical as well as personal items into boxes for soldiers, in one instance making their Christmas worthwhile despite the absence of presents for themselves and in the other reestablishing contact with a beloved absent father.[30]

A few stories also portrayed children meeting the greater challenges forced on them by the war. The first issue of *Our Young Folks* began a serialized story very similar to "The Boy of Chancellorsville." In this case, the young hero, the only son of a widowed mother, survived the Wilderness, befriended a kindly black "Mammy," and ran into John Mosby's men before he was returned to his mother, showing how "God dealt with a little boy who trusted in and prayed to him." Children could contribute in small ways, too; Gertrude, in "The Discontented Girl," was shamed out of her selfishness into scraping lint for soldiers by her patriotic brother and a parrot who screeched, "Gerty wants to secede!"[31]

Aside from their often jaunty tone, the most typical characteristic of northern children's journals was their association of religious virtue with the Union cause. The hero of "The Drummer Boy of Gettysburg," for example, lost an arm but bravely kept a stiff upper lip with the help of his Sunday school

"The Mother's Sacrifice." This early engraving exaggerates the youth of northern drummer boys but conveys a sense of how the war transported children to an adult world. Frank Moore, Women of the War: Their Heroism and Self-Sacrifice *(Hartford, Conn.: S. S. Scranton, 1867), facing p. 545*

training. Readers were also encouraged not to forget about the slaves over whom the war was being fought. Christie Pearl's "The Contraband" stressed that contributions of clothes and toys to freed slaves, if they were to provide the proper moral boost to the givers, had to come from the heart, not from the junk pile, while a family of well-off white children forfeited their Christmas presents to buy their beloved servants' daughter out of slavery in "Christmas, After All." Yet another story featured a family who held a series of miniature sanitary fairs to aid the contraband children in South Carolina's Sea Islands.[32]

A final theme emerging from a number of stories was that despite sectional hatred—and the fact that wild-eyed fire-eaters in the South had plunged the nation into war—all Americans were basically the same. J. T. Trowbridge wrote a series of travelogues for *Our Young Folks* that not only described the sights at places such as Camp Douglas, Fredericksburg, Richmond prisons, and the Shiloh/Corinth area but also contrasted the loyalty of common southerners with the treason of political leaders who had dragged them into war. Many of the prisoners at Camp Douglas, for instance, had taken the oath of allegiance to the United States and were quite happy to be "well-fed, well-clothed, and well cared for in every way" in the cozy prison camp in Chicago. Most southerners, in fact, were actually Yankees by breeding, "differing . . . only as they are warped by slavery or crushed by slave holders."[33]

Children's magazines hardly provided an objective account of the war, and at times they seemed to use stories merely as illustrations of moral issues and attitudes unconnected to the sectional conflict.[34] It is also very difficult to know how many children actually read them, though we do know that Theodore Roosevelt's favorite childhood reading material came out of *Our Young Folks*, while, interestingly enough, Henrietta Dana recalled that one of her favorite war stories was "The Boy of Chancellorsville."[35] Yet the concerns of the publishers of children's periodicals and the concerns of adults writing about childhood war experiences often meshed. In addition to the insistent moralizing that characterized children's literature in the mid-nineteenth century, magazine stories, articles, and editorials, as well as the more personal writing of children themselves, focused on young people's contributions to their respective national war efforts, the hardships they faced, and the significance they attributed to their efforts.

The battle of Chancellorsville was, according to Ernest B. Furgurson, "the high point of the Confederacy" in terms of "tactics and strategy, and in impact on morale North and South."[36] The battle was certainly the crucible of Sue Chancellor's Civil War experiences. Her ancestral home was destroyed, and images and friendships sparked by the fight would remain with her for the rest of her life. Although the postwar career of Robert is unknown, he scarcely could have forgotten the horror, bravery, and urgency that touched his young life on that bloody ground.

Other battles and campaigns affected other children in dozens of different ways. Many southerners mourned the loss of their childhood as a casualty of the war. During the war, Celine Fremaux's "childhood had slipped from me, never to return. Necessity, humane obligations, glory's obligation, family pride, and patriotism had taken entire possession of my little undersized body, and my over developed mental being." Emma LeConte shared that sense of loss. Early in 1865, the sometime refugee and seventeen-year-old daughter of the Confederate chemist Joseph LeConte complained "how dreadfully sick I am of this war." The war had monopolized her adolescence and robbed her of the joys and prerogatives girls of her class expected. "No pleasure, no enjoyment— nothing but rigid economy and hard work—nothing but the stern realities of life." Such tribulations normally would "come later" but because of the war "are made familiar to us at an age when gladness should surround us." She wistfully wondered "if I will ever have my share of fun and happiness." When she reflected on the war years afterward, Elizabeth Allan pitied "the child who was henceforth to look with different eyes into the face of life, having eaten of the tree of knowledge which was forever to shut her out of childhood's Paradise."[37]

Few northern children complained about a lost childhood, although the drudgery endured by Anna Shaw led her to greet the Confederate collapse with relief: "The end of the Civil War brought freedom to me, too," as well as to the slaves with whom she identified as an adolescent abolitionist. In fact, one senses that the war enhanced rather than shortened northern childhoods. Dan Beard cheerfully commented years later that "had a leader of boys arisen in '61, like that emotional shepherd lad who led the children's crusade of 1212, he could have gathered a vast army of small boys to fight for the Union, who . . . would have marched away as joyfully as did the thirty thousand poor little toddlers trailing after the mad French shepherd Stephen."[38] There was no hardening process for most northern children.

The Civil War, according to a woman who was only two when the war began, "made itself felt" even to the youngest children "from the words and looks of those about us; there was some struggle going on in the world which touched all life, brooded in faces, came out in phrases and exclamations and pitiful sights. . . . We knew, by the time we were four years old, what blue coats and brass buttons stood for."[39]

The sprawling battle of Chancellorsville intruded on thousands of lives. Nearly 22,000 soldiers were killed and wounded.[40] The dead left behind thousands of widows and orphans, while civilians in Fredericksburg and the surrounding region witnessed the continued destruction of their homes and farms and personal property. This single battle forced Sue Chancellor and Robert the drummer boy—representing scores of real-life boys present on the actual battlefield—to endure more warfare than most of their peers experienced during the entire conflict, but their stories are at least partially representative of the experiences of all Civil War children. The intense patriotism, exposure to hardship and even combat, expansion of responsibilities and freedoms, and recognition of basic connections between northerners and southerners that appeared in their stories differ only in degree, not in kind, from the experiences of other memoirists and characters in other stories. Chancellorsville blew through their young lives and changed them in ways they had not thought possible two years before—just as the Civil War jarred the lives of tens of thousands of other children.

NOTES

1. Sue M. Chancellor, "Personal Recollections of the Battle of Chancellorsville," *Register of the Kentucky Historical Society* 66 (April 1968): 137–46 (a nearly identical version of "Recollections of Chancellorsville," *Confederate Veteran* 29 [June 1921]: 213–15); Edmund Kirke, "The Boy of Chancellorsville," *Our Young Folks* 1 (September 1865): 600–608. Kirke reports that two adults as well as the title character provided the information for his story

(ibid., 607). All passages in this essay concerning Sue Chancellor and Robert are drawn from these two sources, which, because of their brevity and the consequent ease with which readers can locate material quoted from them, will not be cited again.

2. For Col. Robert McMillen's very similar description of the hospital at Salem Church, see Ernest B. Furgurson, *Chancellorsville 1863: The Souls of the Brave* (New York: Alfred A. Knopf, 1992), 310.

3. Ibid., 111.

4. For examples, see ibid., 246–49.

5. Joanna L. Stratton, *Pioneer Women: Voices from the Kansas Frontier* (New York: Simon and Schuster, 1981), 25–26; John Burnett, ed., *Destiny Obscure: Autobiographies of Childhood, Education, and Family from the 1820s to the 1920s* (London: Penguin, 1982), 10.

6. For works on antebellum children's literature and magazines, see Anne Scott Mac-Leod, *A Moral Tale: Children's Fiction and American Culture, 1820–1860* (Hamden, Conn.: Archon Books, 1975); John B. Crume, "Children's Magazines, 1826–1857," *Journal of Popular Culture* 6 (Spring 1973): 698–707; and John C. Crandall, "Patriotism and Humanitarian Reform in Children's Literature, 1825–1860," *American Quarterly* 21 (Spring 1969): 3–22. R. Gordon Kelly analyzes postwar children's magazines in *Mother Was a Lady: Self and Society in Selected American Children's Periodicals, 1865–1890* (Westport, Conn.: Greenwood, 1974).

7. William M. Tuttle, Jr., explores these and many other themes concerning children living nearly a century later in his *"Daddy's Gone to War": The Second World War in the Lives of America's Children* (New York: Oxford University Press, 1993). See also Robert William Kirk, "Hey Kids!: The Mobilization of American Children in the Second World War" (Ph.D. dissertation, University of California, Davis, Calif., 1991).

8. Carolyn Martin Rutherford, ed., *A Boy of Old Shenandoah* (Parsons, W.Va.: McClain, 1977), 45–46.

9. Furgurson, *Chancellorsville 1863*, 105.

10. Edward Porter Alexander, *Fighting for the Confederacy: The Personal Recollections of General Edward Porter Alexander*, ed. Gary W. Gallagher (Chapel Hill: University of North Carolina Press, 1989), 210.

11. George W. Donaghey, *Autobiography of George W. Donaghey, Governor of Arkansas, 1909–1913* (Benton, Ark.: L. B. White, 1939), 15–16; Annie P. Marmion, *Under Fire: An Experience of the Civil War* (N.p.: William V. Marmion, 1959), 7, 16.

12. Andrew James Miller, *Old School Days* (New York: Abbey, 1900), 37–39.

13. Louise [Wigfall] Wright, *A Southern Girl in '61: The War-Time Memories of a Confederate Senator's Daughter* (New York: Doubleday, Page, 1905), 57–63; Patrick J. Geary, ed., *Celine: Remembering Louisiana, 1850–1871* (Athens: University of Georgia Press, 1987), 65.

14. Evelyn D. Ward, *The Children of Bladensfield* (New York: Viking, 1978), 32; Geary, *Celine*, 99.

15. Dan Beard, *Hardly a Man Is Now Alive: The Autobiography of Dan Beard* (New York: Doubleday, Doran, 1939), 102, 151; Jeannette L. Gilder, *The Autobiography of a Tomboy* (New York: Doubleday, Page, 1900), 205–7, 220–23; [John Bach McMaster], "John Bach McMaster: A Boyhood in New York City," *New York History* 20 (1939): 321; Edward P. Mitchell, *Memoirs of an Editor: Fifty Years of American Journalism* (New York: Charles Scribner's Sons, 1924), 39. More than 500 envelopes from both the Union and the Confederacy can be found in the Civil War Pictorial Envelopes Collection, Southern Historical Collection, Wilson Library, University of North Carolina, Chapel Hill, N.C.

16. Robert Grant, *Fourscore: An Autobiography* (New York: Houghton Mifflin, 1934), 36; Alice E. Kingsbury, *In Old Waterbury: The Memoirs of Alice E. Kingsbury* (Waterbury, Conn.: Mattatuck Historical Society, 1942), 2; Otis Skinner, *Footlights and Spotlights: Recollections of My Life on the Stage* (Indianapolis: Bobbs-Merrill, 1924), 16–17; Henrietta Dana Skinner, *An Echo from Parnassus: Being Girlhood Memories of Longfellow and His Friends* (New York: J. H. Sears, 1928), 175–79.

17. D. F. Morrow, *Then and Now: Reminiscences and Historical Romance, 1856–1865* (Macon, Ga.: J. W. Burke, 1926), 67–73. The rich, if somewhat dated, literature on the political socialization of children includes such works as Fred I. Greenstein, *Children and Politics* (New Haven, Conn.: Yale University Press, 1965); R. W. Connell, *The Child's Construction of Politics* (Melbourne: Melbourne University Press, 1970); and Robert Coles, *The Political Life of Children* (Boston: Atlantic Monthly Press, 1986).

18. For examinations of the ways in which environment and economic considerations created similar patterns of responsibility and freedom in the lives of nineteenth- and early-twentieth-century children, see Elliott West, *Growing Up with the Country: Childhood on the Far-Western Frontier* (Albuquerque: University of New Mexico Press, 1989), and David Nasaw, *Children of the City: At Work and At Play* (New York: Oxford University Press, 1985).

19. Geary, *Celine*, 71, 102, 115–16.

20. Anna Howard Shaw, *The Story of a Pioneer* (New York: Harper, 1915), 52–53.

21. Geary, *Celine*, 106, 129.

22. Opie Read, *I Remember* (New York: Richard R. Smith, 1930), 11–13.

23. William Hamilton Bayly, *Stories of the Battle* (Gettysburg, Pa.: Gettysburg *Compiler* Scrapbook, Gettysburg National Military Park, 1939), 4; Daniel Alexander Skelly, *A Boy's Experiences during the Battle of Gettysburg* (Gettysburg, Pa., 1932), 18–20.

24. Dosia Williams Moore, *War, Reconstruction, and Redemption on Red River: The Memoirs of Dosia Williams Moore*, ed. Carol Wells (Ruston, La.: McGinty Publications, 1990), 8–11; Wright, *A Southern Girl*, 17–18.

25. Moore, *War, Reconstruction, and Redemption*, 13, 61–69; Mrs. W. H. Gregg, "Can Forgive, But Never Forget," in Missouri Division, United Daughters of the Confederacy, *Reminiscences of the Women of Missouri during the Sixties* (Jefferson City, Mo.: Hugh Stephens, n.d.), 30.

26. Moore, *War, Reconstruction, and Redemption*, 42–43, 19–22; Read, *I Remember*, 10.

27. Read, *I Remember*, 16–17; B. H. Wilkins, *"War Boy": A True Story of the Civil War and Re-Construction Days* (Tullahoma, Tenn.: Wilson Brothers, 1990), 4, 16.

28. Ernest B. Furgurson recounts a similar situation at the fighting south of the Chancellor house, when a Mississippian named Willis Hawkins recognized a Yankee who had guarded him as a prisoner at Sharpsburg a year earlier. Lowering his rifle, Hawkins sent the grateful bluecoat—"whose earlier kindness had saved his life"—to the rear (Furgurson, *Chancellorsville 1863*, 243).

29. J. T. Trowbridge, "The Turning of the Leaf," *Our Young Folks* 1 (June 1865): 399.

30. [Anonymous], "The Yankee Zouaves: A Story for Boys," *The Little Pilgrim* 9 (October 1862): 133–34; N. L. E., "The Children's Attic," *The Little Pilgrim* 10 (July 1863): 93–94; Louisa M. Alcott, "Nellie's Hospital," *Our Young Folks* 1 (April 1865): 267–77; Phebe H. Phelps, "A Box for the Soldier," *The Student and Schoolmate* 13 (March 1864): 71–74; [Anonymous], "The Children's Christmas Box," *The Little Pilgrim* 10 (April 1863): 52.

31. [Anonymous], "The Little Prisoner," *Our Young Folks* 1 (January 1865): 32–37, (April

1865): 240–44, (May 1865): 327–29, (July 1865): 462–65; [Anonymous], "The Discontented Girl," *The Little Pilgrim* 9 (November 1862): 150–51.

32. Cousin Mabelle, "The Drummer Boy at Gettysburg," *Our Young Folks* 1 (November 1865): 67–68; Christine Pearl, "The Contraband," *The Student and Schoolmate* 11 (February 1862): 45–48; Gail Hamilton, "Christmas, After All," *The Little Pilgrim* 9 (April 1862): 50–52; L. Maria Child, "The Two Christmas Evenings," *Our Young Folks* 2 (January 1866): 2–13.

33. J. T. Trowbridge, "Three Days at Camp Douglas," *Our Young Folks* 1 (April 1865): 252–60, (May 1865): 291–300, (June 1865): 357–60; "Battle Field of Fredericksburg," *Our Young Folks* 2 (March 1866): 163–70; "Richmond Prisons," *Our Young Folks* (May 1866): 298–304; and "A Tennessee Farm-House," *Our Young Folks* (June 1866): 370–76.

34. Far fewer children's magazines appeared in the Confederacy than in the Union. Shortages of paper and printing facilities and a deteriorating economic situation plagued southern publishers throughout the war. As a result, only a few issues of a handful of southern magazines survive. Nevertheless, they complement northern magazines in their presentation of patriotic narratives and images. The two longest-running periodicals were the *Child's Index* and the *Deaf Mute Casket*. Samuel Boykin published the former as a hard-shell Baptist Sunday school paper, while the North Carolina Institution for the Deaf and Dumb and the Blind published the latter. Other short-lived publications included the *Children's Guide*, a Methodist Sunday school paper, and the *Child's Banner*, another religious publication out of Salisbury, North Carolina. Although their religious content was more prominent than in typical northern magazines, they, too, provided stories and articles that explained the war to children and showed the ways in which children were involved in the war. See Sarah Law Kennerly, "Confederate Juvenile Imprints: Children's Books and Periodicals Published in the Confederate States of America, 1861–1865" (Ph.D. dissertation, University of Michigan, Ann Arbor, Mich., 1956), 250–312.

35. John Morton Blum, ed., *Yesterday's Children: An Anthology Compiled from the Pages of Our Young Folks, 1865–1873* (Boston: Houghton Mifflin, 1959), xv; Henrietta Dana Skinner, *Echo from Parnassus*, 179.

36. Furgurson, *Chancellorsville 1863*, xv.

37. Geary, *Celine*, 102; Emma LeConte, *When the World Ended: The Diary of Emma LeConte*, ed. Earl Schenck Miers (New York: Oxford University Press, 1957), 21–22; Elizabeth Randolph Preston Allan, *A March Past: Reminiscences of Elizabeth Randolph Preston Allan* (Richmond, Va.: Dietz, 1938), 137.

38. Shaw, *Story of a Pioneer*, 54; Beard, *Hardly a Man*, 151.

39. Ruth Huntington Sessions, *Sixty-Odd: A Personal History* (Brattleboro, Vt.: Stephen Daye, 1936), 31.

40. Furgurson, *Chancellorsville 1863*, 364–65. Nearly 7,000 soldiers were reported missing.

Bibliographic Essay

Readers seeking sources pertinent to facets of the Chancellorsville campaign explored in the essays should look first to the notes, which collectively cite many of the most important works on military operations in Virginia between February and June 1863. As with all military (and many nonmilitary) aspects of the Civil War, the great fount of printed primary material is U.S. War Department, *The War of the Rebellion: A Compilation of the Official Records of the Union and Confederate Armies*, 127 vols., index, and atlas (Washington, D.C.: GPO, 1880–1901). Chancellorsville dominates series 1, volume 25, parts 1–2, of the *Official Records*, which offers more than 2,000 pages of reports, correspondence, orders, and other documents. Janet B. Hewett and others, eds., *Supplement to the Official Records of the Union and Confederate Armies*, 3 vols. to date (Wilmington, N.C.: Broadfoot, 1994–), includes heretofore unpublished manuscript material on Chancellorsville similar to that published in the *Official Records*. U.S. Congress, *Report of the Joint Committee on the Conduct of the War, at the Second Session Thirty-Eighth Congress* (Washington, D.C.: GPO, 1865), contains extensive comments about the campaign from various Union officers, including Joseph Hooker, and points up the bickering and political maneuvering that often attended the Army of the Potomac's military defeats. Clifford Dowdey and Louis H. Manarin, eds., *The Wartime Papers of R. E. Lee* (Boston: Little, Brown, 1961), collects virtually all of Lee's crucial letters and reports for the period April–May 1863.

Although campaign and battle narratives on Chancellorsville are less numerous than those on Gettysburg, Vicksburg, and other Civil War operations, several rank with the best examples of this type of historical writing. John Bigelow, Jr.'s, *The Campaign of Chancellorsville: A Strategic and Tactical Study* (New Haven, Conn.: Yale University Press, 1910) towers above most other Civil War operational studies. Impartial (though devoting considerably more attention to Union than Confederate movements), well researched, and clearly written, Bigelow's book also benefits from several dozen superb maps that show in remarkable detail how the action unfolded. Ernest B. Furgurson's engagingly written *Chancellorsville 1863: The Souls of the Brave* (New York: Alfred A. Knopf, 1992) highlights testimony drawn from manuscript sources and nicely complements Bigelow. Douglas Southall Freeman combines sound research and narrative power in examining Chancellorsville from the Confederate side in volume 2 of *Lee's Lieutenants: A Study in Command*, 3 vols. (New York: Charles Scribner's Sons, 1942–44); Bruce Catton performs the same service from a Union viewpoint in *Glory Road* (Garden City, N.Y.: Doubleday, 1952). Shelby Foote's graceful treatment of the campaign in volume 2 of *The Civil War: A Narrative*, 3 vols. (New York: Random House, 1958–74) and Kenneth P. Williams's too-often-neglected assessment in volume 2 of *Lincoln Finds a General*, 5 vols. (New York: Macmillan, 1949–59) merit the attention of all students of Chancellorsville.

Three older works that remain useful are William Allan and Jedediah Hotchkiss's *The Battle-Fields of Virginia: Chancellorsville; Embracing the Operations of the Army of Northern Virginia, from the First Battle of Fredericksburg to the Death of Lieutenant-General Jackson* (New York: D. Van Nostrand, 1867), which is graced by several of Hotchkiss's unexcelled maps; Samuel P. Bates's *The Battle of Chancellorsville* (Meadville, Pa.: Edward T. Bates, 1882), which focuses more on Union than on Confederate activities and includes a number of insights; and Augustus Choate Hamlin's *The Battle of Chancellorsville: The Attack of Stonewall Jackson and His Army upon the Right Flank of the Army of the Potomac at Chancellorsville, Virginia, on Saturday Afternoon, May 2, 1863* (Bangor, Maine: Published by the author, 1896), which covers in detail the unhappy experience of the Eleventh Corps.

A pair of books will prove especially useful to modern visitors to the battlefield. Jay Luvaas and Harold W. Nelson's *The U.S. Army War College Guide to the Battles of Chancellorsville and Fredericksburg* (Carlisle, Pa.: South Mountain Press, 1987) employs modern maps of the area and extensive quotations from battle reports to convey a sense of how participants saw and reacted to the terrain. In *Chancellorsville Battlefield Sites* (Lynchburg, Va.: H. E. Howard, 1990), Noel G. Harrison uses sketch maps, photographs, and period images to direct readers to scores of man-made and natural landmarks associated with the battle.

Veterans wrote extensively about Chancellorsville, creating an important literature readers should approach with an understanding that such authors often reveal as much about postwar controversies and concerns as about the wartime events. Among Confederate accounts, Jubal A. Early's *Lieutenant General Jubal Anderson Early, C.S.A.: Autobiographical Sketch and Narrative of the War Between the States* (Philadelphia: J. B. Lippincott, 1912) is indispensable on Second Fredericksburg and Salem Church, and Edward Porter Alexander's *Military Memoirs of a Confederate: A Critical Narrative* (New York: Charles Scribner's Sons, 1907) and *Fighting for the Confederacy: The Personal Recollections of General Edward Porter Alexander*, ed. Gary W. Gallagher (Chapel Hill: University of North Carolina Press, 1989) boast excellent narratives and astute analyses. For the Union, O. O. Howard's *Autobiography of Oliver Otis Howard, Major General*, 2 vols. (New York: Baker & Taylor, 1907) defends his actions on May 2, while Rice C. Bull's mistitled *Soldiering: The Civil War Diary of Rice C. Bull*, ed. K. Jack Bauer (San Rafael, Calif.: Presidio Press, 1977), which is really a memoir, presents a common soldier's gripping observations about fighting at Chancellorsville.

Among multivolume collections of postwar testimony, Robert Underwood Johnson and Clarence Clough Buel, eds., *Battles and Leaders of the Civil War*, 4 vols. (New York: Century, 1887–88), certainly is the most famous and frequently quoted. Its third volume includes articles on Chancellorsville by O. O. Howard, Darius N. Couch, Alfred Pleasonton, and other leading figures. Three other essential collections are *Papers of the Military Historical Society of Massachusetts*, 14 vols. (1895–1918; reprint, 15 vols. and index, Wilmington, N.C.: Broadfoot, 1989–90), volume 3 of which is most important for Chancellorsville; J. William Jones and others, eds., *Southern Historical Society Papers*, 52 vols. (1876–1959; reprint, with 3-vol. index, Wilmington, N.C.:

Broadfoot, 1990–92); and Walter Clark, ed., *Histories of the Several Regiments and Battalions from North Carolina in the Great War, 1861–1865*, 5 vols. (Raleigh, N.C.: E. M. Uzzell, 1901).

Generally more reliable than postwar memoirs, sets of letters and diaries also have an immediacy unmatched by any other source. Alpheus S. Williams's *From the Cannon's Mouth: The Civil War Letters of General Alpheus S. Williams*, ed. Milo M. Quaife (Detroit: Wayne State University Press, 1959) offers the blunt observations of a division commander in the Union Twelfth Corps; Robert McAllister's *The Civil War Letters of General Robert McAllister*, ed. James I. Robertson, Jr. (New Brunswick, N.J.: Rutgers University Press, 1965) rivals Williams's book and includes a passage describing how McAllister pummeled a panicked member of the Union Eleventh Corps on May 2. Jedediah Hotchkiss's *Make Me a Map of the Valley: The Civil War Journal of Stonewall Jackson's Topographer*, ed. Archie P. McDonald (Dallas: Southern Methodist University Press, 1973) abounds with information about Stonewall Jackson's headquarters and the movements of the Confederate Second Corps, while Bryan Grimes's *Extracts of Letters of Major-General Bryan Grimes to His Wife, Written While in Active Service in the Army of Northern Virginia, Together with Some Personal Recollections of the War, Written by Him After Its Close, etc.*, comp. Pulaski Cowper (Raleigh, N.C.: Edwards, Broughton, 1883) includes a splendid account of fighting along the Confederate Second Corps front on May 3.

Four key actors at Chancellorsville are covered in Douglas Southall Freeman's exhaustive and laudatory *R. E. Lee: A Biography*, 4 vols. (New York: Charles Scribner's Sons, 1934–36), which manages to place part of the blame for Confederate failure to achieve a more complete victory on the absent James Longstreet; Walter H. Hebert's *Fighting Joe Hooker* (Indianapolis: Bobbs-Merrill, 1944), a generally gentle handling of its subject; Frank E. Vandiver's *Mighty Stonewall* (New York: McGraw-Hill, 1957), an engaging portrait of the quirky Virginian; and Richard Elliott Winslow III's *General John Sedgwick: The Story of a Union Corps Commander* (Novato, Calif.: Presidio Press, 1982), which gives Sedgwick high marks for what many historians consider a weak performance at Second Fredericksburg and Salem Church.

The Confederate artillery enjoyed perhaps its finest hour at Chancellorsville, a fact underscored by Jennings C. Wise in *The Long Arm of Lee, or The History of the Artillery of the Army of Northern Virginia, with a Brief Account of Confederate Ordnance*, 2 vols. (Lynchburg, Va.: J. P. Bell, 1915). L. Van Loan Naisawald covers the Union artillery in his standard *Grape and Canister: The Story of the Field Artillery of the Army of the Potomac* (New York: Oxford University Press, 1960). Confederate cavalry operations at Chancellorsville still await careful study, but the mounted Union arm receives excellent coverage in volume 2 of Stephen Z. Starr's *The Union Cavalry in the Civil War*, 3 vols. (Baton Rouge: Louisiana State University Press, 1979–85).

The Confederate victory at Chancellorsville denied northern photographers access to the battlefield, thereby severely limiting the number of images recorded from late April to early May 1863. The best collections of photographs on the campaign are William C. Davis's *The Embattled Confederacy*, vol. 3 of *The Image of War, 1861–1865*, ed. William C. Davis, 6 vols. (Garden City, N.Y.: Doubleday, 1981–84), which contains a chapter on Chancellorsville with a strong text by Robert K. Krick, and Francis Trevelyan Miller's pioneering *The Photographic History of the Civil War*, 10 vols. (New York: Review of Reviews, 1911), the second volume of which, titled *Two Years of Grim War*, includes a section on Hooker's offensive against Lee. William R. Goolrick and the Editors of Time-Life Books, *Rebels Resurgent: Fredericksburg and Chancellorsville* (Alexandria, Va.: Time-Life Books, 1985), reproduces photographs, engravings, paintings (many in color), and other pictorial material relating to the campaign.

In closing this brief canvass of works on Chancellorsville, it is worth emphasizing what certainly must be obvious to most readers: the movements of the two armies and the decisions of their respective generals have dominated the attention of most historians of the campaign. The impact of the battle on the respective home fronts, the ways in which soldiers in each army reacted to the contest, and many other worthy subjects await investigators who will flesh out the full story of the battle and its impact.

Contributors

Keith S. Bohannon earned an M.A. in history from the University of Georgia and received his doctoral training in American history at Pennsylvania State University. The author of *The Giles, Allegheny, and Jackson Artillery*, he is at work on a study of the Civil War in northeast Georgia.

Gary W. Gallagher is a member of the Department of History at Pennsylvania State University and editor of the Civil War America series at the University of North Carolina Press. He is the author of *Stephen Dodson Ramseur: Lee's Gallant General*, editor of *Fighting for the Confederacy: The Personal Recollections of General Edward Porter Alexander*, and editor and coauthor of *The Third Day at Gettysburg and Beyond* and *The Fredericksburg Campaign: Decision on the Rappahannock*.

A. Wilson Greene, who holds degrees in history from Florida State University and Louisiana State University, is executive director of the Pamplin Park Civil War Site and former president of the Association for the Preservation of Civil War Sites. He is the author of *Whatever You Resolve to Be: Essays on Stonewall Jackson* and coauthor of *The National Geographic Guide to the National Civil War Battlefields*.

John J. Hennessy, a graduate of the State University of New York at Albany, has written widely on the Civil War, including *The First Battle of Manassas: An End to Innocence, July 18–21, 1861, Second Manassas Battlefield Map Study*, and *Return to Bull Run: The Campaign and Battle of Second Manassas*.

Robert K. Krick grew up in California but has lived and worked on the Virginia battlefields for more than twenty years. He has written dozens of articles and ten books, the most recent being *Stonewall Jackson at Cedar Mountain* and *Conquering the Valley: Stonewall Jackson at Port Republic*.

James Marten is a member of the Department of History at Marquette University. A specialist in the era of the Civil War, he has written numerous articles as well as *Texas Divided: Loyalty and Dissent in the Lone Star State, 1856–1874*. His principal current project is a book examining the experience of children during the Civil War.

Carol Reardon is the military historian at Pennsylvania State University and author of *Soldiers and Scholars: The U.S. Army and the Uses of Military History, 1865–1920*. A former holder of the Harold Keith Johnson Visiting Professorship in Military History at the U.S. Army Military History Institute and U.S. Army War College, she is completing a book on the image of Pickett's Charge in American history.

James I. Robertson, Jr., is Distinguished Alumni Professor at Virginia Polytechnic

Institute and State University and former executive director of the U.S. Civil War Centennial Commission. His many books on the Civil War include *The Stonewall Brigade*, *Civil War Sites in Virginia: A Tour Guide*, *General A. P. Hill: The Story of a Confederate Warrior*, and *Soldiers Blue and Gray*. He will soon publish a major reinterpretation of Stonewall Jackson.

Index

fantry, 144, 146–47, 151, 158–59, 161, 166; 66th Infantry, 144, 149, 153, 159, 161, 167; 77th Infantry, 187; 88th Infantry, 150; 108th Infantry, 4, 9; 121st Infantry, 2, 5, 190; 123rd Infantry, 186, 190; 124th Infantry, 126; 140th Infantry, 1; 154th Infantry, 187

Norfolk, Va., ix

Norman, Capt. W. M., 197 (n. 18)

North Anna River, 70, 74, 76, 93–94, 97

North Carolina Institution for the Deaf and Dumb and the Blind, 243 (n. 34)

North Carolina units: 6th Infantry, 51; 7th Infantry, 109, 111, 120–21; 16th Infantry, 80; 18th Infantry, 108–9, 111, 113, 119, 121–25, 134; 28th Infantry, 109, 111, 123, 134, 197 (n. 18); 33rd Infantry, 109, 111, 119–20, 125, 138 (n. 24); 37th Infantry, 109, 111, 123, 133–34

O'Brien, Maj. John F., 209

Ohio, 21

Old Mountain Road, 81

Orange & Alexandria Railroad, 68–69, 76, 79, 81, 96

Orange Court House, Va., 74

Orange Plank Road, 41, 43–48, 51–53, 55, 57, 94–95, 109, 113, 115–16, 119–20, 122–24, 132, 135 (n. 2), 138 (n. 29), 144, 147, 150, 153, 156, 167, 170, 184, 204

Orange Springs, Va., 74, 94

Orange Turnpike, 115, 135 (n. 2), 144, 149–51, 156, 163, 167, 170–71, 219

Oregon, 7

Our Young Folks, 219, 237–39

Palmer, Maj. William H., 109, 113, 119, 122

Palmyra, Va., 84

Pamunkey River, 70, 81, 86–87

Parker's Store, 115

Patrick, Marsena R., 23, 97

Paxton, Lt. Wilson, 169

Payne, William H., 60

Pegram, Maj. William R. J., 53

Pelham, John, 66

Pender, Brig. Gen. W. Dorsey, 135 (n. 2)

Pendleton, Brig. Gen. William N., 40, 43–44

Peninsula of Virginia. *See* Virginia Peninsula

Pennsylvania, 20–21, 36

Pennsylvania units: 1st Cavalry, 102 (n. 14); 4th Cavalry, 76; 6th Cavalry, 73–74, 93, 103 (n. 19); 8th Cavalry, 102 (n. 14), 106 (n. 85), 116, 125; 17th Cavalry, 102 (n. 14); 46th Infantry, 120, 126; 53rd Infantry, 144, 159; 73rd Infantry, 27; 81st Infantry, 144, 150; 105th Infantry, 5; 128th Infantry, 120; 139th Infantry, 187; 140th Infantry, 144, 149–51, 158–59, 164–65, 169, 171; 145th Infantry, 144, 159, 166, 168; 148th Infantry, 143–44, 146–47, 150–51, 153, 162–64, 167, 169; 155th Infantry, 2; reserve division, 30 (n. 36)

Perry, William, 146

Phelps, Col. Walter, 3, 27 (n. 4)

Philadelphia, Pa., 180, 233

Pierce, Francis, 4

Pitzer, Lt. Andrew L., 47–49

Pleasonton, Brig. Gen. Alfred, 66, 68, 70, 80, 99, 102 (n. 14), 106 (n. 85)

Plunkett's Ferry, 87

Pollard, Edward A., 58–59

Pope, Maj. Gen. John, 12

Porter, Maj. Gen. Fitz John, 3–4, 14, 16, 20–21

Posey, Brig. Gen. Carnot, 52

Potomac Creek, 65, 184, 186, 189, 191

Potomac River, 68

Powelson, Sgt. Benjamin, 151

Pratt family, 39

Prospect Hill, 40

Purdie, Col. Thomas J., 124, 139 (n. 32)

Shoemaker, John J., 135 (n. 6)

Sickles, Maj. Gen. Daniel E., 16–18

Sigel, Maj. Gen. Franz, 24

Sim, Dr. Thomas, 184–85

Skinner, Charlie, 228

Slocum, Maj. Gen. Henry W., 16, 25–26, 144

Small, Abner, 23

Smith, Lt. Col. Charles H., 88

Smith, James P., 119–20, 122

Smith, Col. Levi B., 211

Smith, Lt. Col. Levi H., 120

Smith, Lloyd T., 113, 136 (n. 12)

Smith, Brig. Gen. W. F. "Baldy," 3–4, 14, 16, 21

Smith, Brig. Gen. William "Extra Billy," 40–41, 45–48, 51–52, 54

Smith, Lt. William H., 213

Smithfield, Va., 39, 43

Sosebee, Pvt. Drewry M., 211

South Anna River, 70, 76, 81, 83, 87–89, 91, 94, 97

South Carolina unit: 2nd Infantry, 157

South Mountain, battle of, 7, 201, 203, 208–11, 213

Spotsylvania County, Va., 15, 65

Spotsylvania Court House, Va., x, 43, 74, 76, 81

Squibb, Dr. Edward, 177

Stafford County, Va., 1, 65

Stansbury's Hill, 41, 45

Stanton, Edwin M., 6, 17, 67, 93, 97

Stanton, Elizabeth C., 230

"Star-Spangled Banner, The," 158, 187

Steele, Capt. Matthew F., 171

Stevens, Dr. George, 187

Stevensburg, Va., 71, 79–80

Stewart, Dr. William S., 189, 197 (n. 22)

Stiles, Robert, 39

Stone, Charles, 16

Stoneman, Brig. Gen. George, x, 68–71, 73–76, 79–81, 83–84, 87, 89–91, 93–100, 106 (n. 80)

Stoneman's raid, 66–99 passim, 102 (n. 14); effect on morale, 96, 98, 100; postwar interpretations of, 98

Stuart, Maj. Gen. J. E. B., xi, 66, 69, 71, 79–80, 95, 98, 115–16, 205, 221, 223

Student and Schoolmate, The, 237

Suckley, George, 198 (n. 39)

Suffolk, Va., 60 (n. 4)

Sulfur Springs, Va., 68

Sumner, Maj. Gen. Edwin V., 3, 14, 23

Sumner, Lt. Edwin V., Jr., 95

Sunken Road (Fredericksburg, Va.), 45, 48

Surgeon General's Office (U.S.), 193

Swinton, William, 98

Swisshelm, Jane, 192–93

Sykes, Maj. Gen. George, 16, 144

Talley, Capt. William H., 210–13

Tappahannock, Va., 91

Taylor, Lt. Murray F., 113, 122, 124, 127–28

Taylor house, 51–52

Taylor's Hill, 41, 45, 48, 55

Telegraph Road, 46–47, 51, 54

Tennessee, 26, 201

Tennessee unit: 14th Infantry, 205

Texas, 226

Thompson's Crossroads, Va., 76, 81, 83–84, 86–90, 99

Three Chopt Road, 90, 105 (n. 60)

Tidball, Capt. John C., 79

Tobie, Edward P., 65

Tolersville, Va., 75, 89, 94

Trevilian Station, Va., 93–94

Trimble, W. S., 168

Trowbridge, J. T., 238

Tucker, Sgt. George W., 113, 127

Tunstall's Station, Va., 87, 97

Turner, Dick, 236

Turner, Thomas, 236

Turner's Gap, 203

Tuscaloosa, Ala., 182

Union corps: First, 13, 18, 28 (n. 8), 184;
    Second, x, 4, 15, 18, 20, 126, 143, 150,
    153; Third, 17–18, 156, 184; Fifth, 16,
    20–21, 70, 144, 150–51, 184; Sixth, 8,
    21, 24, 186; Ninth, 8–9, 18, 30 (n. 36);
    Eleventh, xi, 9, 18, 23–25, 35 (n. 81),
    70, 99, 119, 158, 170, 184, 198 (n. 39);
    Twelfth, 11, 18, 25, 70, 120, 144, 147,
    151, 153, 159, 164, 167; Cavalry Corps,
    10, 12, 66
United States Ford, 80, 112–13, 166, 184,
    191, 223, 232
U.S. Military Academy, 7, 16, 23, 25
U.S. Sanitary Commission, 237
U.S. units: 2nd Artillery, 95; 4th Artillery,
    146; 1st Cavalry, 75, 89, 104 (n. 40);
    5th Cavalry, 73, 83, 89; 6th Cavalry,
    66; 6th Infantry, 147; 1st Sharpshoot-
    ers (Berdan's), 205; 2nd Sharpshoot-
    ers, 207

Valley Forge, 3
Van Wert house, 121–22
Verdiersville, Va., 95
Vermont unit: 2nd Infantry, 15
Victoria Iron Works, 94
Virginia, ix, xi, 2, 4, 13, 25, 65, 71, 100,
    102 (n. 17), 104 (n. 37), 200–201, 222,
    233
Virginia Central Railroad, 70, 80–81, 83,
    86–88, 93–94, 98
Virginia Military Institute, 131
Virginia Peninsula, 20–21, 65, 86–88, 91,
    94, 144, 201–2
Virginia units: Bedford Artillery, 145;
    Rockbridge Artillery, 40; 22nd Battal-
    ion, 116, 132; Breathed's Battery, 111;
    Brooke's Battery, 205; 1st Cavalry, 80;
    9th Cavalry, 69, 75, 80, 90, 113, 115;
    13th Cavalry, 69, 71, 98; 39th Cavalry,
    113, 135 (n. 4), 136 (n. 12); 4th Infantry,
    188; 12th Infantry, 144; 13th Infantry,
    62 (n. 31); 33rd Infantry, 189; 50th

Infantry, 123; 55th Infantry, 116, 122,
    130; 58th Infantry, 62 (n. 31)
Von Borcke, Maj. Heros, 102 (n. 17)
Von Gilsa, Col. Leopold, 23

Wadding, R. M., 167
Wade, Sen. Benjamin F., 18
Wainwright, Col. Charles, 13–14, 17–18,
    20; opinion of Hooker, 7
Walker, Francis A., 20
Walkerton, Va., 87, 91
Ward, Rev. William, 226
Warren, Brig. Gen. Gouverneur, 2, 4, 18;
    views on Jackson's death, 133; criti-
    cizes Eleventh Corps, 184
Warrenton Junction, 69, 74
Washington, D.C., 2, 4, 15–16, 30 (n. 37),
    68, 100, 193, 214; hospitals in, 189,
    191–92; Ford's Theater, 228
Washington, George, 233
Webb, Alexander, 4
Webb, Nathan, 73, 75, 89, 95
Weed, Capt. Stephen H., 172 (n. 5)
Wellford's Furnace. See Catharine
    Furnace
Wellford house, 207
West, Fred H., 157, 162
West, Cpl. Henry, 187
White House Landing, 87
Whiting, Maj. Gen. W. H. C., 209
Whitman, Walt, 191, 194
Wigfall, Louise, 226, 233
Wigfall, Sen. Louis T., 226
Wilbourn, Capt. Richard E., 111–13,
    116, 121, 124, 127; attends to Jackson,
    129–30
Wilcox, Brig. Gen. Cadmus M., 45, 47,
    54
Wilderness, the, x, 15, 43, 53, 65,
    98–100, 107, 115, 123, 144, 151, 184,
    186, 191, 237
Wilderness Church, 115, 185
Wilkins, B. H., 235

Williams, Brig. Gen. Alpheus S., 18, 25, 120

Williamsburg, battle of, 7

Williamsburg, Va., 87

Williamsburg Road, 202

Willis's Hill, 41

Wilson, Sen. Henry, 17

Winchester, Va., 185

Wisconsin, 23

Wisconsin unit: 6th Infantry, 3

Wofford, Brig. Gen. William T., 48, 146

Wood, James R., 66, 98

World War I, 171

Wright, Brig. Gen. Ambrose R., 52

Wright, Dr. Benjamin P., 122; attends to Jackson, 130–31

Wyndham, Col. Percy, 74–75, 83–84, 89–91, 94, 104 (n. 40)

Wynn, W. T., 113, 128

Yanceyville, Va., 76, 89–91, 93–94

York, Capt. Richard W., 51

York River, 87

York River Railroad, 203

Yorktown, Va., 65, 86, 91, 93, 97, 201–2

Zoan Church, x

Zook, Brig. Gen. Samuel K., 146, 149, 153, 158